Fall 1985

# *Methods Toward a Science of Behavior and Experience*

*Second Edition*

**WILLIAM J. RAY**
Pennsylvania State University

**RICHARD RAVIZZA**
Pennsylvania State University

Wadsworth Publishing Company
Belmont, California
A Division of Wadsworth, Inc.

To Adam & Lauren & Susan (wjr)

a child is the most superb research scientist we can get
Buckminster Fuller

To Diane (rr)

Psychology Editor: Kenneth King
Cartoons: Sidney Harris

Cover: *Omega VI;* Alexander Liberman, (1912– ); acrylic on canvas; 79¾ × 60 inches. The Art Museum, Princeton University, Princeton, New Jersey. Gift of the artist.



Printed in the United States of America

1 2 3 4 5 6 7 8 9 10—89 88 87 86 85

ISBN 0-534-04041-1

**Library of Congress Cataloging in Publication Data**

Ray, William J., 1945–
Methods toward a science of behavior and experience.

Bibliography: p.
Includes index.
1. Psychology—Research. 2. Psychology, Experimental.
I. Ravizza, Richard. II. Title.
BF76.5.R38 1984 150'.72 84–17414
ISBN 0–534–04041–1

# CONTENTS

# PREFACE

We live in a time when books on science are setting sales records. Yet, at many universities, the experimental course remains the one that students dread and put off until the last minute. This seems strange to us, since many of our colleagues are excited about what they do in psychology and approach research with a real desire to know. This makes us think that, in the process of teaching experimental psychology, we have often neglected to include our own experience in psychology, especially our reasons for attempting a science of behavior and experience in the first place. Thus, one of our major goals in writing this book is to introduce the student both to the basics of doing science and to the spirit that motivates many scientists.

One idea we try to convey to the student from the very beginning is the relationship of science and philosophy. We do this not only through the introduction of propositional logic in Chapter 2, but through a discussion of individuals who have shaped our ideas about science. For example, in the first two chapters, the student is introduced not only to Newton's rules of reasoning, but to the views of Karl Popper and Thomas Kuhn on how science works. We also show the student how some approaches to science, such as the use of strong inference and the development of a research program, have allowed certain fields to move at an accelerated rate. Likewise, we show the student that science cannot be done without reference to values. We do this not only in our discussion of the ecology of the experimental situation in Chapter 10 and our discussion of ethics in Chapter 13, but throughout the text.

However useful, abstractions alone do not teach the student about science as it is practiced, much less how to practice science themselves. Thus, we also emphasize the concrete. In our discussion of descriptive statistics in Chapter 3, we teach students how to read graphs and how to plot them. In

Chapter 5, we include detailed information on how to use major library reference works, such as *Psychological Abstracts, Index Medicus,* and *Science* and *Social Citation Indexes.* In Chapter 14, we not only teach the student how to write up an experiment, but also include a valuable checklist that can be used both for writing up an article and for presenting a research proposal. Because of our desire to make science concrete for the student, we have included interviews with active psychologists on how they first obtained the ideas for their studies. These interviews are followed by a discussion of how to turn an idea into a testable hypothesis.

Although most students grasp the idea of asking testable questions, they often have an uncertainty of what exactly it is that they are testing in research. To help clarify this point, we have presented the process of hypothesis testing both conceptually and practically. In Chapter 4, we presented a conceptual understanding of inferential statistics, using a popular video game to illustrate probability. We likewise stress the process of making decisions and the importance of logically ruling out alternative hypotheses. Although this process begins in the first chapter and continues throughout the book, Chapter 2 emphasizes the use of logic and drawing conclusions.

In order to help faculty teach this course and students understand the material better, we have made a special effort to define and illustrate what we know to be general problem areas for students. We have also included material at the end of each chapter that not only summarizes the main points in the chapter but also includes questions to test comprehension, and discussion questions and projects for better integration of the material. Included in this section are designs for the students to criticize and conclusions to evaluate. Our talks with faculty across the country have led us to pay special attention to certain topics. For example, the concept of interaction effect is not only illustrated with research examples, but numerous possible outcomes are graphically represented for the student to see. We have also carefully walked the student through the interpretation of interaction effects and explained why an interaction effect must be interpreted before a main effect. These discussions have been facilitated by our explanation of the concept behind the *F*-ratio. Beginning in Chapter 6 and continuing throughout the rest of the text, the logic of the *F*-ratio is used in our discussions of experimental control and variation. By emphasizing the factors that influence either the numerator or the denominator of the *F*-ratio, students are able conceptually to grasp what factors will influence their acceptance or rejection of the null hypothesis. We gave special attention to two other problem areas for students: the meaning of *causation* in science, and the use of the terms *error* and *chance* in relation to experimentation.

By using the title *Methods Toward a Science of Behavior and Experience,* we wanted to convey a sense not only of where experimental psychology has been but of where it might be going. For example, more and more experimental courses in this country are including information on interviews, questionnaires, and survey research. We have included this material in Chapter 12. Even the guidelines for writing up research required by the American Psychological Association change from time to time, and 1984 was such a time. Chapter 14 and Appendixes B and C reflect the new APA publication manual. Likewise, Chapter 13 includes the most recent revision of the APA ethical principles.

Not only does research change in particulars such as formats for publication but the field also matures in terms of broader conceptual approaches and its willingness to consider new topics. We expand on this idea in the final chapter of the book, in which we discuss the potential for a scientific psychology. We point out that psychology was once almost a battleground for those who were interested in behavior and those interested in experience. But today, with scientific studies of attention, awareness, consciousness, and communication between species, we see a new group of scientists who are interested in both behavior *and* experience, not only in others but in themselves.

This book grew out of discussions concerning our experience of science and the role it currently plays in psychology. At this time we would like to acknowledge individuals who joined us in these discussions at various times. We especially appreciate the time Dale Harris spent discussing with us his perspective on the history of the experimental movement in psychology. We also appreciate the willingness of Lance Shotland, Nora Newcombe, and Carolyn Sherif to discuss with us how their ideas came about and how they began their important research programs.

We also appreciate the help of our colleagues Mel Mark and Hoben Thomas for their careful reading of and critical suggestions on the chapters related to inferential statistics and survey research. Some of our colleagues at Penn State shared with us the manner in which they teach experimental methods as well as the values they wish to impart. In particular, we would like to thank Professors Paul Cornwell, Rick Jacobs, Jim Martin, Robert Seibel, and Robert Stern. There are many colleagues throughout the country who shared their experience of teaching with us and in many ways made this book richer. We appreciate these individuals. Some of these individuals presented careful readings of the earlier edition and make invaluable suggestions based on their experience with the book. In particular we would like to acknowledge Mark S. Sanders, California State University at Northridge;

Barbara Tabachnick, California State University at Northridge; Paul Eskildsen, San Francisco State University; Alan C. Kamil, University of Massachusetts; Howard B. Orenstein, Western Maryland College; Elizabeth Lynn, San Diego State University; Henry Gorman, Austin College; Kathryn Schwarz, Scottsdale Community College; Henry Morlock, SUNY Plattsburgh; Robert T. Brown, University of North Carolina, Wilmington; Keith Stanovich, Oakland University; Ronald Rossi, Lyndon State College; Dennis Cogan, Texas Tech University; W. Scott Terry, University of North Carolina, Charlotte; Sheila Zipf, San Francisco State University; Nancy Kirkland, Trinity College; and Les Herold, California State University at San Bernardino, who reviewed the first edition. John M. Knight, Central State University; Earl Babbie; Mark A. Sabol, Creighton University; John J. Meryman, San Jose State University; Elvis C. Jones; Frostburg State College; Judith E. Larkin, Canisius College; Elizabeth Capaldi, Purdue University; and Thomas O. Nelson, University of Washington reviewed the second edition.

We hope the book has not suffered from our inability to implement all of their suggestions. We found the production staff at Wadsworth to be excellent and wish to thank them for their efforts. It is never an easy task to turn a manuscript into a finished product and such efforts often go unnoticed. We also appreciate our association with Ken King, the psychology editor at Wadsworth, for his commitment to this project and to quality publishing. We would also like to invite both students and faculty to write us with their comments concerning the book or examples from their courses or the literature that has helped to clarify the material. You can write us at the Department of Psychology, Pennsylvania State University, University Park, PA 16802.

# INTRODUCTION

You are about to begin a voyage of wonder and curiosity, of questionings and doubts. Historically, it is a voyage that human beings began many generations ago and that young scientists like yourselves embark on every day. It is a voyage into the nature of ourselves and the world in which we live. It is a voyage with a particular focus: science. For some of you, science may offer a new way to view the world. Learning about science, like learning about anything new, will offer added perspective, which can in turn lead to a very real expansion of your own consciousness. For those of you already familiar with science, this book offers a deeper exploration of the science of behavior and experience. It is important to emphasize from the onset that learning about science is an expansion of what you already are. It is an *option,* an alternative that you are free to use or not to use as you explore and interact with our world. You choose how and when to use it. In fact, after taking this course, you may decide it is not a way you wish to view the world at all and you may never use it again!

Some beginning students are hesitant to explore science because they believe it is cold, antihumanistic, and even antireligious. They believe it separates us from our beliefs, our faiths, our feelings, and ourselves. This is a serious and limiting misconception. Many of our colleagues in all fields of science are as open to humanistic and spiritual traditions as they are to science. We believe that science—a science of behavior and experience—will some day assist us in a profoundly deep exploration of the inner teachings of all our great humanistic and spiritual traditions. This task of helping all of us more fully explore and understand our own potential may be the major function of science in the future evolution of human consciousness.

Our voyage into the science of behavior and experience begins by stressing that there are many childlike qualities that we hope will always remain part of us. Genuine laughter, spontaneous play, intimacy, curiosity, and creativity are some childlike qualities that form the very foundation of mature human experience. In a similar way, the scientific method we are about to explore has firm roots in the simple way children go about exploring their world. With this in mind, we begin our exploration of science by viewing ourselves as children who wish to explore. The world awaiting the child includes not only the outside world but also the child's own psychological experience. Through this child, who is one aspect of ourselves, we approach the question of how we go about performing a science of behavior and experience. We will watch the child search for knowledge and mature into three distinct aspects, which we can define as actors in our drama of psychological inquiry.

The first aspect or role is that of the *scientist.* This is the role that you are reading this book to learn about. It is the active role in our drama. The task before you is to learn how the scientist goes about doing science. In this book we will watch the child learn the role of the scientist. We will come to see that many activities of present-day, mature scientists are simply extensions of the way we approached the world as children. As you learn about this role, you will learn about the types of questions scientists ask, the types of answers that they accept, and the manner in which knowledge is approached and verified. You will also learn how to assume this role for yourself and begin your drama of experimentation.

The second aspect or role is that of the *subject.* This is the passive role in our drama. The subject is the particular organism that the scientist chooses to study. In fact, it is the various experiences and behaviors of the subject that form the content of psychology. The paradox for scientists interested in the study of human behavior and experience is that although the subject matter is "out there" in the subjects we study, because we are also human, it is at the same time "in here" in us. In a very real sense, as we study other people and animals, we also study ourselves.

The third role is that of the *witness.* This role is not always recognized, yet in many ways it is the most important because it maintains a balance between the scientist and the subject, the active and passive aspects of this process. The witness, who is also us, stands back and watches the scientist do science and the subject behave and experience the world. One task of the witness is to teach that both the scientist and the subject are *limited* because each sees the world from his or her own perspective.

As the witness teaches us that there is a broader perspective from which we can appreciate both viewpoints simultaneously, we begin to mature and realize the richness of the scientific process and the wonder of approaching knowledge of reality. In this vein, it is the role of the witness to remind us that the experience and understanding of life require more than just a description of miles of blood vessels, reinforcement schedules, and chemicals interacting with each other. It is the witness who asks whether the science of the scientist is relevant, ethical, and generally worth doing. But most important, it is the witness who brings together the procedures of the scientist and the experience of the subject and allows them to have a relationship in the first place.

Once we have developed these aspects of ourselves—the scientist, the subject, and the witness—we will be in a better position to understand the strengths and weaknesses of using science to study ourselves. Until that time, we would like to suggest that you neither accept nor reject the scientific approach but rather that you *allow* that it may have something to offer you. That is, you can allow yourself to become actively involved in trying to solve problems and answer questions using this method while remaining free to remember the problems and limitations of the scientific approach. As in anything else, it is only through active involvement that you will come to understand fully what the method has to offer. Let us now begin the drama of science with a problem—how did we as children come to know the world?—and from this develop methods for a science of behavior and experience.

# ACKNOWLEDGMENTS

**Chapter 5.** Pages 108–109: The interview with Lance Shotland is used by permission of Lance Shotland. Pages 111–112: The interview with Nora Newcombe is used by permission of Nora Newcombe. Pages 118, 119: The excerpt from the subject index in Box 5.2 and the sample abstract on the following page from *Psychological Abstracts,* copyright 1979 by the American Psychological Association, are reprinted by permission of the American Psychological Association, publisher of *Psychological Abstracts* and the PsycINFO Database, and may not be reproduced without its prior permission. Page 121: Portion of a sample page in Box 5.4 from *Science Citation Index,* 1978 Annual, copyright 1979 by the Institute for Scientific Information, is reprinted by permission of the publisher.

**Chapters 6 and 8.** Pages 132, 133, and 178–179: The quotation and Figures 6.1 and 8.1 from J. D. Bransford and M. K. Johnson, "Contextual Prerequisites for Understanding," *Journal of Verbal Learning and Verbal Behavior,* 1972, *11,* 717–726, are used by permission of Academic Press and J. D. Bransford.

**Chapter 7.** Page 156: The random number table in Box 7.1 is reprinted with permission from William Beyer (ed.), *Handbook of Tables for Probability and Statistics,* Second Edition, 1968; copyright The Chemical Rubber Co., CRC Press, Inc.

**Chapter 8.** Pages 194–195: The two figures in Box 8.1 based on Bower et al., 1978, and Bower and Gilligan, 1979, copyright 1978, 1979, by the American Psychological Association, are adapted by permission of the publisher.

**Chapter 13.** Pages 312–314: The ten *Ethical Principles in the Conduct of Research with Human Participants,* copyright 1973 by the American Psychological Association, are reprinted by permission of the publisher. Pages 316–317: The editorial in Box 13.1 from E. F. Loftus and J. F. Fries, "Informed Consent May Be Hazardous to Your Health," *Science,* 1979, *204,* 4388, copyright 1979 by the American Association for the Advancement of Science, is reprinted by permission of the publisher and Elizabeth Loftus.

**Chapter 14.** Pages 330, 332, 335, 338, 340–341: Quotations from D. J. Gaul, W. E. Craighead, and M. J. Mahoney, "Relationship between Eating Rates and Obesity," *Journal of Consulting and Clinical Psychology,* 1975, *43,* 123–125, copyright 1975 by the American Psychological Association, are reprinted by permission of the publisher and W. E. Craighead. Pages 331, 335–337: Quotations from R. L. Shotland and M. K. Straw, "Bystander Response to an Assault," *Journal of Personality and Social Psychology,* 1976, *34,* 990–999, copyright 1976 by the American Psychological Association, are reprinted by permission of the publisher and R. L. Shotland. Pages 332–333: The quotation from K. Ravizza, "Peak Experiences in Sports," *Journal of Humanistic Psychology,* 1977, *17,* 35–40, is reprinted by permission of the publisher and the author. Pages 344–345: The checklist in Box 14.1 from R. R. Holt, "Experimental Methods in Clinical Psychology," in B. B. Wolman (ed.), *Handbook of Clinical Psychology,* McGraw-Hill, 1965, is reprinted by permission of the publisher.

**Chapter 15.** Pages 366–367: The quotation in Box 15.2 from L. Thomas, *The Medusa and the Snail,* Viking, 1979, is reprinted by permission of the author.

**Appendix B.** Pages 383–392: The article by Margaret S. Clark, Sandra Milberg, and Ralph Erber, "Effects of Arousal on Judgments of Others' Emotions," *Journal of Personality and Social Psychology,* 1984, *46,* 551–560, copyright 1984 by the American Psychological Association, is reprinted by permission of the publisher and Margaret S. Clark.

CHAPTER ONE

# *What Is Science?*

## INTRODUCTION

Science is above all a human activity. One obvious meaning of this is that science is done by people. A second and equally accurate meaning is that all people do science in some form. After all, the methods of science are basically simple extensions of the ways all people learn about their world. Science in many ways is very similar to how we have been learning about the world since we were infants. Consequently, because each of you has been using it in one form or another since you first began toddling about and discovering the world, you already know much more about the scientific method than you think you do.

Watch a young child. When something catches his or her eye, the child must examine it, study it, observe it, have fun with it. Next, the child wants to interact with it, touch it, feel it. From passive observations and active interactions, the child slowly learns about the world. Some interactions are fun: "If I tip the glass, I get to see the milk form pretty pictures on the floor." Other interactions are not much fun: "If I touch the red circles on the stove, my fingers hurt!" From each interaction, the child learns a little more about the world.

Like the child, scientists are exploring the unknown and sometimes the known features of the world. Although most scientists have mastered the effects of spilling their milk, all basic research strategies are based on one simple notion: *To discover what the world is like, we must experience it.* To have an idea about the nature of the world is simply not enough. Instead, like the child, scientists experience the world to determine whether their ideas accurately reflect reality. Direct experience is our most important tool because it alone allows us to bridge the gap between our ideas and reality.

In general, there is no single scientific method any more than there is one art or one education or one religion, yet there is a general process that is called *science.* This process consists of experiencing the world and then drawing general conclusions (called *facts*) from observations. Sometimes these conclusions or facts may be descriptive and represented by numbers. For example, we say that it is 238,000 miles to the moon or that the average human heart rate is 72 beats per minute. Other times these facts may be more general and describe a relationship or a process. For example, we say that it is more difficult to learn a second language after puberty than before, or that as we age we hear fewer high-frequency sounds. Whatever the topic, the known facts about a particular subject are called *scientific knowledge.*

Many conceptions of science picture a man or woman in a white lab coat laboriously writing down numbers and later milling about in a cluttered office trying to make theoretical sense out of the findings. This conception may be accurate, but it is not a total picture of science. Here, we will be stressing another aspect of science, which becomes apparent when the available facts are viewed in light of human value. It is this aspect of value that allows us to see one set of numbers as more relevant or potentially more useful than another. This combining of fact and value results in a humanistic approach to scientific understanding. Scientific understanding helps us to see the *how* and *why* of the world, and thereby to understand nature in a fuller perspective. In many cases, this understanding raises new questions, which in turn can be answered by using science to examine the world. In other cases, these new facts may be applied in real-life settings (technology) and make life easier for everyone. Thus, at its best, science begins and ends in human experience.

In the Introduction we described three actors in the drama of science: the subject, the scientist, and the witness. In our study of behavior and experience, it is the scientist who experiences the world and then formulates general facts or conclusions that describe it. The subject is the particular psychological experience of whatever organism we are studying. In the case of studying human consciousness, the subject will also be some aspect of ourselves. Finally, the witness provides the perspective, the concerns for value, and the relation of science and its facts to other aspects of human life.

## SCIENCE AS A WAY OF KNOWING

Some students fall into the trap of viewing science as the best way, or even the only way, to study behavior and experience. If you find this happening to you, beware! Nothing is further from the truth. To emphasize this, we offer science to you as merely one way of examining human nature. There are others; art, philosophy, religion, and literature are all extremely fruitful ways or channels through which we can gain new ideas about human behavior and experience. In the past, psychology has drawn on many of these traditions and will surely continue to do so in the future.

Having a fruitful source of ideas, whether it is our literary, spiritual, scientific, or artistic traditions, is an important part of understanding behavior and experience. However, a second and perhaps even more important aspect of learning about psychology is the process of deciding whether or not a new idea is accurate. In contrast to other ways of knowing, science offers not only a fertile source of new ideas but also a powerful method for evaluating the ideas we have about reality. For example, suppose you go to a lecture by a well-known spiritual leader and he says that if you meditate twice a day you will be happier. Here is an instance when you are confronted with a new idea that may have a very important impact on your life. Because some time and effort are involved, however, you are hesitant to try meditation unless you know it will be profitable. So you are faced with the task of evaluating the suggestion and deciding whether or not meditation is for you. How do you decide this? In the remainder of this section, we will examine several ways people commonly use to decide whether or not to accept new ideas about the world. For a more detailed discussion of these ways of accepting belief, we suggest you consult the work of the American philosopher Charles Peirce (see Cohen & Nagel, 1934; Kerlinger, 1973). Obviously we are biased and believe the best way, especially for society at large, to go about accepting new ideas is to use science first to evaluate them and then use the results to help make a decision.

### Tenacity

Charles Peirce uses the term *tenacity* to refer to an acceptance of a belief because "we have always known it to be this way." People say "women are bad drivers," "you can't teach an old dog new tricks," or "science is always beneficial." These statements are presented over and over again and accepted as true, yet they are never examined and evaluated. Unfortunately, this is an all-too-common method of accepting information. You may notice that some television advertising and political election campaigns use this technique when they present a single phrase or slogan repeatedly. Even an empty phrase repeated often enough becomes "true." As has been said, if you tell people something often enough, they will believe it. As a way of learning about the world, there are two problems with this method. First, the statement may be just an empty phrase and its accuracy may never have been evaluated. The statement may gain wide acceptance through its familiarity alone. Second, tenacity offers no means for correcting erroneous ideas, and this is its greatest problem. That is, once a statement based solely on tenacity is widely accepted, it is very difficult to change. Social psychologists have shown that once a person accepts a belief without data to support it, the person will often create or make up a reason for its truth; the person may even refuse to accept new information that contradicts this erroneous belief. In the case of the meditation example, a decision to meditate simply because it is "known to be beneficial" would be acceptance based on tenacity. Accepting ideas about experience and behavior simply because they are familiar to us or widely believed by others is an extension of the childish behavior of the three-year-old who just copies the words and behaviors of his or her parents. For the child this is an efficient way to learn about the world, but for the rest of us it is very limiting.

### Authority

A second way we may accept a new idea is through some authority figure telling us it is so. Acceptance based on authority is simple, since we have only to repeat and live by what we are told. In many cases, referring to an authority, especially in areas we know nothing about, is not only useful but also beneficial. When we were young, our parents often used the method of authority for directing our behavior. Health care and education in many places were based almost exclusively on authority. If a famous physician or educator said something was true, everyone considered it true. Even today, we often rely on the judgment of an authority whether we are going to physicians, psychologists, scientists, or stockbrokers. Likewise, religious training as it is taught today relies on the authority of the church for establishing correct religious procedures. Although authority brings with it a stability that allows for consistency, it is not without problems. The major problem of accepting authority as having sole access to truth is that authority can be incorrect and thus send people in the wrong directions. For example, as long as everyone accepted the viewpoint that the world was flat or that the earth was the center of the universe, no one thought to look for America or to study the orbit of the earth. Consequently, it is very important to examine the basis of the authority's claims. Are they based on opinion, tradition, revelation, or direct experience? How valid are these sources of information? In the meditation example, if you decided to meditate simply because this well-known spiritual leader advised it, you would be basing your decision solely on his authority. Box 1.1 discusses the transition from authority to experimentation in the beginning of modern science.

---

## *Box 1.1* *Galileo: The Transition from Authority to Empiricism*

Galileo represents for many scientists a symbol of change in the rules of evidence. Of course many individuals influenced the beginning of scientific thought during the Renaissance, beginning with Copernicus and Kepler as well as the philosopher Bacon. However, Galileo and Newton (see Box 1.2) are often referred to as the greatest founders of modern science (cf. Russell, 1945; Holton, 1952). Before their time, intellectual questions were answered by referring to authority, usually the authority of the church. The church of this period in turn looked to the Greek philosopher Aristotle for answers to "material" questions—what today we call *natural science.*

Suppose a person wanted to know which of two balls would hit the ground first if dropped from a tall building. Until the time of Galileo, the method of answering this question would be to refer to Aristotle's theory, which stated that the world is made up of four types of elements—earth, air, water, and fire. Each element, according to Aristotle, acts according to its own nature. To answer the question of which of two bodies would hit the ground first, one would reason that the two objects, composed of the element "earth," would seek to return to earth and thus fall down. If one object weighed more than the other, it would be reasoned that this heavier object contained more of the element "earth" than the lighter one and would naturally fall faster. Thus, it would be concluded that the heavier body would hit the ground before the lighter one. No one would have thought actually to drop two objects from a tower and *observe* which hit the ground first. Answers were always given in terms of authority.

Galileo was part of a revolution that was to challenge authority. He successfully replaced the method of authority with that of experimentation. The movement toward experimentation was greatly aided by Galileo's own inventions, such as a telescope, a thermometer, an improved microscope, and a pendulum-type timing device. Each of these devices allowed people to experiment and to answer for themselves the questions of nature. After establishing that balls rolling down an inclined plane act similarly to falling objects, Galileo successfully challenged the authority of Aristotle concerning two falling weights. With Galileo's work, a new science based on observation and experimentation was beginning.

---

## Reason

Reason and logic are the basic methods of philosophy. Reason often takes the form of a logical syllogism, such as *All men can't count; Dick is a man; therefore Dick can't count.* We all use reason every day as we try to solve problems and understand relationships. Useful as it is to be reasonable, however, reason alone will not always produce the appropriate answer. Why is this so? One potential problem in the reasoned approach is that our original assumption must be correct. If the original assumption is incorrect or at odds with the world in which we live, then logic cannot help us. For example, the syllogism that concluded that Dick can't count is logically valid even though it is based on the absurd premise that all men can't count! The weakness of using reason alone is that we have no way to determine the accuracy of our assumptions. Thus, we can have situations in which our logic is impeccable, but because our original assumption was inaccurate, the conclusion is silly.

## Common Sense

Common sense offers an improvement over acceptance based on tenacity, authority, or reason because it offers an appeal to direct experience. Common sense is based on our own past experiences and our perception of how we think the world is. One problem is that our experiences and perceptions of the world may be quite limited. Whereas common sense may help us deal with the routine aspects of our daily life, it may also form a wall and prevent us from understanding new areas. This can be a problem particularly when we enter realms outside our everyday experience. For example, people considered Einstein's suggestion that time was relative and could be different for different people to be against common sense. Likewise, it was considered against common sense when Freud suggested that we did not always know our own motivations or when Skinner suggested that the concept of free will is meaningless for most individuals.

## Science

The final way we will discuss in which people accept new ideas is through science. The philosopher of science, Alfred North Whitehead (1925), suggested that there are two methods for what he called the "purification of ideas" that are combined in the scientific method. An idea is evaluated and/or corrected through (1) dispassionately observing by means of our bodily senses (for example, vision, hearing, and touch) and (2) using reason to compare various theoretical conceptualizations based on experience.

The first method is a direct extension of the commonsense approach just described. Unlike a given individual's common sense, however, science is open to *anyone's* direct experience. Presumably any observation made by one scientist could be verified by any other individual with normal sensory capacities. To aid individuals in repeating the observations of others, some scientists (see Bridgman, 1927) have emphasized the importance of *operational definitions* in research. As you will see in the next chapter, operational definitions direct *how* observations are to be made and *what* is to be observed and measured.

The second method is a direct application of the principles of logic. In this case, however, logic is combined with experience to rule out any assumptions that do not accurately reflect the world. This blend of direct sensory experience and reason gives science a self-corrective nature, which is not found in other ways of accepting ideas about the world. This means that scientific conclusions are never taken as final but are always open to reinterpretation as new evidence is gained. In other words, the method of science includes a feedback component by which conclusions about the world can be refined over time. It is the refining of ideas through both experimentation and reason that allows science to be a fruitful method for knowing about the world. Box 1.2 describes Sir Isaac Newton's rules of reasoning in science. In many ways these rules are as applicable today as they were 300 years ago.

## THE SCIENTIFIC APPROACH

In this chapter we will acquaint you with the scientific approach through various informal illustrations, examples, and stories. In Chapter 2 we will more formally discuss the methods of natural observation and experimentation. Among other things we will emphasize that a major characteristic of science is a reliance on information that is *verifiable through experience.* That is, it must be possible for different individuals in different places and at different times using a similar method to produce the same results.

Once you know the methods of science and have actually used them in a variety of situations, you will be in a position to evaluate science as a method of knowing about the world that includes the behavior and experience of yourself and others. More important, you will be in a position to decide whether it is the way you choose to understand your world. First, however, let us begin to understand what science is by looking at three early efforts to understand the world better. Although these efforts attempted to be systematic, today we would call them pre-experimental or quasi-experimental. That is, in none of these accounts was an actual experiment conducted. Our purpose is to ask you to focus on the manner in which the problem was resolved. Try to see how the solution was sought, particularly the efforts to be systematic, and what errors were made. You might also recall instances from your own life when you attempted to solve problems in similar ways.

## EARLY APPROACHES

The first example concerns extrasensory perception (ESP). Do you think research on ESP is new? Think again, for the story we are about to relate took place in 447 B.C., more than 2,400 years ago.

---

### *Box 1.2* *Newton's Rules of Reasoning*

Born the year after Galileo's death, Newton represents the beginning of modern science as we know it. Where Galileo had fought with philosophers of his day and was tortured by the church for his belief, Newton was able to live in a new age, in which science through experimentation and reason began to bear fruit.

In the 1680s Newton's classic work, *Principia,* was published (Newton, 1969 reprint). Designated by the historian of science Gerald Holton (1952) as "probably the greatest single book in the history of science," this work described Newton's theories concerning time, space, and motion as well as his rules of reasoning for science. Science, called *natural philosophy* by Newton, is based on four rules of reasoning. These rules, created more than 300 years ago, are still useful for helping scientists to reason and develop hypotheses.

*Rule 1*

*We are to admit no more causes of natural things than such as are both true and sufficient to explain their appearances.*

*To this purpose the philosophers say that Nature does nothing in vain, and more is in vain when less will serve; for Nature is pleased with simplicity, and affects not the pomp of superfluous causes.*

Today we refer to this rule as the law of parsimony. The rule simply states that natural events should be explained in the simplest way possible.

*Rule 2*

*Therefore to the same natural effects we must, as far as possible, assign the same causes.*

*As to respiration in a man and in a beast, the descent of stones in Europe and in America; the light of our culinary fire and of the sun; the reflection of light in the earth, and in the planets.*

This rule reflects Newton's belief in a natural order, which requires that the same gravity causes stones to fall in Europe and in America.

*Rule 3*

*The qualities of bodies, which admit neither intensification nor remission of degrees, and*

According to the historian Herodotus (1942 trans.), Croesus, the king of Lydia, became concerned at the increasing power of the Persian army, because Lydia was located between Persia and Greece. King Croesus knew the Persian armies to be strong and thus did not want to attack them unless it was certain he would win. He needed someone who could foretell the future. As an enlightened consumer, Croesus wanted to know that the information he received was true. To determine this, he constructed a test of the oracles who were said to foretell the future best. The test went as follows: Croesus's assistants were to go out into Greece and Libya where famous oracles lived. The assistants were to visit each oracle on a specific day and at a specific time and ask the following question: What was the king doing at that moment? Since the king told no one what he was actually doing at that moment, he reasoned that only a true oracle capable of ESP could answer correctly. The

---

*which are found to belong to all bodies within the reach of our experiments, are to be esteemed the universal qualities of all bodies whatsoever.*

*For since the qualities of bodies are only known to us by experiments, we are to hold for universal all such as universally agree with experiments; and such as are not liable to diminution can never be quite taken away. We are certainly not to relinquish the evidence of experiments for the sake of dreams and vain fictions of our own devising; nor are we to recede from the analogy of Nature, which is wont to be simple, and always consonant to itself. We no other way know the extension of bodies than by our senses, nor do these reach it in all bodies; but because we perceive extension in all that are sensible, therefore we ascribe it universally to all others also.*

Newton continues with a long discussion of this principle. Briefly, it states that what we learn from our experiments can be applied to other similar structures outside the reach of our experiments. For example, the properties of gravity and inertia should apply to the moon and other planets as they apply to stones and other objects we experiment with.

*Rule 4*

*In experimental philosophy we are to look upon propositions inferred by general induction from phenomena as accurately or very nearly true, notwithstanding any contrary hypotheses that may be imagined, till such time as other phenomena occur, by which they may either be made more accurate, or liable to exceptions.*

*This rule we must follow, that the argument of induction may not be evaded by hypotheses.*

This rule simply states that theories obtained from experiments should be considered true or approximately true until new experimental evidence shows the old to be incorrect. Ideas developed from experiments should not be changed just because we like another hypothesis better.

These four simple rules have directed science for the past 300 years. In this century they have been applied to the social and behavioral sciences as well.

---

assistants all returned to the king and reported their answers. Only one oracle—the oracle at Delphi—knew the correct answer. In fact, according to Herodotus, this oracle answered the question before it was even asked. The king had been making lamb stew.

Although the king had the beginnings of a scientific approach to experience, he had not yet learned the role of chance in science or the nature of the language of science, as we shall soon see. Trusting his research, the king honored the oracle and asked the important political question whether he should go to battle against the Persian armies. The oracle replied that in such a contest, "a mighty empire would be destroyed." This was all the king needed to assemble his armies and attack. When the battle was completed, a mighty empire had been destroyed as the oracle had predicted. The problem for the king was that the empire destroyed was his own and he was a prisoner. As we shall discuss in later chapters, the king, like many others after him, failed to realize that the initial "correct answer" of the oracle may have been only a lucky guess. Likewise, he did not realize that the language of prediction must be quite precise in directing our attention toward possible outcomes that can be tested.

Let us look at another attempt to understand the world, this one dating back almost 2,000 years. In the second century A.D., Galen, a well-known physician, described a woman who complained of insomnia (Mesulam & Perry, 1972). The problem was to determine the factors that led to the insomnia. Galen first decided that the problem was not mainly physical. Following this determination, he began to notice the woman's condition during his examinations. It happened that during one examination, a person returning from the theater mentioned the name of a certain dancer, Pylades. At this point Galen observed that the woman's pulse increased along with a change in her facial color and expression. What did Galen do next? To answer his questions as to what was affecting the woman, he began to experiment. In his own words,

> The next day, I told one of my following that when I went to visit the woman he was to arrive a little later and mention that Morphus was dancing that day. When this was done the patient's pulse was in no way changed. And likewise, on the following day, while I was attending her, the name of the third dancer was mentioned, and in like fashion the pulse was hardly affected at all. I investigated the matter for a fourth time in the evening. Studying the pulse and seeing that it was excited and irregular when mention was made that Pylades was dancing, I concluded that the lady was in love with Pylades, and in the days following, this conclusion was confirmed exactly. (Galen, 1827 trans.)

Galen went past observation and began to ask, "I wonder what will happen if I do this?" He performed what we would now call a *single-subject experiment* (see Chapter 11). It is important for you to notice that Galen checked to determine that it was not the name of just any dancer that produced a change in pulse rate or even just a man's name. Thus, he sought to discover what factors brought on an irregular pulse by examining a number of alternatives. From this investigation, he concluded that only the name of one particular man repeated on different occasions produced the effect.

Let us consider one more story, which took place in Europe 200 years ago. A physician named Semmelweis faced a serious problem when he noticed that healthy women who had just given birth to healthy children were dying. The women died of a condition that included fever, chills, and seizures. Although there were numerous theories offered, which included bad diet, unhealthy water, and even the smell of certain flowers, Semmelweis knew that other women in the same hospital who ate the same food, drank the same water, and smelled the same flowers did not die. Consequently, Semmelweis reasoned that it was not the food, water, or flowers. Yet the fact remained that only women giving birth died of this condition.

Semmelweis became aware of a crucial clue when he learned that an assistant who had accidentally cut his hand during an autopsy had later died of the same symptoms as the mothers. What was the connection between the death of the assistant and those of the mothers? Was there any connection at all? Semmelweis reasoned that the autopsy laboratory where the assistant had worked might be the cause of the mysterious deaths. To evaluate this notion, he traveled to other hospitals and recorded what physicians did just before delivering babies. From these observations, he learned that when the physicians who delivered the babies came directly from a pathology lecture in which diseased tissues were handled or from performing an autopsy, the death rate was highest. He suggested that it was the physicians who were transferring the diseases from the pathological tissue to the healthy mothers, just as the assistant had accidentally infected himself with the knife cut.

As you might imagine, the physicians of the day were outraged at the suggestion that they were the cause of death. Semmelweis found further evidence by demonstrating that in those hospitals where there was an option for a birth by either a midwife or a physician, the mothers with the birth by midwife survived at a much greater rate. In a rather dramatic, though not totally controlled experiment, Semmelweis is said to have placed himself at the door to the delivery ward and forced all physicians who entered to wash their hands first. The number of deaths decreased dramatically. Although not everyone accepted the report of his findings, the data spoke for themselves and modern medical practice has been shaped by this event (Glasser, 1976).

These three stories—of Croesus, Galen, and Semmelweis—show the beginning of a scientific approach to human problems. Croesus faced the problem of how to evaluate information offered by various oracles. To do this, he devised a test—an evaluation of the sources to decide which one he would use to direct his behavior. But we do not consult oracles today, you might argue. This may be true, but we do develop far-reaching social programs and treatments. For example, is "Sesame Street" a useful means for teaching disadvantaged children? In terms of psychotherapy, would you gain more by just talking with your favorite professor than by going to a clinical psychologist? If you want to avoid heart attacks, do you change your diet, run four miles a day, meditate, or just do nothing? To answer these questions, we, like Croesus, need to perform evaluation research, and the methods of science offer us one approach.

Croesus's experience also reminds us of two potential pitfalls to knowing about the world. These are the roles of chance in the events we observe and the need for unambiguous statements. Croesus's single question to the oracle might have been correctly answered by a lucky guess. To decrease the chance of a lucky guess, Croesus might have asked the oracles several questions. In essence, such a safeguard would have constituted a *replication* (repeating a procedure under similar conditions) of his experiment. Today simple replication of a new finding is a powerful way to decrease the likelihood that it is a fluke. In retrospect, Croesus also surely recognized that he misinterpreted the oracle's ambiguous answer about the battle. To minimize the chances of ambiguities, scientists carefully and systematically define their words as precisely as possible.

Galen faced a different problem. He wanted to learn why a particular woman did not sleep. To do this, he first observed the woman; that is, he just spent some time with her and noticed what happened. Once he realized that the woman's heart reacted to a dancer's name, he began to test his observations. Galen at this point moved to a more sophisticated process than Croesus's simple consultation with a fortune-teller. Galen sought evidence for a causal relationship by examining the woman directly. In this he anticipated a major shift concerning how we know about the world. Very briefly, Croesus sought his answers from authority. The authority of his time was the gods, who spoke through the oracles. A more empirical approach would have been for Croesus to develop a system of spies and scouts to provide information about the Persians' strength based on direct experience. In contrast, Galen went beyond the ungrounded opinions or guesses of available authorities and relied on his direct experience. Galen's appeal to direct experience reflects an alternative approach to knowing and in a real way reflects an alternative level of consciousness, toward which modern science has evolved. Indeed, for several generations now science has been rebuilding our knowledge and understanding of the world in terms of direct experience.

In all likelihood, the actual choice of basing our actions on evidence from experience or on unfounded opinion has probably been with us in some form for thousands of years and currently confronts *each of us* countless times every day. Yet basing one's actions on direct experience of the world sometimes initially appears time-consuming and more difficult than simply consulting some expert or acting on a hunch. In the long run, because our actions invariably take place in the world, the wiser alternative is to base actions on experiential knowledge of the "real situation." For you, this may mean beginning to resolve those nagging career decisions by attempting to get some part-time or even volunteer job experience to find out whether you enjoy the job as much as you predicted. Frequently students base their career decisions solely on their own hunches or their parents' opinions. Because it is difficult to get direct experience of many jobs, we often encourage our students to take time off and try out some of their ideas. Mere opinions of others provide a convenient answer, but in the long run, as Croesus found out, reality prevails. We hope the experiences you have in this course, particularly the experimental aspects, will help you decide whether you enjoy "doing science." Use this course as a way of learning about science and yourself as well.

In the third story Semmelweis had a different problem to solve. Why were some healthy women dying after giving birth? To solve this problem, he examined a number of factors. *He observed the patients with a definite purpose in mind.* He asked: How are these women being treated that is different from the way other patients are treated? That is, he sought to determine what was unique to these patients. Was it diet? Flowers? Doctors? What was it? Then an unexpected event occurred; an autopsy assistant died. This gave the clue that led to the solution of the problem. To digress, we want to suggest that science not only is a method that scientists engage in to solve problems and learn about the world, but also is a procedure that allows for unexpected events to play a part, whether in the form of accident or human error. That is to say, one of the rich aspects of science includes unpredictability, serendipity, and what is often called "luck." Keep in mind, however that luck can work either way, as Croesus found out.

In thinking about Semmelweis's work, notice how he used logic and simple common sense to design his tests so that his observations would lead to a better understanding of the problem. Semmelweis tried to understand what was related to the mothers' deaths. For example, because the laboratory assistant died of similar symptoms, Semmelweis reasoned that perhaps he died of the same cause. Semmelweis's observation that more deaths occurred after doctors handled diseased tissue led him to reason that perhaps the cause was somehow related to the diseased tissue. In other cases he tried to rule out *factors that were not responsible* for the deaths. For instance, because women patients who did not die ate the same food and drank the same water, Semmelweis reasoned that these were not possible causes and could be eliminated from further consideration.

There was nothing particularly extraordinary about any of these conclusions. In fact, they reflect the simple common sense we all possess. What was exceptional was that Semmelweis saw relationships that others overlooked. When simple common sense and reason are combined with direct sensory experience, a desire to understand reality, and the courage to accept new facts, science emerges as a powerful means of asking questions about reality.

Our final comment on Semmelweis's work is that his desire to know and understand led to the development of a series of investigations that approached the problem from several directions. Once he had gained the clue from the death of the assistant, he set out to answer his question through a series of observations. First, he saw how the new mothers in his hospital were treated differently from other women; that is, he observed that they were *not* given different food or flowers or treated by different doctors. Second, he allowed himself to consider a possible connection between the death of an assistant and the death of the mothers. Third, he went to other hospitals to determine whether his ideas or hypotheses were limited to his hospital or whether they were true for other hospitals as well. Fourth, he concluded that the problem was that the physicians handled diseased tissue and then delivered babies without washing their hands, even though this was an unpopular idea. Fifth, he performed an indirect test of his theory by comparing the difference in death rates caused by physicians who handled diseased tissue and midwives who did not. Sixth, he began a direct test of his theory by insisting that physicians wash their hands as they came onto the delivery ward. The power of Semmelweis's procedure was not in any one test of his ideas, since it is almost impossible for any single procedure to answer

"TREADMILLS! MAZES! THERE MUST BE MORE TO LIFE THAN THIS."

all questions in science. The power was that he began with a problem and followed it through to the end by means of a series of observations.

## SUMMARY

Let's pause for a moment and review what we have covered so far. In the preceding sections we described the scientific approach to problem solving. We began with children learning about the world through interacting with it. In particular, we suggested that such interaction leads to a notion of science as a way of knowing through experience. We characterized science as a process for drawing conclusions that describe the world. We further discussed science not as a sacred ritual to be worshiped but as the simple extension of the way children and all of us learn about our world.

We then gave an overview of science by relating the stories of Croesus, Galen, and Semmelweis. We pointed out the manner in which aspects of these stories anticipated important issues in present-day behavioral science. These correspondences included the need for unambiguous statements, the need for testing what does not affect behavior as well as what does affect behavior, and the importance of a series of tests or research studies for zeroing in on the solution to a problem. We wanted you to see that science combines experience, reason, and desire to answer questions about our conceptions of reality. In order to accomplish this goal, scientists also create theories to help explain the experiences that they have had. As we shall see later, evaluating ideas and theories is also a large part of what science is all about. Furthermore, the approach to solving problems that we call science is not new, but represents a way of solving problems that we *all* use to some extent every day.

## STUDYING PSYCHOLOGICAL BEHAVIOR AND EXPERIENCE PROCESSES

In the preceding discussion we emphasized that scientists view themselves as using sensory experience to evaluate their ideas concerning the world. This appeal to experience and experimentation as opposed to authority is crucial for two reasons. First, it represents a genuine attempt to pause and observe the external world. Second, reliance on sensory experience means that not only scientists but *any other person* with normal sensory capacities and training could observe the particular behavior under study. The ability of anyone to use his or her own senses to verify the raw data of any scientist provides a strong and essential safeguard that our observations of the world remain as free as possible of the unintended, or even intended, biases of any one particular scientist. The process of relying on sensory experience to verify our ideas about reality is referred to as *empiricism*. Empiricism has been a very important approach in the history of psychology.

As the title of this book implies, we are dealing with two worlds in our study of behavior and experience. One is the objective, physical world in which anyone can observe appearance and *behavior*. The other is the subjective world of personal psychological *experience*, which is, of course, completely private. Science, whether it be biology, physics, chemistry, psychology, sociology, or zoology, focuses on the objective world of appearances and behavior. In the behavior of people, molecules, internal organs, or electrons, what science observes and measures are observable objects in the real world. Psychology has continued this tradition, and many studies you will perform and read about will consist of the observation and measurement of human behavior. However, since the subject matter of psychology focuses in part on humans, psychology is faced with a greater challenge. Not only can we observe humans behaving, but we can also ask them about their inner experiences, whether these be thoughts, feelings, or sensations. Furthermore, because we share the same presumably normal array of psychological processes, we can also observe our own behavior and experiences.

This diversity offers us a challenge. The challenge is to explore and understand scientifically the experiences as well as the behaviors of ourselves and others. E. F. Schumacher (1977) emphasized this diversity when he pointed out that using experience and behavior to study psychological processes in ourselves and others leads to four possible fields of knowledge. For our purposes, we will consider these as four possible ways of studying psychological processes. These ways are summarized in Table 1.1.

Let us consider this table for a moment. The first cell (1) is that with which we are all immediately acquainted. This is our private experience of being who we are and living in our world. It is largely unshared subjective experience open to no one but ourselves. However, as we will suggest to you later, it may be possible to explore this space scientifically and in a systematic manner.

The second cell (2) is the inner world of all beings other than ourselves. We, of course, have no direct experience of the subjective world of others. This cell asks such intriguing yet unanswerable questions as: What does it feel like to be you? Do my cats experience the world as I do? Do you and I both see a red apple as the same color? There are researchers in psychology,

**Table 1.1 Four Ways Of Studying Psychological Processes**

| | *Inner Experience* | *Outer Appearance (Behavior)* |
|---|---|---|
| *"I" (self)* | 1 | 3 |
| *"You" (others)* | 2 | 4 |

however, who try to understand how another individual perceives the world and how this might be represented internally (cf. Sherpard, 1983; Simon, 1978). Such a researcher is interested in the experience of other people as they deal with their world cognitively. For example, Simon and others have sought to describe how expert and novice chess players decide on making a particular move. Do you think that an expert player plans farther ahead in a game of chess than a novice player? The answer is no. This is only one of the many questions that cognitive scientists have posed as they try to understand how we experience and process the world around us. In seeking to understand how someone experiences the world, clinical and personality researchers have studied the types of associations that one has to different categories of knowledge, as well as the manner in which certain groups (e.g., schizophrenics) experience the world. Physiological psychologists also consider questions from the second cell when they ask if the nervous system of a cat produces a view of "reality" different from that produced by the nervous system of a human.

The third cell (3) asks the question: How do I appear in the eyes of others? Some aspects of psychology, such as psychotherapy, may focus on helping someone learn about how others perceive them. We could also ask the somewhat uncommon question: How am I represented in the sensory system of nonhuman organisms?

The fourth cell (4) focuses on those behaviors of other people or animals that anyone can directly observe, measure, or objectify. Included here would be physiological responding, such as heart rate or EEG measure, as well as self-report responses, as in a memory experiment. This cell has been the traditional domain of psychological research in this century.

We can use the four ways of studying psychological processes presented in Table 1.1 to ask how we might conduct a science of behavior and experience. In Cell 1 we would ask the question, "How do I study my own inner experience?" In Cell 2 we ask the question, "How do I study your inner experience?" In Cell 3 the question becomes, "How do I study my own behavior in terms of how others see me?" The fourth cell and the one we focus on most in this book asks the question, "How do I study your behavior?"

But what about the subjective experiences of our subjects in psychological experiments? Can't we study these subjective experiences *directly?* No! At least using the methods that we know today this is not possible. However, we can use a subject's behavior, which includes self-report, as a means of learning about the internal world of our subjects. That we use behavior to study subjective experience indirectly is an important idea. Consequently, it will be helpful to step back and discuss the idea in some depth.

## BEHAVIOR: A ROAD INTO THE SUBJECTIVE EXPERIENCE OF SUBJECTS

Assume you want to know whether an animal sees colors. How would you go about it? You cannot directly experience what the animal experiences in the presence of color; you must find a method for asking the animal. You must accept that you can never scientifically answer the question directly, but you can answer indirectly. That is, you begin by reasoning how the animal's behavior would be different in the presence and in the absence of color. You could create a situation in which being able to experience color is necessary for the animal to solve a certain problem.

One way this problem has been approached by some psychologists is through the use of a Skinner box. A Skinner box is designed for use with small animals such as rats or pigeons; it contains a lever on one wall near a food dish. Most Skinner boxes are electrically automated so that a single press or a certain number of presses on the lever cause food to be dropped into the dish. You could program the delivery system in such a manner that the animal would receive food each time the lever was pressed when a green light was on. When either a blue light or no light was on, the animal would not receive food for pressing the lever. How do you think the animal would respond if it could see colors? How would it respond if it could not see colors? Let's look at the table on the next page.

Imagine yourself as an animal for a second, and we think you will see how we could use the animal's behavior to tell us whether it can distinguish green from blue. If, as an animal, you could see colors, then you would soon learn

| | *COLOR LIGHT* | | |
|---|---|---|---|
| | *Green* | *Blue* | *Light off* |
| Food for lever press in each condition? | yes | no | no |
| Expected behavior if: | | | |
| -animal experiences color | ? | ? | ? |
| -animal doesn't experience color | ? | ? | ? |

to press the lever only when the green light was on and not to press the lever when either the blue light or no light was on. What if you could not see colors? When would you press the lever? You would probably quickly learn not to press the lever when no light was on. But what about when there was a green *or* blue light on? If you could not see colors, you would never distinguish between the blue and the green light. Thus you would probably press whenever either light was on. If we made systematic recordings of your behavior (lever pressing) over a period of time, we would be able to predict whether or not you could discriminate a blue light from a green one. We might then set up other discrimination problems (red versus blue, yellow versus green, and so forth). From this information, we could *infer* indirectly whether you could see colors. In solving this problem, we utilized two techniques for inferring the experience of our subjects. The first is to create a situation in which different experiences give rise to different behaviors. The second technique is to imagine yourself as the subject and role-play the responses to gain an experiential perspective.

As you can see, the scientific study of experience rests on the assumption that the subject's behavior is a manifestation of what he or she is experiencing. This is true whether we are studying how animals see colors or a baby's ability to identify their parents from other adults. (How might you do this experiment?) If we are studying human emotions, we may assume that aggressive attacking behaviors are related in some way to an experience of anger in our subjects. In a similar way, if we are studying factors that facilitate the experience of joy in preschool children, we might use increased laughter as evidence that joyful experiences have actually taken place. In these cases we use the behavior of our subjects (aggressive attacks and laughter) to study their subjective experiences of anger and joy. Seen in this light, *behavior and experience are two sides of the same coin.* In the case of anger, for example, the subject's feeling of anger is the internal and unseen experiential aspect, and the subject's aggressive attacks are the external and observable behavioral aspects. In a preceding section, we saw Galen infer his patient's love for Pylades when he observed her behavioral and physiological reactions to Pylades's name. In a similar way, Semmelweis never *saw* a physician carrying germs into the delivery room—indeed, at that time germs could not even be seen! Yet, using indirect evidence, Semmelweis was able to pinpoint the unobservable yet very real cause of the mothers' deaths.

This use of objective behavior to study subjective experience is by no means new to you. We are all very good at "reading" the psychological states of people from their behavior. If your professor walks into class with a scowl, you immediately assume he or she is experiencing some sort of negative emotion. In science, however, we would go a step further and test our assumption.

It should be stressed that the use of objective behavior and appearances to study indirectly unobservable phenomena, such as subjective experience, is not unique to psychology; it is a common feature of all sciences. For example, in physics we discuss the *construct* "gravity," yet we never see gravity. Instead, we observe the movement of objects toward the earth and make inferences about gravity. Nor do we study magnetism directly, but we do observe the movements of iron filings, iron bars, charged particles, and various types of gauges, and we make inferences about magnetism. *A construct is merely a concept used in a particular theoretical manner that ties together a number of observations.* In a nutshell, many major constructs of science, such as gravity, time, evolution, electricity, genetic transmission, learning, and even life itself, are discussed and examined indirectly through their manifestations in the physical world. Thus in science we use the observation of physical events to make inferences concerning not only the physical world but also the unseen processes that underlie it.

## THE PEOPLE WHO DO SCIENCE (SOON TO BE YOU)

We want to remind you, as we did at the beginning of the chapter, that science is a human activity done only by people, and done by all people in one form or another. A third meaning of this statement is that we do science with the support and communication of other scientists. Because a group of people shares our search and values, it is possible for scientists to work together as a larger body of searchers after truth. Sometimes scientists communicate with each other in almost a storybook manner, and new discoveries and formulations are the result of the work of many different individuals. At times, the opposite is the case. As if in a race, the individual scientist competes against other scientists and even against scientists as a group to be the first to make a discovery.

Remember, doing science is just one role or activity of scientists. Scientists are people, and as people they do what people everywhere do. They love and hate. They have good ideas and they have bad ideas. They have thoughts and feelings. Some may want attention and fame, and others may want to be left alone. Scientists feel lonely and sad as well as happy and gregarious. Science is not a means for avoiding what is human within us, although some scientists, as well as persons who do not do science, certainly try to use science this way. Science is merely a systematic way of using experience to test our ideas about the world.

At times in our history, we have forgotten that scientists are human. We have thought of scientists as *objective,* without feeling and oblivious to the human condition in general and to what is going on around them in particular. To be sure, there have been such instances but in these cases it is the failure of the witness and not of the scientist or the subject that is the basis of the problem. We will develop this idea further at a later time.

The message we wish to emphasize now is that in the final analysis, the human sensitivity of scientists adds life and spirit to the scientific enterprise. Thus, what is unique about science is not that it is performed by superhuman individuals in an all-out search for knowledge but almost the opposite. What is unique about science is not the individuals who are scientists, but their methods, and the relationship of the people who do science with these methods.

## Key Terms and Concepts

1. Nature of science
   a. roles of scientist, subject, and witness
2. Ways of accepting knowledge
   a. tenacity
   b. authority
   c. reason
   d. common sense
   e. science
3. Scientific approach
   a. verifiable through experience
   b. Newton's rules of reasoning

4. Examples of early approaches to science
   a. Croesus and the establishment of criteria for evaluation
   b. Galen and the examination of alternative factors
   c. Semmelweis and the development of a series of studies
5. Studying behavior and experience
   a. empiricism
   b. studying experience through behavior
   c. use of constructs
6. The nature of scientists
   a. science is performed by people
   b. all people do some type of science
   c. science requires the support and communication of others

## Summary


1. The purpose of this chapter was to introduce you to science as an approach to learning about ourselves and our world. As a problem-solving approach, science offers an important means of evaluating ideas.
2. Historically man has used a variety of ways of accepting or rejecting ideas. Based on the work of Charles Peirce, we discussed five of these (tenacity, authority, reason, common sense, and science) in terms of strengths and weaknesses.
3. Science is useful for evaluating ideas since it is self-corrective—that is, results from experiments offer a feedback mechanism to help clarify ideas.
4. For thousands of years, people have tried to understand their world better. We looked at three historical events to help clarify the scientific approach. The stories of Croesus, Galen, and Semmelweis pointed to the need for unambiguous statements, the need for testing factors that both do and do not affect behavior, and the importance of a carefully designed series of observations. In sum, science combines experiene, reason, and a desire to answer questions about reality.
5. Psychology is interested in the study of outer appearances (behavior) as well as inner experiences. Using a schema presented by Schumacher, we asked how we might study the behavior and experience of ourselves and others.
6. There are times when researchers want to know about the interal processing of an organism but either cannot or as we discuss in later chapters do not want to ask directly. Since we can assume that an organism's behavior is related to experience, we can ask such questions as does a cat see colors or can babies tell the difference between their parents and other adults. In this manner we use behavior to make inferences concerning the inner worlds of various organisms.


## Review Questions

1. What are the ways of accepting or rejecting ideas, as suggested by Pierce?
2. Discuss the changes in science before and after the time of Galileo.

3. How is science self-corrective?
4. In simple language, what are Newton's four rules of reasoning?
5. What was progressive about Croesus's approach to the oracles?
6. How was Galen's approach scientific?
7. How did Semmelweis approach the problem of the mothers' dying during childbirth?
8. Give some examples of what would be included when discussing behavior and experience, and how modern psychology approaches these areas.
9. Describe an experiment that would show if animals were color-blind.

## Discussion Questions and Projects

Questions in this section are based on ideas presented in the text, and require you to use what you have learned or to draw from your own experience. In some cases, the questions are designed to stimulate discussion and as such have no single right answer.

1. While watching television, pick out five commercials and notice the way in which they try to convince you that their product is good. Which of Peirce's ways of knowing do they suggest? (Hint: Some of the suggestions may be made nonverbally—e.g., the use of a famous person suggests knowledge through authority.)
2. Discuss the statement "Science is above all a human activity."
3. Discuss how the roles of scientist, subject, and witness are exemplified and portrayed in our society. What different disciplines in a college or university are devoted to each of these?
4. It was suggested that science is a self-corrective process. What are the advantages and disadvantages of a self-corrective system?
5. Develop an experiment that would determine if someone who was unable to speak could experience emotions.
6. Name some constructs that cannot be "seen" yet are important in our everyday lives.
7. Discuss how you might study your own behavior. For example, how would you determine whether you practiced your guitar better in the morning or at night? How could you determine the effects of extra sleep on your school work and feeling in general? What could you do to get your professor to tell better jokes?
8. A researcher was looking for the reasons people fail in college. To help answer this question, the researcher took a group of students who flunked out of college and a group that made good grades. Both groups were given a test of self-esteem. It was found that the group that flunked out had lower self-esteem than the group that did not. From this the researcher concluded that low self-esteem is one of the causes of failure in college. Comment on this conclusion.

CHAPTER TWO

# *Introduction to the Methods of Science*

## INTRODUCTION

Most of us remember how different our first few weeks of college were from anything we had known before. Remember how you expected your roommate or your professors to act, and how you reacted when they did not act that way? If you stop and think about your first reactions to college, you can see that there were three aspects of these experiences. First, there was an idea or expectation concerning what was about to happen in college. Second, there was the actual experience of what did happen during those first few weeks, and it was probably quite different, at least in some respects, from what you had expected. Third, there was the resulting reorganization of your ideas about college and the potential impact of this experience on your life.

The methods of science closely parallel these three aspects of your experience. First, scientists begin with an idea or expectation. As you will learn, a formally stated expectation is called a *hypothesis*. The scientist simply says, "I expect this to happen under these conditions," and thus states the hypothesis. Second, scientists look to experience to evaluate the accuracy of their ideas or expectations about the world. That is, they try to find or create the situation that will allow them to observe what they are interested in studying. Through observation and experimentation, scientists can begin to evaluate their ideas and expectations about the world. As mentioned in Chapter 1, learning about the world through observation and experimentation is an example of *empiricism*, which means nothing more than accepting sensory information as valid. Third, based on their observations and experiments, scientists seek to draw conclusions or inference about their ideas and expectations. They reorganize their ideas and consider the impact of the new information on their theoretical conceptualizations.

As mentioned earlier, science is simply a way of determining what the world is really like. In its simplest form, the scientific method consists of asking a question about the world and then experiencing the world to determine the answer. When we begin an inquiry, what we already know about our topic leaves us in one of two positions. In some cases, we know relatively little about our topic and, consequently, our ideas and questions are very general. For example, what causes mental illness? What factors make a fruitful marriage? If relatively little is known about a particular phenomenon, it is frequently useful simply to watch the phenomenon *occur* naturally and get a general feeling for what is involved by simply describing what naturally occurs. This scientific technique is called *naturalistic observation.* On the other hand, if we already know quite a bit about a given phenomenon, a general description of this sort would probably not add much new information. Instead, we would gain more by seeing how some single factor affects the phenomenon we are studying. To do this, we begin to interact with the phenomenon. *If I do this, what will happen?* For example, will a rat learn to press a lever faster if it is given food each time it presses or only on every fifth press? As our knowledge grows, we may even get to the point of formulating specific predictions. *If I do this, I bet this will happen!* These two scientific methods in which we interact directly with the phenomenon we are studying are examples of the *experimental method.*

Before we continue, we want to emphasize that there is no set number of methods for doing science. Methods are developed in response to specific questions. Often our area of study determines which methods we use. For example, in sciences such as astronomy and zoology, scientists often use *post hoc* (after the fact) methods; like Darwin, they might ask how a certain species came about. Clinical psychologists use similar methods when they speculate on the development of personality or the origin of mental illness. Other areas of psychology may rely on single-subject approaches when the problem they are studying is rare, such as with a specific brain disorder. We will discuss these and other approaches to research later in this book. For the present we will focus on two main approaches: naturalistic observation and experimental manipulation. We do not want to leave you with the impression that these are the only two ways to organize research; that is not the case. However, these two approaches do use very different strategies for answering questions in science and thus it is informative to examine them in some detail.

Let us consider the relationship between the scientist and the subject in each of these methods. With the naturalistic method, it is the job of the scientist to be passive and observe carefully the activity of the subject. In this method, the scientist does not try to change the environment of the subject. The subject simply goes about its normal activity in its normal way and the scientist watches, preferably without his presence influencing the subject's behavior. In this way, the scientist gains a detailed description of some aspect of the subject's natural behavior. In contrast, when using the experimental method, the scientist is more active and the subject is restricted in activities. The scientist intentionally structures the situation so that he or she can study the effect of a particular factor on the subject's behavior.

If you have not noticed already, let us pause and remind you that each of these methods is a simple extension of the way a child explores its world. A common way children and scientists begin to explore a new phenomenon is first simply to watch it occur naturally for a while. As a second step, we continue to learn by beginning to interact with the phenomenon. Once we understand the relationship involved in a particular phenomenon, we can use it profitably in our everyday lives. It works for the child, and it works for scientists, too, although on a more complex level. To provide you with a more accurate conception of how the scientific method is an extension of our everyday activities, we will examine the two fundamental scientific strategies mentioned above: the *naturalistic observation* technique, which is akin to the child's observing a phenomenon, and the *experimental method,* which is akin to the child's interacting with the phenomenon to learn more about it. Let us now turn to a more detailed discussion of each method.

## NATURALISTIC OBSERVATION

Imagine that it is 20,000 years in the future and you have been sent to a strange part of the galaxy to study a particular species that has been described by astronauts as "cultural apes." Assume you could arrive there and remain undetected. How would you go about your mission? . . . Right! Because you know virtually nothing about these cultural apes, the method of naturalistic observation would be an efficient way to get a general idea of what these alien beings are like.

As many others who have studied animals in the wild on nineteenth- and twentieth-century earth, you might set up a "blind," so that you would not be detected, and observe the behavior of these aliens. Often with animals in the wild, scientists try to find a place where the animals come together, such as a watering hole, and set up an observation post near this place. After some preliminary observations, you find that these cultural apes come together every morning in large structures. Consequently, you set up your observation within one of these structures. Assuming you remain undetected, what would you do next?

The answer is simple yet deceptively difficult to do. *You just watch.* "Just watching" is difficult; it might be compared to seeing a movie in a foreign language that you do not understand. It is easy to see that there are interactions between the actors in the movie, yet you can only guess what they mean. In the beginning, the most difficult part of just watching is not to guess constantly. Until you have observed a given interaction repeatedly, you can easily color or even distort what you are seeing by your expectation that it occurs in a certain way. After much observation, you may begin to notice certain patterns of behavior by the aliens. For example, they may say "hello" each time they meet and "good-bye" each time they leave each other. One hallmark of naturalistic observation is the discovery of patterns in the behaviors of different organisms.

An important part of the naturalistic technique is to record what you observe. At one time, the only method of recording was to reduce the observations to written notes or hand-drawn pictures, much as Darwin did when he went to the Galapagos Islands. Today, however, we can record our observations on audio- or videotape. Of course, individual scientists are still an important part of the process, since they select what will be recorded and thus determine the observations for later analysis.

Once we have observed many instances of the typical behavior of this alien species, we can withdraw from our observation post and begin to analyze our recorded observations. It is at this stage that we can begin to make summary statements that characterize the natural ongoing behavior of these aliens.

Coming down to earth, let's consider the work of one scientist who has used the naturalistic method in his research. Several years ago Nikolaas Tinbergen (who later received the Nobel Prize for his research) became interested in autistic children. Because little was known about the overall behavior of autistic children, Tinbergen began by using the *naturalistic observation* method and simply observed autistic children (Tinbergen & Tinbergen, 1972). Autistic children do not communicate with others. Often they just walk around making sounds to themselves or even literally hitting their heads against a wall. As Tinbergen watched these children, he observed that there was a pattern to their abnormal behavior in that the behavior appeared most often when these children were in an unfamiliar social situation. Even a smile from a stranger might be followed by an attempt to withdraw from the situation. Tinbergen was also interested in how autistic children were different from normal children. To understand these differences, Tinbergen observed normal children and also children with varying degrees of autism. He found that some facial expressions displayed by the autistic children differed from those of the normal ones. Thus, the naturalistic method offered a starting point for describing differences between autistic and normal children.

Another scientist who has utilized the naturalistic method of observation is Konrad Lorenz (Lorenz also received the nobel Prize for his behavioral research). In the following passage, Lorenz (1952) describes the behavioral interactions in a colony of birds called jackdaws:

> A jackdaw sits feeding at the communal dish, a second bird approaches ponderously, in an attitude of self-display, with head proudly erected, whereupon the first visitor moves slightly to one side, but otherwise does not allow himself to be disturbed. Now comes a third bird, in a much more modest attitude which, surprisingly enough, puts the first bird to flight; the second, on the other hand, assumes a threatening pose, with his back feathers ruffled, attacks the latest comer and drives him from the spot.

### Naturalistic Observation—Summary

In summary, there are four characteristics of this method. First, the idea of noninterference is of prime importance. It is the task of scientists using this method not to disrupt the process or flow of events that is going on before them. In this way we can see things "as they really are" without influencing the ongoing phenomenon. Second, this method emphasizes the invariants or patterns that exist in the world. For example, if you could observe yourself in a noninterfering manner, you might conclude that your moods vary with the time of day or with particular weather patterns or even with particular thoughts. Third, this method is most useful when we know relatively little about the subject of our investigation. It is most useful for observing the "big picture" and emphasizing a series of events, rather than isolated happenings. Fourth, the naturalistic method may not shed light on those factors that directly influence the behavior observed. The method provides a *description* of a phenomenon; it does not answer the question of why it happened. To understand better how one variable influences another we use the experimental method. This method emphasizes scientists' ability to manipulate important aspects of the topic under study. Through the manipulation, scientists are better able to understand and describe important aspects of our world.

## EXPERIMENTAL METHOD

As we suggested, you already know a great deal about the experimental method. Indeed, each of us has used it in one form or another to explore our world since we were small children. Like the child, the scientist begins to interact with the phenomenon he or she is studying: *If I do this, what will happen?* From these interactions, the scientist gains increased understanding of the phenomenon under study. To test this understanding further, the scientist asks: *Was what happened really because of what I did?*

To give you a more accurate understanding for how the scientist learns from interacting with the environment, consider the following line of fictitious research. Assume that the makers of a children's brand of cereal, which we will call Roasty-Toasties, want to claim that their cereal, eaten for breakfast, helps children to grow. In their enthusiasm to demonstrate the claim and thus add "scientific evidence" to their television commercials, the company designed the following experiment. A group of children were given daily a bowl of Roasty-Toasties with cream, bananas, and sugar. After several months each child was weighed. It was found that they gained an average of eight pounds each. Obviously, the weight increase was due to the nourishing breakfast and, consequently, the company recommended this breakfast for all children. Well, what do you think? Do you see any problems? When a thoughtful scientist heard the results, he admitted to their appeal but added that he was confused about several things. One thing that bothered him quite a bit was that the children also ate lunch and dinner. Consequently, he pointed out, the weight gain may be due to the food eaten at these other meals.

Dismayed that they had not thought of that, the company designed a new experiment. This time it used two groups of children whose average age and weight were the same. One group received the recommended cereal with cream, bananas, and sugar; the other was given scrambled eggs. Both groups ate approximately the same foods for lunch and dinner. Several months later each child was weighed. It was found that there was an average gain of five pounds in the group who received the recommended breakfast cereal and an average gain of only one pound for the children who ate eggs for breakfast. Needless to say, the company was excited and assailed our thoughtful scientist with the new findings confirming the earlier results. The scientist pointed out that he was even more impressed than before. However, he grew silent again, looked up, and meekly said, "Could the weight gain be due to the cream, sugar, and bananas and not to the revolutionary new cereal?" Although the company was confident that the results were due to the cereal, logically, the scientist was right. The entire effect could have been due to the cream, sugar, and bananas and not to the cereal.

Crushed by the scientist's keen insight, the company returned to the laboratory to plan its next experiment. After much debate, it decided to do the following experiment. As before, one group received the cereal with cream, sugar, and bananas for breakfast, but now another group received equal amounts of cream, sugar, and bananas each morning. Once again lunch and dinner were approximately the same for both groups, as were their weights at the onset of the study. The company was confident of replicating the earlier findings, so after several months they weighed each child. Much to their dismay, it was found that children in both groups gained five pounds. The group that received cereal did not gain more weight than the other group.

## Definitions in the Experimental Method

The goal of the third study was to determine whether eating cereal affected the growth of a child. The *hypothesis* or idea being tested was that eating the new cereal influences growth. To test its hypothesis, the company gave its cereal to one group of children and not to a second group. The group that received the cereal was called the *experimental group*. The group that did not receive the cereal was called the *control group*. A control group is a group that is treated exactly like the experimental group except for being given the cereal. In this case, the control group was used to assess growth from all other possible factors *except* the cereal. The study can be charaterized as in Table 2.1.

In any experiment we must define the terms in the hypothesis so that the hypothesis can be tested. To minimize possible confusion, the crucial terms in the hypothesis are clearly defined in reference to concrete operations. This sort of definition is called an *operational definition* and, as you will see, it forms a crucial link between our ideas and the world. Kerlinger (1973)

**Table 2.1 Design of the Final Roasty-Toasties Study**

| | *Pretreatment Weight (Before the Study)* | *Treatment* | *Posttreatment Weight (After Treatment)* |
|---|---|---|---|
| *Group 1 (experimental)* | 50 lb. | cereal with cream, bananas, and sugar | 55 lb. |
| *Group 2 (control)* | 50 lb. | cream, bananas, and sugar without cereal | 55 lb. |

suggests that there are two types of operational definitions. The first type relates to measurement and may specify both *how* observations are to be made and *what* is to be observed and measured. For example, in a study that measures anxiety during certain types of tasks, it would be necessary to define operationally how anxiety was measured. That is, were the anxiety scores derived from self-report measures, physiological measures such as heart rate, or observation of a specific behavior? The second type of operational definition refers to experimentation. This type of operational definition describes how experimental procedures are to be followed. For example, in a study that examines the effects of praise on change in psychotherapy, it would be necessary to define operationally both what praise is and under what conditions it is to be given and withheld. In one sense operational definitions function like a recipe for a cook. In the same way that it would be difficult to follow a recipe that said only "heat eggs, milk, and flour," it would be impossible to understand an experiment that said only "anxiety hurts performance." For a complete understanding, it would be necessary to specify (that is, operationally define) what measure of anxiety was used and how the measurement of performance was made. Thus, one of the first tasks in developing a research study is to specify the operational definitions related to measurement and experimentation.

It should be pointed out that we are using the term operational definition in the more popular and less technical sense. Thus we are not speaking of the total definition of a construct, a point we will discuss in more detail in Chapter 5. (For a more complete discussion of operational definitions and the related concept "reduction sentences" see Suppe, 1977.)

In the cereal experiment, the researchers had to define operationally both what was meant by the construct of growth and how the eating of the cereal was to be manipulated experimentally. The variable that an experimenter manipulates in an experiment is called the *independent variable* or *treatment.* An independent variable is said to be "independent" because its levels are established by the experimenter before the experiment begins and thus the levels are independent of anything that happens during the experiment. In this manner the independent variable is seen to precede and potentially influence the measurements that we take in an experiment.

The aspect of the world that the experimenter feels will be affected by the independent variable is referred to as the *dependent variable.* The dependent variable gets its name because if a relationship does exist, its value will *depend* on the independent variable. In the present experiment, the researchers hoped that growth would be enhanced through ingestion of their new cereal. However, because there are many aspects of growth (physical maturation, height, weight, intellectual or emotional maturation), the task of deciding which aspect to measure is difficult. Notice that their final decision to define growth operationally in terms of weight is quite arbitrary and ignores other aspects of growth that might be evaluated.

The difference in the magnitude of the dependent variable for the control and experimental groups is called the *treatment effect.* The only difference between the experimental and control groups should be the independent variable or treatment. If we are certain of this, then any difference in the magnitude of the dependent variable is said to be due to the independent variable. If there is more than one difference between the two groups, then we would not know which is responsible for any treatment effects we may observe. (Note that there are more complex experimental designs, called *factorial designs,* that allow us to investigate the effects of two or more independent variables in the same experiment. This class of designs will be discussed in Chapter 8.)

If we suspect that some unintended factor may also be operating, then, as we mentioned earlier, the truth or validity of the experiment is seriously threatened and the entire experiment must be questioned. In the second experiment, the fact that the control group did not receive cream, bananas, and sugar constitutes a potential alternative explanation for the group's lower weight gain. Whenever two or more independent variables are operating, the unintended (those not chosen by the experimenter) independent variables are referred to as *confounding variables.* In the second experiment, the cream, sugar, and bananas were confounding variables.

Before we continue, we would like to clear up some confusion experienced by a number of people when the word *caused* is used. In psychology when we speak about an independent variable causing a change in the dependent variable, we mean that these two variables reflect a consistent association. That is, with every change in the independent variable, there comes a related and predictable change in the dependent variable. This means that the idea of causality in science is generally a conclusion or judgment made concerning the relationship between the independent and dependent variables. If research shows that each time we change one aspect of a situation, then a predictable change follows in another aspect, we usually say that the first aspect caused a change in the second. If, as we repeat an experiment in varying situations and under different conditions, the same relationship between the independent variable and the dependent variable continues to hold true, then we have more confidence in our judgment. In this sense many philosophers of science see causation as something we ascribe to the situation and remind us that what we are really doing is making inferences about the world (i.e., epistemology) rather than making statements about what "really exists" (i.e., ontology). As we will discuss later in this chapter, modern physics is now regarded as the study of observations of reality rather than the study of reality itself.

Another way to discuss causation is to see what conditions are required for the occurrence of an event. In particular, we discuss *necessary* and *sufficient* conditions. A necessary condition, as the name implies, is the situation that *must* occur. For example, it is necessary to be a woman to become pregnant. However, just being a woman does not make you pregnant. To do this, we must also show a *sufficient* condition. A sufficient condition is a condition that *can* occur, and when it does occur it always produces the effect. For example, we say that fertilization through intercourse is a sufficient condition for producing an embryo and that feeding milk to a child is a sufficient condition for producing growth. However, these may not be necessary conditions. For example, other substances fed to the child will also produce growth. Thus, if we were looking for *The Cause* of growth, we would reject the idea that milk causes growth, since the administration of milk does not represent both a necessary *and* a sufficient condition for growth. However, as we suggested earlier, when we use the word *cause,* we do not mean *The Cause*—the one and only cause—but rather the case in which two events (the independent and dependent variables) are systematically connected in a variety of situations.

At this point we would like to introduce you briefly to a type of research in which we seek to know the relationship between two variables but we do not attempt to establish how one variable influences the other. These are referred to as *correlational studies.* Correlation is a measure of association that we will present statistically in Chapter 3. In correlational studies the researcher is interested in asking whether there exists an association between two variables, but does not attempt to establish how one variable influences the other. This may be the first step for dealing with a complex problem. For example, a physiological psychologist might ask whether someone's pulse is related to how old they are. To answer this question he could simply measure the person's heart rate and correlate this measure with the person's age. What would this tell us? It would tell us how two variables are related but it would not tell us whether either variable influences the other. If these two variables are related, what might the reason be for the relationship? As you begin to suggest factors that might have produced a high degree of relationship, you realize that a third unspecified variable may have actually influenced the two variables in the correlational study. Thus, the nature of a correlational study is to suggest relationships but not to suggest which variable influences which other variable. As is often said, "Correlation does not imply causality." Let's consider another example. A researcher might want to know whether a relationship exists between the type of food that one eats and heart attacks. One approach would be to examine the diets of people who have heart attacks and those who don't. What if there was a high association between eating steak, for example, and heart attacks: what could you conclude? That's right; you could conclude little other than that there was an association or correlational between the two variables. The association of two factors does not in itself imply that one influences the other. However, since a high degree of association is necessary for establishing that one variable does influence another, a correlational study is often the first step for supporting the need for later experimental research, especially in very complex areas, such as the etiology of both disease and well-being.

### Exploratory Research

Having described the experimental method, it is important to emphasize that psychologists frequently use this method either more or less rigidly depending on how much they already know about the phenomenon they are studying and the types of questions they want to ask. In some cases, following an extensive library search for relevant information, a scientist may realize that almost nothing is known about a particular phenomenon and simply wonder what effect a given treatment will have on subjects' experience. Given this situation, the scientist can use the experimental method in either of two ways. First, when we have no idea what the effect of the independent variables will be, we are sometimes content to give the experimental treatment to a single group of subjects and then informally observe the subjects to get some idea of what aspects of behavior were affected by the independent variable. This initial exploratory use of the experimental method is frequently employed in the initial stages of biofeedback experiments, psychotherapy research, and drug evaluation studies, for example. Strictly speaking, this way of gaining information is not an experiment because it does not involve a control group or test specific hypotheses. It is no more than a simple demonstration that may provide either (1) clues to fruitful independent variables for more refined analysis or (2) potential attributes of behavior that shoud be reflected in the future selection of dependent variables.

The second way we use the experimental method as an exploratory tool occurs when we have some idea which aspects of behavior will be affected by the independent variable and, consequently, have a reasonable idea what sort of dependent variables and control group(s) we should use, yet we do not understand the phenomenon well enough to make a specific prediction. In this way, our understanding of the phenomenon is progressively refined by a more detailed search for influential factors (independent variables that produce treatment effects) and by a more accurate estimate of their influence (measured by the dependent variables) on the phenomenon under study.

At other times, when we actually know a great deal about a particular topic, we can move beyond the exploratory uses of the experimental method. In these cases we are able to formulate specific predictions that reflect a more detailed theoretical understanding of the phenomenon. Because we have a clearer understanding, we are able to *refine* our independent and dependent variables and our use of control groups so that we can more precisely isolate the important relationships involved in our phenomenon.

Whether we use the method of naturalistic observation or the experimental method, the task before us is to make inferences about human experience from the behaviors we observe. These inferences are generally related back to our hypothesis or some larger theory we wish to evaluate. Thus, after we look to the world through these methods, we are faced with the task of deciding how to evaluate new information we receive in the light of both the methods used and our theoretical perspective. To accomplish this task, we use reason and logic. In particular we ask whether the results of our methods as well as our conclusion are valid. In the next section we will focus on the question of validity and differentiate among some common types of validity. We will also summarize briefly the structure of propositional logic. We present this discussion to aid you as you begin to evaluate your own research and that of others.

## LOGIC AND INFERENCE: THE DETECTIVE WORK OF SCIENCE

Perhaps you have heard the story of our friend from Boston who got up every morning, went outside his house, walked around in a circle three times, and yelled at the top of his voice. His neighbor, being somewhat curious after days of this ritual, asked for the purpose behind his strange behavior. The man answered with some certainty that the purpose was to keep away tigers. "But," the neighbor replied quite frankly, "there are no tigers within thousands of miles of here." To which our friend replied, "Works quite well, doesn't it?"

Consider this story for a moment. What is wrong with our friend's method for keeping away tigers? It works, doesn't it? Why not? How could we demonstrate to our friend that his yelling is not causally related to the absence of tigers? One strategy might be to point out that the absence of tigers might have come about for other reasons, including the absence of tigers roaming in the greater Boston area. In technical terms we would say that the absence of tigers was a *necessary* condition but not a *sufficient* condition for showing that yelling *caused* the tigers to stay away. Our friend's reasoning was insufficient because it left unevaluated many other plausible explanations of the obvious absence of tigers.

Logic is particularly important in science as an aid to answering this question: What question should my experimental study answer to test my ideas about the world? That is, logic can help us to answer questions of *inference.* Inference refers to the process by which we look at the evidence available to us and then use our powers of reasoning to reach a conclusion. Like Sherlock Holmes engaged in solving a mystery, we attempt to solve a problem based on the available evidence. Did the butler do it? No, the butler could not have done it because there was blond hair on the knife and the butler had black hair. But perhaps the butler left the blond hair there to fool us. Like a detective, scientists try to determine other factors that may be responsible for the outcome of their experiment or to piece together available information and draw general conclusions about the world. Also, like the detective, the scientist is constantly asking: Given these clues, what inference can I make and is the inference valid? Logic is one method for answering these questions.

## Validity

Logical procedures are also important for helping us to understand the accuracy or *validity* of our ideas and research. Validity means true and capable of being supported. In psychological research we are particularly interested in two general types of validity (Campbell & Stanley, 1963). The first is *internal validity*. The word *internal* refers to the experiment itself. Internal validity asks the question: Is there another reason that might be used to explain the outcome of our experimental procedures? Students are particularly sensitive to questions of internal validity when it is time for final exams. They are able to make a number of alternative suggestions as to what the test actually measures and why it does not measure their knowledge of a particular subject. Like students, scientists look for reasons (threats to internal validity) for a particular piece of research not measuring what it claims to measure. In the case of our friend from Boston, the absence of tigers near his house could have reflected a long-standing absence of tigers in his part of the world rather than the effectiveness of his yelling.

The second type of validity is *external validity*. External validity refers to the ability of a particular set of research results to be applied in another setting. This is often called *generalizability*. Remember the story of Semmelweis. His finding that the deaths of the mothers was the result of the physicians' handling diseased tissue was true not only for his hospital but for all other hospitals as well. Thus, in addressing the question of external validity for the work of Semmelweis, we would conclude that his answers could be generalized to other hospitals with other women and not just to his own original setting. Now consider the story of Galen. We would not fault his research concerning why the woman did not sleep, but we would say that it lacked external validity or generalizability. Although the insomnia of one particular woman was due to a particular male dancer, it is not true that all people who suffer from insomnia react to male dancers, nor that they are all in love. In summary, internal validity refers to the interal consistency or logic of the experiment that allows for the results to be meaningful. External validity, on the other hand, refers to the ability of the results from an internally valid experiment to be applied in other situations and with other subjects.

We logically design our research to rule out as many alternative interpretations of our findings as possible and to have any new facts be applicable to as wide a variety of other situations as possible. Unfortunately, in many real-life situations where external validity is high, it is impossible to rule out alternative interpretations of our findings. In a similar way, in laboratory settings where internal validity is high, the setting is often artificial and in many cases our findings cannot be generalized beyond the laboratory. Consequently, in designing and conducting research, one goal is to maximize *both* internal and external validity. In the next section we will introduce you to propositional logic. However, before you begin this section, we suggest that you try to solve the problem presented in Box 2.1. The problem relies on logical approaches you will learn about in the next section.

## Propositional Logic

In the previous section, we introduced the terms *internal* and *external validity* and emphasized the scientist's attempt to rule out alternative explanations. In this section, we will emphasize the way in which a scientist relies on the rules of formal logic to both *deduce* and *induce* valid conclusions. As a starting point, keep in mind that deduction (to deduce) is the process by which one moves from a general theory to particular data, whereas induction (to induce) is the process by which one moves from a particular set of data to another particular set of data or to a general theory or concept.

If one were to begin with the premise and from this *deduce* the consequences, this would be called the *deductive* approach to knowledge. One uses deductive reasoning when saying, "If it is true that schizophrenia is genetically determined, then we should find greater similarity in the existence of the disorder (either presence or absence) between twins than between strangers." On the other hand, if one were to begin with the consequent and then *induce* the premise, this would be called *inductive* reasoning. Inductive reasoning might be of the form: "I just saw a monkey use sign language and ask me for food; therefore, it is true that monkeys can communicate with humans." In summary, deductive reasoning goes from theory (the premise) to data (the consequent), whereas inductive reasoning goes from data (the consequent) to the theory (the premise).

Suppose a friend said to you, "You know, all experimental textbooks are really dull." You might respond, "That's not true, I am reading one right now that is really interesting." (Well, what did you expect we would have you say?) In terms of logic, you were showing your friend a simple way to disprove the statement "All experimental textbooks are really dull." That is, by finding an exception to a statement, you can show it to be false.

Let's look at this procedure in a formal way. You begin with a premise—"All experimental textbooks are really dull." From this premise, a logical consequence follows. The consequence would be that given an experimental textbook, it would be really dull.

## *Box 2.1 Think Square*

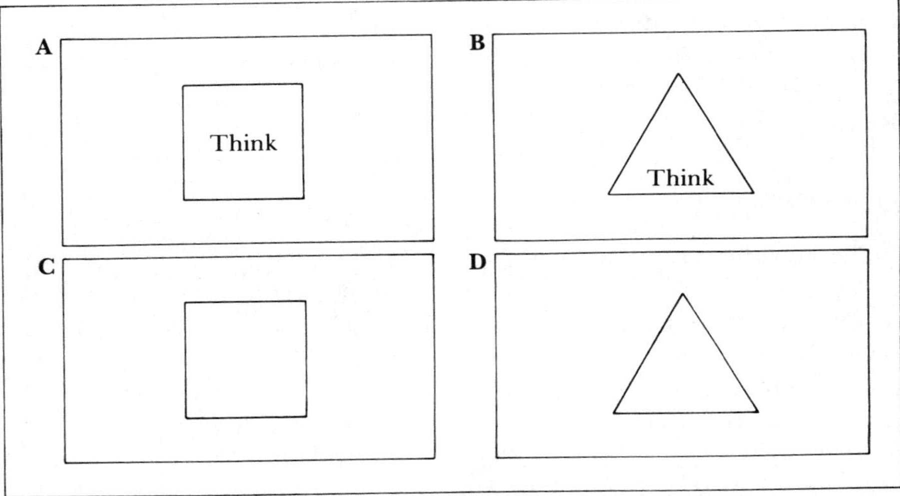


Assume that there are four cards. Each has a square with or without the word "think" on one side and a triangle with or without "think" on the other side. Which of the cards would you have to turn over to determine whether EVERY CARD THAT HAS A *THINK* SQUARE ON ONE SIDE HAS A TRIANGLE WITHOUT *THINK* ON THE OTHER?

We will make a prediction based on previous experience that you chose cards A and D. You may be in good company since many people choose these cards, but you were wrong. However, you were right when you chose card A. As you correctly reasoned, card A must have a triangle without "think" on the other side for the statement to be true. However, if you turn over card D, which we did when we first tried the problem, you missed the point of the statement. The statement talks about what is opposite a "think" square and says nothing about what is opposite a triangle. The other card that we needed to turn over to solve the problem was card B. We needed to demonstrate that the negative of the statement was not true; that is, we needed to demonstrate that there was not a "think" square with a "think" triangle on the other side. Still confused?

We begin with the premise that all "think" squares have empty triangles on the other side, which we sought to test. We then move to the real situation in which there are four cards. In these four cards we see a "think" square and thus can test the truth of the statement just by turning it over. Now comes the problem. We have tested all the "think" squares (card A), so what do we do next? If it is true that all "think" squares have empty triangles on the other side, then it must also be true that no card with a "think" triangle has a "think" square on the other side. Once we realize this, we know that we must look at card B and test this assumption. Thus the correct answer is cards A and B.

After Wason (1977).

Technically, this type of reasoning is referred to as *confirmatory reasoning* or *modus ponens.* Confirmatory reasoning is nothing more than a true premise leading to a true consequent. This is abbreviated as: If $p$, then $q$ (if the premise, then the consequent). Suppose we have an instance where $q$ is correct; what does this say about $p$? That is, if I can find a single experimental textbook that is dull, does that demonstrate the truth of the statement "All experimental textbooks are dull"? The answer is, of course not, because there may be other experimental textbooks that are exciting! Technically this type of reverse confirmatory reasoning is referred to as *affirming the consequent.* Although it is an invalid form of logic, one sees it used almost daily. The cartoon on p. 45 offers one example of this form of reasoning. Consider another example. A person may tell you a story about how she knows someone who is more than 100 years of age and meditates. Therefore, she concludes that meditating makes you live longer. This is an invalid argument of logic, since any single case does not prove that the same is true for an entire group. The premise may indeed be correct in the real world, but we cannot make that conclusion logically from single cases. We believe this point is so important that we will repeat it. It is an invalid form of logic to conclude from a true consequent that the premise is true. If you begin with the idea that beer makes you creative and attempt to prove this by finding a creative person who drinks beer, then you have produced an invalid argument referred to as *affirming the consequent.* As you think about this, you should be able to see that a single study can never *prove* any theory. Research results may support (that is, not refute) a theory, but they cannot prove it (show the theory to be logically true).

Let us take another situation in which the premise is shown to be incorrect. What can we conclude from this? Someone might say that if we show the premise "All experimental textbooks are dull" to be false, then it follows that all experimental textbooks are not dull. Right? Wrong! It might turn out that some textbooks are dull and some are not. Thus a false premise does not necessarily lead to a false consequent; that is, if $p$ is not true, it does not follow that $q$ is not true also. To reason in this way is invalid and referred to technically as *denying the antecedent.* Although this is invalid logic, we still hear individuals suggesting that since Carl Rogers's theory (or Fritz Perls's or B. F. Skinner's or Sigmund Freud's) has been shown to be incorrect, then the therapy is not effective. His therapy may be very effective but just not for the theoretical reasons he suggested.

This brings us to the last situation in which we have a false consequent.

What does this have to say about the premise (if *q* is not true, then *p* is?)? If *q* is not true, then *p* is also not true. In our example, if we can find one experimental textbook that is not dull, then it is not true that "All experimental textbooks are dull." This is a valid form of argument and is referred to technically as *disconfirmatory reasoning* or *modus tollens*. To see how *modus tollens* reasoning might be applied to testing scientific theories, read Box 2.2.

To summarize, we discussed four forms of propositional logic of the form "if *p*, then *q*" where *p* is the premise and *q* is the consequent. These four forms are presented in Table 2.2.

Having presented logical inference in its ideal form, we want to remind

---

### *Box 2.2 Philosophy of Science: Sir Karl Popper (Falsification Approach)*

Popper has devoted much of his career to answering the questions: What is science? How is science performed? Although these questions may at first seem easy to you, consider such areas as astrology and Marxism. Could these approaches be considered scientific? Why not?

*Falsificationism* is the name given to Popper's description of how science is performed. Falsificationism suggests that science should be concerned with disproving or falsifying theories through logic based on observation. How is this accomplished? First, a scientist must create a consistent falsifiable hypothesis. A falsifiable hypothesis is one that can be shown to be false. For example, the hypothesis "It will rain in Tuscaloosa, Alabama, on Tuesday, December 23, 1997" is a testable hypothesis. Likewise the hypothesis "All objects regardless of weight will fall to earth at approximately the same speed" is a testable hypothesis. However, a hypothesis such as "ESP (extrasensory perception) exists" is an untestable hypothesis. Even the hypothesis "Gravity exists" is untestable. It may be true that both ESP and gravity exist, yet until the hypothesis is stated in a form that can be falsified, the hypothesis is not testable. Second, once a scientist has a falsifiable hypothesis, the task is to develop a test of the hypothesis. Third, the hypothesis is tested. Fourth, if the hypothesis is shown to be false, a new bold hypothesis is developed.

Using this model of science, Popper emphasizes science as a process for the elimination of false theories. You may also compare Popper's model for science with the discussion on propositional logic presented in Chapter 2 as well as with Box 2.1 on problem solving. If you study the section on logic and accept the suggestion that all psychological research is inductive in nature, you must then conclude with Popper that the major role of science is the falsification of incorrect theories. This line of reasoning also leads one to conclude that science, particularly psychology, never *proves* a hypothesis. Science, according to Popper, only shows that the hypothesis is not false.

Note: Although Popper is usually discussed in terms of the falsification position, his recent writings emphasize research programs rather than single theories.

---

**Table 2.2 Forms of Propositional Logic**

1. A true premise leads to a true consequent and is called *confirmatory* (modus ponens).
   Example: If "All species are shaped by evolution" is true, then humans (a species) are shaped by evolution.
2. A false premise *does not* lead to a false consequent, and to argue so is a mistake called *denying the antecedent.*
   Example: If "All people are sexually motivated" is false, it does not mean that no one is sexually motivated.
3. A true consequent *does not* lead to a true premise, and to argue so is a mistake called *affirming the consequent.*
   Example: If behavior therapy works in a given case, it does not follow that the theory of behavior therapy is true.
4. A false consequent does lead to a false premise and is called *disconfirmatory* (modus tollens).
   Example: If there is one person over 65 who is productive, then the premise "no one over 65 is productive" is false.

you that logic is a tool of the scientist. Like the experimental method, logic is an approach to knowledge designed to help us evaluate and direct our research questions. Because of the complexity of the world in which we live and the limits of our own minds to perceive this complexity precisely, we find ourselves as scientists using a combination of both inductive and deductive approaches to knowledge in our science as well as in our lives. We often use deductive and inductive approaches as a means of gaining information, which becomes a clue as we attempt to interact with and understand the world in which we live. Logic offers us a means of evaluating the inferences we draw from these clues. Logic helps us to understand the limits to our claims of certitude. Quite often logic helps us to see that we do not know enough to make any claim. In this manner logic tends to make the scientific process conservative in its claims. It does not follow that our research topics, our ideas, or our theories also need to be conservative, however.

## SCIENTIFIC OBSERVATION: THE RAW DATA OF SCIENCE

Have you ever heard the question: If a tree fell in the middle of the forest without anyone around, would there be any sound? This question reflects a philosophical problem in science that was solved in physics at the beginning of this century. Until that time, the notion of physicists was that they study *events* in the world. The job of the scientist in this earlier world view was to be the passive observer and accurately watch events that take place either in the real world or in experiments. There was no thought that the process of observing might influence the perception of the very events being observed.

According to modern physics, scientists do not record events. Instead, scientists record their *observations* of events. They record their experience of the world and consequently base their science on these perceptions. This development amounts to a simple acceptance of the fact that in science we can get no closer to the world than our observations of it.

Let's return for a moment to the child who is discovering the world for the first time. Imagine for a moment that you are that small child who is still crawling and cannot stand up yet. As you go around your world, what do you see? What do you know about events that take place and objects that are more than three feet above the ground? Some events you may know by their sound, like a passing car or your father's electric razor. Other events you may recognize only by smell, like the cooking of bacon or the bleach being added to the wash. Other events you could know only from the sensation involved, such as your father or mother picking you up and throwing you in the air and catching you. Suppose someone could talk with you at this age and asked you to describe what the world was like: what would you say? How would the adult that you were talking to react to your description? Would he or she say it was a true, accurate, and acceptable view of the world?

As you begin to answer these questions, you see that your description as a child was from your own perspective. You may also realize that it is difficult to say whether this account was true or false. From your viewpoint as an adult, it was incomplete. In the same way that the view of a child's world is relative to where and when the child lives and observes the world, the view of the scientist and consequently the *facts* of science are *relative* to the current notions of working scientists and the instruments they use to make observations (see Box 2.3). The current notions concerning science and accepted methods, which encompass a philosophical way of seeing the world, are referred to as a *paradigm*. Although there is much debate as to the exact meaning of the word *paradigm,* most scientists understand it to mean shared beliefs, which include topics to be studied and the types of answers that will be given. For example, the current scientific paradigm in psychology emphasizes the importance of quantitative measurement. Thus scientific psychology, as you will learn it, directs you toward topics that can be measured quantitatively.

"IT MUST BE ACUPUNCTURE. MY TOOTHACHE IS GONE."

Not only are the results and conclusions of our research relative to our current notions of science, but they may also relate to our own psychology. Consider the role of the experimenter (soon to be you) in the psychological experiment. Do you think your own state (hungry, sad, tired, excited, and so forth) could influence the data of an experiment? That is just one of the factors we will consider later in this book. The important point now is to realize that the state of the experimenter is relative and important. Since the scientist is not passive but is *actively* searching for answers, then he or she can actually influence the event being recorded by the very manner in which the observation is being made. Although you may not fully realize it yet, the scientist can actually change the world and our understanding of it. Thus, the scientist is more than a passive observer; he or she is a real actor in the drama of science.

---

### *Box 2.3 Philosophy of Science: Thomas Kuhn*

When Newton said, "I stand on the shoulders of giants," he was referring to those individuals who came before him and on whose work he was able to build his scientific system. Many of us have similar ideas when it comes to the progression of science. We think that each new discovery is simply added to old discoveries with the result being a gradual accumulation of knowledge.

In 1962, Thomas Kuhn suggested that this view is wrong. Kuhn proposed that science actually goes through a series of revolutions. Following each revolution, a new system or method for performing science is instituted. The new system or world view is referred to as a *paradigm* or set of assumptions, which guide scientific activity until a new revolution and paradigm shift take place. The stable period between revolutions is referred to as *normal science*. Normal science is the process of problem solving, which most of us think of when someone uses the term *science*. Normal science for Kuhn is always science performed in relation to a particular paradigm.

As an example of the role of paradigms, assume you were a mapmaker before the time of Columbus. You would draw your maps as if the world were flat, since that was the accepted belief. You, as a mapmaker, would never think to question this belief; it was a given in your task of drawing maps. Then in the Middle Ages, there was the mapmaker's version of a scientific revolution. The paradigm shifted to that of a world that was round. As a mapmaker, you would now draw the world as if it were round and you would continue with this system until a new revolution came along. This, of course, was the replacing of the earth as the center of the solar system with the sun as the center. In the same way that mapmakers work in relation to present-day assumptions and beliefs about the world, Kuhn suggests that scientists also work in relation to a set of beliefs or paradigms until these are replaced by a revolution.

---

## EVALUATING SCIENTIFIC RESEARCH

Regardless of the amount of work involved in scientific research, an extremely important aspect of *any* research endeavor is whether or not the final product is worthy of being reported to the scientific community. We must ask whether our conclusions are *accurate,* Whether they are capable of being *replicated,* and whether they have *relevance* to others. In this book we will emphasize four ways to ensure the high quality of our research. The first is through impartial systematic observation using logically sound experimental design. Since the experimental method is the most powerful class of research design currently available, we will emphasize this technique in the initial chapters of this book and later discuss some other scientific approaches. The second way we ensure meaningful research is through statistical description and inference. We will show you how statistics help us decide whether our results are due to some causal agent or merely to chance. The third method of quality control is through reason and logic. In discussing logic, we will emphasize types of validity as well as types of propositional logic and how they help us evaluate research. The fourth and final way is by emphasizing perspective and context. In particular we will suggest that you view your conclusions from the perspectives of the scientist, the subject, and the witness. Although this book emphasizes the perspective of the scientist, it is important to remember the experiences of the subject as well as the perspective of the witness if our conclusions are to have meaning. We believe that through these four ways of evaluating research you can come to understand science and maintain the high level of excellence that a science of behavior and experience requires.

## COMMUNICATION IN SCIENCE

Unlike the child who is busy learning about the world, the scientist must share what he or she learns about the world with other people, especially other scientists. More than 2,000 years ago, Aristotle emphasized this when he taught that science had two parts: inquiry and argument. In modern terms, inquiry is represented by the research itself, which answers our questions about the world, and argument refers in part to the scientist's responsibility to inform others of his findings. Consequently, we design our research, record our observations, and summarize our findings in a manner that others can understand. For a scientist to answer a question only in terms that he or she can understand would not be complete science because it is not shared knowledge. The final product of mature science is and has always been a communication that summarizes a conclusion about the world and is directed to both scientists and nonscientists.

Learning to communicate in science may be compared to learning a foreign language. One of your first tasks is to learn the vocabulary of science. You need to understand what a scientist means by a certain word. Initially, you may say that is easy since most scientists speak English anyway. That may be true, but it can also be a problem since English words have slightly different or even totally different meanings when used in the context of a scientific statement. For example, suppose you were reading a newspaper article concerning a new discovery in subatomic physics. The article is about particles with "color" and "charm." If you were to talk to a physicist, you would find that "color" and "charm" have nothing to do with colors or with the particles being appealing. These words have special meaning for the physicist. Likewise in psychology, common words may be used in a special or technical way. For example, B. F. Skinner discusses "negative reinforcements" as applied to people, yet "negative reinforcements" have nothing to do with punishment as many people think. Likewise, Carl Jung used the words "extrovert" and "introvert," which have a technical meaning very different from their usages in newspapers and magazines. Even as common a word as "sex" was used scientifically by Freud in a manner almost as distinctive as the terms "color" and "charm" as used by the physicists. Sound confusing? At first the language of science may seem strange. Yet, as with any language, once you learn some words and phrases, you can begin to understand what is going on. This understanding will be useful not only to those of you who pursue careers as scientists, but also to all of us in our daily interactions with the world as we try to understand what we read about science and strive to become more educated consumers. The point to be made is that you have in front of you a twofold task. First, you must seek to understand how words are used in research in a technical way. You cannot just assume that because you have heard the word you already know its meaning. Second, in your own report writing you must seek to define your words and ideas in as precise a way as possible so that others can understand and follow what you are saying.

## Key Terms and Concepts

1. Overview of science
   a. hypothesis
   b. observation and experimentation
   c. inference and conclusion

All cats have four legs.
I have four legs.
Therefore, I am a cat.
S. Harris

2. Types of questions
   a. "If I do this, what will happen?"
   b. "If I do this, I bet this will happen!"
3. Role of scientist
   a. in naturalistic observation
   b. in experimental method
4. Naturalistic observation
   a. four characteristics
      - noninterference
      - determining patterns
      - useful for "big picture"
      - descriptive
5. Experimental method
   a. key question
      - "Was what happened really because of what I did?"
   b. definitions
      - hypothesis
      - experimental group
      - control group
      - operational definition, types of
      - independent variable (also called treatment variable)
      - dependent variable
      - treatment effect
      - confounding variables
6. Causation in science
   a. necessary conditions
   b. sufficient conditions
   c. correlation
7. Validity
   a. internal validity
   b. external validity and generalizability
8. Forms of propositional logic
   a. correct reasoning
      - confirmatory (modus ponens)
      - disconfirmatory (modus tollens)
   b. incorrect reasoning
      - denying the antecedent
      - affirming the consequent
9. Falsificationism
   a. Karl Popper
10. Paradigm
    a. Thomas Kuhn
11. The language of science

## Summary

1. Science is one way of learning about the world that involves articulating an idea or hypothesis, using experience developed in research to evaluate the idea, and drawing conclusions or inferences from experimentation and observation concerning the idea or hypothesis.
2. Observation is an important part of science. The naturalistic observation procedure emphasizes observation and has four characteristics. These are (1) noninterference, (2) observations of patterns and invariants, (3) developing the "big picture" or learning about an unknown process, and (4) providing descriptions rather than pinpointing specific factors that influence one another.
3. Experimentation is also an important part of science. It offers a means of creating control and determining the manner in which one factor influences another. This determination is aided by the use of a control group, which allows you to evaluate the effects of the independent variable on the dependent variable.
4. Another type of research is referred to as correlational study. The purpose of this research is to determine the association between two variables but not the manner in which one variable affects another.
5. A very important part of science is the use of logic and inference. The particular task is to draw conclusions and rule out alternative hypotheses. The study of propositional logic points to both logical and illogical conclusions that are drawn from research results.
6. A researcher must question the validity of conclusions drawn from research. Two major types of validity are discussed. Internal validity refers to the experiment itself and asks whether there are alternative explanation (such as confounds) that would invalidate the reported relationship between the independent and dependent variables. External validity poses the question of generalizability and asks to what other groups or situations a particular set of findings might be applicable.
7. Science reflects a history of observations of events. As a recorder of observations, it is important for you to be sensitive to factors that can influence this record and to understand that any record is always presented from a certain perspective, which has recently been referred to as a "paradigm." It is likewise important that communication in science be clear and be stated in such a manner that it can be evaluated.

## Review Questions

1. What are four characteristics of naturalistic observation?
2. What is an experimental group and what is a control group?
3. What is an operational definition and is there more than one type?
4. In the example given (cereal experiment), describe the independent variable and the dependent variable.

5. Distinguish between a sufficient and a necessary cause.
6. What is meant by the terms *internal validity* and *external validity*?
7. What does the term *falsificationism* mean in science?
8. How would modern physics answer this question: if a tree fell in the forest with no one around, would there be sound?
9. What are the two invalid forms of logic? Give an example of each.
10. What are the valid forms of reasoning? Give examples.

## Discussion Questions and Projects

1. Use the library as the site for a naturalistic observation study. For this you will go to the library, find a place from which you can observe, and simply record what you see. One focus might be the pattern of interactions among individuals in the library. If you were an outsider looking at these data, what might you conclude about the function of the library for students?
2. Give the "Think Square" problem to some of your friends. Using naturalistic observation, record what they do as they go about solving the problem. You might time them, record what they say (if anything), notice facial expressions, etc.
3. Have another group verbalize what they are thinking as they try to solve the "Think Square" problem. You might decide whether there are similarities in the verbalizations of the different people. If you tape-record the verbalizations, it will make the task easier. How do you go about deciding if the verbalizations of two different individuals are similar? What categories do you look for?
4. Put people who are knowledgeable about a sport (e.g., football, baseball, soccer, gymnastics) in one group and those who know little about it in another group. A knowledgeable person should describe in detail some particular play or move from the sport; you then ask for recall of what was said. Notice if there is any difference between the two groups in amount of recall. What other differences are there between the two groups?
5. Discuss how you might turn the demonstrations in Questions 3 and 4 into experiments. What would be the independent and the dependent variables?
6. Assume that you followed the directions in Question number 4 and found that people who knew about the sport remembered more. Discuss the following conclusion: this experiment demonstrates that playing sports helps to increase your ability to remember and thus sports should be required in all schools.
7. Discuss the statement "Scientists do not record events but only their observation of events."

8. An experimenter was interested in creativity. In particular she wanted to know whether a person is more creative at one time of day than another. At the time, she was teaching two sections of an introductory psychology course. One class met from 8:00 to 9:00 A.M. and the other from 4:30 to 5:30 in the afternoon. She used a well-known creativity test and gave the test to each of her classes. When she scored the test she found that those who took the test in the morning did better than those who took it in the afternoon. The experimenter then concluded that in general, college students are more creative in the morning than the afternoon. Discuss this conclusion. Are there other ways in which these data might be interpreted?

CHAPTER THREE

# Description of Behavior Through Numerical Representation

## INTRODUCTION

Behavior can be described in many ways. In naturalistic observation studies, descriptions may consist of simple lists of behaviors or behavior sequences. An ethologist, for example, might describe the detailed movements in the feeding behavior of some common fish. In experimental studies, behaviors are usually expressed in more quantitative terms. Some examples of these measurements are the number of millimeters an observer overestimates the length of a line in a visual illusion experiment, the number of words recalled in a memory experiment, the change in heart rate experienced from watching an emotionally laden film, and the results of an IQ test taken under different conditions. In this chapter we will examine three distinct topics related to the description of behavior through numbers. These are (1) measurement, (2) summary or descriptive statistics, and (3) graphic procedures.

## MEASUREMENT

How we measure things is part of the field of study referred to as measurement theory (Krantz, Luce, Suppes, & Tversky, 1971). One of the first questions we are faced with in doing research is finding what we can measure, and what the measurements mean. Unlike a rose, a number is not always a number. A number may be used in a variety of ways. Sometimes numbers are used to identify particular objects or events, as when a friend tells you she lives at 45 Glenn Road. Sometimes numbers are used to mean "more than," as when a child says that a bike must cost a million dollars more than a candy bar. We adults do the same thing when we tell someone that we woke up in the middle of the night and stayed awake for hours. Numbers can also be used to specify an exact relationship or unit of measure. We know that 25 cents is half of 50 cents and that the difference between 70° and 90° is the same as the difference between 30° and 50°. We can discuss the different ways in which a number is used through the concept of scales of measurement. In the next section we will introduce four important scales: the nominal, ordinal, interval, and ratio. Our discussion will be somewhat brief; for more technical presentations of this information see Combs, Raiffa, and Thrall (1954); Stevens (1946, 1951, 1957); and Roberts (1979).

## SCALES OF MEASUREMENT

### Nominal Measurement

Nominal (sometimes called *categorical*) measurement occurs when subjects are simply placed into different categories. This form of measurement is a classifying or naming activity (hence the term *nominal*). For example, you can classify your subjects as men or women, as right-handed or left-handed, as Catholic or Protestant. The differences between categories are of kind (qualitative) and not of degree (quantitative). In many research problems, it is sufficient to determine simply whether the number of individuals in a given category varies as a function of some treatment in which you are interested. For example, you might want to determine whether the percentage of people willing to try a new product is altered by a particular type of advertising. In this example, your behavioral measure would simply be whether or not an individual is willing to try a new product. Numbers themselves can sometimes be used as nominal categories. For example, the numbers on baseball jerseys, telephone numbers, and zip codes illustrate nominal uses of numbers, as well as coding data (e.g., male = 1, female = 2).

### Ordinal Measurement

In the case of ordinal measurement, there is usually a single continuum that underlies a particular classification system. College football standings, pop charts, and class standings are widely used examples of ordinal measurement. In a psychological experiment, you may divide your subjects on the basis of creativity and end up with three categories: noncreative, creative, and highly creative, which can be given the values 1, 2, and 3. These scores reflect an underlying continuum: the *relative amount* or *magnitude* of creativity. An ordinal scale represents some degree of quantitative difference, whereas a nominal scale does not. Ordinal scales can be obtained whenever you rank subjects or events along a single dimension. With ordinal measures, you are making statements only about order; the differences between consecutive values are not necessarily equal. Notice that numbers used in ordinal measurement have no mathematical properties other than providing categories and rank. Nothing is implied about the magnitude of the intervals between the categories. For example, in the case of the top 20 ranked football teams, there is no assumption that the difference in excellence between the number 1 and 4 football teams is the same as that between the number 6 and 9 football teams. Furthermore, it does not make sense to say that the number 1 and 4 teams equal the number 2 and 3 teams.

What we are really doing is transforming information expressed in one form to that expressed in another. For example, think of the food you ate for supper last night. One way of presenting this information is to name it. We could make a list: pizza, soft drink, salad, green stuff. (No one really knows what green stuff is but every college cafeteria has a large supply of it.) We can take this list of food and transform it into numerical representations. One simple method uses the property of identity. We can assign numbers to our list of food in such a way as to identify or distinguish single foods or groups. For example, we might let a 1 represent all food that we feel better after eating and a 0 stand for all food that we feel worse after eating . You guessed it. Pizza, soft drink, and salad would get a 1 and green stuff would get a 0. Technically speaking we have mapped the aspects of one set onto another set. All this means is that we have found another way (other than just listing) for presenting our data (the list of foods). But this is not the only way that we can represent our data. We could also assign numbers to refer to how much we like the food. We could assign pizza a 1, salad a 2, soft drink a 3, and green stuff a 4. We have now presented the data in terms of the characteristic of magnitude. From this you know that pizza is ranked higher than soft drink but, as with a list of finishers in a race, you don't know anything about how much distance exists between each one. If you want to know about the distance between the numbers then you must assign numbers in such a way that equal intervals are involved. Equal intervals tell us that a given difference between two scores has the same meaning throughout. For example if we were to represent our list of food according to calorie content, we would know that the relationship between the 300-calorie salad and the

150-calorie soft drink was the same as that between the 300-calorie salad and the 450-calorie pizza; there is a 150-calorie difference between each pair. We could also describe the foods in terms of nutritional value such as its ability to support life or vitamin content. As you begin to make this mapping you realize the necessity for having an absolute zero point. There is no way that green stuff could ever support life, much less contain vitamins. Thus we could use numbers to represent the amount of a particular vitamin in the food. Pizza might have 33 units, soft drink 12 units, salad 52 units, and of course green stuff would have 0 units. Zero in this case means that the vitamin is not present at all; 0 represents an actual quantity. This is different than the case in the winter when we say it is 0°F outside. Here we do not mean that there is no temperature, but only that 0 is assigned a certain place on the scale. In conclusion, a given number may convey different types of information depending upon how it is used.

We have just discussed four ways in which numbers may be used in terms of four specific properties: identity, magnitude, equal intervals, and absolute zero. We can use these properties to help us define levels of measurement, or scales of measurement as they are sometimes referred to. We commonly discuss four basic levels or scales of measurement. These are nominal, ordinal, interval, and ratio. These are summarized in Table 3.1 and discussed in the following sections.

### Interval Measurement

For interval data, the scale values are related by a single, underlying quantitative dimension (like ordinal data) and *also* there are *equal* intervals between consecutive scale values. Equal intervals mean that there are equal amounts of the quantity being measured between every two successive numbers on the scale. Thus, on an interval scale, the interval between 1 and 4 equals the interval between 6 and 9. The household thermometer is an example of an interval scale. The degree lines are equal distances apart and, consequently, reflect equal volumes of mercury so that the difference between 20° and 40° is equivalent to the difference between 50° and 70°.

### Ratio Measurement

For ratio data, scores are related by a single quantitative dimension (as with interval or ordinal); they are also separated by equal intervals (as with interval), *and* there is an absolute zero. The most common ratio scales are found in the measurement of the physical attributes of objects, such as weight or length. There is no length shorter than 0 inches, no weight lighter than 0 pounds.

## IDENTIFYING SCALES OF MEASUREMENT

Most frequently, the scale of measurement question is related to the device (scale, questionnaire, etc.) used for measuring the particular concept under study. Even clear examples from the physical sciences that are normally viewed as being an interval or ratio measure (e.g., temperature or length) could not be so termed if the measuring instrument itself was not well constructed. In turn, the measuring instrument is closely related to a theoretical understanding of the underlying concept. For example, until the development of the kinetic theory of heat, the measurement of temperature was inconsistent. There were a large number of devices, each giving different results that could not be converted from one scale to another as they can now (e.g., Celsius to Fahrenheit). Once there existed a theoretical description of how to consider heat, problems of measurement were reduced. This may also be the case in psychology, with our many concepts lacking well-developed theory (e.g., anxiety or intelligence). The point to remember is that scales of measurement are related to how a particular concept is being measured and the questions being asked. For example if we were to

**Table 3.1 Scales of Measurement**

| *Levels* | *Properties* | *Examples* |
|---|---|---|
| Nominal | Identity | Phone numbers, numbers on uniforms, races, brands of soup, employment statuses, diagnostic categories (schizophrenic, paranoid, neurotic, etc.) |
| Ordinal | Identity, magnitude | Class standing, weekly college football polls |
| Interval | Identity, magnitude, equal intervals | Temperature (Fahrenheit or Celsius), scores on intelligence tests, scores on personality adjustment inventories |
| Ratio | Identity, magnitude, equal intervals, absolute zero point | Length, weight, time, reaction time, number of responses made by a subject |

record the order of finish in a marathon we would have an ordinal scale, whereas if we were to record times for the race we would have a ratio scale. We are also interested in measuring devices that reflect a concern for both reliability and validity, which we will discuss in more detail throughout this book.

## MEASUREMENT AND STATISTICS

When we were in college taking "methods" courses, it was commonly taught that a direct relationship existed between the particular scale of measurement (nominal, ordinal, interval ratio) that you were using and a statistic (e.g., *t* test and sign text) appropriate to use with it. This idea, along with the idea of scales of measurement, was introduced by S. S. Stevens in the 1940s (Stevens, 1946). Statisticians as well as present-day experimentalists do not hold this view and continually point out that where a number comes from is not one of the requirements for performing a statistical test. Gaito (1980) has presented a brief but clearly stated review of this issue, and the interested person should consult his *Psychological Bulletin* article. The main point to be made is that no statistical reason exists for limiting a particular scale of measurement to a particular statistical procedure. The numbers don't care what you do to them. Lord (1953) in a humorous manner illustrated this point with football numbers and further pointed out that "the numbers do not remember where they came from." Like a computer, a statistical technique does not care what numbers it uses or where they come from. Numbers are numbers as far as a machine or statistic is concerned. However, if you want to make reasonable conceptual decisions based on your numbers, then it becomes important to be concerned about where your numbers came from—but this is an issue of measurement and not statistics. Using measurement theory we try to assign numbers in such a manner as to make sense out of what we are doing. But to restate, your statistics do not know and do not care where your numbers come from. It does not matter to a statistic if your numbers mean what you claim they do, much less whether your experiment was performed well or poorly. As we will see, statistics tell us about numbers.

## PICTORIAL DESCRIPTION OF FREQUENCY INFORMATION

### Frequency Distribution

A useful way to begin analyzing the results of any experiment is to convert your numerical data to pictorial form and then simply look at it. One way to depict the results of an experiment is to draw a frequency distribution; that is, simply plot how frequently each score appears in your data. Suppose you were interested in dreaming. One initial baseline measurement might be to ask 20 subjects to write down their dreams for a week. To get an idea of how often people dream, you might begin your analysis by seeing how many dreams each subject recalled. Table 3.2 shows the number of dreams each subject remembered dreaming.

Figure 3.1 shows a frequency distribution for these data. The vertical or $y$-axis (ordinate) labeled *frequency* is the number of subjects who fall into each category, and the horizontal or $x$-axis (abscissa) is the number of dreams recalled. This type of graph is referred to as a *bar graph.*

In Figure 3.1, the two blocks above a 0 score mean that two people reported no dreams during the entire week. Thus, we simply count squares and learn that three people reported only one dream, four people reported two dreams, and so forth. Since the measurements along the $x$-axis may be treated as interval data, we could also present them in the form of a *frequency polygon.* A frequency polygon of the dream data is presented in Figure 3.2

Upon closer inspection, it appears that measurements for most subjects tended to be clustered either to the left or to the right on the $x$-axis. This means that for these twenty subjects as least, dreams were recalled either relatively infrequently (one or two dreams) or relatively often (five, six, or seven dreams). This particular type of distribution, in which the subjects tend to fall into two groups, is called a *bimodal distribution.*

**Table 3.2 Hypothetical Dream Study**

| *Subject* | *Number of Dreams Recalled* | *Subject* | *Number of Dreams Recalled* |
|---|---|---|---|
| 1 | 1 | 11 | 7 |
| 2 | 4 | 12 | 1 |
| 3 | 5 | 13 | 2 |
| 4 | 2 | 14 | 5 |
| 5 | 0 | 15 | 6 |
| 6 | 2 | 16 | 5 |
| 7 | 0 | 17 | 2 |
| 8 | 6 | 18 | 6 |
| 9 | 1 | 19 | 7 |
| 10 | 3 | 20 | 5 |

Some common types of distributions you might encounter are illustrated in Figure 3.3.

For our present purpose, we call a distribution *normal* if it approximates a *bell-shaped* distribution (see A in Figure 3.3). We will present a more exact definition later but for now we will say a distribution is normal if most of the scores are concentrated in the center of the abscissa with relatively few at the extremes. Intelligence test scores for 1,000 randomly selected people will approximate a normal distribution. As we saw in Figure 3.1, a *bimodal distribution,* the scores tend to be concentrated at two points along the abscissa (also see B in Figure 3.3). The distribution of heights for an equal number of men and women will also tend to be bimodal. A *skewed distribution* occurs when more scores occur at either end of the abscissa (see C and D in Figure 3.3). A distribution of verbal SAT scores among honors English majors would be skewed since relatively few individuals with low verbal SAT scores would be included in this group. A skewed distribution can be skewed in either a positive or a negative direction. The direction of the general slope indicates whether it is positive or negative. A slope to the right is positively skewed, and a slope to the left is negatively skewed.

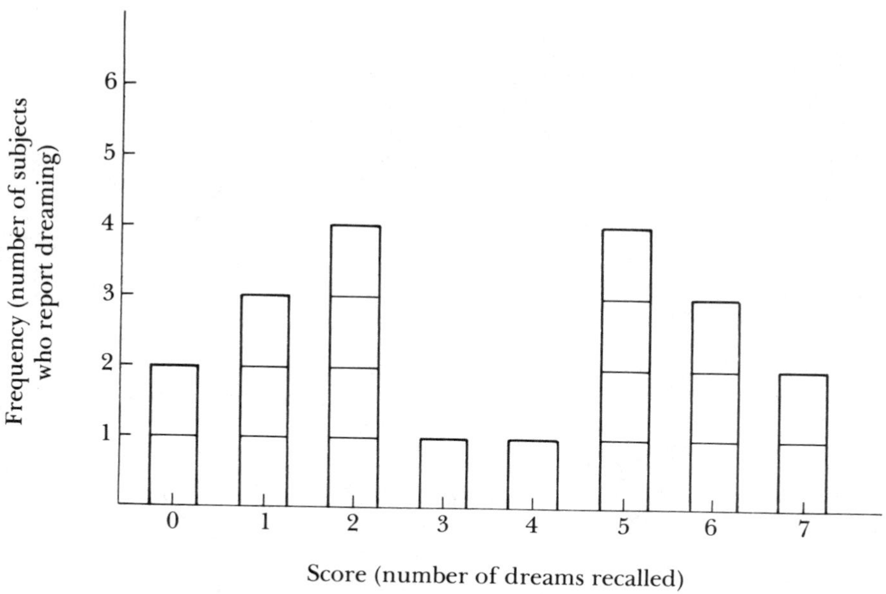


**Figure 3.1.** Bar graph of dream data.

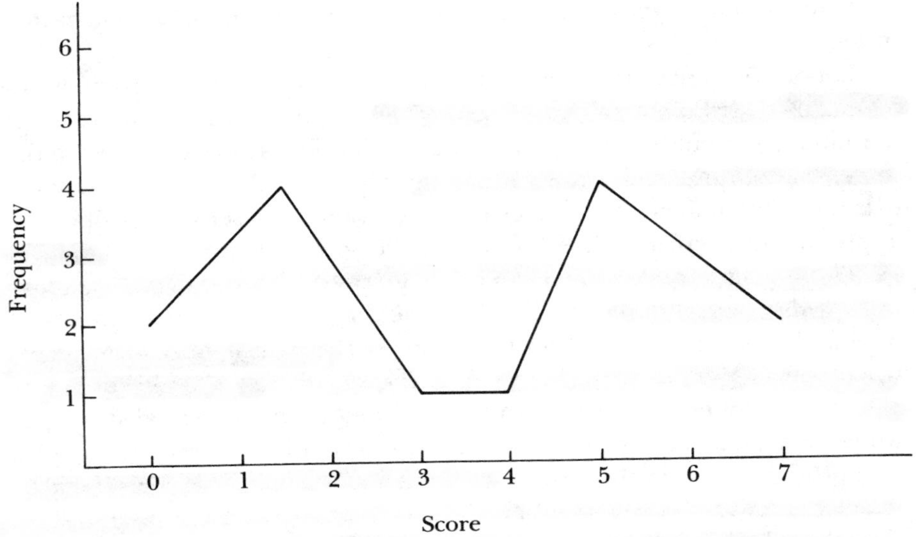


**Figure 3.2.** Frequency polygon of dream data.

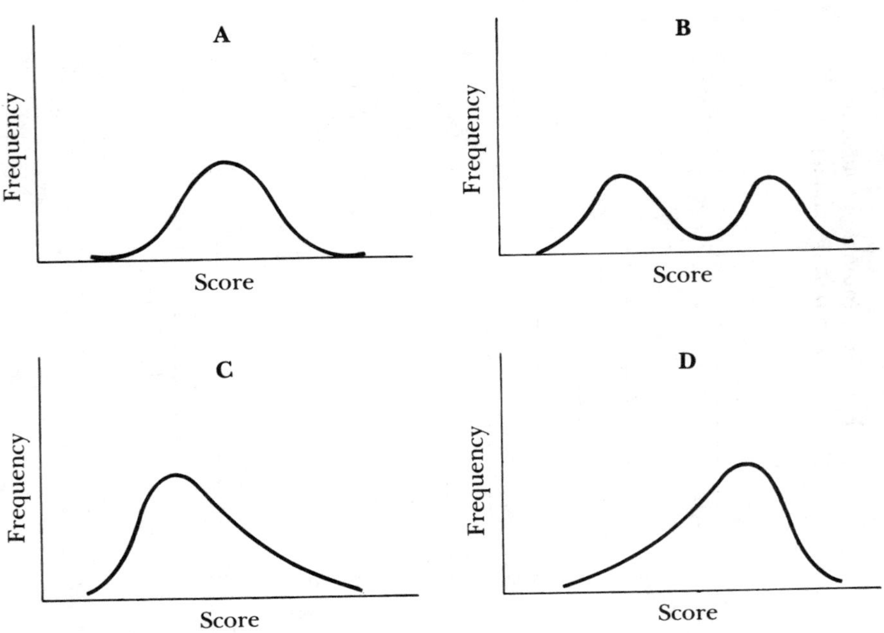


**Figure 3.3.** Four types of frequency distributions are shown: A normal; B, bimodal; C, positively skewed; and D, negatively skewed.

## DESCRIPTIVE STATISTICS

### Measures of Central Tendency

There are three measures of central tendency that we will discuss in this section. These are the mean, the median, and the mode. If you listen carefully to the television news, you will notice that these measures are used frequently to describe the way we "typically" live. You will hear one report discussing the median income of college professors while another discusses the mean price of a new house in different cities in America. Less often we hear about modal (mode) descriptions, although this measure is used from time to time.

**Mean** Of the three measures of central tendency, the *mean* is the most frequently used. The mean of a set of scores is the arithmetic average of those scores. It is obtained simply by adding the scores and dividing the total by the number of scores. In our dream data, a total of 75 dreams recalled was reported by 20 subjects.

$$\text{Mean} = \frac{\text{sum of scores}}{\text{number of scores}} = \frac{\text{number of dreams recalled}}{\text{number of subjects}} = \frac{75}{20} = 3.75$$

average number of dream recalled per subject.

In this particular example, 75 divided by 20 equals exactly 3.75. However, other times the answer may give us a recurring decimal, which must be rounded off to a given number of decimal places. For example, if the total score for 7 subjects was 100, the mean would equal 100/7, or 14.285714285714. . . . The simple rule used by most researchers is to round up if the number is greater than or equal to five and to round down if it is less than five. In this case, if we were to round to four decimal places the mean would be 14.2857, whereas if we were to round to two decimal places the mean would be 14.29. We will follow this rounding rule for any calculation performed in this book.

**Median** The *median* of a set of scores is the middle score—that is, the score that has an equal number of scores both above and below it. To calculate the median of a set of scores, simply list all the scores and the median will be the middle score or, in the case of an even number of scores, the score halfway between the two middle scores. In our dream data, the two middle scores are 3 and 4. Consequently, the median is 3.5

A slight problem in calculating the median is encountered when the median interval contains a large number of scores. In this case, we must interpolate so that an equal number of scores lie above and below the median. This procedure will not be required in this book and is discussed in various statistics books, such as McCall (1980, pp. 64–66).

**Mode** The *mode* is simply the most frequently occurring score. The only mathematical calculation required to compute the mode of a distribution of scores is to count the frequency of each score. The score that occurs most frequently is the mode. If there are two scores with the same frequency, we simply report two modes. For example, the dream data presented earlier had two modes: one at 2 and one at 5 dreams recalled.

Given these three measures, you may be wondering which provides the best estimate of central tendency. As is often the case, there is no clear-cut answer. The appropriate choice varies with the particular frequency distribution and the intent of the researcher. For example, as A in Figure 3.4 indicates, for a normal distribution, the mode, median, and mean all have the same value.

As you can see from B in Figure 3.4, in a skewed distribution, the mean is affected by extreme scores. For example, before you take a job in a company where the mean salary is $100,000 a year, you might want to find out the median salary. A mean of $100,000 could simply be produced by 10 people making $10,000 each and 1 person making $1,000,000 (1,100,000/11 = 100,000). If you were a stock market analyst concerned with how much a company pays out in salaries, however, the mean would be the appropriate measure. In other words, if you are interested in the scores of a total group, then the mean is the most appropriate measure. However, if you are more interested in a representative score for any given individual, then the median is more appropriate. In psychological research, we tend to use the mean most often both for historical reasons and because it fits into already developed statistical theory.

In summary, the measure of central tendency that you use depends on the question you are asking. Thus, in the final analysis, you must use your judgment to determine which measure of central tendency to use.

## TRANSFORMING DATA

After collecting her data a researcher may discover that the numbers she has are either too large or too small to work with comfortably, or are even beyond the range of her calculator or small-computer program. At this point the question arises: Is there a way I can change these data to make them easier to work with? The answer to this question is yes. The procedure is to transform the data. There are a variety of techniques for accomplishing this goal depending both on the type of data and the desired outcome of the transformation. In this section we will only briefly introduce you to the topic.

If you were to travel to Canada, Mexico, or Europe, you might be surprised to look at the temperature listed and see it was only 30° when you were sweating. The explanation, of course, is that these countries use the Celsius scale whereas the United States uses the Fahrenheit scale. Water freezes at 0° on the Celsius scale and boils at 100°. To convert to the Fahrenheit, you multiple the Celsius reading by $\frac{9}{5}$ and add 32. Thus our reading of 30° Celsius would equal 86° Fahrenheit. No wonder you were sweating.

When we converted the temperature in Celsius to Fahrenheit we performed what is referred to as a *linear transformation.* All this means in essence is that if we were to draw a graph of the relationship between the temperature in Fahrenheit and Celsius, the resulting figure would be a straight line. You might try this for yourself by looking in a newspaper (e.g., *The New York Times*) and recording the temperatures from around the world, then con-

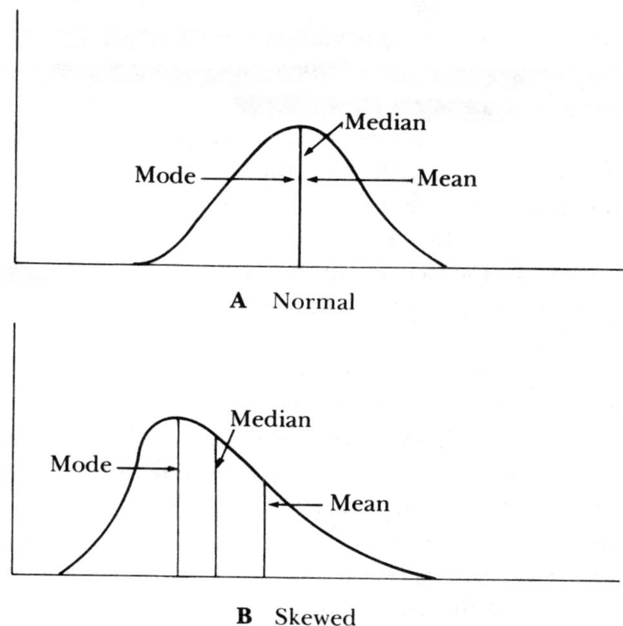


**Figure 3.4** Mean, median, and mode of a normal distribution (A) and a skewed ditribution (B).

verting these into Celsius and plotting the relationship between Celsius and Fahrenheit. Using the example of temperature, we can see that there is a general formula that describes a linear transformation. Using three values that remain constant (A, B, and C), the formula is as follows:

$$\text{New number} = \frac{A}{B}\ \text{Old number} + C.$$

Since the values A, B, and C may be either positive or negative as well as ones, this means that we can add, substract, and multiply or divide the values or perform a combination of these operations in a linear transformation.

There are a number of reasons for the importance of transformations. The first is simply their ability to compare data collected using one scale with that collected using another. For example, in a biofeedback study designed to determine how well subjects can raise their hand temperature, some researchers might report their data using Fahrenheit and others Celsius. By transforming the reported data it would be possible to compare the results. We will have more to say about this type of transformation in relation to the concept of meaningfulness. Another reason for the importance of data transformation relates to statistical assumptions that are suggested for performing inferential statistical comparisons. Sometimes if you violate one of the assumptions, the results are difficult to interpret; the researcher can seek to avoid this problem by transforming the data so that the assumption is not violated. This topic is discussed in some advanced texts referred to in the section on inferential statistics.

We can now introduce a concept that Roberts refers to as *meaningfulness* (Roberts, 1979). Roberts refers to the ability to transform from one scale as *meaningfulness.* He holds that a statement is meaningful if the truth or falsity of the statement remains unchanged when one scale is replaced by another. To understand this better let us look at one example. Imagine that you have performed a study in which you measured the weight of individuals after a certain amount of exercise. One group received more exercise than the other. If we were to transform our data from weight in pounds to weight in kilograms, we would still be able to make meaningful statements concerning the relationship between the two groups. However, in other cases this might not be true. For example, one measure (and underlying theory) of anxiety might reflect a scale construction different from that of another and thus prevent meaningful comparative statements, since the scores from one anxiety scale could not be transformed to the other.

## Measures of Variability

As we have seen, a measure of central tendency gives us some information concerning a set of scores; however, it does not give any information about how the scores are distributed. To obtain a more complete description of a set of data, we use a second measure in addition to the measure of central tendency. This is a measure of *variability*. Measures of variability are merely attempts to indicate how spread-out the scores are. We can also refer to this variability as *dispersion*. One common measure of dispersion is the *range*, which reflects the difference between the largest and smallest scores in a set of data. The actual computational formula given for the range in most introductory statistics books is the largest score minus the smallest score. In the dream data presented earlier, the range is 7 ($7 - 0 = 7$). This is technically referred to as the *exclusive range* (Keppel & Suafley, 1980). Although the computation is easy, the range tells us only about the two extreme scores; it provides no information about the dispersion of the remaining scores if we know nothing concerning the underlying distribution.

Let us now demonstrate this graphically. Consider the following two sets of data for group A and group B:

| *Group A* | *Group B* |
|---|---|
| 2 | 2 |
| 3 | 5 |
| 4 | 5 |
| 5 | 6 |
| 6 | 6 |
| 7 | 6 |
| 8 | 7 |
| 9 | 7 |
| 10 | 10 |

In these two distributions, the ranges are the same (8) and the means are the same (6), yet the actual shapes of the distributions are very different (see Figure 3.5). The scores in group B appear more concentrated in the center of the distribution, yet our estimate of range does not reflect this. To provide a more sensitive description of the dispersion of *all* the scores, a second measure of the variability of data is used. This measure is called the *variance*.

Simply stated, the variance is a description of how much each score varies from the mean. One way to describe the dispersion of *all* the scores would be to subtract each score from the mean and then add these deviations and divide the total by the number of scores. Unfortunately, for both technical and practical reasons, this approach does not give us the type of information we need. Since the sum of the positive deviations is always equal to the sum of the negative deviations from the mean, adding these deviations gives a sum of 0. Instead, we square each deviation, add the squares, and then divide the total by the number of deviations. This gives us a description of how much each score varies from the mean. From this we arrive at the definition of *variance: the average of the squared deviations from the mean.* In order to determine variance, we must first calculate what is called the *sum of the squares;* that is, we add the numbers squared. The sum of the squares is often abbreviated as *SS*. The first formula for *SS* that we will show you is called the deviation method:

Sum of squares = sum of squared deviation scores = $\Sigma(X - \bar{X})^2$. Thus,

$$SS = \Sigma(X - \bar{X})^2$$

where $\Sigma$ = sum of, $X$ = individual score, and $\bar{X}$ = mean of scores.

The deviation method is a useful teaching device because it requires that

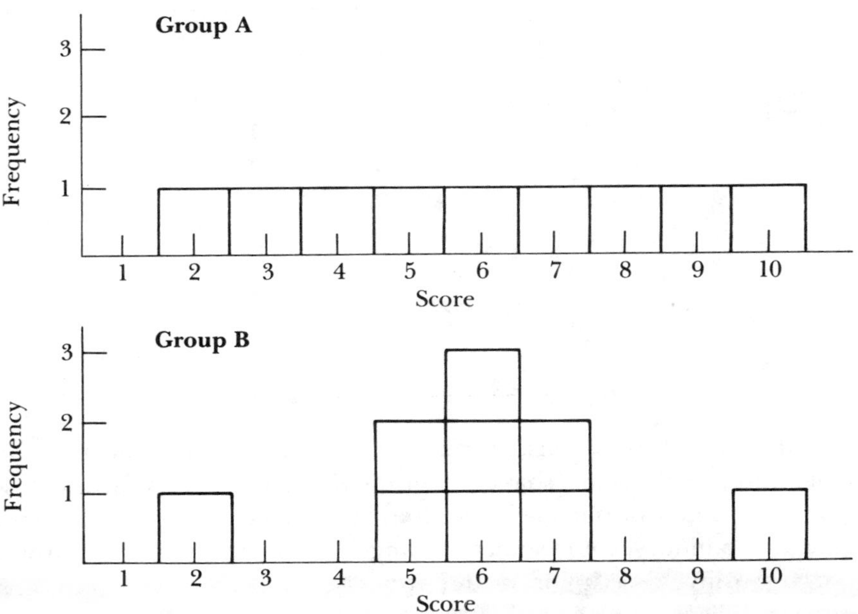


**Figure 3.5** Two different distributions with the same range and mean but different dispersions of scores.

you compute the actual deviations for each score. The method is cumbersome, however, and once you master the concept, you might want to consider a second way to calculate the sum of squares. This is called the *computational formula* and is sometimes used simply because it requires less work, particularly on hand calculators:

$$SS = \Sigma X^2 - \frac{(\Sigma X)^2}{N}$$

where $X$ = individual score and $N$ = number of observations.

In Tables 3.3 and 3.4, the sum of squares of a set of data is calculated by both the computational and the deviation methods. The difference in $SS$ for the two methods reflects the rounding of the data to two decimal places during computation.

**Table 3.3 Deviation Method**

| *Individual Scores, (X)* | *Deviation, $(X - \bar{X})$* | *Deviation², $(X - \bar{X})^2$* | |
|---|---|---|---|
| 1 | −2.75 | 7.56 | |
| 4 | 0.25 | 0.06 | |
| 5 | 1.25 | 1.56 | $\bar{X} = 3.75$ |
| 2 | −1.75 | 3.06 | |
| 0 | −3.75 | 14.06 | $SS = \Sigma(X - \bar{X})^2$ |
| 2 | −1.75 | 3.06 | |
| 5 | 1.25 | 1.56 | $= 93.70$ |
| 6 | −2.25 | 5.06 | |
| 1 | −2.75 | 7.56 | |
| 3 | −0.75 | 0.56 | |
| 7 | 3.25 | 10.56 | |
| 1 | −2.75 | 7.56 | |
| 2 | −1.75 | 3.06 | |
| 5 | 1.25 | 1.56 | |
| 6 | 2.25 | 5.06 | |
| 5 | 1.25 | 1.56 | |
| 2 | −1.75 | 3.06 | |
| 6 | 2.25 | 5.06 | |
| 7 | 3.25 | 10.56 | |
| 5 | 1.25 | 1.56 | |
| | Sum (Σ) = 0 | Sum (Σ) = 93.70 | |

If you remember the definition of variance—the average of the squared deviations from the mean—you will realize that we must now determine the average of the sum of squares. However, in determining the variance, we divide by $N$ for a description of a single population (or $N - 1$ for inference to a larger group, for which see the inferential statistics section on page 97).

$$\text{variance} = \frac{\text{sum of squares}}{\text{number of scores}}$$
$$= \frac{SS}{N}$$

Using the example in Table 3.4, in which the sum of squares equals 93.75, we determine variance by dividng this sum by the number of scores

**Table 3.4 Computational Method**

| *Individual Scores (X)* | *$(X)^2$* | |
|---|---|---|
| 1 | 1 | |
| 4 | 16 | |
| 5 | 25 | |
| 2 | 4 | $SS = \Sigma X^2 - \frac{(\Sigma X)^2}{N}$ |
| 0 | 0 | |
| 2 | 4 | |
| 5 | 25 | $= 375 - \frac{(75)^2}{20}$ |
| 6 | 36 | |
| 1 | 1 | |
| 3 | 9 | $= 375 - \frac{5{,}625}{20}$ |
| 7 | 49 | |
| 1 | 1 | |
| 2 | 4 | $= 375 - 281.25$ |
| 5 | 25 | |
| 6 | 36 | |
| 5 | 25 | $= 93.75$ |
| 2 | 4 | |
| 6 | 36 | |
| 7 | 49 | |
| 5 | 25 | |
| Sum $(\Sigma)$ = 75 | Sum $(\Sigma)$ = 375 | |

(20). Thus,

$$\text{variance} = \frac{SS}{N} = \frac{93.75}{20} = 4.69.$$

This calculation formula for variance would now appear as follows:

$$\text{variance} = \frac{\Sigma X^2 - \frac{(\Sigma X)^2}{N}}{N}.$$

At this point, let's return to the two sets of data used in Figure 3.5. We saw that even though these distributions look quite different, the range for each distribution is the same. Granting for the moment that variance is a more sensitive measure of dispersion, let's see whether it provides a more useful tool for describing the dispersion about the mean of a group of scores. Tables 3.5 and 3.6 show the calculation of the variance for each of these samples using the deviation method.

Thus, group B has less variance than group A and, consequently, this supports our earlier subjective analysis, which indicated less variability or dispersion in group B than in group A. Because variance uses squared

**Table 3.5 Group A Variance**

| *Group A* | $(X-\bar{X})$ | $(X-\bar{X})^2$ |
|---|---|---|
| 2 | −4 | 16 |
| 3 | −3 | 9 |
| 4 | −2 | 4 |
| 5 | −1 | 1 |
| 6 | 0 | 0 |
| 7 | +1 | 1 |
| 8 | +2 | 4 |
| 9 | +3 | 9 |
| 10 | +4 | 16 |
| | Σ = 0 | Σ = 60 |

$$\text{Variance} = \frac{\Sigma(X-\bar{X})^2}{N} = \frac{60}{9} = 6.67$$

scores, however, the variance does not describe the amount of variability in the same units of measurement as the original scores; that is, a variance of 6.67 exceeds the greatest absolute deviation in either sample! Consequently, many researchers prefer simply to use the square root of variance as their estimate of variability. The square root of the variance is called the *standard deviation* (*SD*):

$$\text{standard deviation} = \sqrt{\text{variance}}$$

**Table 3.6 Group B Variance**

| *Group B* | $(X - \bar{X})$ | $(X - \bar{X})^2$ |
|---|---|---|
| 2 | −4 | 16 |
| 5 | −1 | 1 |
| 5 | −1 | 1 |
| 6 | 0 | 0 |
| 6 | 0 | 0 |
| 6 | 0 | 0 |
| 7 | +1 | 1 |
| 7 | +1 | 1 |
| 10 | +4 | 16 |
| | $\Sigma = 0$ | $\Sigma = 36$ |

$$\text{Variance} = \frac{\Sigma(X - \bar{X})^2}{N} = \frac{36}{9} = 4$$

To illustrate:

Group A variance = 6.67,
$SD = \sqrt{6.67} = 2.58$.

Group B variance = 4,
$SD = \sqrt{4} = 2$.

As stated previously, by making this transformation we return to the original units of measurement and can therefore make meaningful comparative statements.

## PICTORIAL DESCRIPTIONS USING MEASURES OF CENTRAL TENDENCY

In addition to using numerical descriptions of data such as frequency counts, measures of central tendency, and variance, it is usually helpful to use graphs to describe our results pictorially.

In psychology we have borrowed graphing procedures from other fields, such as mathematics, and we use many of their conventions. For example, the independent variable is placed on the *x*-axis and the dependent variable on the *y*-axis. There are two main types of graphs used: line graphs and bar graphs.

*Line graphs* are used when the independent variable represents a point along a continuum. For example, you could graph the data from a study of the effects of room temperature on running rates in rats as follows:

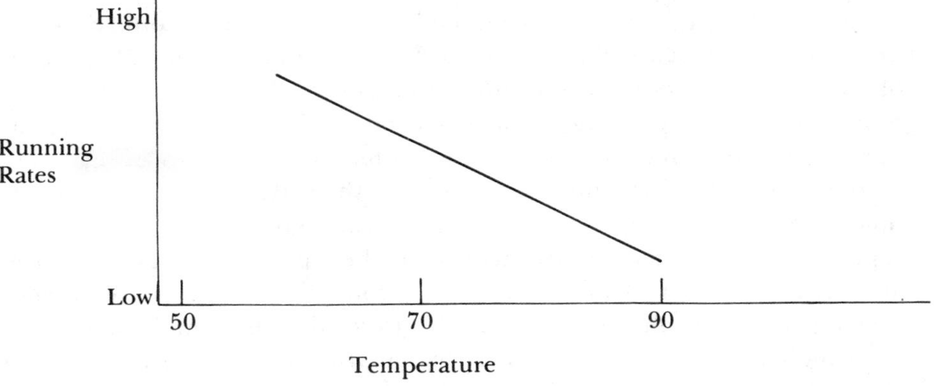


*Bar graphs* are used to depict information that is categorical. For example, the results of a study that examined the effects of different forms of therapy could be illustrated as shown on the next page. It would not be appropriate in this case to draw lines since these types of therapy do not lie along a continuum, although it would have been appropriate if the independent variable had been the amount of a particular drug given, since dosage levels of the *same* drug would form a continuum.

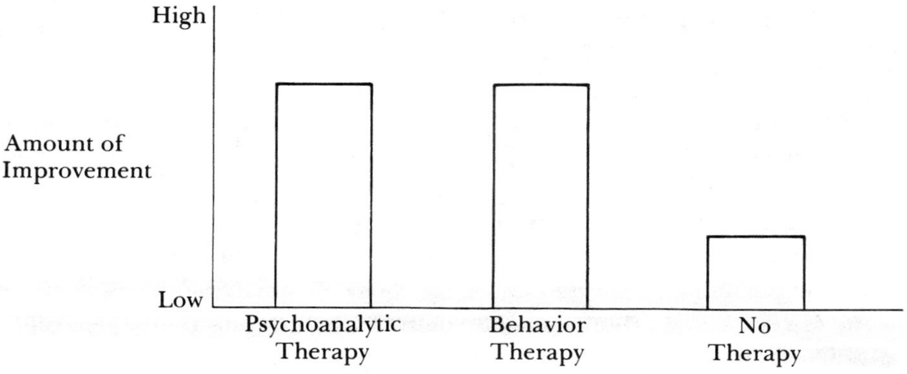


## MEASURE OF ASSOCIATION

Psychologists have long been interested in the question of whether our behavior and self-report go together—that is, whether we actually do what we say we will. In order to understand this question better we could develop a questionnaire that asked people how often they would help people in need of assistance. We could also set up a situation in which there were many opportunities to help another. If we had conducted this study, we could plot our data as shown in Figure 3.6. In this graph, referred to as a *scatterplot,* the score on the helpfulness questionnaire is on the $x$-axis and the number of times the people helped is on the $y$-axis. Each point on the scatterplot represents one person, and two scores: (1) the score on the questionnaire and (2) the number of times that the person helped in the experiment. Looking at this graph you should be able to see that those individuals who score high on one measure also score high on the other measure. Likewise, those who score low on one also score low on the other. A useful statistic to apply to this type of analysis is the correlation. A correlation helps us to understand the relationship or degree of association between two measures. When we perform a correlation we derive a correlation coefficient, which ranges between +1 and –1. A positive correlation represents a linear relationship between two factors such that large values of one measure is associated with larger values of another. In our example, a positive correlation would show a positive association between reporting that one would help in a situation and actually helping in a situation (see Figure 3.6). A 0 correlation would show no relationship. That is, how a subject filled out the questionnaire was in no way related to what he or she actually did. A negative correlation (–1) on the other hand would be found for individuals who either said they would help but did not or said they would not help but did.

A negative association is found in Figure 3.7. We will create a set of data to illustrate how you would determine one particular correlation coefficient, the Pearson *r*, using hypothetical scores from our measures of helping behavior (see Box 3.1). In your own class you might measure everyone's height and weight, and then compute a similar correlation coefficient.

An important question now arises: What can you say about the underlying casual relationship between the two measures under study (e.g., height and weight, or self-report and observed measures of helping)? The answer, plain and simple, is nothing. Correlations have to do with association between two measures; they tell us nothing about the causal relationship between the two variables. We do not know whether either measure caused

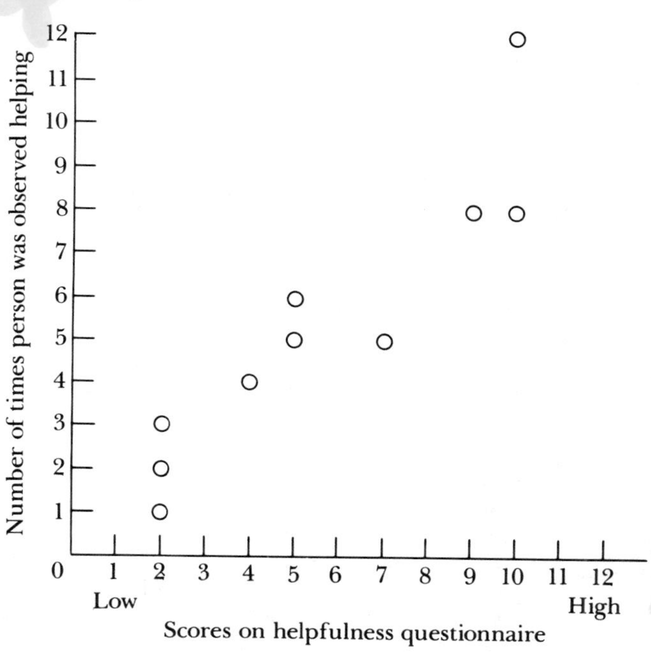


**Figure 3.6** Scatterplot showing positive relationship between two measures.

the other, or even whether both measures were influenced by a third unstudied variable. For example, we could tell you our latest theory, stating that the size of your feet determines how fast you read. We could then show you our data, collected from thousands of children, showing that as foot size increases, so does reading speed. Great theory, right? Although it may be a great theory, a positive correlation coefficient will do nothing to support it. Correlations do not help us to understand causality, since there are numerous factors that are not in any way considered. In our example both size of feet and reading speed were related to development and had nothing to do with each other.

One other quick point must be made concerning correlations, and this has to do with the underlying distribution. If the relationship of the two variables we are studying is not linear, then the correlation that we obtain will not adequately inform us of the underlying relationship. In this case, a graphic representation would supply more valuable information. For example if we were to plot age in months against the number of words that a very

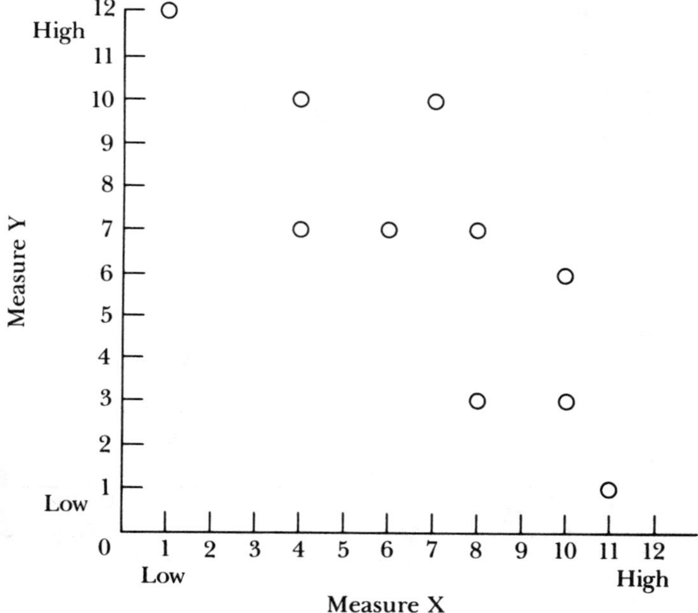


**Figure 3.7** Scatterplot showing negative relationship between two measures.

"THIS IS THE PART I ALWAYS HATE."

## *BOX 3.1 Pearson Correlation Coefficient*

Using hypothetical scores from the helping experiment, we will compute a Pearson correlation coefficient. In this example there are 10 subjects with two scores each. The score on the helpfulness questionnaire we will call *X* and the score derived from the observation of the person we will call *Y*. More information concerning this and other types of correlation coefficients can be obtained in most statistical textbooks. There also exist statistical "cookbooks" that show you how to perform these calculations step by step (e.g., Bruning & Kintz, 1968; Linton & Gallo, 1975). For those of you with personal computers, some books also include BASIC computer programs for finding correlation coefficients (e.g., Cohen & Holliday, 1982).

| Subject(*N*) | Questionnaire Score *X* | $X^2$ | Observation Score *Y* | $Y^2$ | *XY* |
|---|---|---|---|---|---|
| 1 | 2 | 4 | 3 | 9 | 6 |
| 2 | 10 | 100 | 12 | 144 | 120 |
| 3 | 9 | 81 | 8 | 64 | 72 |
| 4 | 4 | 16 | 4 | 16 | 16 |
| 5 | 7 | 49 | 5 | 25 | 35 |
| 6 | 10 | 100 | 8 | 64 | 80 |
| 7 | 1 | 1 | 2 | 4 | 2 |
| 8 | 5 | 25 | 6 | 36 | 30 |
| 9 | 2 | 4 | 1 | 1 | 2 |
| 10 | 5 | 25 | 5 | 25 | 25 |
| | $\Sigma X = 55$ | $\Sigma X^2 = 405$ | $\Sigma Y = 54$ | $\Sigma Y^3 = 388$ | $\Sigma XY = 388$ |
| | $(\Sigma X)^2 = 3{,}025$ | | | $(\Sigma Y)^2 = 2{,}916$ | |

$$r = \frac{N\Sigma XY - (\Sigma X)(\Sigma Y)}{\sqrt{[N\Sigma X^2 - (\Sigma X)^2]\,[N\Sigma Y^2 - (\Sigma Y)^2]}}$$

$$= \frac{(10)(388) - (55)(54)}{\sqrt{[(10)(405) - (3{,}025)]\,[(10)(388) - (2{,}916)]}}$$

$$= \frac{3{,}880 - 2{,}970}{\sqrt{(4{,}050 - 3{,}025)(3{,}880 - 2{,}916)}}$$

$$= \frac{910}{994.03} = .915$$

young child speaks we would see that there is a sudden and dramatic shift. Another example of a nonlinear relationship would be the "U"-shaped curve that is said to relate motivation and performance. In this example one would perform most poorly under conditions of high motivation or low motivation. The best performance would occur when there is a moderate amount of motivation. A correlation would not accurately represent this relationship, which is referred to as curvilinear. Thus for a correlation to give us the information that we desire, the underlying relationship between the variables must be a linear one. In closing, it should be noted that there are correlation coefficients in addition to the Pearson $r$. These are designed for use when one's data are in terms of rank orders (e.g., Spearman $\rho$) or dichotomous data (e.g., point-biserial). These and other types of correlation coefficients are included in many textbooks and handbooks on statistics.

## Key Terms and Concepts

**1.** Measurement
   a. scales of measurement
      - nominal
      - ordinal
      - interval
      - ratio
   b. measurement and statistics
   c. transforming data
   d. meaningfulness

**2.** Frequency distribution
   a. bar graph
   b. frequency polygon
   c. bimodal distribution
   d. positive skew
   e. negative skew
   f. normal distribution

**3.** Measures of central tendency
   a. mean
   b. median
   c. mode

**4.** Measures of variability
   a. range
   b. variance
   c. sum of the squares
   d. degrees of freedom
   e. standard deviation

5. Graphs
   a. line graphs
   b. bar graphs
6. Measure of association
   a. scatterplot
   b. positive correlation
   c. negative correlation

## Summary

1. An important question in research is what we measure and what these measurements mean. One aspect of this question is the realization that not every number means the same thing. When we use a nominal scale of measurement, differences between categories are qualitative but not quantitive. Ordinal data reflect amount or magnitude along a continuum. Interval data reflect magnitude in terms of equal intervals between successive scale values. For ratio data, scores are related by a single continuum, like interval and ordinal; have equal intervals, like interval; and have an absolute zero.
2. A pictorial or graphic presentation of data is an extremely important first step. The vertical axis of a graph is referred to as the *y*-axis or ordinate. The horizontal axis is referred to as the *x*-axis or abscissa. There are a variety of graphs, one of the more commonly used referred to as a bar graph.
3. Common distributions have special names. Those presented in this chapter were normal, bimodal, positively skewed, and negatively skewed.
4. Three important measures of central tendency are the mean (determined by adding the scores and then dividing by the number of scores), the median (the middle score), and the mode (the most frequently occurring score).
5. A score may sometimes be transformed from one scale to another, as when temperature in the Fahrenheit scale is transformed to that on the Celsius scale. If such a transformation can be made, statements made about the original data would also apply to the transformed data. This is referred to as "meaningfulness."
6. Measures of variability are very important in psychological research. Variability or dispersion is related to how spread-out a set of scores is. Most common measures of variability are range, variance, and standard deviation.
7. Special statistical techniques have been developed to ask how two sets of data are associated with one another. One such technique is the correlation. A correlation aids us in understanding how two sets of scores are related but does not tell us whether one score influences the other, or whether both scores were influenced by a third unmeasured factor. Certain distributions, such as curvilinear ones, are not accurately reflected in a correlation coefficient.

## Review Questions

1. What is measurement?
2. What are the four scales of measurement? Give an example of each.
3. Describe the bar graph presented in Figure 3.1 and name the type of distribution shown (e.g., normal curve and bimodal).
4. What is the formula for the mean?
5. What is a median?
6. What is a mode?
7. What is the simple definition of variance?
8. What is meant by the term *SS* and how is it calculated?
9. What is the relationship between standard deviation and variance?
10. Describe the different types of data that you would use with a line graph and with a bar graph.

## Discussion Questions and Projects

1. Find out the number of dreams the people in your class have had this week. Using this data, construct a frequency distribution and present it graphically.
2. Determine the mean, median, and mode as well as variance and standard deviation for the temperature in your area for the month of April.
3. Construct a set of numbers in which the mean, median, and mode are the same, and another set in which they are different.
4. Why do some people say you can lie with statistics?
5. What are the differences between measurement and statistics?
6. Why do some people say that in science if you can't measure it, it does not exist? What do you think?
7. Ask the people in your class to write on a piece of paper two things. The first thing is the size of their high school and the second is a rating of how well they enjoyed their first weeks at college. How might you do this in such a way that you can obtain a measure of association between the two? Would this prove (or disprove) that coming from a small high school makes one enjoy college more in the first weeks? What are the problems with making such a statement?
8. Each day for a period of time pick out any two numbers from a newspaper. For example you might pick out the temperature in Redwood City, California, and the Dow Jones Industrial Average. Determine the correlation between these numbers and discuss what conclusions you can draw.

CHAPTER FOUR

# *Inferential Statistics: Making Statistical Decisions*

## INTRODUCTION

Most of us are able to learn from experience. Like the child who touches a hot stove, we make decisions concerning future events based on past experiences. Like the child, we create for ourselves subjective probabilities about what the future will bring and what will happen if we touch the same hot stove again. We can do the same in regard to research. As we will see, one way to view research statistically is to ask what results we could expect if we ran the same experiment over and over again. The answer most of us would give is that we would expect the results to be similar. When we answer this way we carry with us a long heritage of science, best examplified by the Newtonian approach to physics. Using such a classic approach it does not matter where or when we conduct an experiment as long as certain conditions are met. As Newton suggested in his second law, force is always related to mass and acceleration in the same manner. Thus, to infer the results from one experiment to a number of similar experiments poses no major problem. Likewise in simple chemical studies, it does not matter which actual sample of a pure element one uses. There would be little question that the results found with one piece of pure gold would generalize to all pieces of pure gold. In such situations there would be little reason to invoke an inferential statistical procedure; to do so would be like trying to predict what card would be drawn from a deck of all aces. However, there are situations in which we have reason to believe that the particular sample we are working with may *not* be like every other possible sample, and that it may contain more or less of some measure. In such situations we attempt to understand the properties of all possible samples (referred to as the *population*) from looking at the particular sample we are working with. This process requires *inferential statistics.*

In more technical language, inferential statistics is used to infer from a given sample of scores on some measure the characteristics or parameters related to the set of all possible scores from which that sample was drawn. Implicit in this statement is the assumption that the sample we are discussing was the result of random sampling or some systematic form of sampling. That is, each element (e.g., each person in the population of all people) is equally likely to be included in the sample with some known probability. We will have more to say about random sampling later. For now, the important thing to remember is that inferential statistics constitutes a set of tools for inferring from a particular sample to larger populations. One way of viewing this conceptually is to ask how the parameters of my sample (i.e., the mean and standard deviation) match the actual mean and standard deviation of the entire population (the population values). Thus, the purpose of inferential statistics is to estimate these population characteristics. Another way of viewing the inferential process conceptually is to assume that the same experiment was run an infinite number of times, each time with a different sample of individuals chosen from the entire population. If we were to plot the parameters from each experiment, the population of estimates would then represent all the possible outcomes of the experiment. For our purposes it does not matter which conceptual approach you use; they are equally valid for understanding the logic of inferential statistics. In order to understand the logic of inferential statistics we must introduce the related topic of probability.

## PROBABILITY

We know that simply by using the terms *statistics, probability,* and *sampling,* we have pulled off one of the greater hypnotic acts of the century: we have made half of you cut your minds off completely. Right now there are a number of persons reading this page with no comprehension at all. That's really not much benefit to either you or us. It may help you to know that questions of probability date back thousands of years. The Roman Cicero, who lived in the first century B.C., tried to understand how one should interpret the event in which four dice were thrown and they all came up the same. Was this an act of the gods or a rare event of chance? Read *De*

*Divinatione* (preferably in Latin) for the answer. You might also want to look into the modern-day roots of probability theory—gambling. In fact, much of what we know today came about because some individuals wanted to make games of chance less of a chance, especially for them. It may also be interesting to know that making better beer was one of the practical problems that lead to the development of one popular statistical technique, Student's *t*. The practical question asked what a person could infer concerning an entire batch of beer from sampling a small portion of it. In other terms this asks what the probability is that this particular sample is similar to the entire batch. Before you go off to perform some experiential sampling procedures on your own, let's see if we can work through the theory of probability and inferential statistics with some consciousness.

## Video Games

To make things easier we will talk about video games. Perhaps you have played some; if you haven't, just look at Figure 4.1. I am the circle. When I see the triangle coming I ask myself which way I should go so the triangle will not eat me. At this point in Figure 4.1, the triangle can go one of two ways: left or right. If the program that runs the triangle choses a direction randomly, then the triangle is equally likely to go right or left. One half of the time it will go one way and the other half the other. Thus there is a 50% probability that it will go right and a 50% probability that it will go left. If the program that controls the triangle was written so that the triangle always turns right, we would say there was a 100% probability that it would go right; in every case it would go right and it would never go left. Even if we waited for years it would always go right. However, since we assume there exists a 50% probability for right turns, half the time we expect the triangle to go left and half the time right (even though we may subjectively feel that whatever direction we take the triangle will follow).

Let's assume that you watch me play this game and record whether the triangle goes right or left at each choice point. The triangle comes to a choice point and it goes right. Now it comes to another choice point. Which way will the triangle go this time? That's right; you still don't know. It may be right or it may be left. The triangle has no memory (although it could be programmed to have one). It doesn't remember which direction it went before, and thus every choice point is like starting all over again. If you think triangles remember, you are committing what is called the "gambler's fallacy." You are failing to realize that triangles have no memory—neither do games of chance and hence the name gambler's fallacy. Every time the triangle comes to a choice point it is starting over and thus equally likely to go either direction. In more technical terms we say that each outcome is *independent;* that is, the direction taken at one choice point is not influenced by (i.e., dependent on) the direction taken at the previous one. In Figure 4.1, whether the triangle turns right or left at point A will not influence whether the triangle turns right or left at the next point. Likewise, if it arrived at point C, there would still be a 50-50 chance to go right or left. Given the two choices right and left, and given that the triangle must make one choice, we could also say there would be one chance out of two that the triangle will go right; likewise there is a one-in-two chance that it will go left.

Now, what if we were to look at a number of moves and ask what the probability is that the triangle will arrive at point C after two moves. One way of answering this question would be to draw all the possible choices that the triangle had. Figure 4.2 shows us there are four possible routes for the triangle. Thus, the triangle had a one-in-four chance of arriving at point C. You can also obtain this answer by multiplying the probabilities at each choice point. Since the probability at point A is $\frac{1}{2}$ and the probability at point B is $\frac{1}{2}$, then $\frac{1}{2} \times \frac{1}{2}$ equals $\frac{1}{4}$. How about the probability of arriving at location Y? That's right, the probability at A, B, and C are each $\frac{1}{2}$ and thus $\frac{1}{2} \times \frac{1}{2} \times \frac{1}{2} = \frac{1}{8}$. Thus there is a one-in-eight possibility of arriving at point Y. (You could also draw out the eight possible routes of the triangle if you want to check this). You can of course continue this process to determine the probability of our triangle beginning in any one place and ending in any other. If you are

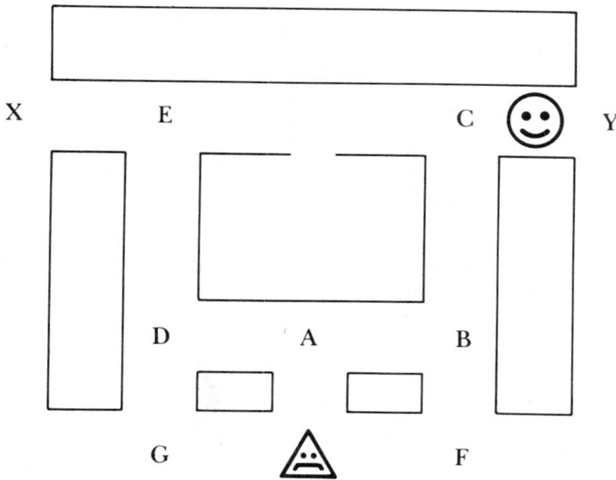


**Figure 4.1** Layout of video game.

having a hard time following this, you might want to take a break and then reread the material. Once you catch on, it's fairly easy.

### *I Ching*

Now that you have had a break, we want to tell you about a friend of ours left over from the 1960s. He was using the *I Ching* the other night. As you may know, the *I Ching* is a Chinese text, aspects of which may be as old as 8,000 years. Although it is best known as a method for divination based on both Confucian and Taoist wisdom, it has also been considered important for the information that it contains. Leibniz, known along with Newton for the invention of calculus, believed that one *I Ching* scholar (Fu Hsi, in the eleventh century) had used the symbols in the *I Ching* to denote binary notation, which lies at the heart of the modern-day digital computer. Although there exists a very elaborate system for using the *I Ching,* most individuals simply take three coins and toss them six times. On the basis of these tosses, one is able to construct a symbol called a hexagram, made up of solid and broken lines. (You can see one in Figure 4.3.) According to popular tradition, contained in this hexagram and the accompanying *I Ching* text are the answers to whatever questions you may ask. We thought, "Why not?" and consulted the text on how we should teach probability. Not having the

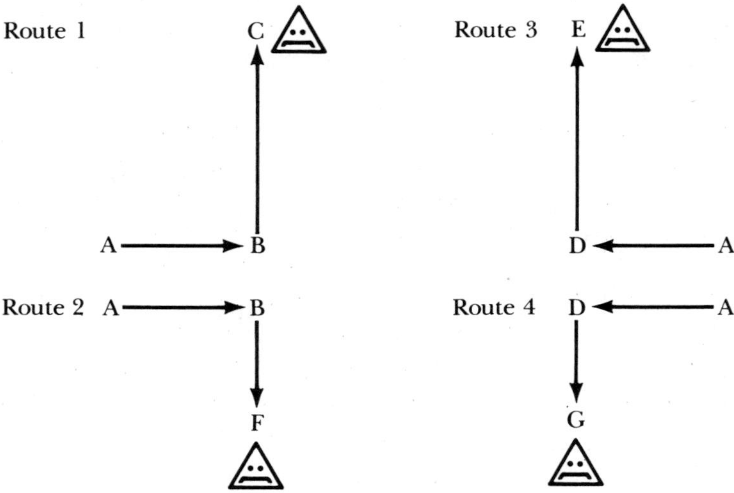


**Figure 4.2** The chances of a triangle.

traditional 50 yarrow stalks, each 1 to 2 feet long, we took the common alternative of throwing three coins six times. The first time the coins came up two tails and one head. The second, three heads; the third, two heads and a tail; the fourth, three tails; the fifth, three tails; and the sixth, two tails and one head. This pattern is associated with Hexagram 31 and produces the pattern shown in Figure 4.3. (There is also a second hexagram associated with this toss but we will save that for the advanced course.) For the interested, Martin Gardner, in *Scientific American,* discusses the mathematical properties of the *I Ching* (Gardner, 1974). A good translation of the basic text is the one from Wilhelm, published by Princeton University Press (*I Ching,* 1967).

Let's look at the first time we threw the coins. The outcome of throwing three coins was two tails and one head. Now we want to ask you a question. What is the probability of throwing three coins and having them land *head, tail, tail?* If you answered "one in eight," then you were correct. This problem is solved in the same way as the video-game problem. For our purposes it might be easier to consider throwing the coins one at a time. The probability of obtaining a head on the first coin-toss is one out of two or $\frac{1}{2}$, as is the probability of obtaining a tail on the second coin-toss, as is the probability of obtaining a tail on the third coin-toss. Multiplying $\frac{1}{2} \times \frac{1}{2} \times \frac{1}{2} = \frac{1}{8}$. It may be easier for you to list the coins and see graphically how the same answer would be reached. Hint: It might be easier to list the possibilities for just two coins and then add the third. The arrangement of two coins is shown in Figure 4.4(A). (Part B is discussed later.) By listing the third coin along with the first two, you should arrive at eight possible outcomes and thus determine that an outcome of *head, tail, tail* has a one-in-eight possibility of coming up.

Now we want to ask the question a little differently, and this is where many people become confused. We could also ask what the probability is of throwing three coins and coming up with two tails and one head, in any order. Before you give the same answer as before, let's reexamine the question and see if we can clear up the potential confusion. The first

| | | Hexagram 31 |
|---|---|---|
| Toss 6 | TTH | — — |
| Toss 5 | TTT | —— |
| Toss 4 | TTT | —— |
| Toss 3 | HHT | —— |
| Toss 2 | HHH | — — |
| Toss 1 | TTH | — — |

**Figure 4.3** Coin tosses leading to Hexagram 31.

question asked was what is the probability of obtaining the order *head, tail, tail.* Looking at Figure 4.4 we saw that there was only one of eight possible orders that would give the sequence *head, tail, tail.* However, if we do not care about the order and just want to know how many patterns have one head and two tails we see that the answer is three. One order is, of course, *head, tail, tail.* Another is *tail, tail, head,* and the one remaining possibility is *tail, head, tail;* all three orders give the desired result of one head and two tails. We could also have obtained the answer mathematically, by using what is called the additive law of probability. That is, we could have taken the individual probabilities of each particular order and added them. The probability of the specific order *head, tail, tail* equals one out of eight, as does the probability of the specific order *tail, head, tail* and likewise the order *tail, tail, head.* The probability of two tails and one head in any order is thus $\frac{1}{8} + \frac{1}{8} + \frac{1}{8}$, equaling $\frac{3}{8}$.

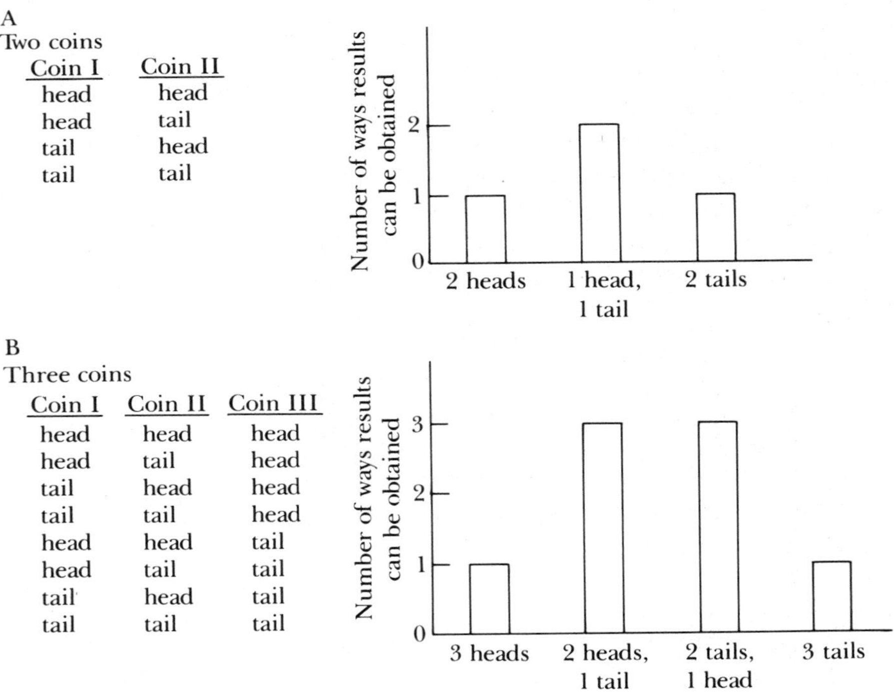


**Figure 4.4** A. Possible outcomes of tossing two and three coins. B. Probability distributions for tossing two and three coins.

PROBABILITY LABS
USUALLY OPEN 9-12
OFTEN OPEN 1-5
S. Harris

Thus far we have discussed the probability of an event as the number of ways that an event can occur divided by the number of all possible events. In the video-game example, the total number of possible events was two (it could go left or right), which was divided into the number of ways the specific outcome (either going right or going left) could occur, which was one. In the *I Ching* coin example, there were three possible ways of having one head and two tails out of eight possible combinations of the three coins. Thus the probability of an event equals

$$\frac{\text{number of ways event can occur}}{\text{total number of possible events}}$$

The probability of the triangle turning right could also be written as $p(\text{right}) = \frac{1}{2} = .50$, as could the probability of having two tails and one head be written $p(2 \text{ tails}, 1 \text{ head}) = .375 = \frac{3}{8}$. We saw how these probabilities could be derived graphically or mathematically. We mathematically discussed the multiplicative law of probability, which we use when we are interested in the probability of two or more events occuring in a particular sequence. In finding the probability of obtaining two tails and one head in the order *head, tail, tail,* we multiplied the probability of each occurrence and obtained $\frac{1}{8}$. That is, the probability of *head, tail, tail,* which can also be written $p(\text{head, tail, tail}) = p(\text{head}) \times p(\text{tail}) \times p(\text{tail}) = \frac{1}{2} \times \frac{1}{2} \times \frac{1}{2} = \frac{1}{8}$. Mathematically we also discuss the additive law of probability. Obtaining one head and two tails in any order equals the sum of probabilities of obtaining each possible sequence. Since the probability of obtaining a specific sequence of three coins was $\frac{1}{8}$, the probability of obtaining the three possible sequences that gave one head and two tails was $\frac{3}{8}$ $(\frac{1}{8} + \frac{1}{8} + \frac{1}{8} = \frac{3}{8})$.

However, there is more to the additive formula. What we have told you thus far works only as long as it is impossible for the events to occur at the same time. For example, it is impossible to throw three coins and obtain on one toss both the sequence *head, tail, tail* and *tail, tail, head.* If it is possible for the events to occur together then the additive formula must be modified. An example will make this clearer. Count the number of people in your class and specify how many are male and how many are female. Now specify how many are 20 years of age or older and how many are under 20. Let's assume that the numbers came out as shown in Table 4.1. If you were to put everybody's name in a hat and draw one name, what would be the probability of picking a male? If out of 40 students, 20 are male, then the probability of picking a male would be 20/40, which equals 1/2 or .50. What would be the probability of picking someone under 20? Since there are 28

**Table 4.1 Number of Students According to Age and Sex in Class**

| | *Male* | *Female* | *Totals* |
|---|---|---|---|
| Age 20 or older | 5 | 7 | 12 |
| Under 20 years of age | 15 | 13 | 28 |
| Totals | 20 | 20 | 40 |

people out of the class of 40 who are under 20 years of age, then the probability would be 28/40, which equals 7/10 or .70. How about the probability of picking someone who is under 20 *or* male? Notice the "or"—unlike the coin-tossing experiment, this one holds the possibility of someone's being both under 20 and male. Technically, we say these events are not *mutually exclusive;* that is, one event does not exclude the other, and we must take this into account in order to determine the probabilities. When we wish to find the probability of drawing the name of someone who is either male or under 20, we add the probabilities of each event occurring alone and then subtract from that the probability of both events occurring together. In our example, the probability of drawing the name of someone male or under 20 equals the probability of drawing someone male 20/40 or ($p$ = .50) plus the probability of drawing someone under 20 28/40 or ($p$ = .70) minus the probability of drawing a male under 20 15/40 or ($p$ = 3/8). Thus the probability of drawing a male or someone under 20 equals 20/40 + 28/40 – 15/40 = .50 + .70 – .375 = .825. By the way, you may be wondering what the *I Ching* text for Hexagram 31 had to say on how we should go about teaching probability. Among other things, it advised that "perseverance furthers."

## THE NORMAL DISTRIBUTION

Let us return to the example of tossing coins. In Figure 4.4 we not only listed the various outcomes of tossing two and three coins but also presented a graphic representation of the number of possible combinations of each toss. Because we know that the probability of an event equals the number of ways that an event can occur divided by the total number of possible events, we can use this same information to create a probability distribution. In fact that is exactly what the two graphs in Figure 4.4(B) are, distributions of probability. If we were to extend these figures to include 10 coins we would find that there are 1,024 possible combinations—quite a change from the 8 possible combinations with three coins. A probability distribution for tossing 10 coins is shown in Figure 4.5. If we were to continue this process and develop probability distributions for even larger numbers of coins, we would eventually arrive at a distribution like the one shown in Figure 4.6. This distribution is like a normal probability curve, or a normal distribution.

The normal distribution has a number of interesting properties both practically and mathematically. For example, some characteristics of humans, such as height, intelligence, and even shoe size, tend to form this distribution. That is, the majority of people wear similarly sized shoes, with only a few wearing very large or very small sizes. To obtain this relationship we would plot shoe size along the *x*-axis (horizontal axis) and number of individuals who wear that size along the *y*-axis (vertical). If we were to identify the places where the curve changes direction (e.g., points of inflection) and draw lines from these perpendicular to the *x*-axis, we would find that these lines divide the *x* = axis into segments each equal to one standard deviation from the mean. If we let the area under the curve equal 100%, or the whole population, then we can describe how much of the population is found in each standard deviation (see Figure 4.7). You can approximate this information by plotting a probability distribution for tossing a coin a large number of times and then counting the numbers that fall under these

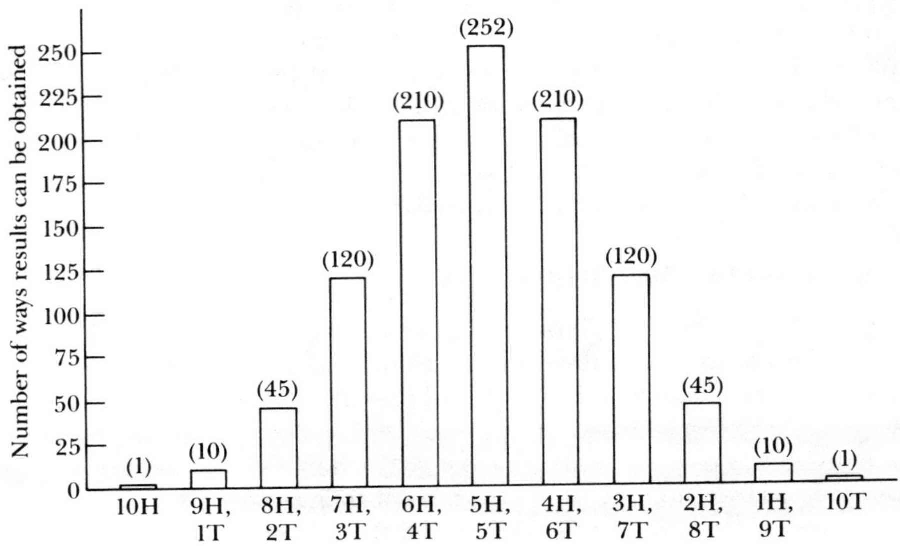


**Figure 4.5** Probability distribution for tossing 10 coins.

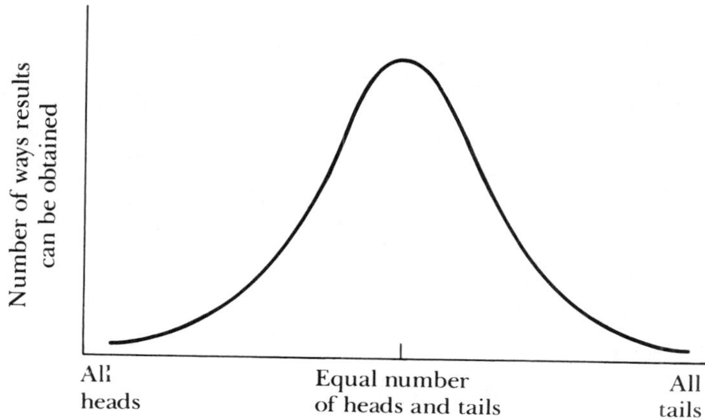


**Figure 4.6** Probability distribution for an extremely large number of coin-tosses.

areas. Let us assume that shoe size distribution constitutes a normal curve: you could then know that 68.26% of all people wear a shoe size that falls within one deviation in each direction from the mean. Alternatively, we could say that given any individual (randomly chosen) there is a 68.26% chance that he or she would wear a shoe size within one standard deviation of the mean size. Within two standard deviations of the mean (in both directions) fall over 95% of all individuals. As to probability, you would have over a 95% chance, choosing any individual at random, of finding that the person's shoe size falls within two standard deviations of the mean.

Unless you run a shoe company, however, you probably don't care very much what shoe size people wear. What does this have to do with research? What this has to do with research is that we can use this normal distribution for making inferences from our research. We could generate a graph of the possible outcomes if we performed the same study over and over again (similar to assuming a normal distribution for people who wear different size shoes). For example, most of you took some type of college admission test, such as the Scholastic Aptitude Test (SAT). Let's assume that we have access to all the scores on this test from students across the country. Then we have a computer randomly pick out a sample of names and determine the mean and standard deviation of this sample. Since computers don't care what they do, or how often, we might have the computer repeat this procedure a large number of times; then we could draw a plot of the distribution of the means found in all the samples. What do you think this plot would look like? Right;

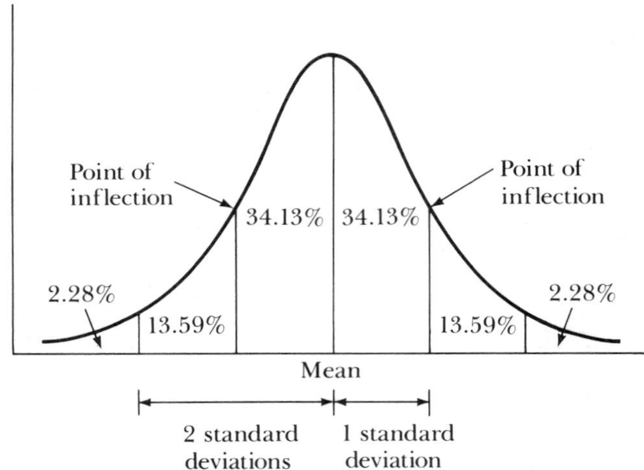


**Figure 4.7** Normal distribution, showing standard deviation.

it would look very much like the normal curve presented in Figures 4.6 and 4.7. Let's make sure you know how to create this graph for the SAT example (Figure 4.8). The $x$-axis represents the mean score found in a particular sample and the $y$-axis represents the number of cases in which that particular mean was found. From this graph we see that many more of the samples had a mean of around 500 than of around 750. Now, what if someone asked you whether it is more probable that in your next sample the mean would be about 500 or about 750? If you said "750," put your money in a bank and never place a bet. It would of course be more probable for the mean to be about 500, since from past experience we know that it is common for a sample to have a mean of 500 but not very common for a sample to have a mean of 750. This is what we learn from the graph in Figure 4.8. This is the basic logic of inferential statistics in general and hypothesis testing in particular.

## HYPOTHESIS TESTING

Hypothesis testing is one of the main branches of inferential statistics. In testing a hypothesis statistically, we simply make a statement, such as "the mean equals 500" or "the mean equals 750." "The mean of what?" you should ask. The answer is the mean of the population. Let's work through the logic of this for a moment to make it clear. Suppose you claim that the students in your class scored higher than students around the country on the SAT. What in essence you are claiming is that the students in your class come

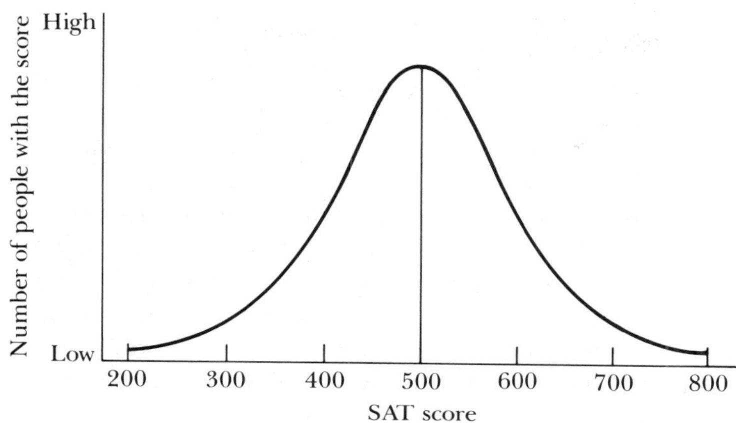


**Figure 4.8** Hypothetical distribution derived from giving a standard test to large numbers of students.

from a population (the population of high-scoring students) that is different from the population of all students taking the SAT. We can use what we have learned so far to test this assumption. What if you are wrong and the students in your class do not come from a different population but rather from the population make up of all students taking the SAT? How would we expect the mean of your sample to be related to the population mean of all students taking the SAT? That's right; they should be similar. If there is no difference between your sample and the population of all students taking the SAT, we would predict that the population mean would be very similar to the sample mean. This particular hypothesis, that the population mean is the same as the sample mean, is referred to as the *null hypothesis* and was developed by Sir Ronald Fisher. If the null hypothesis cannot be rejected, then we cannot claim that your class comes from a different population.

On the other hand, what if we can reject the null hypothesis? If the null hypothesis can be rejected, then we make a statistical statement concerning the null hypothesis. Assume that the mean of your class was 750 on the SAT. What would be the probability of finding this mean in a random sample drawn from the population of all individuals taking the SAT? The probability would be very low but it would be possible. We can make a statement of probability that a sample mean is associated with a certain population mean some percentage of the time. We might say that a sample mean of 750 could have been drawn from a population with a mean of 500 one time in a thousand. Thus although we may reject the null hypothesis, we make this rejection with a conditional statement concerning the probability of our being wrong. (We will have more to say about this in Chapter 5, in Box 5.1. Likewise in Chapter 5 we will discuss in greater detail what the rejection of the null hypothesis allows us to say conceptually.)

Before concluding, we want to point out that in the psychological literature, the null hypothesis has taken on a broader meaning, resulting from the common practice of using two or more groups to test a particular treatment. For example, in the cereal experiment of Chapter 2, we wanted to know if the cereal affected one group more than the other. In such a situation the null hypothesis as commonly used states that no differences exist between the two groups. Most students then assume that we are testing to see whether a difference exists between the means of the two groups (that is, does the mean of Group 1 equal the mean of Group 2?). Although this may appeal to our common sense, what we are actually doing statistically is asking whether these two groups came from the same population; *inferential statistics always refers to a population.* It should also be pointed out that although we spoke only about the mean in our discussion, a number of other parameters, such as the population variance (which we discussed in Chapter 3) and the size of the sample, are also important considerations and play a role in statistical hypothesis testing.

## Example of Inferential Statistics: The *t*-test

In the previous section of this chapter we discussed the idea of statistically testing the null hypothesis, which states that two samples came from the same population. Although we will discuss this in more detail throughout the book, we want to move at this time from a more conceptual to a more computational approach. In this section we want to remind you of one of the more popular inferential statistical techniques, that of the *t*-test. We say "remind" because most likely you learned about this previously in a statistics course. Thus, we encourage you to review your previous course as required.

Let us quickly run through some important terms. Throughout this chapter we have discussed a population and a sample from that population. In Chapter 3 we discussed the mean, variance, and standard deviation. We use different symbols to refer to the mean, variance, and standard deviation of the population and to those characteristics of the sample. We speak of population *parameters* and use the following Greek letters:

mean $= \mu$
variance $= \sigma^2$
standard deviation $= \sigma$

In discussion of the sample, we say *sample statistics* or *characteristics* and use Roman letters as follows:

| | |
|---|---|
| sample mean | $= M$ or $\bar{X}$ |
| sample variance | $= S^2$ |
| sample standard deviation | $= S$ |

As you probably remember from your statistics course, when we find the variance of the population, we use a slightly different formula from that used for sample variance, presented in Chapter 3 in our discussion of descriptive statistics. When we are estimating the population variance as with intentional statistics, we use a different formula. Rather than divide the sum of squares by the number of scores, we divide by $N - 1$. The denominator is technically referred to as the *degrees of freedom.* Thus the formula becomes:

$$\text{sample variance} = \frac{\text{sum of squares}}{\text{number of scores minus 1}}$$

This is also written $S^2 = SS/df$.

Although a formal discussion of degrees of freedom is beyond the scope of this discussion, the basic idea is simple. Degrees of freedom refers to the number of scores that are free to vary. To illustrate this, imagine that you and two friends are eating out and you are waiting for your order to come. One of you orders chicken salad on rye, another orders a yogurt and fruit cup, and the third, pastrami on white bread with mayonnaise. The waiter comes with the food, but he has forgotten who ordered what. From his standpoint, he has a number of degrees of freedom in that he can place the dishes in any of several different combinations. However, if you were to remind him that you ordered chicken salad and the friend on your right the yogurt, this would limit his degrees of freedom. How many would he now have? Right, he would not have any; that is, once you had fixed the order in two of the three selections, the third was determined and not free to vary. Thus, the general idea behind the term *degrees of freedom* reflects how many scores are free to vary.

Let us assume that we had run the cereal experiment discussed in Chapter 2 and obtained the results presented in Table 4.2. We could then perform a *t*-test on the posttreatment scores for the experimental and control groups. The particular formula that we would use follows:

$$t = \frac{\bar{X}_1 - \bar{X}_2}{\sqrt{\dfrac{SS_1 + SS_2}{(N_1 - 1) + (N_2 - 1)}\left(\dfrac{1}{N_1} + \dfrac{1}{N_2}\right)}}$$

where $\bar{X}$ = mean of Group 1 (experimental), $N_1$ = number of subjects in Group 1, and $SS_1$ = sum of squares of Group 1.

From Table 4.2 we can see that there are 7 subjects in each group, with the mean of Group 1 being 7.86 and that of Group 2 being 3 (these numbers are rounded). We can use the computation formula for determining sum of squares (see page 70 in Chapter 3):

$$SS = \Sigma X^2 - \frac{(\Sigma X)^2}{N}$$

or in terms of actual numbers:

$$SS^1 = 455 - \frac{55^2}{7} = 22.857$$

$$SS^2 = 103 - \frac{21^2}{7} = 40$$

Substituting these numbers into the formula for $t$:

$$t = \frac{7.857 - 3}{\sqrt{\dfrac{22.857 + 40}{(7-1) + (7-1)}\left(\dfrac{1}{7} + \dfrac{1}{7}\right)}} = \frac{4.857}{\sqrt{1.497}}$$

$$t = 3.98$$

Thus in the common language of research we would say the two groups differ statistically significantly. However, as we will show you in the next chapter, there is more to research than just the statistical decision related to the null hypothesis. We must make a decision concerning what can be inferred from our data on a number of levels. Generally said, we must develop the meaning of the data.

**Table 4.2 Cereal Experiment Results: Weight Gain**

| *Experimental Group* | | | *Control Group* | | |
|---|---|---|---|---|---|
| *Subject* | $X_1$ | $X_1^2$ | *Subject* | $X_2$ | $X_2^2$ |
| 1 | 10 | 100 | 1 | 0 | 0 |
| 2 | 10 | 100 | 2 | 3 | 9 |
| 3 | 7 | 49 | 3 | 2 | 4 |
| 4 | 6 | 36 | 4 | 1 | 1 |
| 5 | 5 | 25 | 5 | 7 | 49 |
| 6 | 8 | 64 | 6 | 6 | 36 |
| 7 | 9 | 81 | 7 | 2 | 4 |
| | $\Sigma X_1 = 55$<br>$\bar{X}_1 = 7.857$ | $\Sigma X_1^2 = 455$ | | $\Sigma X_2 = 21$<br>$\bar{X}_2 = 3$ | $\Sigma X_2^2 = 103$ |

## Key Terms and Concepts

1. Inferential statistics
   a. sample
   b. population
2. Probability
   a. independent events
   b. mutually exclusive events
   c. additive law of probability
   d. multiplicative law of probability
3. Normal distribution
   a. distribution of probability
   b. distribution of scores
4. Hypothesis testing
   a. null hypothesis
5. *t*-test

## Summary

1. Using inferential statistics, we attempt to understand the characteristics of a population (all possible samples) from looking at a particular sample.
2. Using the video game example and the *I Ching,* we introduced the topic of probability. The multiplicative and additive law of probability we discussed mathematically.
3. In the same way that we can create a distribution of scores we can also create a distribution of probability. For example, if we were to flip a large number of coins repeatedly and plot the results, we would create a distribution that looked very similar to a normal distribution.

4. The fundamentals of probability can be used to aid researchers in testing statistical hypotheses in research. The major statistical hypothesis tested is the null hypothesis, which suggests that no difference exists between the population mean and a particular sample mean.
5. Using the example of SAT scores, the question was asked whether a sample with a mean of 750 could be drawn from a population with a mean of 500. The answer was that it is possible but very rare. A graphic illustration of a probability distribution of SAT scores helped to illustrate this point.
6. One of the more common statistical tests used in psychological research is the *t*-test. This procedure was illustrated in the chapter.

## Review Questions

1. What is inferential statistics?
2. What is the "gambler's fallacy"?
3. Describe events that would be "independent."
4. In what situations would you use the additive law of probability?
5. What is the multiplicative law of probability?
6. What does it mean for events to be mutually exclusive?
7. Describe the normal distribution.
8. In the SAT score example, which would be more likely: to draw a sample with a mean of 400 or one with a mean of 502?
9. Describe hypothesis testing.
10. Discuss the null hypothesis.

## Discussion Questions and Projects

1. Name some common uses of inferential statistics that you see in your everyday life.
2. Discuss some ways in which you see others using the gambler's fallacy in their everyday lives.
3. If you put all the names of the people in your class in a hat, what would be the probability of your name being picked out? What would be the probability of drawing the name of someone who has heard of your professor's favorite singing group? What would the probability of drawing the name of someone who has one brother but no sister? Who has one brother and one sister? Who has one brother *or* one sister?
4. Plot the number of hours of sleep the people in your class reported having last night. Determine how you would statistically test the hypothesis that there is a sexually determined difference in amount of sleep people report. Draw a graph for males and one for females.

CHAPTER FIVE

# *Developing the Hypothesis*

## INTRODUCTION

Imagine that your instructor in this course has just announced that you are to begin an *experiment* of your own and that you are to start right *now*. What do you do? Where do you begin? This chapter is specifically intended to answer these questions and to help you begin your first experiment. As Lewis Carroll once said, the best place to begin is at the beginning.

As with any other human activity, excellence and enjoyment in research begin with genuine interest in some topic. When confronted with their first experiment, many beginning students panic and forget that research begins with interest. Consequently, your first task is simply to sit back and let your interests emerge. Some of you have already done this and are aware of your interests in various areas of psychology. For most of you, however, strong interests have not yet begun to emerge. One way to facilitate this process is to begin exploring various areas of psychology and watch yourself to see what you are interested in.

For example, you may look through your introductory psychology book and see which areas grab your attention. Once you realize the areas that interest you, you might go to the library and look through some textbooks or other books specifically devoted to these areas. You might also talk with psychologists who live in your community and learn more about what they do and what type of questions they ask. However, if no interests emerge, beware; you might want to consider changing majors or even taking a few semesters off. If you have made a mistake in selecting psychology as a major, it is better to try to find areas that do interest you now than after you graduate. It can be very boring to work in an area in which you are not internally motivated by strong personal interest.

As you watch your interests unfold, keep in mind that the interests of even the most dedicated person are not constant. They fluctuate from day to day, sometimes strong and sometimes forgotten. Over a period of years, a scientist may change interests many times. Indeed, some scientists even decide not to be scientists anymore. The key idea here is that interests can be a valuable guide to enable us to enjoy our interactions with the world.

When researchers are interested in a given topic, they learn all they can about it. They go to the library and read about the topic. They talk to other researchers about it. They actively think about the topic. After a time, many researchers find their topic spontaneously arising in their thoughts as they take showers, fall asleep, and eat breakfast. Like a child playing with a new toy, scientists consider their topics from ever-changing perspectives. Some researchers even amuse themselves by trying to describe their topic as if all their ideas about it were backward. The main idea is that they *play* with their thoughts to gain new perspectives on their topic.

## MAKING OUR HYPOTHESES ABOUT REALITY CONCRETE

The essence of a scientific experiment is to see whether our ideas about the world are accurate. In its simplest form it is an interface, a meeting point, between our ideas and reality, between our psychological world and the physical world. This distinction is one aspect of the distinction we made in Chapter 1 between experience (psychological world) and behavior (physical world). To bridge this gap successfully, we must first realize that our intellectual ideas or hypotheses about the world, like our emotions or sensory experiences, are personal experiences. They cannot be shared directly with other people no matter how hard we try. They are private knowledge. Yet science is objective in that its conclusions can be seen and checked by *anyone.* This raises a dilemma: How can we scientifically evaluate our completely private ideas about the world? One answer is to define or represent our private ideas in terms of specific behavior or concrete activities that anyone can witness or repeat. These representations of psychological events in the physical world are called *operational definitions.* An operational definition gives our idea a concrete meaning in reality. For example, the idea that watching violence on television increases aggression is certainly a reasonable and potentially important notion. Yet before we can test it, we must define exactly what is meant by violence on television. Is a program with an unseen murder more violent than an exciting boxing match? Should the violence be rated by how many minutes it is shown on the screen, by the particular type of crime, by how much blood you see, or by a combination of all three? Likewise, to perform this research we would need to devise some measure of aggression. Let's take another example. Assume we wanted to test the idea that psychotherapy is effective. Before we could do that, we must define what psychotherapy is and what could be considered a measure of effectiveness. We would have to adopt operational definitions.

An operational definition takes a general concept, such as aggression or effectiveness, and places it within a given context; that is, *it redefines the concept in terms of clearly observable operations that anyone can see and repeat.* For example, we might define aggression as the number of times a child hits a toy doll after watching a violent television show. Likewise, we might define effectiveness in psychotherapy as measured by a score on a personality test. We could also use the number of days that a person stays out of a mental hospital as an operational definition of the effectiveness of psychotherapy. In each of these cases we have redefined an idea in terms of specified operations. We define an idea (psychological world) in terms of operations (physical world) that are required to produce the phenomenon (physical world) the idea (psychological world) represents. Circular? Of course; that is what science is all about—movement back and forth between our ideas and physical reality. Operational definitions make it possible to tie our ideas and hypotheses to objects and operations in physical reality.

One problem we face with operational definitions is that a given concept may be defined in several possible ways. Similarly, a given operational definition guarantees only a single instance of the original concept. Although we all realize that the grade you receive on a multiple-choice final exam is a narrow facet of all you may have learned in a college course, it is, strictly speaking, an adequate operational definition of your performance. Suppose we were interested in studying the effectiveness of a new form of psychotherapy on severely depressed individuals. Regardless of the research design we use, one task we would face is operationally defining the dependent variable: depression. Before beginning our research, we know that depression can manifest itself in a variety of ways (see Figure 5.1). Each of these ways can then become the focus of an operational definition of depression. For example, we know that the biochemistry of depressed patients undergoes certain changes, so these characteristics would constitute an adequate operational definition of depression. We also know that therapists generally agree on which patients are depressed, so we might operationally define the degree of depression in our subjects by the estimates of various therapists. However, the question of which operational definition is best is tricky. Ideally, it is safest to use several operational definitions. In this

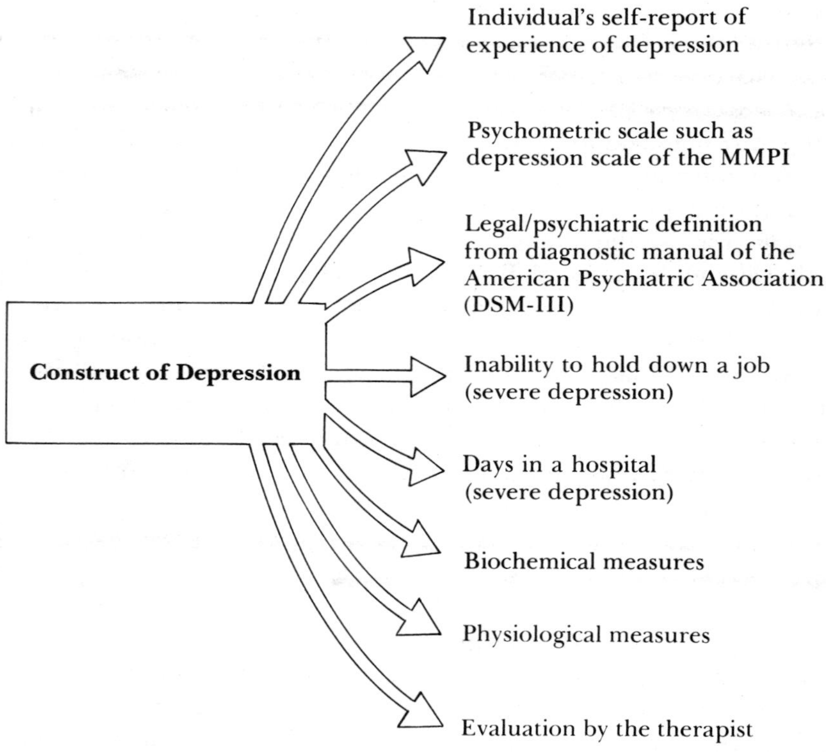


**Figure 5.1** From any one global construct, there are several possible operational definitions depending on the questions asked and the type of population studied (for example, college students or mental hospital patients).

case, we might define depression as a certain score on some depression test plus a "depressed" rating by a therapist and the subject's subjective report of feeling depressed. If this battery of operational definitions is not possible, then at least we should select one that is known to be correlated with others. In selecting operational definitions, remember that they are arbitrary, but are often stipulated or guided by previous research in the area.

When we specify the operational definition, we are helping others to understand the manner in which our measurements took place. As Cronbach and Meehl (1955) point out, however, it is rare for a researcher to accept an operational definition as the sole and exclusive definition of the construct that is being studied. Although we may define hunger operationally in an animal experiment as "amount of time since last feeding," Cronbach and Meehl suggest that we also have other ideas in mind when we use the construct *hunger*. For example, the construct of hunger might also be related to the amount of energy that an animal would expend to seek food. This multiplicity of meaning represents such an important point that Cronbach and Meehl suggest that we need to be concerned about a particular type of validity they refer to as *construct validity*. Construct validity asks whether the procedure that we are using is actually an adequate definition of the construct that we are measuring. Said in other terms, how valid is our inference about the construct we are measuring, based on the specific manipulations and measurements used in our experiment? Thus, one must ask if dropping an apple gives us an adequate basis for making inferences about the construct of gravity. Likewise, in our depression example one must ask whether a particular measure of depression allows us to make valid inferences about the construct of depression.

## MAKING OUR HYPOTHESES LOGICAL

As mentioned in Chapter 2, when we begin our experiment we are in either of two positions concerning what we already know about a research area. In some cases we already know a great deal and can use the experimental method to test specific predictions and hypotheses. Hypotheses of this type take the form "I bet this will happen if. . . ." In other cases we know relatively little and use the experimental method as an exploratory tool. Hypotheses of this type take the form "I wonder what will happen if? . . ." As it turns out, the types of logic underlying these two types of hypotheses are fundamentally different.

### The "I Wonder What Will Happen If" Hypothesis and Inductive Reasoning

If we are working in a relatively new area and know little about the phenomenon we are studying, we have no clear ideas from which to make specific predictions. In this case we use either naturalistic observation or the experimental method to generate new data from which we can begin to formulate a preliminary notion about how the phenomenon is organized. This process of generalizing from a specific instance or even several new facts to a more general idea is called *inductive reasoning* (see Figure 5.2). We use inductive reasoning to increase our knowledge by generalizing new facts to a new understanding. For example, we use inductive reasoning when we observe a chimpanzee using sign language to communicate with a person and we conclude that chimpanzees can communicate with humans. We are generalizing from a specific event to a general idea about how the world is. The danger with this form of logic is overlooking unobserved factors that may be responsible for the effects we observe. For example, you may know someone who is 106 years old and eats yogurt. From this observation, you may conclude that yogurt makes people live longer. This is an invalid use of inductive reasoning since there may be any number of other factors that contribute to this person's longevity. As mentioned in Chapter 2, the *internal validity* supporting this conclusion is questionable.

### The "I Bet This Would Happen If" Hypothesis and Deductive Reasoning

If we already knew a great deal about a particular phenomenon and had formulated a clear-cut idea or theory, then we might *deduce* a specific hypothesis to predict how unexamined but related phenomena operate. In its simplest form, deductive reasoning takes the form of an if–then statement: If my idea about the world is correct, then this cause should produce the following effect. For example, we use deductive reasoning when we say: If it is true that schizophrenia is genetically determined (general idea about world), then we should find a greater incidence of the disorder between twins than between strangers (specific consequence of heredity). The terms of the hypothesis could be operationally defined, an experiment could be conducted, and a decision made about the accuracy of this particular hypothesis. If the hypothesis is supported, then this new fact strengthens the confidence we have that schizophrenia is genetically determined. If it is not supported, then we have reason to question our idea that schizophrenia is genetically determined. Regardless of the outcome, our deduction is logically correct in that if schizophrenia is genetically determined, then we should find a greater incidence among twins than among strangers because twins are known to be more genetically similar than strangers. It only remains to determine empirically whether this logically correct deduction accurately reflects the world. To decide this we use the experimental method.

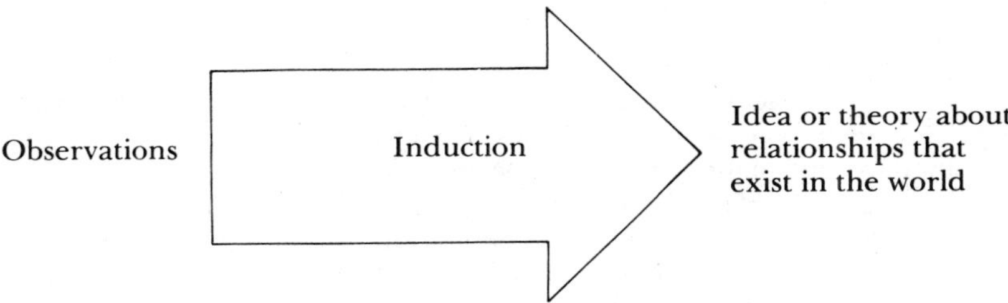


In the early stages of studying a phenomenon, scientists move from observations to theory. Some philosophers of science, such as Karl Popper, believe that psychology is at this stage and thus induction remains the main experimental method of psychological research.

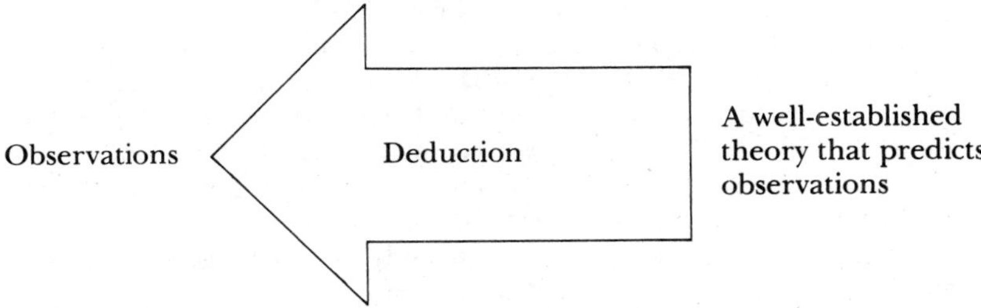


Once a comprehensive theory is developed, predictions can be made from the theory and tested through experimentation. Classical physics is a clear example of a science that uses this procedure.

**Figure 5.2** Inductive and deductive relationships between observations and theory.

## IDEAS COME FROM EVERYWHERE

Every experiment begins with an idea. These ideas can come from anywhere. As we shall see, we may get our ideas from other people, newspapers, television, other scientists, students, ourselves, or just "out of the air." One of our colleagues, Lance Shotland, is a social psychologist who was discussing bystander behavior with his class. Their conversation turned to factors that influenced whether one person will help another in times of trouble. This particular discussion raised questions that led him to conduct a series of studies. Suppose we let him tell how his idea developed:

> While teaching social psychology I got interested in why people don't seem to act when men attack women. For a long time I gave the standard explanation of why people don't help. What happened was that students in the class began to give me other explanations to account for why people don't help. The questions from students gave me the idea that the standard explanation may not be the total answer. What I did was go back to an actual situation in which a woman named Kitty Genovese was killed in front of over thirty people in the streets of New York without anyone calling the police or giving aid. The story is that at 3:00 A.M. a woman named Kitty Genovese arrived home and parked her car in a parking lot across from her home. She walked across the street from the parking lot and started to walk toward her home. She became uneasy as she was walking since someone was walking toward her and she didn't like the way he looked. She became extremely uneasy and turned around and started to walk toward a police telephone. She never reached the police callbox. He overtook her and stabbed her. She screamed, "OH MY GOD, I HAVE BEEN STABBED." With that scream, windows were opened, people's heads came out, and lights came on. The people shouted. With that, the man got scared and ran off. He then jumped into his car and drove away. A bus then came by and people got out of the bus. People in the houses then closed their windows and went back to sleep. She apparently was not helped by anybody. She managed to crawl to another building and the man came back and overtook her and stabbed again. Again she screamed. Again, windows opened and lights came on. Again the people shouted and the man again ran off. The third time, he came back again and this time he killed her. The entire event took over a half an hour.
>
> This is a true event that happened in New York City in 1964. No one who looked out of the apartment windows had done anything that was effective except to scare him off. To have been really effective, the people would have to have helped her, but no one bothered to do that. At that time, the New York papers said "What's going on in New York?" and talked about apathy. A couple of psychologists named Latane and Darley

> decided to research the question of bystander intervention. In their research, Latane and Darley concluded that numbers in themselves may not be important and in fact people in large crowds may leave it to others. These psychologists called this "diffusion of responsibility." Also, the fact that other people are not intervening gives others the feeling that they are not really seeing the situation correctly. Well, this is what I always told my class and my class felt there were other things going on. So I returned to a book that was composed of interviews with the people who watched the Kitty Genovese murder. In this book, *Thirty-eight Witnesses,* I read the bystanders' own accounts of what was going on. One of the things they said was that they were scared. I really don't know why because they were safe in their homes. But also what they seemed to say was that they thought it was a lovers' quarrel. I became interested in that and what I did was to go to *The New York Times* and I started to search through several years looking for cases where men were attacking women and what I found is that it does occur with fair frequency since *The New York Times* generally does not report crime news. Another case happened in the middle 1970s. There was a situation where a man raped a woman in full view of some thirty people. They watched the whole thing. They didn't do anything and it was only a half a block away from a police station. Again, what you find from interviews was that the people thought it was her boyfriend. I began to wonder if this was the controlling factor in the behavior of the bystanders. What I did was to test this. I also went further and wondered what bystanders assume if they don't know the relationship between people. The first thing I wanted to test was if bystanders perceive a relationship between a woman and her attacker, will they intervene less frequently than if it is a situation where a strange man is attacking a strange woman?

At this point, Dr. Shotland had an idea, an educated guess, which stemmed partly from his students' dissatisfaction with the standard explanation and partly from his reading of first-person accounts of crimes. His idea was that one of the important factors that determine whether a woman would be helped or not is related to whether the man and woman are perceived to have a relationship. As a social scientist, Dr. Shotland wanted to test this idea in an experiment. Before he could design the experiment, however, he had to restate the idea in a statement or hypothesis that could be tested in a scientific manner.

What were the steps that Dr. Shotland needed to go through before he could begin an experiment? These are outlined in Figure 5.3. We have already discussed the first two steps: (1) being interested in a topic and having an idea, and (2) considering and thinking about the topic from different perspectives. The third step is the formulation of the initial question: whether a bystander's perception of the relationship was important for a woman to be helped. The fourth step is his reformulating the question into a research hypothesis.

The specific research hypothesis that Dr. Shotland sought to test was this: If bystanders perceive a relationship between a woman and her attacker, they will be less likely to intervene than if the victim and the attacker are perceived to be strangers. To test this hypothesis, Dr. Shotland designed an experiment in which a staged fight took place between a man and a woman. Suppose you were a subject in the experiment. What would you do if you walked out of a classroom and saw a man and woman fighting and yelling at each other? Do you think you would be more likely to intervene if the woman yelled, "I don't know why I ever married you" or if she yelled, "I don't know you"?

In this study what would be the dependent and independent variables? To help you answer this, let's reexamine the structure of a research hypothesis. When a researcher sets up a hypothesis, it is of the general form—if I do this (independent variable), then this will happen (dependent variable). What did Dr. Shotland do in his study? What did he manipulate? He

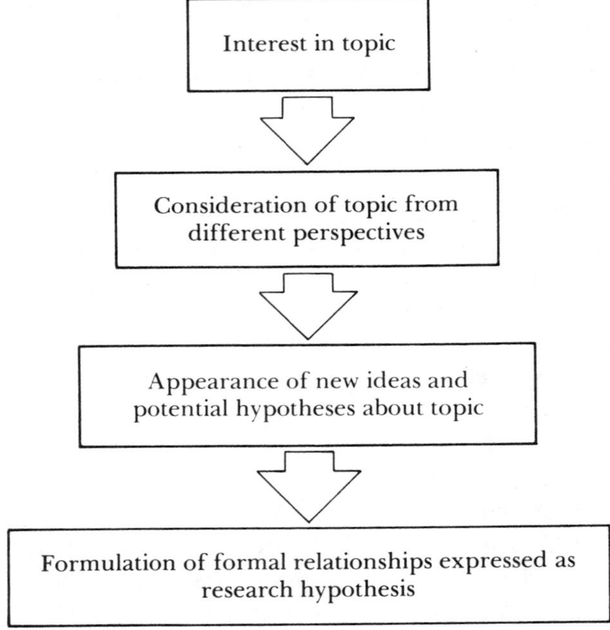


**Figure 5.3** Steps involved in formulating a research hypothesis.

manipulated the bystander's perception of the relationship between the man and the woman. In one condition the man and woman were portrayed as married ("I don't know why I ever married you") and in the other, as strangers ("I don't know you"). Thus the independent variable (that variable under Dr. Shotland's control) was the relationship between the man and the woman. What was the dependent variable, (that is, what was measured)? What was measured was whether or not the subject, who was a genuine bystander in the experiment, intervened. A good question at this point is: What do you mean by "intervene"? Dr. Shotland operationally defined *intervene* as any one of four activities: (1) called the police on a nearby phone, (2) asked a person working nearby to help, (3) shouted at the man attacking the woman, or (4) tried to stop the fight. Now that you know what was measured, an extremely important question arises: How was the dependent variable measured? In this study Dr. Shotland used a very simple procedure; he just counted the number of people who did or did not intervene in the staged fight.

Before we leave this study, let us quickly look at part of the results. How do you think the study came out? The results were consistent with his hypothesis. Under the condition in which there was an apparent marriage relationship, 20% of the subjects intervened, whereas in the "stranger" condition, 80% of the subjects intervened. It should be pointed out that Dr. Shotland did not stop at this point but performed additional studies that controlled for alternative explanations of the data (Shotland & Straw, 1976). The entire article illustrates well how scientists perform research, control for alternative explanations, and modify their studies as new information comes to light. (Following these studies the research was extended to examining what type of cry for help brought the most help [Shotland & Stebbins, 1980], as well as what behaviors and attributions would be necessary in a perceived dating situation for bystanders to decide that rape was involved [Shotland & Goodstein, 1983].)

Let us now turn to another researcher and see how she obtained her ideas. The researcher is a developmental psychologist, Nora Newcombe.

> It all began in graduate school when I shared an office with another woman. One day she asked me what I thought about studying how children go about saying what they want. That is, how they express imperative intent (for example, saying, "Bring me some orange juice"). I thought that was a very interesting idea. It is interesting to me because there is a theoretical position presented by Robin Lakoff that adult men and women differ in how they express imperatives. She stated that women are more tentative and unsure. According to Lakoff, women say

> things like "Would you please open the door" rather than "Open the door" or even hint by saying "It's hot in here" rather than "Open the window." Assuming Lakoff was right, I thought it would be interesting to see if children already showed this type of sex role differentiation. But first I wanted to test Lakeoff's theory with adults. You see, Lakoff is a linguist and had presented her ideas in the form of a theory but had never tested them in a scientific manner. That is, she never collected data from men and women to see if their speech styles indeed did differ.
>
> Another woman, Diane Arnkoff, and I began our research at this point. We did what seemed most straightforward, which was to bring people in and ask them to talk with each other. We brought people in two at a time, either two men, or two women, or a man and a woman. We did this because we thought it was probably important to determine not only if men and women differed in their speech styles but also whether they differed according to whether they were talking to a member of the same sex or opposite sex. In our first study, the people didn't know each other. We gave them a set of topics to talk about, but also told them they could talk about anything else they liked. We then turned a tape recorder on and left them for fifteen minutes.

In performing this study, Dr. Newcombe sought to test the general idea that men and women speak differently, especially when asking for something or giving commands.

Again, if we look at the general pattern of *if I do this, what will happen?*, we can see that Dr. Newcombe paired men-men, women-women, and men-women and then observed the outcomes. The next question we ask is "What was measured?" The general dependent variable was speech style, which was operationally defined in relation to Lakoff's theory. Specifically, the number of qualifiers (such as "you know," "kinda," "I guess," and "maybe") and the number of indirect statements (such as "It is really cold in here, isn't it?") were noticed. The next question is *how* these were measured. Dr. Newcombe used two measures. The first was to count the number of qualifiers and indirect statements spoken during the 15 minutes of recording. Can you imagine some other factors that might influence this measure? You probably realized that one very important factor would be the actual amount of time a person spoke. That is, if one person in the pair spoke almost all the time and the other one said little, then it would be difficult to draw conclusions from the frequency numbers alone. Thus, Dr. Newcombe used a second measure, which was the number of qualifiers divided by the time that a person spoke. Likewise she measured the number of indirect statements divided by the time that a person spoke. What did she find? She found that there were no differences between the speech styles of men and women as operationally defined.

Thus far we have described the manner in which two particular scientists came upon research ideas. We also want to point out that few researchers perform just one study to answer their questions; rather, they conduct a series of studies in which they can clarify their ideas (see Box 5.1). Also, as we hope you begin to see, scientists are people, and as people they differ in the manner in which they discover and develop ideas. Some individuals learn from their classes, some from talking to other people, some from reading the work (scientific or not) of others, and for some the ideas just seem to come out of the air.

## INTUITION AND REVELATION

Depending on the particular century in which you live, ideas that seem to "pop" into your mind have been considered voices of God, meaningless chatter, nonscientific, mystical as well as meaningful, an activation of the right hemisphere of the brain, or an example of psychological intuition. We really do not know much about the workings of our brain, especially when it comes to our own thought processes. At this point in our understanding of the process of science and how we obtain our ideas, we are much like the little baby in the first chapter who watches and tries to see the world. Although we do not know where spontaneous ideas come from, we can observe some examples in which spontaneous or intuitive ideas have influenced the course of science and the work of individual scientists.

One of the most famous stories of an idea just "popping" into the consciousness of a scientist is that of Albert Einstein. When asked how he came upon ideas and solved problems, Einstein replied:

> The words or the language, as they are written or spoken, do not seem to play any role in my mechanism of thought. . . . The above mentioned elements are, in any case, of visual and some of muscular type. Conventional words or other signs have to be sought for laboriously only in a secondary stage. (Koestler, 1964, p. 171)

In other places, Einstein speaks of having a bodily sensation concerning the answer to a problem, or he says that ideas just came to him while sailing. However, he goes on to state that often the translation from the body state to scientific notation required years. Einstein's image of a man riding on a beam of light proved to be one intuitive vision that changed science. Although this vision came in one instant, Einstein spent considerable time working this out and communicating it to other scientists.

Another interesting example of ideas coming from unexpected places is the case of the German chemist Kekulé in 1865. Kekulé was sitting in a chair watching the fire when he fell asleep and later reported the following dream:

> Again the atoms were gambolling before my eyes. This time the small groups kept modestly in the background. My mental eye, rendered more acute by repeated visions of this kind, could now distinguish larger structures, of manifold conformation; long rows, sometimes more closely fitted together; all twining and twisting in a snakelike motion. But

---

### *Box 5.1 Strong Inference: John Platt*

John Platt proposes that certain fields of science have progressed very quickly because of the adoption of a certain method. This method he refers to as *strong inference*. Strong inference is characterized by the following four steps:

1. Devise alternative hypotheses.
2. Devise a crucial experiment (or several experiments) with alternative possible outcomes, each of which would exclude one or more of the hypotheses.
3. Carry out the experiment so as to get clear results.
4. Return to Step 1 with further refinements of the supported hypothesis.

Assume you lived during the time of Galileo and wanted to apply this procedure to the study of falling weights. A simple example would be to drop two weights and hypothesize that if the heavier hit first, then Aristotle would be supported, whereas if they hit at the same time, Galileo would be supported. Once it was determined that Galileo's hypothesis was supported, then a scientist could begin further refinements of the theory. Platt likens the procedure of strong inference to climbing a tree, when each choice point is dependent on the previous one taken. Platt sees strong inference not only as a method for rapid progress in science but also at the heart of every scientist's thinking.

> Obviously it should be applied as much to one's own thinking as to others'. It consists of asking in your own mind, on hearing any scientific explanation or theory put forward, "But sir what experiment could *dis*prove your hypothesis?"; or on hearing a scientific experiment described, "But sir what hypothesis does your experiment disprove?" (Platt, 1964, p. 352).

Platt's procedure of strong inference emphasizes the problem-solving aspects of science and the search for adequate theoretical conceptualizations. It can also serve as a heuristic to help you determine whether your ideas about the world are stated in the form of a testable hypothesis. To help you understand this procedure better, take the hypothesis you are currently developing and ask how you could use the ideas of strong inference to create a line of research through which to test your ideas.

---

> look! What was that? One of the snakes had seized hold of its own tail, and the form whirled mockingly before my eyes. As if by a flash of lightning I awoke. (Koestler, 1964, p. 118)

This simple dream of a snake biting its own tail led to the idea of a circular ring of carbon atoms, which led to research that changed the field of organic chemistry. Through this dream, Kekulé came to suggest the idea that certain chemical compounds are best described as closed rings. Not bad for a night's work, you might say!

Lest you conclude that the best thing for you to do is go sailing as Einstein was fond of doing or take a visionary nap in the middle of class, let us remind you that the insights of these scientists were preceded by years of intensive work in their respective areas of interest. Furthermore, their insight or idea had to be translated into the language and workings of science, which requires not only effort on the part of the scientist but also adequate preparation for understanding the insight in the first place. What can you do to help your ideas along and to prepare yourself for the insights and ideas that lead to new research?

## THE SCIENTIST'S GUIDE TO HAVING AN IDEA

In the 1920s Graham Wallas became interested in how scientists solved problems. Because very little was known about this process, Wallas began by reading the works of famous scientists, particularly Helmholtz and Poincaré. Wallas (1926) concluded that the scientific process could be described in four stages. The first stage is the *preparation* stage. This is the stage in which a person becomes interested in a problem, learns all he or she can about it, and examines it from varied perspectives. Although we do not know why we become interested in the topics that we do, at some point one topic or idea becomes more interesting to us than others. It was at this stage that Dr. Shotland became interested in the alternative reasons his class gave for people's failure to help a woman who is being attacked. This initial stage begins with the scientist's interest and then involves assembling available information on the subject. As you might imagine, assembling available information to get an accurate picture of a research area may take many trips to the library and may involve reading and rereading many crucial articles. As you remember, Dr. Shotland not only talked with his class but also read all he could about bystander behavior and went to eyewitness accounts to hear other people talk about the event. Now you have prepared yourself, but you still do not know what question to ask. What do you do? Actually, the answer is "nothing".

The next stage described by Wallas is called the *incubation stage.* This is the stage in which Einstein goes sailing or Kekulé takes a nap. This stage is very close to meditating on a topic but not thinking about it. One common report is that these new ideas frequently appear spontaneously and catch us by surprise while we are thinking about something else. Brain researchers use the metaphor of letting the right hemisphere take over. Using Wallas's terms, the incubation stage may involve the right hemisphere, whereas the initial survey of the area was primarily left-hemisphere activity (Ornstein, 1977). Keep in mind also that the incubation stage may take years, as it did with Einstein.

The third stage of the process described by Wallas is called *illumination.* It is at this point that the idea or solution begins to emerge into consciousness. This emerging idea could take the form of the dream of Kekulé or the bodily sensations of Einstein, or it could be simply an idea that comes out of nowhere. In this stage one sees a new answer that was not seen before or even a totally different method of viewing the world. It would be like growing up in the Middle Ages and being taught that the world was flat. Then all of a sudden one day you change and see a picture of a round world.

For a scientist, seeing the picture is not enough, and this brings us to the fourth stage—*verification.* This occurs when you test your idea or hypothesis to see whether it fits the real world. The verification stage is what the remainder of this book is all about. Yet we consider it very important that you also realize that there are some very human aspects to doing science, which involve learning everything you can about a topic that interests you, then mulling all this information over and over, and finally permitting yourself to find your answers in strange places.

In trying to understand how scientists obtain the ideas for their experiments, keep in mind that they are already familiar with much of the published work in their areas of interest. At this time in your development, you do not have that advantage. Consequently, an essential first step for all of you is to spend time in the library becoming familiar with various content areas in which you might be interested. To facilitate this process, the next section of this chapter describes several resource tools psychologists commonly use to explore new areas of interest.

## TOOLS FOR LIBRARY RESEARCH

### Journals

Sometimes people are interested in a general area and would like to learn more about it before they attempt to perform an experiment. For example, beginning psychology students may say they want to study biofeedback or ESP or what makes someone go crazy. Where can they go for more information? They could, of course, go directly to experience and attempt to learn more about the topic from the world itself. They could also read what others have written on the topic in either books or journal articles. You can look up books in the card catalog in your library or in a catalog called *Books in Print,* which lists all the currently available books that can be ordered from a bookstore. You may also search for journal articles on your topic. Most published scientific work is found in journals. A journal is nothing more than a collection of experiment reports and other articles written by scientists. There are journals for most areas of psychology; for example, there are the *Journal of Experimental Psychology, Journal of Abnormal Psychology, Developmental Psychology, Journal of Humanistic Psychology, Journal of Applied Behavioral Analysis,* among others. Your reference librarian will help you find out which journals your library carries. If you go to the library, you will notice that the articles in a journal, like those in a newspaper, may be on different topics within a given area. In general, a journal serves as a type of newspaper for scientists, telling of the latest experiments that have been performed in each general area of psychology. But if you want articles on a given topic, what do you do? There are a number of ways to conduct this search. One is to use one of the large computer data bases available at many libraries; your reference librarian will know what your library has available for this purpose. Another way to conduct your search for journal articles is to look in one of the major indexes for the specific area you need. The major indexes that cover psychological research are *Psychological Abstracts, Science Citation Index, Social Science Citation Index,* and *Index Medicus.*

### Psychological Abstracts

*Psychological Abstracts* is published each month and an index volume is published every six months. There are also cumulative indexes covering a number of years. Let us give you an example to illustrate the use of *Psychological Abstracts.* Suppose you had read about biofeedback in the newspaper and wanted to learn about the research concerning biofeedback. How would you do this? Simply go to the most recent index issue of *Psychological Abstracts* and look up the term "biofeedback." You will find two listings: one for biofeedback and one for biofeedback training. Looking at the sample page of *Psychological Abstracts* in Box 5.2, you see a large number of articles. Where do you begin? It depends on what type of question you are asking. If you want only general scientific information, a good place to begin is with a review article. *Psychological Abstracts* notes when the article is a literature review. Notice at the bottom of the second column the following citation:

> Biofeedback training, visceral learning & modification, therapeutic implications, literature review, 10455

---

## *Box 5.2 Psychological Abstracts*

*Psychological Abstracts* is published by the American Psychological Association and includes summaries and listings of recent research of a psychological nature. At the end of each six-month period, an index is published for the preceding six months. Following is a portion of a sample page from the index for the second half of 1979. The number at the end of each listing corresponds to a specific abstract in the monthly issues of *Psychological Abstracts.*

**Biofeedback** *SUBJECT INDEX* **Biofeedback Training**

biofeedback & cognitive-behavioral treatment, myofascial pain dysfunction syndrome, 16–34 yr olds, 6707
biofeedback hardware, book, 32
biofeedback, voluntary control of sexual arousal, unmarried college females, 7988
biofeedback vs instructions & adaptation control, systolic blood pressure control, 2990
cognitive & interpersonal considerations, biofeedback treatment of hypertension vs psychotherapeutic approach, 1456
continuous tumescence feedback & contingent erotic film, voluntary facilitation of erection, men with psychogenic erectile dysfunction, 1630
dichotic stimuli with varying amounts of articulatory feature similarity & EMG feedback, frontalis muscle activity & subvocal muscle activity, right handed Ss, 13087
EEG biofeedback & computer analysis, brain region interactions, cats, implications for experimental design for biofeedback research, 10052
EMG biofeedback & progressive relaxation training, relaxation, tense & anxious vs heterogeneous male alcoholics, 6688
EMG biofeedback, regulation of stuttering, adult stutterers, 6770
false heart rate feedback, sexual arousal, pedophiles, 1610
feedback time & schedule, EMG response, hospitalized males, 7995
frontalis muscle EMG biofeedback vs transcendental meditation muscle tension & locus of control, college students, 5397
hypnosis vs electromyographic biofeedback vs Jacobson progressive relaxation, prefrontal muscle contraction headache, patients, 14063
increased vs decreased vs constant vs noncontingent reinforcement of frontalis muscle activity, verbal decision making task performance, male college students, 3005
information frequency & feedback timing, instructed heart rate speeding, 534
locus of control, dropout from biofeedback treatment program, alcoholics, 6889
manipulation of pulse rate with biofeedback, subjective rating of marihuana intoxication, female 19–30 yr old experienced marihuana users, 5452

biofeedback & relaxation techniques, control of essential hypertension, literature review, 11486
biofeedback assisted muscle relaxation, anxiety & cognitive processes, physical rehabilitation patients, 6656
biofeedback involving frontalis EMG feedback &/or peripheral temperature feedback, muscle contraction headache, patients, posttreatment followup, 14271
biofeedback mediated relaxation training, primary process manifestations in free association, 8968
biofeedback mediated relaxation, depression & anxiety, heroin addicts in methadone maintenance program, 9395
biofeedback monitored relaxation training, writing performance, college students, 516
biofeedback signals & signal aversiveness & reformation value, frontalis muscle relaxation acquisition, patients & normal Ss, 9129
biofeedback thermal training, retainment of biofeedback handwarming skills, 18–24 yr olds, 519
biofeedback training, control of surface skin temperature & response specificity, college students, 13077
biofeedback training, detection of sexual arousal at lower levels of excitation, women, 14229
biofeedback training involving blood volume pulse & frontalis muscle EMG, control of temporal artery vasoconstriction & muscle activity, 2 female 34 & 54 yr olds with combined migraine-muscle contraction headaches, 11516
biofeedback training, treatment of spasmotic torticollis, 60 yr old male, 6627
biofeedback training, visceral learning & modification, therapeutic implications, literature review, 10455 ←
biofeedback training &/vs brief individual psychotherapy, gastrointestinal disorders, college students, 1433
biofeedback vs hypnosis, tension headaches, 14029
biofeedback &/vs relaxation training, psycho-physical measures of stress manifestations, nursing & retirement home residents, 1647
biofeedback &/vs relaxation training, treatment of psychosomatic & functional disorders, literature review, 9144
biofeedback vs voluntary control, heart rate & subjective cold tolerance, 18–25 yr [illegible]

If we now look up the number 10455 in the abstracts, we find the following:

> 10455. **Miller, Neal E.** (Rockefeller U) **Biofeedback and visceral learning.** *Annual Review of Psychology,* 1978, Vol 29, 373–404. —After a clarification of what biofeedback is, methodological and substantive findings in biofeedback research are reviewed in terms of 3 basic scientific issues: (a) the visceral and other responses believed to be unmodifiable that actually can be modified by instrumental training procedures; (b) the types of learned effects involved (indirect or direct); and (c) the law and parameters governing the learned modification of such responses. Implications for therapy are also considered for each area. (218 ref)

This tells us that Neal Miller of Rockefeller University wrote an article entitled "Biofeedback and visceral learning" published in the *Annual Review of Psychology* in 1978. The specific reference is Volume 29, pages 373–404. The abstract tells us what information is covered in the article and that the article includes 218 references (218 ref). From reading the abstract, you can see whether the article covers the information you are interested in or relates to the question you are trying to answer. In addition to literature reviews, *Psychological Abstracts* covers research articles, some books, and Ph.D. dissertations.

### Index Medicus

Whereas *Psychological Abstracts* covers published material of interest to psychologists, *Index Medicus* performs the same function for medical journals. Most of the time, topics of interest to psychological researchers, such as Dr. Shotland's research on bystander intervention, are not found in *Index Medicus.* However, if the topic also deals with treatment factors, as with biofeedback, one can find articles in *Index Medicus* that are not reviewed in *Psychological Abstracts.* If we were to look up "biofeedback" in the July 1978 issue, we would see two references that were not reported in *Psychological Abstracts.* The first refers to an article in the *American Journal of Occupational Therapy.* By looking up the initials *AJOT* in the index, we find the name of the journal. *Index Medicus* does not provide abstracts but only lists the original article by title, authors, and journal. The second reference is to an article on respiratory feedback published in a German journal. You can determine that the article is in German by the (GER) at the end of the article and by the name of the journal: *Zeitschrift für Psychosomatische Medizin und Psychoanalyse.* As with *Psychological Abstracts,* at the end of the year *Index Medicus* publishes a complete listing of articles for the entire year. An example of a *Cumulated Index Medicus* listing of biofeedback articles up to 1979 is shown in Box 5.3.

---

## *Box 5.3 Index Medicus*

*Index Medicus* is published by the National Institutes of Health of the U.S. government. Although the index covers medical journals most fully, areas of psychology related to the health sciences are also included. Unlike *Psychological Abstracts, Index Medicus* does not present a summary of the article but, as the name implies, serves as an index to articles in a given area. Following is part of a page referring to biofeedback work from the 1979 *Cumulated Index Medicus.* Each listing begins with the title of the article, the authors, and then the journal name. The journal name is abbreviated—*Journal of Consulting and Clinical Psychology* would appear as *J Consult Clin Psychol*—and all abbreviations used appear in a special table in *Index Medicus.*

**1979** **CUMULATED INDEX MEDICUS**

board meeting: Center's Board identifies key issues, reorganizes, starts task forces. **Hosp Prog** 60(1):28–9, Jan 79

In vitro fertilization: a moratorium is in order. Diamond EF. **Hosp Prog** 60(5):66–8, 80, May 79

In vitro fertilization: legal and ethical implications. Horan DJ. **Hosp Prog** 60(5):60–5, May 79

Bioethical issues and the moral matrix of U.S. health care. McCormick RA. **Hosp Prog** 60(5):42–5, May 79

Creation, the eschaton, and bioethics. Moraczewski AS. **Hosp Prog** 60(9):61–3, 94, Sep 79

All the President's bioethicists. Annas GJ. **Inquiry** 9(1):14–5, Feb 79

Bioethics and informed consent in American health care delivery. Barkes P. **J Adv Nurs** 4(1):23–38, Jan 79

Nephrology and bioethics. Berman LB, et al. **JAMA** 241(13):1402–3, 30 Mar 79

The role of the nurse in the bioethical decision-making process. Lumpp F. **Nurs Clin North Am** 14(1):13–21, Mar 79

Symposium on bioethical issues in nursing. Shriver EK. **Nurs Clin North Am** 14(1):1–81, Mar 79

Books on bioethics--a commentary. Jonsen AR. **Pharos** 41(3):39–43, Jul 78

### BIOFEEDBACK (PSYCHOLOGY)

Biofeedback, mediated biofeedback and hypnosis in peripheral vasodilation training. Barabasz AF, et al. **Am J Clin Hypn** 21(1):28–37, Jul 78

A biofeedback service by nurses. Putt AM. **Am J Nurs** 79(1):88–9, Jan 79

Biofeedback of accommodation to reduce functional myopia: a case report. Trachtman JN. **Am J Optom Physiol Opt** 55(6):400–6, Jun 78

Bioconverter for upper extremity rehabilitation. Brown DM, et al. **Am J Phys Med** 57(5):233–8, Oct 78

Electromyographic biofeedback in the reeducation of facial palsy. Brown DM, et al. **Am J Phys Med** 57(4):183–90, Aug 78

Biofeedback training of knee control in the above-knee amputee. Fernie G, et al. **Am J Phys Med** 57(4):161–6, Aug 78

Effect of electromyographic feedback and static stretching on artificially induced muscle soreness. McGlynn GH, et al. **Am J Phys Med** 58(3):139–48, Jun 79

Effects of training schedule and biofeedback on speech dysfluency. Weiss T, et al. ... 4 Mar 79

the recent experimental literature. Williamson DA, et al. **Biofeedback Self Regul** 4(1):1–34, Mar 79 (102 ref.)

Heart rate and blood pressure biofeedback: II. A review and integration of recent theoretical models. Williamson DA, et al. **Biofeedback Self Regul** 4(1):35–50, Mar 79

Voluntary heart rate control: the role of individual differences. Carrol LD. **Biol Psychol** 8(2):137–57, Mar 79

Effects of frontalis EMG feedback on frontalis tension level, cardiac activity and electrodermal activity. Siddle DA, et al. **Biol Psychol** 7(3):169–73, Nov 78

Three experiments on the effects of information frequency and feedback timing on instructed heart rate speeding. Twentyman CT. **Biol Psychol** 8(1):1–29, Feb 79

Clinical applications of biofeedback. Johnston D. **Br J Hosp Med** 20(5):561–6, Nov 78

Biofeedback in the treatment of detrusor instability. Cardozo L, et al. **Br J Urol** 50(4):250–4, Jun 78

Idiopathic bladder instability treated by biofeedback. Cardozo LD, et al. **Br J Urol** 50(7):521–3, Dec 78

Yoga and biofeedback in the management of 'stress' in hypertensive patients. Patel C. **Clin Sci Mol Med** 48 Suppl 2:171s–174s, Jun 75

Biofeedback training for stress diseases. Shealy CN. **Compr Ther** 4(9):46–50, Sep 78

EEG feedback training of epileptic patients: clinical and electroencephalographic analysis. Kuhlman WN. **Electroencephalogr Clin Neurophysiol** 45(6):699–710, Dec 78

EEG operant conditioning for control of epilepsy. Wyler AR, et al. **Epilepsia** 20(3):279–86, Jun 79

Effects of sensorimotor EEG feedback training on seizure susceptibility in the rhesus monkey. Sterman MB, et al. **Exp Neurol** 62(3):735–47, Dec 78

Biofeedback--the light at the end of the tunnel? [editorial] Almy TP, et al. **Gastroenterology** 76(4):874–6, Apr 79

Progress in biofeedback conditioning for fecal incontinence. Cerulli MA, et al. **Gastroenterology** 76(4):742–6, Apr 79

The clinical application of EMG biofeedback therapy for muscle contraction headaches. Tsushima WT, et al. **Hawaii Med J** 37(9):270–1, Sep 78

Clinical applications of biofeedback: a summary of research 1974–1978. Wedding D, et al. **Hawaii Med J** 38(1):9–12, Jan 79 (32 ref.)

The value of biofeedback in the treatment of chronic headache: a five-year retrospective study. Diamond S, et al. **Headache** 19(2):90–6, Mar 79

Biofeedback and hea... Diamond S. **Headache** 19(3):180–4. A...

Biofee / pati / Mar / A con / bruxi / Jul 7 / Locus / rate / **J Pe** / Self-f / al. / Rest / wi / F / Eff / Ne / w / **J** / Uroo / sph / 122( / Biofee / obse / 79 / From / phe / **JA** / Helpi / the / Use o / cont / 17(2) / A my / feedb / Jan 7 / Effect o / Pinel / Erythro / **Nurs** / Pain c / train / Inforn / con / per / Au

---

## *Science Citation Index* and *Social Science Citation Index*

The *Science Citation Index* and the *Social Science Citation Index* list articles published in either the sciences (such as physics, chemistry, and biology) or the social sciences (such as sociology and economics). Parts of psychology are referenced in either or both depending on the area of study. *Science Citation Index (SCI)*, as you can see from the example in Box 5.4, lists articles by topic and author. This makes it particularly useful for finding specific types of studies within a general area. For example, when we look under "biofeedback," we see specific areas such as blood pressure, EEG, migraine, temperature biofeedback, and so forth (only EEG and temperature are seen in the example below). Next to the topic is the author's name. We then look up the author's name and find a listing that tells the journal in which the article was published.

### Box 5.4 Science Citation Index

*Science Citation Index* is published by the Institute for Scientific Information in Philadelphia. The index is actually composed of three separate indexes. The first is the subject index, which lists articles related to a specific topic. The second is called the source index and lists authors and the articles or books they published during the period covered. The third index is the citation index, which lists articles published during a certain period that cite as a reference a particular article. By using this third index, one can determine what work has followed up a specific research article. Presented here is a portion of a sample page from the subject index of the *Science Citation Index*.

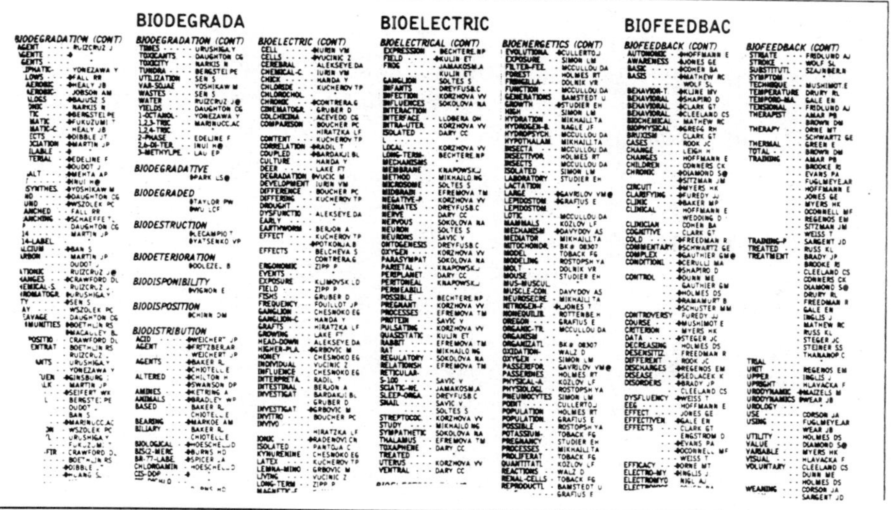

BIODEGRADA

BIOELECTRIC

BIOFEEDBAC

One advantage of the *SCI* over other indexes is that it includes in a separate volume a listing of all studies that cited a particular study (hence the name *Science Citation Index*). This would be particularly useful to a researcher like Dr. Newcombe. As she was beginning to plan her study examining sex and speech types according to the theory of Robin Lakoff, she would want to know whether anyone else had tested this theory. Since, as you will see later, scientists refer in their articles to the research and theories of others, it would be possible to find all the studies that refer to Dr. Lakoff's work. To do this, Dr. Newcombe would look up R. T. Lakoff and note all the articles that cited her work. Dr. Newcombe could then check these articles to see whether any other scientists had asked the specific question in which she was interested.

We have now discussed developing the hypothesis, including the use of operational definitions, how various scientists have arrived at their ideas for research, and some library resources that you will use as you begin to explore your own ideas. You should be able to consider your own research study. Before moving into the question of experimentation presented in the next chapter, however, we want to expand on our discussion of creating testable hypotheses, since many beginning students have difficulty with this.

## CREATING TESTABLE RESEARCH HYPOTHESES AND THE PROBLEM OF MEASUREMENT

Making the transition from a general idea to a testable research hypothesis is not always a simple task. Most beginning students present their ideas in the form of a general statement and tend to ask global questions. It is only with considerable work and practice that a generally interesting idea can be rephrased into a testable hypothesis that clearly spells out a specific relationship between variables. It may even be that many areas of psychology are ignored simply because of the difficulty in making the transition to adequate research hypotheses. Areas such as romantic love, creativity, extrasensory perception, consciousness, and mental illness may be some examples. Because of the nature of the questions, other areas may even be outside the realm of testability, as illustrated by the cartoon on p. 123. Even for the experienced scientist, the transition from a general idea to a specific research hypothesis can be a difficult process.

One aspect of the transition to a testable research hypothesis is measurement. Measurement considerations underlie the way we develop our operational definitions. We touched on this issue when we discussed the work of Dr. Shotland and Dr. Newcombe. At this time we will briefly introduce you

"IT MAY VERY WELL BRING ABOUT IMMORTALITY, BUT IT WILL TAKE FOREVER TO TEST IT."

to two important aspects of measurement: reliability and validity. For a measurement to be *reliable* means that the measure is consistent. There are many everyday examples of reliable measuring devices; for example, the ideal bathroom scale will give you the same weight no matter how many times you stand on it unless, of course, your weight actually does change between weighings. For a measurement to be *valid* it must be accurate. In the case of the bathroom scale, the reading must accurately reflect your weight in some unit of measurement such as pounds. Now suppose your boyfriend or girlfriend wanted you to lose weight, so he or she set your scale at five pounds overweight. At five pounds overweight, your scale would still be reliable; that is, it would continue to give you and anyone else a *consistent* weight each time you weighed. However, at five pounds overweight, the measurement would not be *valid;* that is, the scale would not reflect your *true* weight. To be valid a measurement must reflect the *true* score within limits. The "within limits" is determined by what we know scientifically about a given construct. Thus, our goal is to use measurements that as much as possible are both true (valid) and consistent (reliable) in our experiments.

Let us say that again. For a measure to be valid, it must *accurately* reflect the construct in question. For a measure to be reliable, it must *consistently* give the same information. To understand this better, consider two clocks, one that was stopped at four o'clock and one that is always five minutes fast. Which is reliable and which is valid? If you say that the fast clock is reliable, you are right. This clock *consistently* gives the same time in relation to the actual time of day. How about validity? Neither clock is totally valid. You could argue that the fast clock was never valid, whereas the stopped clock was valid twice a day, although that would be of very little use to us.

To return to your psychological experiment, it is your task to choose measurements that are both accurate (validity) and consistent (reliability) in relation to the question you are asking. Yet how do you as a beginning student select methods of measurement that are both reliable and valid for your purposes? You have two alternatives. You can either (1) begin from scratch and demonstrate that your measures are indeed reliable and valid or (2) review the literature and determine what measures have been used by others and adopt them. Since the first option for many areas of study is a difficult and lengthy process requiring highly technical expertise, we recommend that you choose the second option and pattern your measurement devices on those that have been established in the literature. We do not recommend that you do this blindly, however, but that you continue to remember the problems of reliability and validity. For example, even if you are merely having a rat press a lever for food, you must still determine what construct lever pressing validly measures. Or, said in the other way, if you were interested in the construct "learning" in animals, you would first ask what would be a good measure of "learning." You would look for a measure with numerous empirical studies to support it, and you might conclude that lever pressing was one such measure. In the final analysis, the task of choosing good measures is yours, although you are greatly aided by previously published studies as well as your own experience in experimentation.

## CONCLUSION

It may seem as if you have many decisions to make and in a sense you do, but you must also remember that much of the process of doing science is learned through experience. By this we mean that although there are guidelines for how to perform experiments and answer questions through science, many of the procedures that have to be devised are learned through performing experiments.

As you become more familiar with the process of experimentation, you will come to see which considerations of good experimental design are most appropriate in which situations. For now you must mainly rely on understanding the logic of experimentation.

As we pointed out, all experiments begin with an idea or consideration of the world in which we live. This consideration or idea is then formulated in terms of a general statement or question. For example, you may think that schizophrenia is related to diet or that anxiety is related to too much homework, or you might be interested in the factors that produce helping behavior. You might even think that students would be less anxious if they were not given homework. Whatever your idea, you must then translate it into a *specific* research question or hypothesis; that is, you must develop a testable statement that points out what *specific* variables are to be examined and the hypothesized relationship between them. It is at this point that you rely on operational definitions, as we discussed previously. If at this point you have clearly stated (1) your independent and dependent variables; (2) how each is measured, taking into account reliability and validity; (3) the hypothesized relationship between the independent and dependent variables; and (4) how this hypothesized relationship is to be tested, then you have passed one of the major hurdles of performing a scientific experiment (See Figure 5.4). Once you have overcome this hurdle, you are ready to move on and consider the process of experimentation itself.

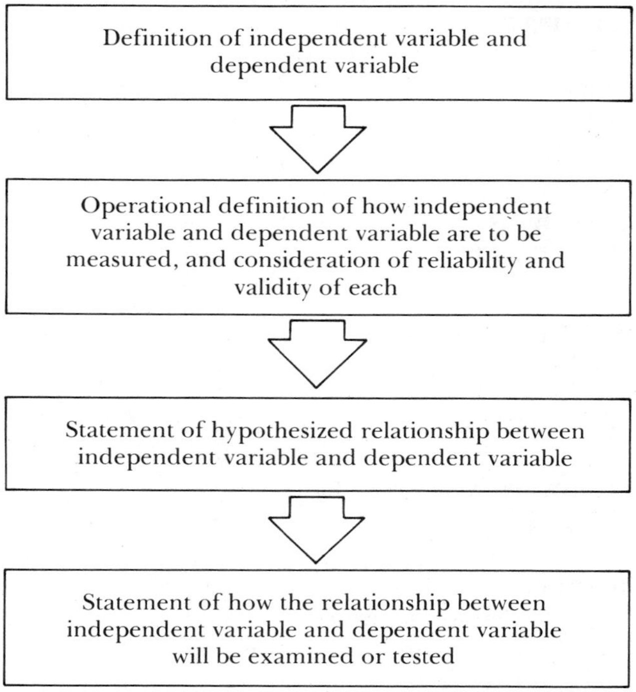

Definition of independent variable and dependent variable

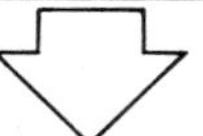

Operational definition of how independent variable and dependent variable are to be measured, and consideration of reliability and validity of each

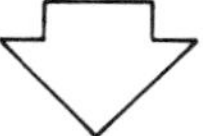

Statement of hypothesized relationship between independent variable and dependent variable

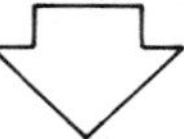

Statement of how the relationship between independent variable and dependent variable will be examined or tested

**Figure 5.4** Steps required prior to experimentation.

## Key Terms and Concepts

**1.** Making hypotheses concrete
   a. operational definition
   b. construct validity

**2.** Types of reasoning
   a. inductive
   b. deductive

**3.** Developing ideas
   a. Lance Shotland
   b. Nora Newcombe

**4.** Strong inference
   a. four steps according to Platt
      - alternative hypotheses
      - crucial experiment
      - obtain clear results
      - repeat with supported hypothesis

5. Wallas's four stages
   a. preparation
   b. incubation
   c. illumination
   d. verification
6. Library tools
   a. *Psychological Abstracts*
   b. *Index Medicus*
   c. *Science Citation Index*
   d. *Social Science Citation Index*
7. Measurement
   a. reliability
   b. validity

## Summary

1. Unlike the character in *Alice in Wonderland* who said that when I use a word it means exactly what I want it to mean, nothing more and nothing less, a researcher needs to present ideas in a form that others can understand. Creating an operational definition is one way researchers clarify their ideas and make their hypotheses more concrete. That is to say, an operational definition presents a hypothesis in terms of observable operations that others can see and repeat.
2. "Construct validity" refers to whether the procedure that we are using is an adequate definition of the construct we are measuring. For example, a person could define "intelligence" operationally as the time required to respond to a stimulus. The question of construct validity would then arise, asking whether response time was a valid measure of the construct of intelligence.
3. Inductive and deductive forms of reasoning, discussed also in Chapter 2, were reviewed as related to hypotheses.
4. Scientists obtain ideas for research from a variety of sources. Dr. Shotland explains how reading the newspaper and listening to his class helped him to develop a productive line of research. Dr. Newcombe explains how talking a friend leads to her thinking about the manner in which men and women ask for what they want. Passages from Einstein and Kekulé suggest that ideas and solutions may also come in terms of vague bodily sensations or even dreams.
5. Graham Wallas was interested in how scientists solve problems. He suggested four stages: preparation, incubation, illumination, and verification.
6. Since science represents a history of observation and theory development, it is important to know what others have observed and said about a particular topic. Reference libraries contain important tools for helping us find articles related to our interests. Four library tools that are important in psychological research are *Psychological Abstracts, Index Medicus, Science Citation Index,* and *Social Science Citation Index.*

7. The chapter concludes with a return to the problem of measurement and the concerns of reliability and validity. "Reliability" refers to the consistency of a measuring instrument. "Validity" refers to accuracy.
8. In performing research you begin with an idea or theory. Through operational definitions, this idea must be turned into a testable hypothesis. This may be seen as a four-part process: first, the definition of the independent and dependent variable; second, a statement of how the independent and dependent variables are to be measured, considering issues of reliability and validity; third, a statement of the hypothesized relationship between the independent and dependent variables; and fourth, a statement of how this relationship is to be examined or tested.

## Review Questions

1. Discuss what operational definitions are and give some examples.
2. What is construct validity?
3. Describe Dr. Shotland's study in terms of the independent variable, the dependent variable, and operational definitions.
4. How does "intuition and revelation" play a role in research?
5. What is meant by the term "strong inference?"
6. Name the reference work in which you would find a summary of most psychological articles.
7. Using a bathroom scale as an example, describe the difference between reliability and validity.

## Discussion Questions and Projects

1. Give some examples of inductive and deductive reasoning from newspapers, magazines, or television.
2. Discuss the topics you are most interested in researching and describe how you might construct an experiment to study these areas.
3. Discuss some important and interesting topics that may be difficult or impossible to research experimentally.
4. Find the reference section of your library and list five studies performed in the past 10 years that look at the relationship between watching television and aggression.
5. Design a study to demonstrate that people who take vitamins make better grades. What are the steps necessary to design such a study? What control groups would you need? What might some of the rival hypotheses be in such a study?
6. How might you design a study that would still be useful even if your hypothesis was refuted?
7. Assume that there exists a construct related to achievement called "motive to achieve." Describe a way to measure this construct that would be very reliable but would have no validity whatsoever.

CHAPTER SIX

# *Testing the Hypothesis: A Conceptual Introduction*

## INTRODUCTION

Once you have developed your research hypothesis, what do you do next? Most beginning students answer, "I perform an experiment to prove that my hypothesis is correct." It is true that your hypothesis needs to be evaluated in the light of an actual experiment. However, contrary to the manner in which science is sometimes portrayed, the evaluation of a hypothesis is a complex process that takes place on a number of levels. In fact, three separate questions need to be asked in order to evaluate your original research hypothesis. The first question is related to statistics and asks whether the *numbers* found in an experiment could be due to chance factors alone. The second question is related to alternative explanations for the research findings and asks whether the results of the study could be due to factors other than the independent variable as hypothesized; that is, are there threats to the internal validity of the study? The third question concerns the research hypothesis and asks what support exists for assuming that the independent variable is directly related to the results.

Thus we find ourselves like detectives who sort through one set of clues and then another, hoping to determine how a particular situation occurred. What caused this event; who did it? Although the detective always looks to the butler, in research we begin with the curious possibility that *no one did it;* that is, we ask whether the experimental results as we found them happened not because of a crucial factor (the independent variable) but because of chance. Once we determine that chance alone did not produce the results, we are ready to look for other factors. "If it was not chance, then it was our independent variable," the naive young detective might say. "Not yet," the sage of experience admonishes. "Let us first look to unknown factors that might be responsible for our experimental outcome." "But how can we know the unknown, Pop?" the number-one son of Charlie Chan always asks on the late show. "Through logic, common sense, and a thorough knowledge of the literature" is the answer.

Let us expand and repeat these considerations. Interpreting the results of an experiment is a three-stage decision process. The first stage does not directly involve our research hypothesis at all! Instead it involves the possibility that chance fluctuations between the performance of our groups may be solely responsible for any differences. The possibility that there are no differences between groups makes us consider the *null hypothesis.* Because chance is always involved in our sampling and observations of the world, the null hypothesis is *always* one possible interpretation of even the most striking differences between our groups that must be evaluated. This means that regardless of how great the differences are between our groups on whatever dependent measure we are using, it is always possible that the results are due to chance fluctuations. Thus, when we make a statement about cause and effect in a psychological experiment, we never state that the independent variable *absolutely* caused the effect on the dependent variable. Rather, we make a probabilistic statement that we can be relatively certain that our results were not due to chance factors alone. It was a realization of the probabilistic nature of experimental outcomes that led to the development of statistical procedures at the beginning of this century. Because of the central importance of chance in modern science, we will have much to say about chance, the null hypothesis, and the importance of statistics. (See also Chapter 4.) In the meantime, an essential idea to keep in mind is that the initial phase of interpreting the outcome of any experiment is a *statistical decision process.* Thus, when confronted with differences between our groups, we first use statistics to determine the probability that these differences are due to chance (null hypothesis).

Once we have satisfied ourselves that our results are probably not due to chance, we must turn to the second stage and examine another possibility—that our results are due to some systematic but unspecified factor, which we call a *confound.* If indeed our results are due to some factor other than our independent variable, then, as mentioned in Chapter 1, the internal validity of the experiment is threatened. In the fictitious series of breakfast cereal experiments described in Chapter 2, we saw that the weight gain that occurred in the experimental groups was not due to the new cereal, as the manufacturers had hoped, but to the cream, bananas, and sugar. In confounded experiments like this one, the treatment effect is not due to the independent variable, but to one or more overlooked factors. Because it is always possible that the internal validity of an experiment is weakened by some unknown factor causing the observed differences, we routinely scrutinize the both published experiments of others and our own work for the possibility that some confound occurred. However, even with careful scrutiny we can *never be certain* that some unknown factor other than the independent variable is not responsible for the experimental results.

Once we have rejected the null hypothesis and the confound hypothesis as interpretations of our results, we can turn to the third consideration. This is the assumption that our results reflect an action on the part of the independent variable; that is, there is now a greater probability that our research hypothesis is accurate. At this point we are ready to interpret our data in relation to the research hypothesis. As a digression we want to point out that many people who are not familiar with the process of science tend to view it as consisting of only this third consideration. Most scientists, however, do not speak so much about "proving a hypothesis" as they do about "controlling and seeking alternative explanations." In fact, many research scientists argue that the heart of experimentation lies in ruling out alternative explanations. In this chapter we will emphasize the process of minimizing the likelihood of alternative explanations through a discussion of the null and confound hypotheses. In the next chapter we will emphasize experimental control through a discussion of techniques for controlling, reducing, and eliminating various potential confounds.

Before we continue, let us remind you that throughout this and the next chapter, we will discuss the interpretation of experimental results and experimental design from the standpoint of the *scientist.* We will be presenting the experimental method in its ideal form. Consequently, keep in mind that although internal validity and eventual statistical analysis are important determiners of experimental design, they are by no means the only factors to consider when conducting research. In later chapters we will return to the perspectives of the *subject* and the *witness.* Specifically, we will return to questions of *external validity* and *ecological validity.* Through external validity we will examine in more depth the generalizability of research findings. Through ecological validity we will focus on research in a broader context as well as the scientist-subject relationship. Finally, we will emphasize value by asking questions of ethics and meaning. Now let us turn to an actual experiment and observe how we evaluate the three possible interpretations of experimental results discussed previously.

## THE CONTEXT OF EXPERIMENTATION: AN EXAMPLE

In the early 1970s Bransford and Johnson (1972) performed an experiment to explore some of the factors that influence how we remember and encode what we hear. In particular, they were interested in the role of context in the comprehension and recall of information. Imagine you are a subject in that experiment and you are asked to listen to and later recall the following passage:

> If the balloons popped, the sound wouldn't be able to carry since everything would be too far away from the correct floor. A closed window would also prevent the sound from carrying, since most buildings tend to be well insulated. Since the whole operation depends on a steady flow of electricity, a break in the middle of the wire would also cause problems. Of course, the fellow could shout, but the human voice is not loud enough to carry that far. An additional problem is that a string could break on the instrument. Then there could be no accompaniment to the message. It is clear that the best situation would involve less distance. Then there would be fewer potential problems. With face-to-face contact, the least number of things could go wrong.

After the passage was read, the subjects in the experiment were asked to rate it for comprehensibility; that is, they were asked to rate how well they understood the passage, with a rating of 7 meaning it was highly comprehensible. You might try that yourself. If you are like the subjects in the experiment, you would rate the material as incomprehensible. Their actual average rating was 2.3 on the seven-point scale. The next task for the subjects was to recall what they had read. Here they were instructed to write the main ideas that they remembered from the passage. How many ideas did you remember? The subjects in the experiment recalled on the average 3.6 ideas out of a possible 14.

Bransford and Johnson also included a second group of subjects who were shown Figure 6.1 before they heard the passage. As with the no-picture group, the task was to recall as many ideas from the story as possible. If we were to discuss these two groups in terms of the independent variable (the picture), we would say that one group received the complete independent variable and the other group received a zero level of the independent variable. One could also present other levels of the independent variable between the total picture and zero picture. Bransford and Johnson actually did this in their complete experiment, but that is beyond our discussion. After you have seen the picture, go back and read the passage. How would you rate its comprehensibility now? The subjects in the second experimental group rated comprehensibility more than twice as high as those in the group who did not see the picture (mean rating of 6.1 versus 2.3 on the seven-point scale). This second group also recalled many more ideas than the first group (8 versus 3.6 ideas). Although the Bransford and Johnson experiment is much more complex than we have presented it thus far, we will draw on this

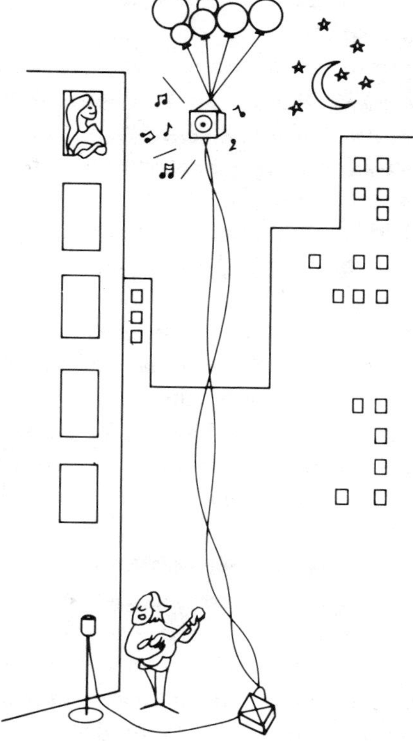

**Figure 6.1** Complete context picture. (Bransford & Johnson, 1972).

simplified version as a means of illustrating the task of evaluating the null, confound, and research hypotheses. We will begin with a discussion of statistical interpretation.

## Statistical Interpretation

Philosophers for centuries have told us that everything varies, and in psychology we know this all too well. Some things vary a little; some things vary a lot. Some factors vary systematically; some factors vary by chance. In the process of experimentation we have set the goal of understanding what part of our results may be attributed to *systematic* variation (for example, the influence of the independent variable on the dependent variable) and what part is due to *chance* variation.

Chance variation may also be called *error* variation. Since the words *chance* and *error* have a similar technical meaning in this context, it is important that you understand this meaning. Chance or error variation refers to factors that influence the performance of the subjects in a *nonsystematic* manner. This means that *from the frame of reference of the experiment,* chance variation cannot be ascribed to any given set of factors. This is not to say that we cannot find an explanation for the particular performance of a given individual subject. It does say, however, that the explanation given for any one individual cannot be ascribed to the group as a whole. Consider a memory experiment such as that of Bransford and Johnson. One person in the experiment might have performed poorly because he did not sleep well the night before. Another person might have done very well because she had just received some good news from home. Another might have had too much coffee, whereas another could have been anxious because of a test the next period. Each of these factors would be considered as a chance factor or error factor *from the standpoint of the group* of subjects who took part in the experiment.

When we discuss *systematic variations,* we are referring to those factors that influence one group of subjects as a whole. It is our hope that any systematic variation between groups is due to the influence of our independent variable on the dependent variable, although this may not always be the case. It may happen that some confound systematically influences our data and thus contributes an source of unwanted systematic variation. We will discuss the problem of confounds later in the chapter. Thus far we have suggested that the variation in the scores of subjects in an experiment may be due to three major factors: (1) nonsystematic variation ascribed to chance factors, (2) systematic variation due to some confound, and (3) systematic variation due to our independent variable.

To continue with the Bransford and Johnson example, one group of subjects heard the story without seeing the picture whereas the other group heard the story after being shown the picture. Once we have collected the results, we are faced with the task of interpretation. In light of the preceding discussion, our overall task both statistically and theoretically is to interpret the results in relation to three possibilities. These are: (1) there are no differences between our groups (null hypothesis); (2) the results were produced by some systematic influence *other than* the independent variable, that is, a confound; and (3) the results were produced in a systematic fashion by the independent variable.

Ignoring the question of confounds for a moment, let us discuss our results in terms of the effects of the independent variable and of chance or error. In the Bransford and Johnson study, we are trying to determine how much influence seeing the picture had on remembering the passage. To answer this question, we begin with what some students feel is a backward approach. We ask the question: What if seeing the picture had no effect on memory? What would the results look like then? We already know the answer theoretically. The two groups would look like each other. Since the groups were presumably chosen as being similar, they would continue to be similar if the independent variable (and confounds) did not influence them.

We can now present this same point in a more technical way. First, let us use a more statistically oriented language—that of the $F$-ratio. In this case, $F$ stands for Sir Ronald Fisher, the man who developed the statistical technique of analysis of variance. The particular terms we will use in this ratio are *within-groups variance* and *between-groups variance*. In the Bransford and Johnson study, within-groups variance reflects those factors we referred to as chance or error variance. These are factors that influence particular subjects in each group. Factors such as mental alertness, physical health, and emotional state are expected to have a random or chance effect on the groups as a whole and thus do not contribute to any systematic differences between the two groups *randomly* selected. Factors that systematically influence a group of subjects, such as showing one group the picture before the memory task, are reflected in the between-groups variance. In other words, between-groups variance reflects the difference between the experimental and control groups—that is, the effect of the treatment. Further, we need to say that chance factors also contribute to the total between-groups variance, although when the term is used conceptually we are mainly referring to the effect of systematic variations. Thus, between-groups variance equals the effect of treatment plus error variance, whereas within-groups variance reflects chance or error variance alone.

Consider the relationship of between-groups variance and within-groups variance if the independent variable has no effect in a study. That is, if showing one group the picture has no effect on their remembering the passage, what is the relationship of between-groups variance and within-groups variance? That's right; they are the same. In the form of a ratio,

$$\frac{\text{between-groups variance}}{\text{within-groups variance}} = \frac{\text{treatment effects} + \text{chance variance}}{\text{chance variance}}.$$

If there are no treatment effects, then

$$\frac{\text{between-groups variance}}{\text{within-groups variance}} = \frac{0 + \text{chance variance}}{\text{chance variance}}.$$

Let us ignore confounds for another moment and again assume that the independent variable has no effect on the dependent variable. What would the preceding ratio equal? Before you claim that your great-great-grandmother died of math anxiety, consider the answer from a conceptual point of view. Even if you had to reread the last page, you should realize that if the independent variable has no effect, the ratio will be equal to one. Thus if the independent variable (and confounds) does not systematically influence the results, then

$$\frac{\text{variance between groups}}{\text{variance within groups}} = 1.$$

So what, you might be saying to yourself. Before we discuss why we consider the ratio of between-groups variance to within-groups variance to be important in experimental design and interpretation, take a moment to consider mathematically what factors could cause this ratio to change—that is, become larger. You might also consider how a ratio of 1 would be involved in addressing our three considerations of (1) chance variation, (2) systematic variation due to confounds, and (3) systematic variation due to the independent variable. Also consider how the null hypothesis is related to the ratio.

Let us begin with the null hypothesis. If we cannot reject the null hypothesis (there are no differences between our groups), then the ratio will be equal to or close to 1. If, on the other hand, the ratio is equal to a very large number, then we would want to reject the null hypothesis and explore the possibility that there are real differences between our groups. Thus as a general rule we can see that the larger the ratio, the more relatively certain we are that there are real differences between our groups that are not caused by chance alone. We also see that the smaller the ratio, the less certain we can be that the results are not due to chance. Actually, we are never certain that our results are or are not due to chance. Instead we use statistics to help us make a best guess or bet by assigning a probability to our statement that the results are not due to chance alone. That is, we may say that results from our study could have happened by chance only one time out of every hundred. In the published literature you will see this written as $p<.01$. Our ratio is statistically called an *F-ratio,* and you also see this number in published papers as $F$ equals some number—for example, $F=5.8$. If you look on page 400 in Chapter 14 you will see one such example ($F=68.2, p<.001$). Thus, in this example we would expect that the particular differences between groups would occur by chance less than 1 time in 1000. As with any bet based on probability, we can be wrong and we do make mistakes. In relation to rejecting and failing to reject the null hypothesis, we have given our mistakes special names. We call them *Type I* and *Type II* errors, and these are described in Box 6.1.

From our discussion thus far you should have drawn some important conclusions related to the $F$-ratio. First, the closer the number produced by the ratio is to 1, the greater the probability of not rejecting the null hypothesis. Second, the larger the number produced by the ratio, the greater the chance of rejecting the null hypothesis and assuming that some systematic factor influenced the results. Third, a large $F$-ratio can be produced mathematically by either *increasing the between-groups variance* or *reducing the within-groups variance.* The practical implication of this is that positive experimental results can be obtained either by having a strong independent variable or by *controlling* the error variance. The presentation of the independent variable may be made stronger by using extreme levels of the independent variable. For example, a zero level of a drug might be given to one group and a high-dosage level given to another. Controlling error variance will be discussed in greater detail in the next chapter.

## Types of Variation

On a conceptual level we suggested that the variability in an experiment can be divided into three parts: (1) variation due to chance, (2) systematic variation due to confounds, and (3) systematic variation due to the independent variable. Let us repeat these with a slightly different terminology as used by Kerlinger (1973). The first aspect of the total variation in an experiment is called the *error variance*. Error variance refers to those fluctuations in scores that result solely from chance factors as seen from the standpoint of the group. In psychological research, error variance is generally attributed to *individual* differences in our subjects and can sometimes be rather large.

Another aspect of the total variance in any experiment is called *secondary* or *uncontrolled systematic variance.* Secondary variance results from variables (secondary variables) other than the independent variable that can affect our experiment in either of two ways. They may occur along with the independent variable and thus differentially affect the performance of our two groups. This confounding effect of secondary variables is what we have referred to as *confounds* in our previous discussion. A portion of the remainder of this chapter will focus on this class of secondary variables. Secondary variables can also occur independently of our independent variable, and in this case they tend to have a similar impact on the performance of our two groups of subjects. Secondary variables that fall into this class are often called *extraneous variables.* Typical extraneous variables are time of day, season of the year, color of the room, temperature in the experimental setting, and so forth. These variables could have been controlled for by the experimenter but were not (a point that will be elaborated in the next section). Sometimes they are unknown, and sometimes we realize their existence and decide they are not worth eliminating. Because extraneous variables affect both groups, they can be ignored as not influencing the internal validity of our experiments. However, as we shall see, they do contribute to the overall subject variability and thereby affect the acceptance or rejection of the null hypothesis.

The other aspect of variation in an experiment is called *primary* or *controlled systematic variance.* Primary variance reflects the "real" effect of the independent variable (occasionally called the *primary* variable).

Table 6.1 summarizes these possible changes and shows how they affect the between- and within-groups variance of the $F$-ratio.

On a statistical level we must decide whether or not our groups are equal (null hypothesis). There are many kinds of inferential statistics that can be used in a variety of situations. In the final analysis, these statistical manipulations boil down to a consideration of the size of our treatment effect and the amount of subject variation in our experiment. This comparison takes the form of the *F*-ratio.

As discussed previously, the numerator of this ratio reflects the difference between the scores of the experimental and control groups on the dependent variable. This difference is also referred to as the *treatment effect,* and it is assumed that it results in part from the independent variable. The difference *between* the experimental and control groups on the dependent measure is reflected in the statistical measure of *between-groups variance.*

The denominator of the *F*-ratio simply reflects the amount of variability on our dependent measure among the subjects in this experiment. Because the subject variability is calculated by determining the amount of variation

---

### *Box 6.1* *Type I and Type II Errors*

Suppose we reject the null hypothesis and assume our results are not simply due to chance. In this case our decision may accurately reflect the world (correct rejection of the null hypothesis) or it may not (incorrect rejection of the null hypothesis). An incorrect rejection of the null hypothesis is referred to as a *Type I error.* A Type I error occurs whenever we incorrectly reject the null hypothesis and the true state is that chance fluctuations are solely responsible for the differences between our groups. Suppose, on the other hand, we accept the null hypothesis and bet that our results are merely due to chance. Our decision may accurately reflect the world (correct acceptance of the null hypothesis) or it may not (incorrect acceptance of the null hypothesis). An incorrect acceptance of the null hypothesis is referred to as a *Type II error.* A Type II error occurs when factors other than chance (for example, the independent variable) are responsible for the differences between our groups and we conclude that they are not.

| Null Hypothesis Decision | True State of Affairs: Chance is responsible | True State of Affairs: Chance is not responsible |
|---|---|---|
| Fail to Reject | Correct acceptance | Type II error (incorrect acceptance) |
| Reject | Type I error (incorrect rejection) | Correct rejection |

---

**Table 6.1 Effects of Four Types of Changes on Within-Groups and Between-Groups Variance**

| *Type of Change* | *Effect on Variance* |
|---|---|
| 1. Random changes in subjects | Increase within-groups variance (may also increase between-groups variance) |
| 2. Systematic changes that influence both groups equally | Increase within-groups variance |
| 3. Systematic changes (not independent variable) that affect groups differently (confounds) | Increase between-groups variance |
| 4. Systematic changes (independent variable) that affect groups differently | Increase between-groups variance |

of our subjects *within* each group, it is sometimes called the *within-groups variance.* If there is a lot of subject variability on the dependent measure within our experimental and control groups, we would say that the within-group variance is high, and as a matter of common sense, we would insist that the treatment effects be quite large before assuming that any treatment effects were due to any cause other than chance. In contrast, if there were only very small individual differences on the dependent measure among the subjects in each group (low within-groups variance), it would be reasonable to consider that smaller differences between the experimental and control groups were not caused by chance.

Thus, our confidence that the treatment effect is not due to chance fluctuations in the performance of the subjects in our two groups is directly related to the size of the treatment effect and inversely related to the variability of scores within our groups.

Once we have made a decision about whether or not to reject the null hypothesis, we can turn to the second stage of our decision process. If we have not rejected the null hypothesis, which states that our groups are equal after treatment, we simply interpret our data theoretically to mean that the independent variable did not affect the dependent variable. If, on the other hand, we reject the null hypothesis, we must decide what did produce the results of our experiment. Since the $F$-ratio cannot tell us whether the systematic variation reflects the independent variable or a confound, we must logically and conceptually deduce the source of the systematic influence. To do this, we turn first to the question of confounds and then finally to our independent variable. At each stage of this process we are attempting to become more and more certain of whether the independent variable affected the dependent variable.

## SYSTEMATIC FACTORS NOT RELATED TO THE INDEPENDENT VARIABLE

From our previous consideration of the $F$-ratio, we have a better understanding of how we conclude that the numbers found in our research did not result from chance. However, this or any other statistic cannot tell us *what* did cause the difference between our groups. Statistics only tell that there is a difference, which is probably not due to chance factors. To determine what caused the differences between our groups, we move to a more conceptual level. To aid us in these decisions, we rely on logic, common sense, and the published literature. Depending on the nature of our research, sometimes we rely on one of these factors more than the others. If we know a lot about an area, then the published literature is a tremendous aid in helping us to interpret the crucial factors in our research results. If we know little about an area, however, we must repeatedly rule out alternative hypotheses through the use of logic and common sense. It is only when alternative factors have been ruled out that we can conclude that the independent variable did indeed influence our results. Like a court of law, we refrain from implicating the independent variable until we can conclude without a reasonable doubt that the independent variable did it. Although the detective always looks to the butler, researchers look to confounds as the most likely suspect.

What is a confound? Almost anything can be a confound. It is something that systematically biases the results of our research. It may be the fact that the day before we ran the experimental group in a social psychology experiment on conformity, there was a television special on how we always do what other people tell us. Or, a confound may be introduced into a weight-reduction experiment by asking one group to lose weight at a time of the year when people eat less and their gastrointestinal system works faster (summer) whereas another group was started at a time when people eat more (winter). A confound may be introduced when one group is made up of more men than women. In one biofeedback study, the control group was instructed by young inexperienced technicians whereas the experimental group was instructed by an older, more experienced physician, and this may have produced a confound in the results. As you consider these and other possible confounds, you quickly realize that some confounds can be prevented or controlled. In the next chapter we will emphasize techniques for controlling systematic bias. Other factors, however, can never be controlled. You cannot control world events, but you can ask whether there is any reason to believe that a particular event that took place inside or outside of the laboratory could have influenced one group more than another and thus introduced a confound.

## THREATS TO INTERNAL VALIDITY

Every confound is a threat to the internal validity of our experiments. As you remember, internal validity asks whether the experimental treatment makes a difference in a specific experimental instance. In order to aid researchers in answering this question, Campbell and Stanley (1963) and more recently Cook and Campbell (1979) presented a list of possible threats to internal validity that must be considered. We present this list for two reasons. First, we want to introduce you to some of the possible confounds that can influence the groups in our experiments differently. Keep in mind that the list does not include every possible confound, because many confounds are related to the specific type of research being performed and thus cannot be listed in a general manner. Second, we want you to begin thinking about ways in which you might control for the effects of these confounds. You already know one way, which is through the use of appropriate control groups. This discussion should help to set up your thinking in preparation for an introduction to experimental design. Let us now turn to several examples of threats to internal validity.

### History

*History* refers to events that take place between measurements in an experiment and that are not related to the independent variable. In general, the longer the time between two measurements—a pretest and a posttest for example—the greater the possibility for outside events to influence the situation. In the cereal experiment described in Chapter 2, the availability of other foods made it impossible to know whether the experimental cereal caused the weight gain. Some confounds are subtle and difficult to detect. For example, in a long-term treatment study with psychiatric patients, such factors as new staff or a change of diet can influence the outcome. Cunningham (1979) has shown that the amount of sunshine present during a helping

"OF COURSE I'VE BECOME MORE MATURE SINCE YOU STARTED TREATING ME. YOU'VE BEEN AT IT SINCE I WAS 14 YEARS OLD."

behavior experiment influences the degree to which participants aid an interviewer. Even more subtle confounds may be introduced simply by a person taking part in research. For example, in clinical research studies where individuals come in for the treatment of some specific disorder such as alcoholism or child abuse, it has been noted that once the person is defined as a "patient" under "treatment," his or her family and friends begin to act differently toward the person. Thus it is impossible to know whether any change came about because of the treatment or because of relationships outside the treatment setting.

### Maturation

*Maturation* refers to problems of interpretation resulting from the subject growing older, wiser, stronger, healthier, as well as more tired, more bored, and so forth. The cartoon on p. 143 illustrates this problem. If a scientist is conducting a study that lasts for a period of time, it is imperative that maturational factors be controlled. This is accomplished by the use of a control group. Confounds of this type plague many beginning students because they often have their subjects perform too many tasks over too long a time. The subjects become bored and frustrated, and then the results are due to boredom and not to the independent variable in the study.

### Testing

*Testing* refers to the problems that result from repeated measurement of the same subject. For example, if an individual is given the same math test repeatedly, then both the practice of taking the test and the memory of certain items could influence the results. Another example is when blood pressure is taken once a minute for 30 minutes. With the standard cuff method of measuring blood pressure (as in the physician's office), each inflation and deflation of the cuff results in temporary changes in the tissue of the arm itself. Thus just taking repeated measurements during a short time results in a change in blood pressure readings. Another example of testing as a confound occurs when subjects are monitored for certain behaviors, and after repeated observations they become sensitive to the behaviors the experimenter is recording.

## Instrumentation

The problem of instrumentation is related to changes that occur in the measuring device, be it a person or a machine, during the course of an experiment. For example, if you are measuring aggressive behavior in children, you would become more accurate at making ratings as the study continues, and this could influence your results. To avoid this problem, such researchers as Newcombe and Arnkoff (1979) in the study of speech styles discussed in Chapter 5 had more than one rater of the same material and compared the ratings for consistency. If possible it is also important that the ratings for each group be made concurrently so that any improvement in ratings does not systematically influence the groups in the study. Another possible source of confounds is the use of machines. Many individuals believe that machines are always more reliable, but this does not mean that they are always perfect. For example, psychophysiological equipment such as that used to measure heart rate, electrodermal response, or skin temperature may require a certain warm-up time to give accurate results.

## Statistical Regression

A simple example of this problem occurs when subjects are selected because of some score or measurement that turns out to be extreme. On the next testing, the score may return to normal. If this had happened during an experimental treatment, we might conclude that the change in the score was the result of the treatment when in fact it represented only a regression to the mean or average score. Statistical regression thus occurs when extreme scores (very high or very low) change over time (low scores become higher and high scores become lower) without any treatment. A related problem is found in medical, psychotherapy, biofeedback, and drug studies that use individuals who come into a professional's office. Most individuals go to see a professional when a given disorder such as a cold is at its worst. With such disorders, some improvement can be seen over time without any treatment, and thus we may conclude incorrectly that the improvement is related to the treatment alone.

## Selection

Selection confounds occur when the subjects in one group differ initially from the subjects in another group. Suppose you were testing a new speed-reading technique. For the experimental group you used people who came to the reading clinic, and these people received the treatment. For the control group you might use students in a psychology course. There are at least three possible problems with this design. First, there could be a difference (in IQ, reading level, achievement, and other factors) in the types of people who come to a reading clinic and those in a psychology class. Second, those who come to the clinic might have a lower reading score initially and be able to improve more than the students, who may already be reading at their optimal level. Third, the subjects who come to the clinic would probably be more motivated and work harder at learning to read faster no matter what technique was used. This third type of problem must be guarded against in any treatment study (for example, drug, relaxation training, meditation) when the group receiving the treatment seeks the treatment and the control group does not. In each of these cases some characteristics of the subjects might initially constitute important differences in the groups even before the independent variable is introduced. Thus it is best to have the experimental and control groups *both* come from people seeking treatment. In this way the groups are most likely to be similar at the beginning of the experiment.

### Mortality

This problem occurs when subjects drop out or refuse to take part in any experiment. The problem is greatest when subjects differentially drop out of one group. For example, suppose you want to measure whether children are more creative after playing with dull toys than with fun toys. You first classify the toys as dull or fun and then establish your measure of creativity. As you run the experiment, some of the children who play with dull toys might leave the experiment or not return for other sessions. Thus after a period of weeks the fun-toy group might be composed of all the subjects who began the experiment whereas the dull-toy group is composed of only half of the original children. If you try to analyze these results, you are faced with the possibility that only a certain type of child remained in the dull-toy group. The dull-toy group would then consist of a different subject population than the fun-toy group, thus making your conclusions invalid.

### Selection-Maturation Interaction

This broad category refers to the situation when one group of subjects changes along a given dimension faster than another group. For example, lower- and middle-class children develop cognitive abilities at different rates. If this is not taken into account, the experimenter could ascribe the difference to a specific treatment. Likewise, girls develop verbal abilities before boys; when working with preschool children, this differential development must be taken into account. Another possibility in this broad category is selection-testing interaction. For example, Fry and Greenfield (1980) examined job-related attitudes in a midwestern city. They collected data from 529 policemen and 21 policewomen. Assume that this represented the total police force of the city and that other researchers were also collecting various data from these individuals. One possibility that could occur is that every policewoman was used in every study, whereas only some of the 529 policemen were used in every study. This could cause each policewoman to be more sophisticated and experienced at being a subject in an experiment, whereas it would remain a relatively new experience for any given policeman. Thus experimental results that compared policemen and policewomen in this city could be biased because of the policewomen's greater participation in psychological research. Cook and Campbell (1979) expand this category to include also selection-history and selection-instrumentation interactions.

### Diffusion or Imitation of Treatments

This occurs when subjects in an experiment can and do communicate with each other and by this communication reduce the differences between groups. If the difference between the experimental and control groups is that one group has information that the other does not have, then if the subjects communicate with each other, it is possible that this difference may be reduced or even removed completely. Consider what would happen if a subject in the picture condition of the Bransford and Johnson study mentioned to a friend that he was in a psychology experiment and described the experiment and the picture he saw. If the friend was later in the experiment and assigned to the no-picture group, his results would be greatly influenced by the previous knowledge. The sharing of information among subjects is a problem particularly when the subjects are drawn from a group that has daily contact. Dr. Shotland avoided this problem in his simulated attack study by helping the subjects to understand the importance of his research and the necessity that they tell no one of the experiment until the study was completed. This may take place in the debriefing process, which we will discuss in Chapter 13.

## CONCLUSION

After ruling out the null hypothesis and the confound hypothesis, we can assume that the results reflect the action of the independent variable. Thus we go back and reexamine our numerical results in light of the assumption that our independent variable is the crucial agent. We likewise begin to generalize from our one set of data and consider the implications of our results both for other groups of subjects and for the theoretical implications the data hold. Sometimes we are led to new ideas, which in turn generate new research hypotheses, which can be interpreted with additional experiments.

Figure 6.2 presents a simplified outline of this procedure, which reflects the evolutionary nature of science. The steps are (1) the development of the

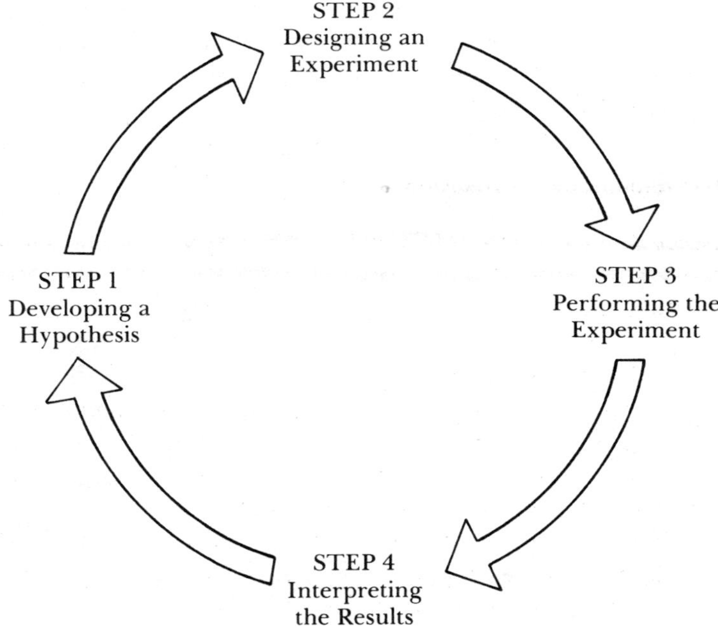


**Figure 6.2** Schematic representation of the four major steps in the process of experimentation.

hypothesis, (2) the translation of this hypothesis into an actual research design, (3) the running of the experiment, and (4) the interpretation of the results. You will notice that there is also an arrow from Step 4 back to Step 1. In this way researchers take the results and interpretations of their studies and create new research studies that refine the previous hypothesis.

Although Figure 6.2 may appear to be circular, it would be better represented by a spiral in which each rotation adds additional information to our knowledge. This is the idea underlying the self-correcting nature of science as discussed in Chapter 1. The overall goal of the process is to help us understand more about what we are studying and to lead us in new directions we could not have discovered by reasoning alone; that is, experimentation gives us an interaction with reality that is not available to reason alone.

## Key Terms and Concepts

1. Types of hypotheses
   a. statistical (null hypothesis)
   b. confound hypothesis
   c. research hypothesis
2. Variation
   a. chance and error variation
   b. systematic variation
      - due to confound
      - due to independent variable
3. Variance
   a. within-groups
   b. between-groups
   c. ratio of between-groups and within-groups variance
   d. factors that influence ratio of between- and within-groups variance
4. Type I and Type II errors
5. Confounds
6. Threats to internal validity
   a. history
   b. maturation
   c. testing
   d. instrumentation
   e. statistical regression
   f. selection
   g. mortality
   h. selection-maturation interaction
   i. diffusion or imitation of treatments

## Summary

1. Interpreting the results of an experiment may be seen as a three-part process, each part consisting of a separate hypothesis. The first consideration relates to the null hypothesis and concerns us with a statistical decision process, such as the one we discussed in Chapters 4 and 5. The second consideration relates to the possibility of rival hypotheses, such as confounds, that influenced the results in our research. The third consideration relates to the manner in which the independent variable influenced the dependent variable.
2. Variation is an important concept in research. We hope that systematic variations between groups in an experiment are planned and result from the influence of the independent variable on the dependent variable. Variations in an experiment may also be nonsystematic and result from chance; these are also called error variations.
3. The $F$-ratio is a common inferential statistic in research. This ratio reflects the effects of the independent variable plus chance, divided by the effects of chance variation alone. In more technical language this is referred to as between-groups variance divided by within-groups variance. If there were no treatment effects, this ratio would be equal to 1.
4. An $F$-ratio equal to 1 would not allow us to reject the null hypothesis. To be able to reject the null hypothesis we would need an $F$-ratio larger than 1—how large depends on a number of factors such as the number of subjects in each group. Conceptually a researcher could increase the size of the $F$-ratio in two ways. The first way would be to decrease the amount of chance or error variance. This may be accomplished through careful control. The second way is to increase the size of the treatment effect.
5. Even if the null hypothesis is rejected, it is still necessary to consider factors other than the independent variable that might have influenced the results. These other factors or confounds have been referred to as threats to internal validity by Campbell and Stanley. These threats include such possibilities as history, maturation, testing, instrumentation, statistical regression, selection, mortality, interactions, and diffusion of treatments.
6. The conclusion that the independent variable influences the dependent variable is considered only after the null hypothesis and the confound hypothesis have been ruled out.
7. The process of experimentation may be considered as a spiral that consists of four major steps, continually repeated. These are (1) the development of the hypothesis, (2) the translation of the hypothesis into a research design, (3) the running of the experiment, and (4) the interpretation of the results, which leads back to the development of a better hypothesis.

## Review Questions

1. How are a scientist and a detective alike?
2. Describe the hypotheses that a researcher must consider in performing research.

3. Describe the Bransford and Johnson study in terms of independent variable, dependent variable, and hypotheses.
4. What is the meaning of "error" when discussing error or chance variations?
5. What factors influence within-groups variance?
6. What factors influence between-groups variance?
7. If no systematic variation affected the results of a study, what would the following ratio equal?

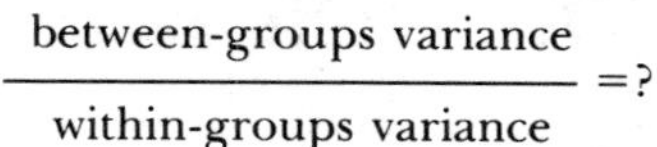

$$\frac{\text{between-groups variance}}{\text{within-groups variance}} = ?$$

8. What is the difference between a Type I and Type II error?
9. Name Campbell and Stanley's threats to internal validity.

## Discussion Questions and Projects

1. Discuss the meaning of chance in science. In an experiment, how is chance related to the individual? To the group?
2. Using the Bransford and Johnson study as an example, (1) How could between-groups variance be increased? Be decreased? (2) How could within-groups variance be increased? Be decreased?
3. A company gives its employees money to lose weight. Records of weight loss are kept over a six-month period. A control group also tries to lose weight but are not given money. The results will determine whether it will become part of company policy to reward employees for weight loss in the future. What would a Type I and Type II error mean in this study?
4. The President announces on television that he has just completed a study in which he applied his economic program to the economy and found positive results. Assume that he presents a graph showing the economy improving, beginning with the introduction of his economic policy. Discuss the President's presentation in terms of possible confounds.
5. Discuss the Bransford and Johnson study in terms of threats to internal validity.

CHAPTER SEVEN

# *Control: The Keystone of the Experimental Method*

## INTRODUCTION

In the past chapters we have followed the transformation of an idea into a research hypothesis. We have also begun the process of interpreting experimental results in terms of not one but three separate hypotheses. These hypotheses are (1) the chance hypothesis (the results are influenced by chance) and its inverse, the null hypothesis (there are *no* differences between groups); (2) the confound hypothesis (the systematic results are influenced by a factor other than the independent variable); and (3) the research hypothesis (the results are related to the independent variable). We also developed the conceptual thinking underlying the $F$-ratio and pointed out how this ratio is related to differences between groups in an experiment (between-groups variance) and error or chance variation (within-groups variance). Our ultimate goal in both a conceptual and a practical manner is to understand what influence, if any, the independent variable has on the dependent variable. We want to be certain in our experiments that once we reject the null hypothesis, the differences between our groups are indeed due to the independent variable and not to other factors such as confounds.

In psychological research we have some powerful techniques to help us achieve this aim. Unlike the detective who must always reconstruct events after the fact, the researcher has the advantage of being able to create a new situation in which to test ideas. This would be like the homicide detective being able to bring back to life the dead man and place him in the presence of each suspect until the murder is reenacted. Although such a reenactment of ruling out every possible suspect may lack suspense and not make it in prime time, it does increase the relative certainty of knowing who committed the murder. Increased certainty is a large part of the experimental process. Scientists increase certainty by creating an artificial situation, the experiment, in which important factors can be controlled and manipulated. Through control and manipulation, individual variables may be examined in detail and the influence of one variable on another may be determined with certainty. As a digression we want to point out that since the experiment is an artificial environment created to answer a small number of specific questions, it may not in every case mirror the "real world." In these cases we are often faced with a problem of generalizability and threats to the *external validity* of our research. We will approach these questions in Chapter 10. For now we will assume that our research does reflect the real world. In this discussion we will present research in its more ideal form from the standpoint of the scientist, with an emphasis on techniques for reducing threats to the internal validity of an experiment. Throughout the chapter we will emphasize the theme of control in three ways: first, control as related to subject assignment; second, control as related to experimental design and the assurance of internal validity; and third, control as related to the logic of experimentation.

## CONTROL ACHIEVED THROUGH SUBJECT ASSIGNMENT AND SUBJECT SELECTION

To illustrate some techniques available for subject assignment, let us begin with the simple illustration of a class designing an experiment. This particular class began with the idea that people can be taught to estimate time more accurately if they are given feedback concerning their performance. From this idea came a formal research hypothesis followed by a discussion of how to conduct the experiment. We pick up the discussion as someone suggests that the experiment simply consist of two groups. One group of subjects will receive verbal feedback on how accurate their estimates of a given time interval are, and the other group will not be given feedback. Thus, we would have two levels of the independent variable—a zero level and a high level. The first question asked is: "How do we go about assigning subjects to groups in this experiment?" It is suggested that someone could contact an equal number of male and female subjects. They could then place the male subjects in one group and the female subjects in the other group. After thinking about this for a moment, the group disagrees. They argue that there might be differences between men and women in the ability to estimate time; that is, perhaps either men are better time estimators than women or women are better time estimators than men, and that this inherent difference might actually create unequal groups before the experiment even begins. Indeed, one person points out that in her recent readings in psychological literature on time estimation she came upon a study indicating that there are sex differences in subjects' ability to estimate time. More specifically, she found that men are more accurate in estimating given intervals of time than women. As it turns out, this student had seen only one part of a larger and somewhat confusing story. Some of the published literature reports sex differences in time estimation and some does not (see Roeckelein, 1972, for a more detailed discussion of this literature). Faced with such ambiguity, the students need to decide how to control for possible sex differences. Note that the first objection stemmed from common sense, namely that men and women *might* differ in their ability to estimate time. Furthermore, the fact that one student was familiar with experimental evidence that this commonsense idea is correct greatly strengthened this objection. In view of their concern and the evidence supporting their arguments, the group decides not to have all the women in one group and all the men in another group because if they do this, they would never be sure whether any difference between the two groups was due to feedback or to a difference in men's and women's abilities to estimate time. In a very real sense, the experiment would be confounded because they would not know which of the variables—that is, feedback or sex differences between the groups—caused any treatment effects they might observe. Although they might obtain a treatment effect, they could not be sure what the causal factor is.

"Wait a minute!" someone in class yells out. "All of you are getting ahead of yourselves. Even before assigning subjects to groups, we must establish who our subjects are, how many we should use, and only then, how we are going to select them." The question of who our subjects are is, of course, related ultimately to the topic we are studying. If we are interested in time estimation in college students, then college students are the appropriate population. If we decide to use our own college, then we have to ask whether it is in any way different from colleges across the nation. Although this consideration does *not* affect the internal validity of our results, it does influence the generalizability or external validity of our results. The question of how many subjects to use depends in part on the question being asked. We suggest that the literature is the best guide for this consideration. Although using a number of subjects similar to those used in other experiments is not infallible (they can be wrong), it is a good guide. For the sake of illustration, the present study was designed with 10 subjects (5 men and 5 women) in each group. "We could select our subjects by just calling them on the phone," another student suggests. "That's true," someone says, "but you may just call your friends and they may not be a representative sample of all college students. Also, you would probably start calling and just keep on calling until you found 10 men and 10 women. Although we don't know," the student continued, "the set of people you find in their dorm rooms at a given hour may be different from the set of college students in general. Thus you could select a biased group of subjects related to activities and the amount of time students spend near their phones." Our technique for avoiding this last criticism is to use a procedure known as *random selection* or **random sampling**. With random selection, every person in the potential subject pool is equally likely to be selected for the study. There are a number of ways random sampling can be accomplished. Box 7.1 illustrates the most common technique—the use of a random number table. Random selection helps to control systematic confounds that could be introduced unknowingly into the subject selection process and to ensure that subjects reflect the population of people we are studying. After the 20 subjects have been randomly selected, the next question is how to assign them to groups.

The group then considers how they can avoid the potential confound created by sex differences in subject assignment to the two groups. One person points out that one way to eliminate this potential confound would be to limit the subjects to one sex. Then, quite correctly, he points out that if they used this *elimination procedure* to remove the potential confound due to sex differences, they would be limiting the generality of the finding tremendously because any new facts they uncover would pertain to only one sex. (This person's concern about the generality of the results is very important and we will return to a more extended discussion of its importance in Chapter 10.) Someone then suggests that they could assign subjects so that an equal number of men and women are in each group. This process of attempting to equate by assigning equal attributes to each group in called a *matching procedure*. In this particular experiment, matching for sex differences consists of simply placing the same number of men and women in each group. In this case, because we know there may be sex differences in time estimation ability, matching provides an important control for not mistaking differences in men's and women's abilities to estimate time with differences caused by our independent variable—verbal feedback—in the accuracy of their estimates.

Before proceeding, it is important to understand exactly how matching controls for a possible confound due to sex differences. To begin, this procedure *does not eliminate sex differences* as does the elimination procedure,

---

## *Box 7.1* Random Number Table

A random number table is a table of numbers ordered in such a manner that their occurrence cannot be predicted from a mathematical formula. There are entire books of such numbers that researchers can use for selecting subjects randomly. Look at the random number table in this box. Since there is no order to random number tables, it does not matter whether you read up the page, down the page, across the page, in either direction, or even diagonally. All that matters is that you state beforehand how you will use the table. A simple example would be to use the table to pick out 10 subjects from a possible 63 for use in the study. First, you might decide that you will use only the last two digits in each number. Second, you might decide you will read the numbers from the bottom to the top of the page. Third, you might decide you will ignore any number greater than 63.

Assume you turned to the page shown in this box. You would begin by closing your eyes and placing your finger on some part of the page, or any other method you wish to use. Once you have your first number (91511), you simply read up the page using only the last two digits. The first 10 numbers are as follows—11, 95, 24, 45, 25, 75, 50, 18, 06, 71. Since you cannot use numbers larger than 63, you ignore 95, 75, and 71 and keep reading upward until you find three numbers less than 64. These are 54, 33, and 25. Since 25 occurred twice, you need to pick one final number, which is 05. At this time you could take your list of 63 possible subjects and pick subjects who are listed in positions 11, 24, 45, 25, 50, 18, 06, 54, 33, 05. You now have a group of randomly selected subjects.

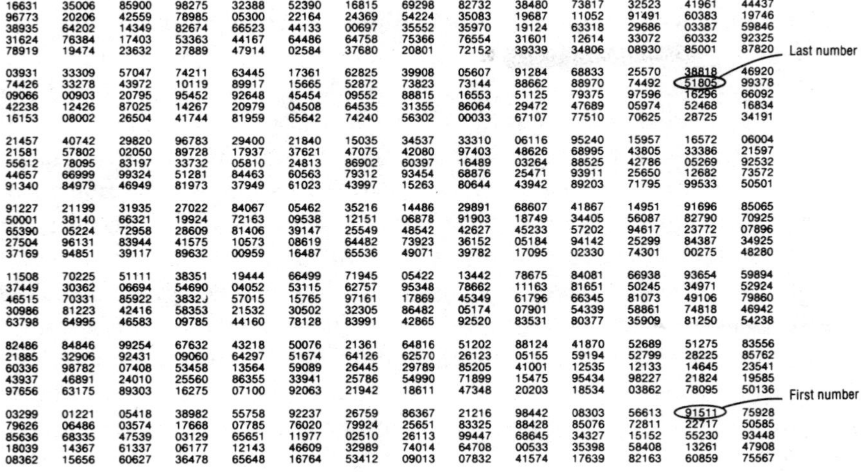

| | | | | | | | | | | | | | | |
|---|---|---|---|---|---|---|---|---|---|---|---|---|---|---|
| 16631 | 35006 | 85900 | 98275 | 32388 | 52390 | 16815 | 69298 | 82732 | 38480 | 73817 | 32523 | 41961 | 44437 | |
| 96773 | 20206 | 42559 | 78985 | 05300 | 22164 | 24369 | 54224 | 35083 | 19687 | 11052 | 91491 | 60383 | 19746 | |
| 38935 | 64202 | 14349 | 82674 | 66523 | 44133 | 00697 | 35552 | 35970 | 19124 | 63318 | 29686 | 03387 | 59846 | |
| 31624 | 76384 | 17403 | 53363 | 44167 | 64486 | 64758 | 75366 | 76554 | 31601 | 12614 | 33072 | 60332 | 92325 | |
| 78919 | 19474 | 23632 | 27889 | 47914 | 02584 | 37680 | 20801 | 72152 | 39339 | 34806 | 08930 | 85001 | 87820 | Last number |
| 03931 | 33309 | 57047 | 74211 | 63445 | 17361 | 62825 | 39908 | 05607 | 91284 | 68833 | 25570 | 38818 | 46920 | |
| 74426 | 33278 | 43972 | 10119 | 89917 | 15665 | 52872 | 73823 | 73144 | 88662 | 88970 | 74492 | 51805 | 99378 | |
| 09066 | 00903 | 20795 | 95452 | 92648 | 45454 | 09552 | 88815 | 16553 | 51125 | 79375 | 97596 | 16296 | 66092 | |
| 42238 | 12426 | 87025 | 14267 | 20979 | 04508 | 64535 | 31355 | 86064 | 29472 | 47689 | 05974 | 52468 | 16834 | |
| 16153 | 08002 | 26504 | 41744 | 81959 | 65642 | 74240 | 56302 | 00033 | 67107 | 77510 | 70625 | 28725 | 34191 | |
| 21457 | 40742 | 29820 | 96783 | 29400 | 21840 | 15035 | 34537 | 33310 | 06116 | 95240 | 15957 | 16572 | 06004 | |
| 21581 | 57802 | 02050 | 89728 | 17937 | 37621 | 47075 | 42080 | 97403 | 48626 | 68995 | 43805 | 33386 | 21597 | |
| 55612 | 78095 | 83197 | 33732 | 05810 | 24813 | 86902 | 60397 | 16489 | 03264 | 88525 | 42786 | 05269 | 92532 | |
| 44657 | 66999 | 99324 | 51281 | 84463 | 60563 | 79312 | 93454 | 68876 | 25471 | 93911 | 25650 | 12682 | 73572 | |
| 91340 | 84979 | 46949 | 81973 | 37949 | 61023 | 43997 | 15263 | 80644 | 43942 | 89203 | 71795 | 99533 | 50501 | |
| 91227 | 21199 | 31935 | 27022 | 84067 | 05462 | 35216 | 14486 | 29891 | 68607 | 41867 | 14951 | 91696 | 85065 | |
| 50001 | 38140 | 66321 | 19924 | 72163 | 09538 | 12151 | 06878 | 91903 | 18749 | 34405 | 56087 | 82790 | 70925 | |
| 65390 | 05224 | 72958 | 28609 | 81406 | 39147 | 25549 | 48542 | 42627 | 45233 | 57202 | 94617 | 23772 | 07896 | |
| 27504 | 96131 | 83944 | 41575 | 10573 | 08619 | 64482 | 73923 | 36152 | 05184 | 94142 | 25299 | 84387 | 34925 | |
| 37169 | 94851 | 39117 | 89632 | 00959 | 16487 | 65536 | 49071 | 39782 | 17095 | 02330 | 74301 | 00275 | 48280 | |
| 11508 | 70225 | 51111 | 38351 | 19444 | 66499 | 71945 | 05422 | 13442 | 78675 | 84081 | 66938 | 93654 | 59894 | |
| 37449 | 30362 | 06694 | 54690 | 04052 | 53115 | 62757 | 95348 | 78662 | 11163 | 81651 | 50245 | 34971 | 52924 | |
| 46515 | 70331 | 85922 | 3832J | 57015 | 15765 | 97161 | 17869 | 45349 | 61796 | 66345 | 81073 | 49106 | 79860 | |
| 30986 | 81223 | 42416 | 58353 | 21532 | 30502 | 32305 | 86482 | 05174 | 07901 | 54339 | 58861 | 74818 | 46942 | |
| 63798 | 64995 | 46583 | 09785 | 44160 | 78128 | 83991 | 42865 | 92520 | 83531 | 80377 | 35909 | 81250 | 54238 | |
| 82486 | 84846 | 99254 | 67632 | 43218 | 50076 | 21361 | 64816 | 51202 | 88124 | 41870 | 52689 | 51275 | 83556 | |
| 21885 | 32906 | 92431 | 09060 | 64297 | 51674 | 64126 | 62570 | 26123 | 05155 | 59194 | 52799 | 28225 | 85762 | |
| 60336 | 98782 | 07408 | 53458 | 13564 | 59089 | 26445 | 29789 | 85205 | 41001 | 12535 | 12133 | 14645 | 23541 | |
| 43937 | 46891 | 24010 | 25560 | 86355 | 33941 | 25786 | 54990 | 71899 | 15475 | 95434 | 98227 | 21824 | 19585 | |
| 97656 | 63175 | 89303 | 16275 | 07100 | 92063 | 21942 | 18611 | 47348 | 20203 | 18534 | 03862 | 78095 | 50136 | First number |
| 03299 | 01221 | 05418 | 38982 | 55758 | 92237 | 26759 | 86367 | 21216 | 98442 | 08303 | 56613 | 91511 | 75928 | |
| 79626 | 06486 | 03574 | 17668 | 07785 | 76020 | 79924 | 25651 | 83325 | 88428 | 85076 | 72811 | 22717 | 50585 | |
| 85636 | 68335 | 47539 | 03129 | 65651 | 11977 | 02510 | 26113 | 99447 | 68645 | 34327 | 15152 | 55230 | 93448 | |
| 18039 | 14367 | 61337 | 06177 | 12143 | 46609 | 32989 | 74014 | 64708 | 00533 | 35398 | 58408 | 13261 | 47908 | |
| 08362 | 15656 | 60627 | 36478 | 65648 | 16764 | 53412 | 09013 | 07832 | 41574 | 17639 | 82163 | 60859 | 75567 | |

which would limit the experiment to only men or only women. Instead, by placing an equal number of men and women in each group, *we control for any sex differences by distributing them evenly between our experimental and control groups.* In this way, any sex differences in time estimation affect both groups equally and, consequently, no longer differentially affect our experimental and control groups. Thus, matching for sex differences eliminates a potential confound from this experiment. The original experimental design and the revised design are contrasted in Figure 7.1

One member of the group then suggests that they could ask all 20 subjects to report to the laboratory at 2 P.M. As the subjects arrive, they could simply assign the first 5 men and 5 women to the experimental group and the second 5 men and 5 women to the control group. After a moment's hesitation, someone points out that one group would be made up of the subjects who arrived on time and the other would include subjects who arrived somewhat later. If there is a relationship between one's ability to get to an experiment on time and the ability to estimate time, another confound would be introduced. Although no one had encountered any published evidence of a relationship between one's ability to get to an experiment on time and ultimate accuracy in estimating time, it is reasonable to suspect that

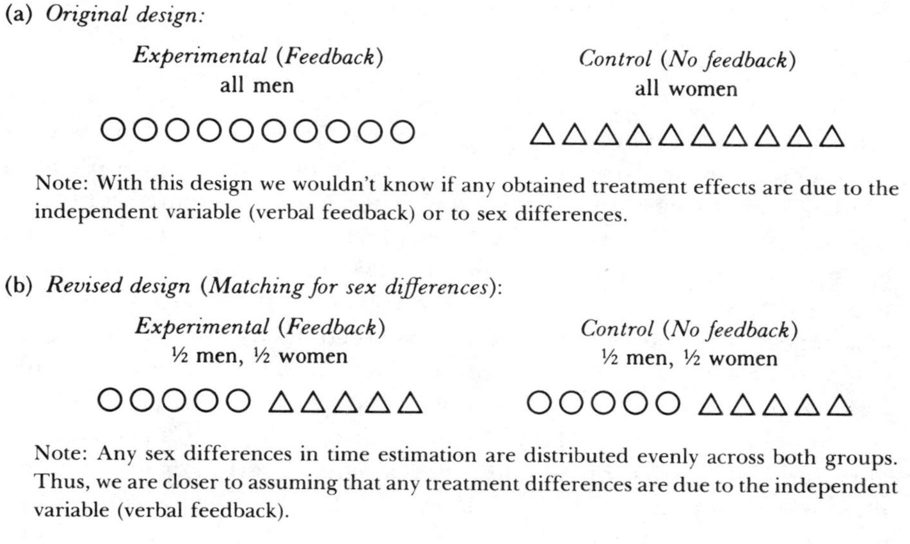

(a) *Original design:*

| *Experimental (Feedback)* all men | *Control (No feedback)* all women |
|---|---|
| ○○○○○○○○○○ | △△△△△△△△△△ |

Note: With this design we wouldn't know if any obtained treatment effects are due to the independent variable (verbal feedback) or to sex differences.

(b) *Revised design (Matching for sex differences):*

| *Experimental (Feedback)* ½ men, ½ women | *Control (No feedback)* ½ men, ½ women |
|---|---|
| ○○○○○ △△△△△ | ○○○○○ △△△△△ |

Note: Any sex differences in time estimation are distributed evenly across both groups. Thus, we are closer to assuming that any treatment differences are due to the independent variable (verbal feedback).

**Figure 7.1** Original experimental design and revised experimental design.

there might well be a correlation. In this case, we would not know whether the ultimate treatment effect is due to the feedback or to the fact that there are a lot of on-time people in one group and not-on-time people in another group. Consequently, it is agreed to control for a possible confound due to the subjects' arrival time as well as sex.

As to exactly how they might do this, one student suggests that they simply alternately assign subjects as they arrive to either the experimental (E) or the control (C) group. With this alternating assignment procedure, subjects would be assigned as follows: ECECECEC. . . . Another disagrees, saying that because E always precedes C, this would create a small but possibly relevant bias. He then suggests assigning subjects the way they used to "choose up" baseball teams in fifth grade: first choice to one team, next two choices to the next team, fourth choice to the first team, and then repeat the sequence until all players are chosen. Although he did not realize it then, he and his fifth-grade teammates had reinvented a commonly used *counterbalancing* procedure. With this particular procedure, subjects would be assigned as follows: ECCE, ECCE, ECCE. . . . Like simple alternation, counterbalancing ensures that each condition (early versus late arrival) appears equally often, and it has the additional advantage that each condition precedes and follows the other condition an equal number of times. In Figure 7.2, this counterbalanced design is contrasted with the previous design, which controlled for sex differences but ignored the potentially confounding influence of arrival time.

By using these matching and counterbalancing procedures, our students arrive at the final experimental design depicted in Figure 7.2. This design is far superior to their original plan to place all men in one group and all women in another because it adequately rules out two potential confounds that may have inadvertently produced unequal groups even before the experiment began. These confounds are: (1) time estimation performance may be different for men and women, and (2) time estimation may be related to a subject's ability to get to an experiment on time. By using matching and counterbalancing, the students feel confident that they have a confound-free design and decide to go ahead with their experiment.

Pause for a moment and think about their final design. Can you think of any other factors that might constitute potential confounds in an experiment designed to determine the effect of verbal feedback on time estimation? Remember, if you suspect that some factor may constitute a potential confound, you will greatly strengthen your argument if you can find some evidence supporting your concern (as the student did when she cited evi-

(a) *Revised design (which matched for sex differences but ignored arrival time):*

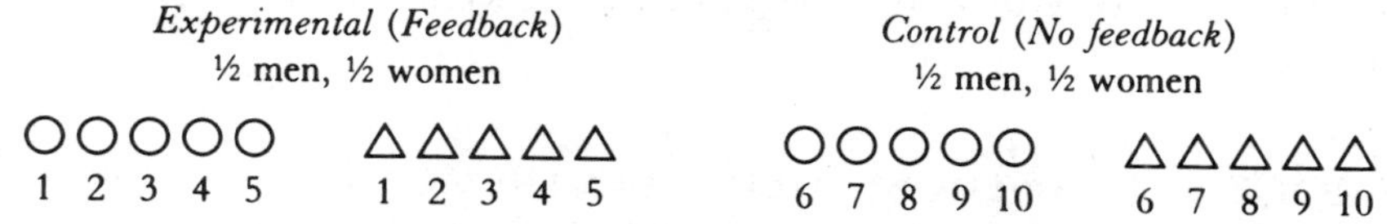

| *Experimental (Feedback)* ½ men, ½ women | | *Control (No feedback)* ½ men, ½ women | |
|---|---|---|---|
| ○○○○○ | △△△△△ | ○○○○○ | △△△△△ |
| 1 2 3 4 5 | 1 2 3 4 5 | 6 7 8 9 10 | 6 7 8 9 10 |

Note: With this design, although we've controlled for sex differences, we still don't know if any eventual treatment differences are due to feedback or to some relationship between the ability to get to an experiment on time and the ability to estimate time. The numbers under each figure represent the arrival order of each man and woman.

(b) *Final design (matching for sex and counterbalancing for arrival time):*

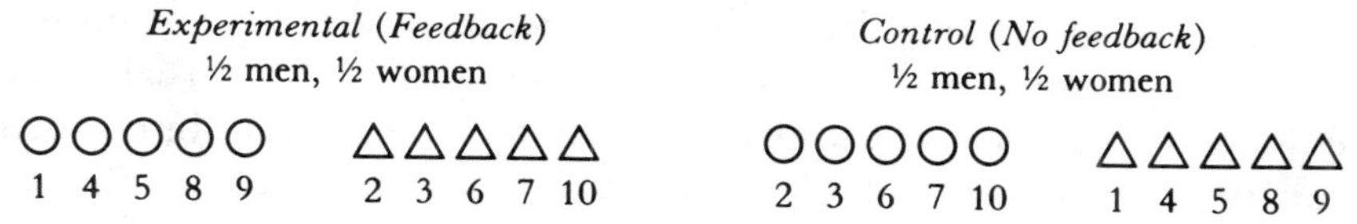

| *Experimental (Feedback)* ½ men, ½ women | | *Control (No feedback)* ½ men, ½ women | |
|---|---|---|---|
| ○○○○○ | △△△△△ | ○○○○○ | △△△△△ |
| 1 4 5 8 9 | 2 3 6 7 10 | 2 3 6 7 10 | 1 4 5 8 9 |

Note: Both sex differences and arrival time differences are now evenly distributed across our two groups. Because this design balances for both sex and arrival-time differences, any experimental effect can be assumed with greater probability to be due to the independent variable.

**Figure 7.2** Revised experimental design and final experimental design using matching and counterbalancing procedures.

dence that men and women differ in their ability to estimate time). In lieu of direct evidence, however, common sense can be a useful tool. For example, it would not surprise us if subjects who could get to an experiment on time were better time estimators, so it is reasonable to control for this factor. In a similar way, our common sense tells us that other factors such as where the subject was born are probably not related to the ability to estimate time; consequently, we would not bother to control for the place of birth of our subjects. As you become increasingly familiar with doing experiments and a research area, you will gain a better idea of what factors are reasonable to control for and what factors can be safely ignored. As we pointed out in Chapter 1, although common sense can be a useful tool, it can sometimes mislead even seasoned researchers. For example, in reaction time experiments, very few researchers bother to control for eye color. Yet one study indicates that people with dark eyes have slightly faster reaction times than people with light eyes (Landers, Obermier & Patterson, 1976). Because of such possible confounds, random assignment of subjects to groups is generally the best procedure to follow, as we shall see in the next section of this chapter.

## PROCEDURES FOR SUBJECT ASSIGNMENT: MATCHING, COUNTERBALANCING, AND RANDOMIZATION

In the preceding discussion, our students use matching and counterbalancing procedures to ensure that their experiment is not confounded by either sex differences or arrival-time differences between their two groups. If either of these variables is permitted to affect our groups differentially, a serious confound would result. We would not know whether any difference between our experimental and control groups is due to verbal feedback (independent variable) or to sex or arrival-time differences in our groups (confound). To control the impact of these potentially confounding variables, we typically utilize procedures such as matching, counterbalancing, and randomization to distribute their influence between our two groups.

In this section we will discuss each of these procedures for equating groups at the onset of our experiment. Whenever possible we will compare these procedures with one another so that the advantages and disadvantages of each will be evident. In terms of our earlier discussion of subject variability (within-groups variance), notice that when we distribute the impact of these potentially confounding variables between our two groups, we end up *increasing* the amount of subject variability in our experiment! Thus we are often confronted by a choice between a variable influencing a single group (thereby acting as a confound) or having its influence evenly distributed between both groups (thereby serving only to increase subject variability). Given this dilemma, the lesser of two evils is definitely increased subject variability!

*Matching* consists of assigning subjects to our experimental and control groups so that each group possesses equal attributes of any dimension we wish to equate. Put simply, a design that incorporates matching procedures in subject selection must first evaluate each subject along some relevant dimension and then, on the basis of each subject's score, assign that subject to either the experimental or the control group so that each group possesses an equal amount of the attribute being "matched." Matching groups on the basis of pretest scores can equate groups along any physical or psychological dimension that can be measured: intelligence, anxiety level, racial prejudice, and others. In the time estimation experiment, our students simply placed an equal number of men and women in each group. Another way they might have used matching would have been to equate their groups for the ability to estimate time before the experiment began. (Perhaps you thought of this as you were reading the previous section.) To match the groups for time estimation ability, we would first have to use a pretest or a previous measurement to evaluate each subject's ability to estimate time. Then we would assign subjects so that the two groups are approximately equal in the pretest measure of this attribute. We would then say that the groups are "matched" for their ability to estimate time before the experiment begins.

Matching is most frequently used when we are dealing with a limited number of subjects because it is with a small group that we are most likely to get an uneven distribution of a given attribute if we assign subjects on the basis of chance alone. When matching groups, keep in mind that it is not necessary to match along every possible dimension. Instead it is only necessary to equate our groups along those dimensions that may be related to our subjects' performance on the dependent measure. So, in the time estimation experiment, we would not bother to match for attributes such as body weight, religious background, or intelligence. The only requirements involved in matching are that (1) we already know those attributes of our subjects that, if unevenly distributed between groups, may be confounded with the effect of our independent variables; and (2) our pretest measure of these attributes is adequate.

One disadvantage of matching is that the groups are equated only along the dimension measured by the pretest. For all other attributes we have no assurance that the groups are equal, particularly when dealing with small groups. The danger with this procedure is that if we overlook an attribute that constitutes a potential confound, there is a good chance it will be unevenly distributed between our two groups. This disadvantage can be overcome if we match subjects into pairs and then randomly assign one of each pair to one group and the other to the second group. We will discuss this approach later. A second disadvantage of matching is that it may require that the subjects visit the laboratory twice: once for the measure on which the subjects will be matched (a pretest) and once for the experiment itself. This can be avoided if we match on the basis of available measures (such as SAT scores) or attributes (such as sex or eye color). Thus a pretest is not needed in every situation.

A second procedure used to eliminate potential confounds from experimental designs is *counterbalancing*. To counterbalance the assignment of subjects to experimental and control groups, certain conditions must be met.

First, each condition must occur equally often, and second, each condition must precede and follow all other conditions an equal number of times. Thus counterbalancing is a matching procedure with the added restriction that each condition must precede and follow all other conditions an equal number of times. To counterbalance subjects between two groups, we must first rank order all our subjects along the dimension we wish to counterbalance. In the time estimation experiment, our students used counterbalancing to control for the possibility that there may be a relationship between the subject's ability to get to the experiment on time and their ability to estimate time. They simply assigned the first man to arrive to one condition (experimental group), the next two to the other condition (control group), the fourth to the first group, and so on. This generates an ABBA counterbalancing sequence, and they simply repeat it until all male subjects are assigned to a group and then until all female subjects are assigned. Notice that counterbalancing subjects can be done along any physical or psychological dimension once the overall order of scores is known. Thus we could counterbalance our subjects' height, age, intelligence, or emotionality. When considering counterbalancing, keep in mind that more than two factors can be counterbalanced as long as each condition appears equally often and precedes and follows all other conditions an equal number of times. For example, with a counterbalancing procedure, subjects could be assigned to three conditions in the following order: ABCCBA. . . .

Because counterbalancing is a specialized form of matching, its advantages and disadvantages are similar to those described for matching. Like matching, counterbalancing is particularly useful when we are dealing with a limited number of subjects because it eliminates the uneven distribution of conditions that might result from chance or the random assignment of subjects. Similarly, one disadvantage of counterbalancing is that the groups are equated only along the dimension measured by the pretest. This means that because it is usually used with small groups, if we overlook an attribute that constitutes a potential confound, there is a good chance it will be unevenly distributed between our two groups.

A third procedure and the most powerful technique we have for eliminating unintended subject assignment confounds from the design of experiments is *randomization.* Randomization simply involves making subject assignments solely on the basis of chance. For example, a simple way to assign subjects randomly to either of two groups is to flip a coin. If the outcome is heads we would assign the first subject to one group, if it is tails we would assign the first subject to the other group. We would continue this process until one group is completely filled and then simply place the remaining subjects in the other group. Another common method of making random assignments is to use a random number table (see Box 7.1). In this case we would use the table to assign each one of our previously selected subjects to groups in the experiment.

Let us take a moment to differentiate two terms that are sometimes confused. These are *random sampling* and *random assignment.* Briefly, random sampling refers to the selection of subjects from a larger population to participate in a piece of research. Random assignment refers to the assignment of selected subjects to groups—for example, experimental and control—in an experiment. Let us now discuss these in more detail.

Random sampling concerns the selection of the entire group of subjects who will participate in an experiment. As we will later emphasize in our discussion of external and ecological validity, when we conduct an experiment we want our conclusions to have relevance for more people than just those who took part in the experiment. One way we ensure this relevance is to have our subjects constitute a representative sample of the entire population in which we are interested. By *representative,* we mean that our sample is similar to the overall population from which it is taken in all major aspects. For example, if I am interested in the time estimation ability of adult men, I must randomly sample my subjects from the entire adult male population in such a way that all men in the population have an equally likely chance of being selected. I would want to be sure that the local lawyer has just as much chance of being selected as the local garbage collector. In a similar way, I would want to be sure that a given 21-year-old man is just as likely to be selected as the town's only Revolutionary War veteran. The importance of randomly sampling a large population of subjects to obtain the samples we work with in our psychological experiments is crucial to the task of generalizing from the data we obtain in the laboratory back to the entire population. For example, as most of you know, most research done in experimental psychology has involved college sophomores. In a very real sense, our psychology is a psychology of college sophomores and may not generalize to the normal adult population. We will return to this consideration later in this book.

After we have *randomly selected* our subjects from the larger population we are studying, we can *randomly assign* them to our experimental and control groups as a way of equating groups prior to the application of our experimental treatment. The most important advantage of randomly assigning subjects over other procedures for equating groups is that randomization controls for both *known* and *unknown* potentially confounding variables. Unlike the matching and counterbalancing procedures, which attempt to equate our two groups directly on known relevant dimensions, the basic idea behind randomization is to leave the assignment of our subjects to a group solely up to chance. In this way, not only will any *suspected* subject selection biases between our two groups, such as the sex or arrival time or eye color differences, be nullified, but also any other differences, even *unknown* or *unsuspected* differences, will be nullified by randomly distributing them among our two groups. Indeed, it is not an overstatement to say that *randomization randomizes everything*.

As with matching and counterbalancing, it is important to realize that randomization does not remove the differences between the people in our experiment. They are still in our experiment. However, rather than influencing one group as opposed to the other, these subject differences are no longer differentially affecting either group. In this way, randomization provides a powerful tool for control because the impact of both known and unknown potentially confounding assignment biases can be evenly distributed between our experimental and control groups.

## CONTROL ACHIEVED THROUGH EXPERIMENTAL DESIGN

As we have emphasized throughout this book, science is a way of asking questions about the world. The quality of the answers we receive is influenced by several factors, one of the most important being the structure we use to reach our answers. In research this structure is determined by our experimental design. Somewhat like a blueprint, the experimental design directs our procedures and gives form to the experiment. In essence, an experimental design is a plan for how a study is to be structured. In an outline form, a design tells us what will be done to whom and when. To be evaluated favorably, a design must perform two related functions. First, it must provide a logical structure that enables us to pinpoint the effects of the independent variable on the dependent variable and thus answer our research questions. Second, it must help us to rule out confounds as an alternative explanation for our findings. In this section we will discuss experimental designs and introduce you to three specific designs that meet these criteria. In the following chapters we will discuss experimental design in greater detail.

A sound design must allow us to determine logically the effect of the independent variable on the dependent variable and to rule out alternative explanations. We informally introduced you to this idea in Chapter 2 with the cereal experiment. As you remember, the cereal company first tried to demonstrate the value of the cereal by giving it to a group of children and then weighing them several months later. If we were to diagram the design of this study, it would be as follows:

| Select group of children | Give cereal | Take weight of children |
|---|---|---|

We could also illustrate the design in a more generalized manner as follows:

| Group A | Treatment | Measurement |
|---|---|---|

Such a design would not be much help in pinpointing the effect of the independent variable on the dependent variable, nor would it rule out confounds. As was pointed out in Chapter 2, a stronger design would involve a control group. This design would appear as follows:

| Experimental group | Cereal | Measurement |
|---|---|---|
| Control group | No cereal | Measurement |

Again, we could diagram this in a more generalized manner using T as an abbreviation for treatment and M as an abbreviation for measurement:

| Group A | T | M |
|---|---|---|
| Group B | T (zero level) | M |

This new design helps us to determine the effects of the independent variable. However, does it help us to rule out the various threats to internal validity as presented in the preceding chapter? The answer is no. In particular, we could not rule out the possibility of biased subject selection unless we had randomly assigned subjects to the two groups. To denote this in a design, simply place an R before each group. Campbell and Stanley (1963) refer to this as a posttest-only control group design. The design is diagramed as follows:

| | | |
|---|---|---|
| R Group A | T | M |
| R Group B | T (zero level) | M |

Look at this design closely and see whether you can remember which study that we have discussed used this design. That's right—the Bransford and Johnson study discussed in Chapter 5 used such a design. In this example, T represents the presentation of the picture and M is the passage-recall measure.

Let us now consider a modification of this design that is similar to the final cereal experiment discussed in Chapter 2. This new design adds a measurement before the treatment. Such measurements are called *pretests,* whereas the measurements after the treatment are called *posttests.* In the terminology of Campbell and Stanley, this design is referred to as a *pretest-posttest control group design.* It is diagramed as follows:

| | | | |
|---|---|---|---|
| R Group A | M | T | M |
| R Group B | M | T (zero level) | M |

This design would allow us to determine the effects of the independent variable on the dependent variable as well as to control for the threats to internal validity discussed in Chapter 6.

Let us briefly review the threats to internal validity presented by Campbell and Stanley (1963) in relation to the pretest-posttest control group design. History is controlled by the inclusion of a control group, and thus any effects of history on one group would equally affect the other group. Maturation is similarly controlled in that any changes during the course of experimentation would affect both groups equally. Likewise, testing would affect both groups similarly. Notice that when we use the word *controlled,* we use it in the sense of being constant and not just in the sense that we can manipulate some factor. To control a factor in experimentation is the same as holding the effect of that factor constant for all groups throughout a research study. Such threats as subject selection and statistical regression would be controlled since the groups were randomly assigned in the first place. Mortality or the dropping out of the subjects would likewise not be expected to occur more frequently in one group than the other since the subjects were randomly assigned. Random assignment would also control for the subject-maturation interaction. As you can see, this same design without random assignment would be much weaker.

As a digression it must be noted that although Campbell and Stanley recommend the designs presented in this section as useful in controlling threats to internal validity, they do not mean that the designs are perfect. Confounds such as history can be introduced easily if subjects are not treated consistently throughout a study. Common sense would tell that if you are very nice to one group of subjects and nasty to another group, a confound will be introduced that could affect the results. Likewise in a rating study, if you rate the entire control group before the experimental group, an instrumentation confound may be introduced if your rating ability improves over time. The simple point is that designs serve their function only if used correctly.

A design such as the pretest-posttest control group design has been used by social psychologists as they study the persuasive effects of movies and lectures on the attitudes of individuals. Using this design, they randomly assign subjects to one of two groups. Subjects are then given a questionnaire concerning their attitude toward a certain topic—being politically conservative for example. The experimental group may be shown a movie supporting an extremely conservative position while the control group sees no movie. Following this, each group receives a questionnaire concerning their attitude on conservatism. Using this design, it is possible to measure the amount of attitude change brought about by the movie by comparing the change scores on the pretest and posttest questionnaires of the experimental and control groups.

As researchers used this type of design, it became apparent that the administration of a pretest alone could influence the persuasiveness of a movie or lecture; that is, if someone was asked his or her views on being conservative and was then shown a movie encouraging agreement with an extreme conservative position, the questionnaire alone could reduce the attitude change produced by the movie. To control for this problem, Solomon (1949) suggested the use of a four-group design. Groups 1 and 2 would be the experimental and control groups described previously. Groups 3 and 4 would be like the experimental and control groups except neither Group 3 nor Group 4 would receive the pretreatment questionnaire. The design could be outlined as follows:

| | | | |
|---|---|---|---|
| Randomly assigned Group 1 | Pretest | Treatment | Posttest |
| Randomly assigned Group 2 | Pretest | | Posttest |
| Randomly assigned Group 3 | | Treatment | Posttest |
| Randomly assigned Group 4 | | | Posttest |

By using the *Solomon four-group design,* researchers are able to determine not only the effects of the treatment but also the interaction of the treatment with the presence or absence of a pretest. One can also use this design to determine the effects of maturation and history by comparing the posttest of the fourth group with the pretest of Groups 1 and 2.

The three designs presented in this section (posttest only, pretest-posttest, and Solomon four-group) are considered by Campbell and Stanley (1963) to be examples of experimental designs that lead to "true experiments." A true experiment includes at least three characteristics and sometimes a fourth. The first characteristic is that subjects are *randomly assigned* to groups such that a given subject is equally likely to be assigned to any of the groups. As we already mentioned, there are a number of procedures for accomplishing this goal, including the use of a random number table. In certain cases, you may want to match the subjects before they are randomly assigned to groups. A simple procedure after the matching has been done is to flip a coin and allow the heads or tails to determine in which group the first subject of the pair is placed. The second characteristic of a true experiment is that there are at least two levels of the independent variable. One level can, of course, be a zero level as in the Bransford and Johnson study cited earlier; that is, not to present one group with the picture is the same as presenting a zero level of the independent variable. The third characteristic of a true experiment is that it can control for the major threats to internal validity, which we discussed in Chapter 6. Sometimes a fourth characteristic is included, which is of a theoretical nature. Although not agreed upon by all researchers, this characteristic requires that a true experiment compare two alternative theoretical positions. We introduced you to this idea in Box 5.1 with Platt's discussion of strong inference. In this box we used the example of falling weights, lending support to either Galileo's theory or the theory of Aristotle. This example illustrates the fourth criterion.

In this section we presented the most ideal cases of experimental design. Specifically, we presented three designs that can lead to true experiments and reduce the threats to internal validity. However, a general point needs to be made, which we will continue to develop throughout this book: Research designs are created in response to the needs of researchers as they attempt to answer specific questions and rule out alternative explanations. This being the case, designs are not sacred in themselves but are valuable only through the manner in which they allow us to make accurate interpretations of experimental results. Thus, an experimental design is never a replacement for an understanding of your research area. With such an understanding, it is important to create useful experimental designs that actually control for the important factors involved. Although true experimental designs aid greatly in our search for understanding, they can never replace logic, common sense, and a thorough knowledge of our research area.

## CONTROL AS RELATED TO THE LOGIC OF EXPERIMENTATION

In this section we want to pull together some of the themes related to the logic of experimentation. Let us do this through the simple illustration in Figure 7.3. Imagine an experiment in which subjects are selected and then randomly assigned to one of two groups. It is diagramed as follows:

| | | |
|---|---|---|
| R Group A | T | M |
| R Group B | | M |

Let us first turn to Steps 1 and 2 of Figure 7.3. To help us logically determine the effect of the independent variable on the dependent variable, we must first ask whether Group A is equal to Group B before any treatment (independent variable) is introduced. We can assume this to be the case if we have randomly assigned subjects to these two groups. What would the $F$-ratio equal at this point (assuming we had a measure of the dependent variable in each group)? Conceptually the $F$-ratio would equal 1. Follow this reasoning for a second. If the two groups are chosen as equal, then we can assume that there are no systematic effects on one group as compared with the other *before* the independent variable is introduced. There should only be variations due to chance. As you remember, between-groups variance is influenced by differences between the groups as well as chance variation. Within-groups variance is influenced mainly by chance variation. Thus,

$$F = \frac{\text{between-groups variance}}{\text{within-groups variance}} = 1 = \frac{\text{treatment effect + error}}{\text{error}}$$

If, for some reason, the two groups were unequal at the beginning of the experiment, then the $F$-ratio would be greater than 1 *before* the independent variable is ever introduced! In this situation we might find ourselves rejecting the null hypothesis (Group A = Group B) and drawing an inappropriate conclusion. Thus it is imperative that we control subject assignment to groups for the logic of experimentation to be valid. The best method for ensuring that subject groups are equal is through the random assignment of subjects to groups. This is especially true when our design lacks a pretest measure from which our assumption of equal groups can be verified.

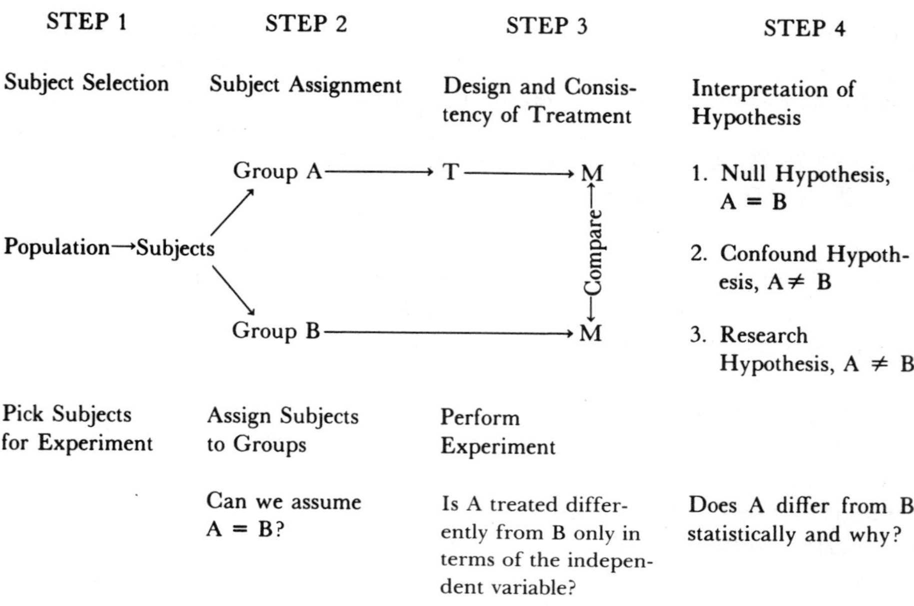


**Figure 7.3** Conceptual steps in experimentation.

Moving to Step 3 of Figure 7.3, we arrive at the introduction of the independent variable. In relation to the logic of experimentation, the main question that we ask here is: Are the different levels of the independent variable the *only* way in which Group A is treated differently from Group B? If the answer is no, then we face a possible confound, which makes interpretation of the data difficult if not impossible. Thus, we must be able to control the experimental situation at Step 3 or else the logic of our experimental design falls apart. Statistics cannot help us at this point since any systematic change in Group A as compared with Group B because of either the independent variable or a confound will increase the between-groups variance and may cause us erroneously to reject the null hypothesis. For the sake of completeness, we want to point out that if an extraneous variable affects *both* Groups A and B, then the within-groups variance is increased, thus making it more difficult to reject the null hypothesis and to see the effect of the independent variable on the dependent variable. For example, if a study withan independent variable that provoked anxiety was performed at the same time that college students (both men and women) were being called into the army on short notice, some students (those who could be drafted) might show higher anxiety scores, which would lead to greater variability than normal, making it more difficult to see changes related to the independent variable. As pointed out earlier, the more variability in an experiment, the greater the within-groups variance. On the other hand, if we treat all our subjects the same and every subject is exposed to exactly the same experimental situation, then the within-groups variance is minimized. The simple rule is that the more consistently subjects are treated in every way, the less the within-groups variance.

A simple rule for internal validity is to achieve as much control as possible over the experimental situation and to use this control to make the experiment as similar as possible for all subjects. The first type of control that we exercise at Step 3 is the control gained by a good experimental design. A design with sound structure helps us to rule out possible confounds or threats to internal validity. The second type of control we exercise at this point is consistent treatment of our subjects. Consistency of treatment helps us to reduce *needless* variation.

The final point in Figure 7.3 is Step 4, which represents the interpretation of our experimental results. We discussed this in detail in Chapter 6. If we achieved control in Steps 1, 2, and 3 of our experiment, then interpretation of the experimental results becomes a relatively easy task. That is, once we have controlled group differences through random assignment of subjects and we have controlled confounds through experimental design and minimizing needless variability among subjects, we can assume that our results are due to the independent variable.

## Key Terms and Concepts

1. Subject assignment
   a. matching
   b. counterbalancing
   c. random assignment
2. Subject selection
3. Random number table
4. Difference between random sampling and random assignment
5. Experimental designs
   a. posttest only
   b. pretest-posttest
   c. Solomon four-group

6. True experiments
   a. characteristics
      - subjects randomly assigned
      - at least two levels of independent variable
      - controls for major threats to internal validity
7. Control as related to logic of experimentation and $F$-ratio

## Summary

1. Controlling the experimental situation is an important way that the researcher can make more accurate inferences concerning how the independent variable influences the dependent variable.
2. There are a variety of methods for equating groups to ensure that differences in an experiment are not due to biased subject assignment. Three of these are matching, counterbalancing, and randomization.
3. Two terms sometimes confused are random sampling and random assignment. Random sampling refers to the selection of subjects from a larger population. Random assignment refers to the assignment of selected subjects to particular group in an experiment.
4. Strong experimental designs help to rule out alternative factors that may account for the results in an experiment. Although no design is perfect, the posttest design, the pretest-posttest, and the Solomon four-group design help to rule out a number of potential threats to internal validity, and because of this ability are referred to "true experimental designs" by Campbell and Stanley.
5. Three characteristics (and sometimes a fourth) are seen as representative of a true experiment. The first is that subjects are randomly assigned to groups. The second is that there are at least two levels of the independent variable. The third is that the design can control for the major threats to internal validity. The fourth characteristic is that the experiment compares two alternative theoretical positions. This final characteristic is not required by some researchers.
6. Figure 7.3 presented in a schematic fashion the major steps in experimentation once the hypothesis had been developed. These include subject selection, subject assignment, experimental design, and the interpretation of the hypothesis.

## Review Questions

1. Describe a random number table and tell how it is used.
2. What are the disadvantages of using matching as an assignment procedure?
3. What is the difference between random assignment and random sampling?
4. What is the purpose of random assignment of subjects to groups?
5. Diagram a posttest-only control group design.

6. What threats to internal validity does a Solomon four-group design control for?
7. Name three characteristics of a "true experiment."
8. In terms of the null hypothesis, why is it important that all groups be equal at the beginning of the experiment?

## Discussion Questions and Projects

1. A university sets up a computer lab that students can use as they wish. At the end of the year the administration decides to determine whether using the lab helps to increase a student's grade. To answer this question, the administration divides the students into two groups, those who have used the computer lab and those who have not. They determine grade point average of the two groups and conclude that using the computer results in a student's making better grades. Discuss this conclusion.
2. Assume another university was about to install a computer lab and asked you to help them design a study for determining its effect on grades. How might you design such a study?
3. If you could either randomly select subjects *or* randomly assign subjects to groups in an experiment, which would be the better procedure? What would be some of the problems in the interpretation of the data in each case?
4. How might one determine what factors subjects need to be matched on? Give an example of a situation in which matching might offer an advantage over randomization. What would be some of the problems in making inferences from such a study?
5. A large corporation wanted to develop a long-term project to test a series of leadership training courses that it was designing. These training courses were to be offered after work for low-level employees. These courses were to be run on a volunteer basis and the workers not paid for staying late at work. To evaluate the effectiveness of the course at the conclusion of 5 and 10 years, the corporation decided that the measure of effectiveness would be how many of the individuals who took the course had assumed levels of leadership in comparison to those who did not take the course. Discuss this design. Assume that after 10 years it was found that those who took the leadership course were in higher positions of leadership than those who did not. The corporation then could conclude that the leadership course produced leaders. Comment on this conclusion.

CHAPTER EIGHT

# *Applying the Logic of Experimentation: Between-Subjects Designs*

## INTRODUCTION

In Chapter 7 we emphasized the importance of control in experimentation, and we presented concepts underlying the design of experiments. We introduced you to the idea of the "true experiment" and its advantages in helping us make causal inferences. Specifically, we presented you with the blueprints for three designs that give us a large degree of control over the experimental situation. In this manner, potential confounds are reduced, thus limiting the threats to the internal validity of our experiments. We want to build on that discussion in this chapter. We will show how the potential usefulness of experimental designs can be increased by using more than two levels of the independent variable. We will also introduce you to designs that examine the effects of more than one independent variable on the dependent variable; these are referred to as *factorial designs*.

From the onset of this discussion, it is important that you realize that no design is perfect. Each design has its own strengths and weaknesses in relation to the specific scientific questions being asked. Part of your task as a scientist is to learn which designs are best suited to certain types of questions and how existing designs may be modified to answer future questions. Whenever possible, we will make specific suggestions as to the appropriateness of designs and point out potential problems with certain designs. However, without an exploration of the specific context in which a given design is to be used, it is impossible to evaluate fully the appropriateness of a given design. Some students feel perplexed at this point. Yet part of becoming a mature researcher is seeing that psychological experimentation is more than learning a set of rules and applying them to research. Research in psychology is *work.* It may be fun work, but it is still work, which requires thinking, common sense, and a knowledge of the published literature. It is in this spirit that we suggest you approach the next chapters—not only as an introduction to different types of experimental designs but also as a development of research approaches that you can learn from and modify as needed at a later stage in your career.

## BETWEEN-SUBJECTS DESIGN: TERMINOLOGY

Between-subjects designs are a general class of designs in which different subjects are used in each of our groups. To be more precise, these designs involve comparisons *between* different groups of subjects. In the illustrations of research presented thus far in this book, we have emphasized between-subjects designs. For example, the cereal experiment presented in Chapter 2 compared the weight gained by a group of children who ate cereal with that of a group that did not. The "true" experimental designs presented in Chapter 7 are also between-subjects designs. One characteristic of the between-subjects design is that *any given subject* receives *only one level* of the independent variable. Another characteristic is that only one score for each subject is used in the analysis of the results. Although the children in the cereal experiment were weighed more than once (before and after the treatment), the comparison between groups were related to the difference between these two measurements; a single score reflected the amount of weight gained.

The alternative to between-subjects designs is *within-subjects* designs. These designs present different levels of the independent variable to the *same* group of subjects. For example, we could determine the value of feedback in shooting basketballs through a within-subjects design by having you shoot baskets blindfolded (zero level of feedback) and then without the blindfold (high level of feedback). In this case you would receive both levels of the independent variable as well as have more than one measure of the dependent variable. We will examine these designs in much greater detail in the next chapter.

## COMPLETELY RANDOMIZED DESIGN

One of the simplest between-subjects designs is the completely randomized design, which is also referred to as the simple randomized design or the simple random subject design. In this type of design, the assignment of subjects is completely randomized between groups. In its simplest form, it is composed of two levels of the independent variable. In Chapter 7 we used the following type of diagram:

| | | | |
|---|---|---|---|
| R | Group A | T(high level) | M |
| R | Group B | T(zero level) | M |

As you remember from that chapter, Group A received a high level of the independent variable and Group B received a zero level. Let us quickly go through the procedure for using this design. Assume that we have already chosen 50 subjects for our experiment for two groups of 25 each. The next task is to assign randomly 25 subjects to Group A and 25 to Group B. As mentioned earlier, this may be accomplished in several ways—for example, with a random number table—with the outcome being that every subject is equally likely to be placed in either Group A or Group B. It is this process of randomization that initially equates our two groups and enables us ultimately to infer that the independent variable influenced the dependent variable. The next task prescribed by the design is for Group A to receive a high level of the independent variable and Group B to receive a zero level. The task then is the measurement of the dependent variable for each group. Finally, the dependent variable is compared between the groups, which gives us our treatment effect.

## MULTILEVELED COMPLETELY RANDOMIZED DESIGNS

The completely randomized design can also contain more than two levels of the independent variable. Such a design is called a *multileveled completely randomized design* and can be diagramed as follows:

| | | | |
|---|---|---|---|
| R | Group A | Level 1 T | M |
| R | Group B | Level 2 T | M |
| R | Group C | Level 3 T | M |
| R | Group D | Level 4 T | M |

As an example of a completely randomized design with four levels of the independent variable, consider a study of the effects of drinking coffee on flying an airplane. Each group would be given a prescribed number of cups of coffee and then tested in a laboratory equipped with a flight simulator. The number of errors made by each group would serve as the dependent variable. In this hypothetical example, Level 4 could equal six cups of coffee, Level 3 could equal four cups, Level 2 could equal two cups, and Level 1 could equal zero cups.

In Chapter 6 we presented the Bransford and Johnson (1972) study in a simple two-group form with one group seeing the entire picture before hearing the passage and the other group seeing no picture. That was an incomplete description of the actual study. In the actual study there were five groups, which would qualify the study as a multileveled completely randomized design. In addition to the two groups described previously, Bransford and Johnson included three other groups. As you remember, their independent variable was the amount of context (prior knowledge), with the appropriate picture representing total context (Group 1). Group 2 also saw a picture before hearing the passage; however, the picture presented to Group 2 represented only a partial context for the passage, although the individual components were the same as those presented to Group 1 (see Figure 8.1). The third group was presented with a zero level of the independent variable and saw no picture before hearing the passage. There were also a fourth and fifth group that served as controls. Group 4 saw the picture representing the total context but not until *after* the passage had been heard. Group 5 heard the passage twice but did not see the picture. This study is pictorially represented in Figure 8.1.

The most common way to analyze a completely randomized design is to use a single-factor analysis of variance. In this case the null hypothesis would state that every group equals every other group. If we did reject the null hypothesis and found that one or more groups differed significantly, we would then need to apply what are called *post hoc tests* and compare the differences between the groups taken as pairs. In the hypothetical study of the effect of drinking coffee on flying an airplane, we would want to know not only whether the groups as a whole statistically differ from one another, but also which particular groups differ from which other groups. After doing such a post hoc analysis, we might find that six cups of coffee cause different results from no cups of coffee but do not cause any statistical differences compared with two or four cups of coffee. The alternative to using post hoc tests is to plan particular comparisons *before* the study is performed. This is the statistical approach taken by Bransford and Johnson. To be specific, they compared the "context before" condition (Group 1 in Figure 8.1) with each of the four other conditions. For this comparison, they used something called Dunnett's test, which is beyond the scope of this book.

|  |  | |
|---|---|---|
| Group 1 (seeing appropriate picture before hearing passage) | If the balloons popped, the sound wouldn't be able to carry since everything would be too far away from the correct floor. A closed window would also prevent the sound from carrying, since most buildings tend to be well insulated. Since the whole operation depends on a steady flow of electricity, a break in the middle of the wire would also cause problems. Of course, the fellow could shout, but the human voice is not loud enough to carry that far. An additional problem is that a string could break on the instrument. Then there could be no accompaniment to the message. It is clear that the best situation would involve less distance. Then there would be fewer potential problems. With face to face contact, the least number of things could go wrong. | Recall Measure |
| Group 2 (seeing partial context picture before hearing passage) | If the balloons popped, the sound wouldn't be able to carry since everything would be too far away from the correct floor. A closed window would also prevent the sound from carrying, since most buildings tend to be well insulated. Since the whole operation depends on a steady flow of electricity, a break in the middle of the wire would also cause problems. Of course, the fellow could shout, but the human voice is not loud enough to carry that far. An additional problem is that a string could break on the instrument. Then there could be no accompaniment to the message. It is clear that the best situation would involve less distance. Then there would be fewer potential problems. With face to face contact, the least number of things could go wrong. | Recall Measure |
| Group 3 (hearing passage | If the balloons popped, the sound wouldn't be able to carry since everything would be too far away from the correct floor. A closed window would also prevent the sound from carrying, since most buildings tend to be well insulated. Since the whole operation depends on a steady flow of electricity, a break in the middle of the wire would also cause problems. Of | Recall Measure |

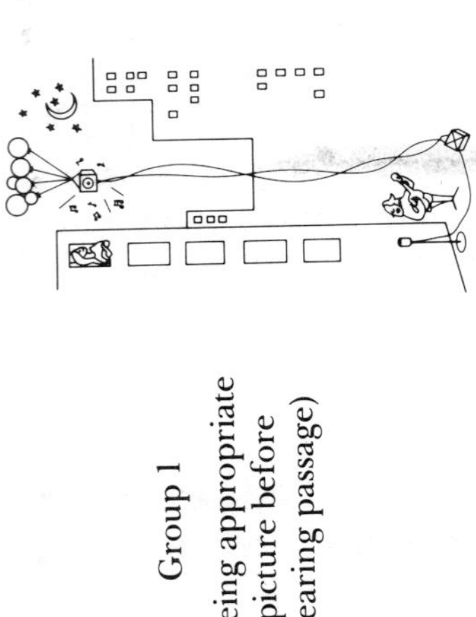

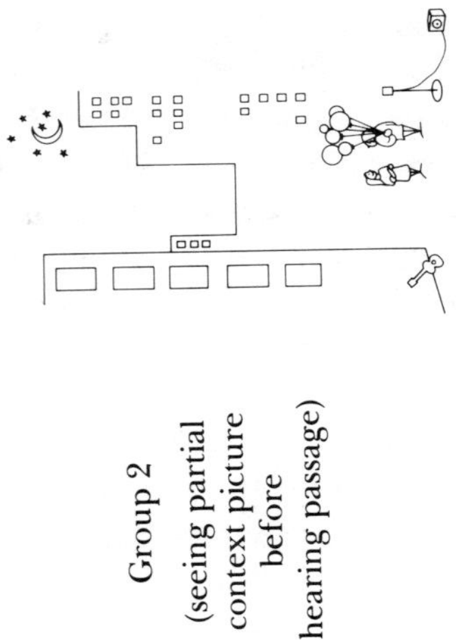

**Figure 8.1** Pictorial representation of the Bransford and Johnson study.

without seeing picture)

course, the fellow could shout, but the human voice is not loud enough to carry that far. An additional problem is that a string could break on the instrument. Then there could be no accompaniment to the message. It is clear that the best situation would involve less distance. Then there would be fewer potential problems. With face to face contact, the least number of things could go wrong.

Group 4 (seeing appropriate picture after hearing passage

If the balloons popped, the sound wouldn't be able to carry since everything would be too far away from the correct floor. A closed window would also prevent the sound from carrying, since most buildings tend to be well insulated. Since the whole operation depends on a steady flow of electricity, a break in the middle of the wire would also cause problems. Of course, the fellow could shout, but the human voice is not loud enough to carry that far. An additional problem is that a string could break on the instrument. Then there could be no accompaniment to the message. It is clear that the best situation would involve less distance. Then there would be fewer potential problems. With face to face contact, the least number of things could go wrong.

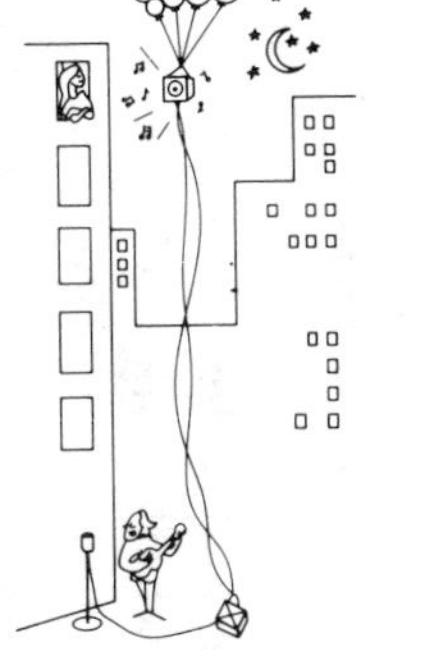

Recall Measure

Group 5 (hearing passage twice)

If the balloons popped, the sound wouldn't be able to carry since everything would be too far away from the correct floor. A closed window would also prevent the sound from carrying, since most buildings tend to be well insulated. Since the whole operation depends on a steady flow of electricity, a break in the middle of the wire would also cause problems. Of course, the fellow could shout, but the human voice is not loud enough to carry that far. An additional problem is that a string could break on the instrument. Then there could be no accompaniment to the message. It is clear that the best situation would involve less distance. Then there would be fewer potential problems. With face to face contact, the least number of things could go wrong.

If the balloons popped, the sound wouldn't be able to carry since everything would be too far away from the correct floor. A closed window would also prevent the sound from carrying, since most buildings tend to be well insulated. Since the whole operation depends on a steady flow of electricity, a break in the middle of the wire would also cause problems. Of course, the fellow could shout, but the human voice is not loud enough to carry that far. An additional problem is that a string could break on the instrument. Then there could be no accompaniment to the message. It is clear that the best situation would involve less distance. Then there would be fewer potential problems. With face to face contact, the least number of things could go wrong.

Recall Measure

Another illustration of a between-subjects design comes from clinical research. Strupp and Hadley (1979) asked how important technical skills are for the therapist in the process of psychotherapy; that is, does a professional psychotherapist learn certain skills or techniques that are required for a successful outcome in psychotherapy? To answer this question, these researchers compared the psychological improvement of clients seeing experienced psychotherapists with that of clients seeing college professors chosen for their ability to form good human relationships. Notice how Strupp and Hadley were attempting to control for the relationship factor in their study. In essence they were asking whether something more than a good relationship is needed for successful psychotherapy to take place. For subjects in the study, they used college students who requested therapy and who scored high on certain scales of a traditional psychological test (the Minnesota Multiphasic Personality Inventory). Based on traditional diagnostic systems, the subjects were classified as having "neurotic depression" or an "anxiety reaction." The design of the study called for students to be randomly assigned to one of three groups. Group 1 was treated by experienced psychotherapists; Group 2 talked with college professors chosen for their ability to form good relationships; and Group 3 was referred to as a "minimal treatment" group. This third group was told that treatment would be delayed, and thus it served as a no-treatment control during the time the first two groups received therapy. The design of the study was as follows:

| | | | | |
|---|---|---|---|---|
| R | Group 1 | M | T (experienced therapist, therapy skills plus good relationship) | M |
| R | Group 2 | M | T (college professor, good relationship) | M |
| R | Group 3 | M | T (waiting list no treatment) | M |

As you can see, this is a multileveled completely randomized design with pretest-posttest measures. In the actual study, a number of dependent variables were used, which included changes in psychological tests and ratings of change by the therapists, students, and outside clinicians allowing Strupp and Hadley to assess changes over time. What do you think the results were? Better yet, you should read this study yourself. The complete title is listed in the Bibliography of this book. This study is a good example of how to perform clinical research and illustrates some factors that must be controlled to achieve a scientific understanding of such clinical processes as psychotherapy.

Let us quickly turn to the logic of hypothesis testing as it is related to multileveled between-subjects designs. As with the simple two-level completely randomized experiments presented earlier in the book, we must still answer three questions. First, are the results due to chance? Second, are the results due to a confound? And third, are the results due to the independent variable? The first question is approached through a statistical test of the null hypothesis, which states that no differences exist between the groups. Thus, the null hypothesis for a three-level design states that group 1 = group 2 = group 3. Again we evaluate this through the $F$-ratio. If the $F$-ratio is statistically significant, then we know there is a difference between the groups; *however, we do not know which group or groups caused this difference*. To determine whether there is a statistically significant difference between any combination of groups, we must use a post hoc test (these tests are described in most advanced statistics books—for example, Winer, 1971).

After you have rejected the null hypothesis, you turn to the question concerning confounds and utilize the same logic we presented to track down factors that might have played a role in the results. As you can see, if we were not able to assume that our groups were equal before we began the treatment, it would be impossible to conclude what effect, if any, the independent variable had on the dependent variable. Even if you do not read the random number table every night before you go to bed, we hope you have come to understand the extreme importance of the random assignment of subjects to your groups in an experiment. When we are reasonably sure that no significant confounds are present in our study, we can consider our third question concerning the independent variable. If we reject the null hypothesis and rule out confounds, then we may conclude that the independent variable influenced our results and theoretically interpret this relationship.

## FACTORIAL DESIGN

A survey of published psychological research reported that most research using inferential statistics relied on more complex designs such as factorial designs (Edgington, 1974). The popularity of factorial designs seems related to our acceptance of the fact that there are few, if any, isolated cause-and-effect relationships in psychological processing. Rather, most psychological processes have several causes that *interact* with each other in various ways and cannot be determined from simple experimental designs such as those we have discussed thus far. The advantage of factorial designs is that they allow us to examine scientifically the effects of more than one independent variable, both individually and collectively, on the dependent variable.

An easy way to conceptualize factorial designs is to view them as a composite of several simple completely randomized designs such as those we have discussed previously. Let us illustrate this point. Consider a completely randomized design to determine the effect of money on memory in psychological experiments. A simple design would be to randomly assign subjects to two groups. Each group would hear the same passage. The subjects in one group would receive 1¢ for every idea remembered and those in the other group would receive $1 for every idea remembered. This would be diagramed as follows:

| | | | |
|---|---|---|---|
| R | Group 1 | T (1¢) | M (recall task) |
| R | Group 2 | T ($1) | M (recall task) |

Now consider a second completely randomized design such as the two-treatment version of Bransford and Johnson's study presented in Chapter 6. We described this study as consisting of a zero level of the independent variable (no picture) and a high level of the independent variable (appropriate context picture). This single-factor experiment can be diagramed as follows:

| | | | |
|---|---|---|---|
| R | Group 1 | T (picture—high context) | M (recall task) |
| R | Group 2 | T (no picture—zero context) | M (recall task) |

We could perform these two studies separately; however, then we could not determine the collective effect of both independent variables (money and context) on the dependent variable. This is referred to as the *interaction effect*, but we are getting ahead of ourselves. First let us see how we might go about combining these two separate studies into one experiment.

An alternative to performing these studies separately would be to combine them into a factorial design. For ease of representation, let us diagram the first experiment in a horizontal fashion as follows:

| Money | |
|---|---|
| Level 1 (1¢) | Level 2 ($1) |
| Group 1 | Group 2 |

We can likewise diagram the second experiment in a vertical fashion:

| | | |
|---|---|---|
| Prior Knowledge | Level 1 (no picture) | Group 1 |
| | Level 2 (picture) | Group 2 |

Now if we simply combine our graphic representations of these two studies, the diagram appears as follows:

| | | Money Factor | |
|---|---|---|---|
| | | Level 1 (1¢) | Level 2 ($1) |
| Prior Knowledge Factor | Level 1 (no picture) | Group A | Group C |
| | Level 2 (picture) | Group B | Group D |

Notice that with this design we have four *separate* groups, with each subject receiving one level of *each* independent variable. Group A will receive 1¢ for each correct idea recalled and will be given the minimum context or prior knowledge (no picture). Group B will be given 1¢ for each correct idea recalled and will be given the maximum context or prior knowledge (picture). Group C will receive $1 for each idea recalled and minimum context (no picture). Group D will receive $1 for each idea recalled and maximum context (picture).

This type of design is referred to as a 2 × 2 *design* (read "two by two"). In this notation 2 × 2 refers to there being two levels of one independent variable and two levels of another. The independent variables are also referred to as *factors*. If, instead, we had a design involving six levels of factor A and two levels of factor B, then it would be called a 6 × 2 factorial design. Similarly, a design that consisted of two levels of factor A, three levels of factor B, and four levels of factor C would be called 2 × 3 × 4 factorial design.

The treatment differences (between levels of a given factor) in a factorial design are referred to as *main effects*. Thus it is possible to determine the main effect for each factor. In our previous example, this would be equivalent to performing two single-factor experiments; one would compare the amounts of money given for recall and one would compare the levels of pictorial context. However, in factorial designs the independent variables may combine in various ways in their effects on the dependent variable. Such a combined effect is referred to as an *interaction effect*. Interaction effects cannot be determined by performing separate single-factor studies and thus are unique to factorial designs.

A general representation of a 2 × 2 design:

| | | Factor A Level 1 $A_1$ | Factor A Level 2 $A_2$ |
|---|---|---|---|
| Factor B | Level 1 $B_1$ | $A_1B_1$ | $A_2B_1$ |
| | Level 2 $B_2$ | $A_1B_2$ | $A_2B_2$ |

A general representation of a 3 × 3 factorial design:

| | | Factor A Level 1 $A_1$ | Factor A Level 2 $A_2$ | Factor A Level 3 $A_3$ |
|---|---|---|---|---|
| Factor B | Level 1 $B_1$ | $A_1B_1$ | $A_2B_1$ | $A_3B_1$ |
| | Level 2 $B_2$ | $A_1B_2$ | $A_2B_2$ | $A_3B_2$ |
| | Level 3 $B_3$ | $A_1B_3$ | $A_2B_3$ | $A_3B_3$ |

**Figure 8.2** This figure is a schematic representation of 2 × 2, 3 × 3, and 2 × 3 × 2 (opposite page) factorial designs. Note that the total number of treatment conditions in each design can be obtained by multiplying the number of levels of each factor.

A general representation of a 2 × 3 × 2 design:

Factor C

Level 1 $C_1$

| Factor B | Factor A: $A_1$ | $A_2$ |
|---|---|---|
| $B_1$ | $A_1B_1C_1$ | $A_2B_1C_1$ |
| $B_2$ | $A_1B_2C_1$ | $A_2B_2C_1$ |
| $B_3$ | $A_1B_3C_1$ | $A_2B_3C_1$ |

Level 2 $C_2$

| Factor B | Factor A: $A_1$ | $A_2$ |
|---|---|---|
| $B_1$ | $A_1B_1C_2$ | $A_2B_1C_2$ |
| $B_2$ | $A_1B_2C_2$ | $A_2B_2C_2$ |
| $B_3$ | $A_1B_3C_2$ | $A_2B_3C_2$ |

A 2 × 3 × 2 design can also be diagramed as follows:

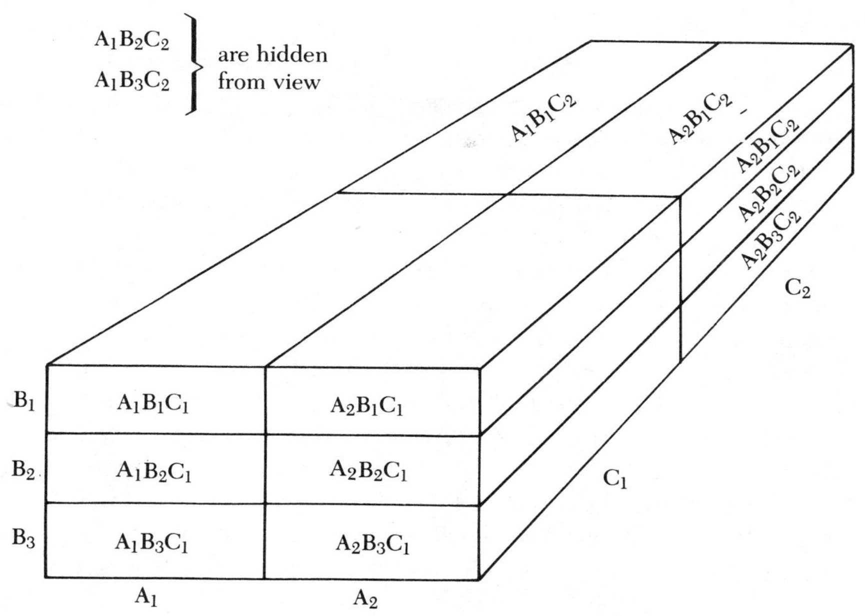

What is an interaction effect? An interaction effect is the result of two independent variables combining to produce a result different from that produced by either variable alone. To give you an extreme example, we know that combining moderate levels of barbiturates and alcohol leads to severe illness and sometimes death, whereas moderate levels of either drug alone do not, for most individuals. Thus it is only in combination that the interaction effect is produced. This is only one type of interaction. We will present additional possible interaction effects later in this chapter.

Before we leave the question of terminology, let us look at schematic diagrams of three different factorial designs (see Figure 8.2 on pp. 184–185). The blocks in the diagram are called *cells*. Notice that the individual cells are labeled according to the level of each independent variable that affects the cell. For example, the group of subjects that receive Level 1 of Factor A and Level 2 of Factor B is labeled $A_1B_2$. Remember that in between-subjects designs, which we are discussing here, each cell represents a different group of subjects that have been randomly assigned to that cell.

## FACTORIAL DESIGNS: THE LOGIC OF EXPERIMENTATION AND THE INTERACTION EFFECT

The logic of experimentation for factorial designs is similar to that already described for single-factor experiments. As with these other experiments, in factorial designs we must be able to assume that our groups are equal before any of the treatments are presented. Once we can make this assumption, we may turn to an evaluation of our hypotheses. As with other designs, we will seek the role of (1) chance, (2) confounds, and (3) the independent variable in the results of our experiment.

Because a factorial design involves the simultaneous evaluation of two or more factors and their interactions, the evaluation process is more involved than in a single-factor design. For example, in a factorial design there is not one but many null hypotheses. There is a null hypothesis for each factor of our design. As in a simple design, this null hypothesis states that every level of a factor is equal to every other level. In our 2 × 2 example, one null hypothesis would state that Level 1 of factor A is the same as Level 2 of factor A. A second null hypothesis would state that Level 1 of factor B is the same as Level 2 of factor B. A third null hypothesis is also required. This null hypothesis states that there are no interaction effects. It is theoretically possible for any combination of these three null hypotheses in a 2 × 2 design to be accepted or rejected. Once we have made this determination, we can then continue to look for confounds and eventually conclude what effects, if any, the independent variables have on the dependent variable. With more than one independent variable, the logic of searching for confounds is similar to that of the single-factor study, although the complexity is increased.

Let us continue to illustrate factorial designs and their evaluation with a hypothetical experiment. In this experiment we want to study two factors and their effects on the learning ability of old mice (see Warren, Zerwick, & Anthony, 1982, for an actual study in this area). The dependent variable will be the number of errors in running a maze. One factor is whether the mice live in an "enriched" environment, with other mice and many "playthings," or live alone in a standard laboratory cage. The second factor concerns the feeding schedule of these old mice. More specifically, we want to determine whether unlimited access to food and water (called an *ad libitum* or *ad lib* schedule) affects these old mice differently from a feeding of enough food once a day to maintain normal body weight. In our tentative design we have designated the living environment as factor A (with $A_1$ = enriched, $A_2$ = standard) and the feeding schedule as factor B (with $B_1$ = ad lib, $B_2$ = once a day). Consequently, in this design there are four possible combinations of the two independent variables: $A_1B_1$, $A_2B_1$, $A_1B_2$, and $A_2B_2$. This particular design is represented by the matrix in Figure 8.3. Each cell of the matrix contains one of the four possible combinations of our two independent variables.

In actually executing such a factorial design, we would first obtain, say, 40 mice to participate in our experiment. Our subjects would then be randomly assigned to any one of these four possible combinations of independent variables until there was an equal number of subjects in each cell of the matrix. This hypothetical experiment is depicted in Figure 8.4. Next, the subjects in the upper left-hand cell would receive the first level of independent variables A and B ($A_1B_1$ = enriched housing/ad lib feeding). Consequently, their performance on our dependent measure (the number of errors in running a maze) would reflect a combined effect of enriched housing and ad lib feeding. Subjects in the upper right-hand cell of the matrix would receive the second level of independent variable A and the first level of independent variable B ($A_2B_1$ = standard housing/ad lib feeding). Their performance would reflect the influence of standard housing and ad lib feeding. The same holds for the combinations $A_1B_2$ (enriched housing/fed once a day) and $A_2B_2$ (standard housing/fed once a day).

In analyzing the outcome of any factorial design, we are interested in two major questions. First, *does either of our independent variables produce a statistically significant treatment effect?* As mentioned earlier, in a factorial design we call the treatment effect of each independent variable the *main effect* of that

| | | Factor A (living condition) | |
|---|---|---|---|
| | | *$A_1$ (enriched)* | *$A_2$ (standard)* |
| *Factor B (feeding schedule)* | *$B_1$ (ad lib)* | $A_1B_1$ (enriched/ad lib) | $A_2B_1$ (standard/ad lib) |
| | *$B_2$ (once a day)* | $A_1B_2$ (enriched/once a day) | $A_2B_2$ (standard/once a day) |

**Figure 8.3** This matrix shows the four possible combinations of each of the two levels of a 2 × 2 factorial random subject design. Notice that each cell contains one of the four possible combinations of our two independent variables (living condition and feeding schedule).

variable. In the preceding experiment we have two main effects: type of housing and type of feeding schedule. To determine the extent of the main effect of each independent variable, we compare the different levels of each of our two independent variables. We calculate the performance on our dependent measure for each row and column of our matrix.

For example, Table 8.1 shows hypothetical data from 40 old mice tested on our dependent variable following a six-month period of living under our two experimental conditions. To determine the main effect of the type of housing, we compare the mean score for all animals housed in the enriched condition with the mean score for all animals housed in standard cages (10 versus 18 errors in Table 8.1). To determine the main effect of the type of feeding schedule, we compare the mean score for all animals who were fed ad lib with the mean score for all animals who were fed once a day (14 versus 14 errors in Table 8.1). Just from glancing at these data, it appears that the type of housing had a definite effect on the final performance of the old mice on our dependent variable, whereas the type of feeding schedule apparently did not result in differences in performance. These data must be subjected to appropriate statistical tests before drawing any final conclusions regarding the null hypotheses.

The second question we want to ask for a factorial design is: *As our two independent variables occur together, do they influence each other or do they remain relatively independent of one another?* The extent to which the impact of one independent variable varies as a function of the level of the other indepen-

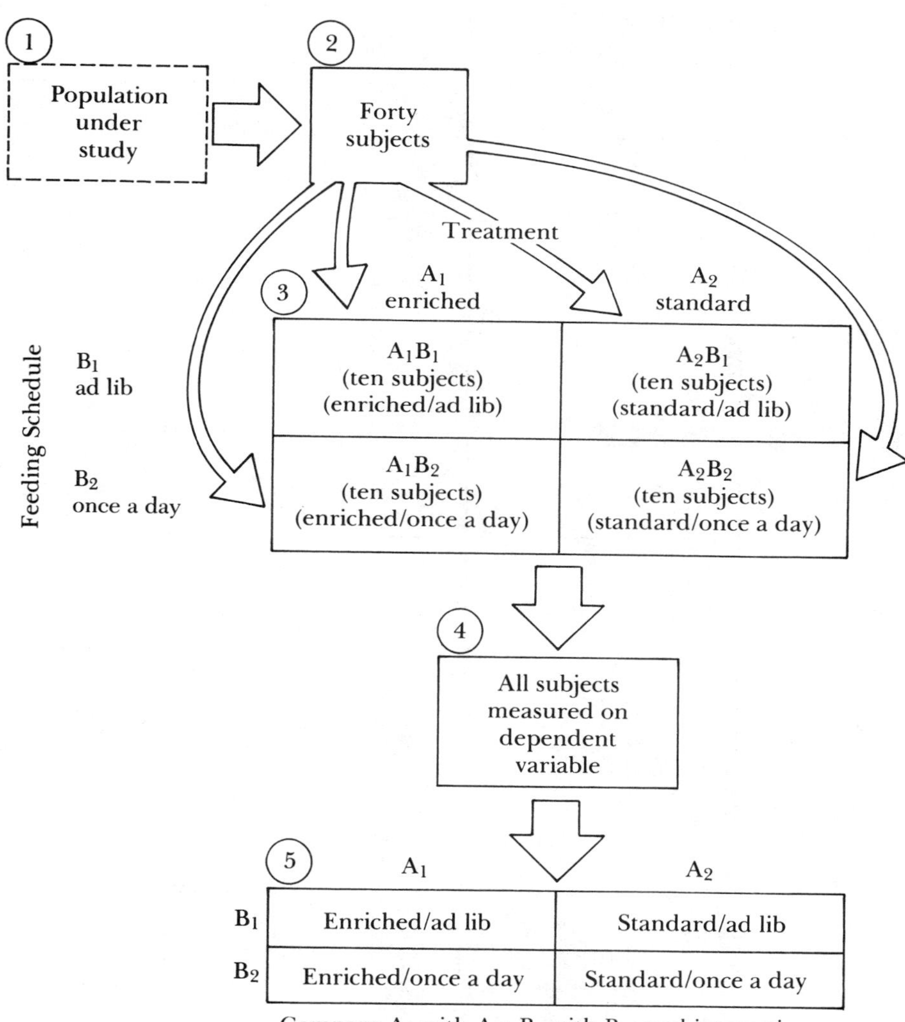


**Figure 8.4** This is a schematic representation of the five steps involved in a factorial random subject design involving two levels of each of two independent variables. (1) The entire group of 40 mice is obtained from a commercial animal supplier. (2) These 40 mice are randomly assigned to four groups of 10 each. (3) Each group is exposed to the appropriate level of each factor. (4) All subjects are measured on our dependent variable. (5) We determine whether the interaction effect and the main effect are statistically significant.

**Table 8.1 Hypothetical Number of Errors on the Dependent Variable for Forty Old Mice**

| *Feeding Schedule* | *Type of Housing* | | *Row Mean* |
|---|---|---|---|
| | *Enriched* | *Standard* | |
| *Ad lib* | 6<br>4<br>8<br>5<br>7<br>7 $\bar{x} = 6$<br>5<br>6<br>4<br>8 | 21<br>23<br>22<br>22<br>24<br>20 $\bar{x} = 22$<br>20<br>24<br>22<br>22 | 14 |
| *Once a Day* | 13<br>15<br>15<br>13<br>18<br>16 $\bar{x} = 14$<br>10<br>12<br>14<br>14 | 14<br>14<br>13<br>15<br>12<br>16 $\bar{x} = 14$<br>14<br>14<br>15<br>13 | 14 |
| *Column Mean* | 10 | 18 | |

dent variable in the experiment is referred to as the *interaction effect.* The manner in which we assess interaction effects involves determining whether the difference between the means of the levels of one independent variable varies as a function of the levels of the other independent variable. (Keep reading; this will become clear.)

Consider the hypothetical data shown in Table 8.1 for the 40 mice tested on the learning task. As we pointed out, animals housed in the enriched environment learned the maze with fewer errors than animals housed in standard cages. In contrast, the type of feeding schedule *did not* have an effect on overall maze performance (14 versus 14 errors). Although there was no overall difference in the mean number of errors for the mice on ad lib versus once a day feeding schedules, the performance of these mice was quite different depending on whether they lived in enriched or standard cages. More specifically, the animals fed once a day all performed about average regardless of housing (14 versus 14 errors). In contrast, the mean performance of the ad lib animals ranged from very good (only 6 errors) for the mice that lived in enriched housing to very poor (22 errors) for the mice that lived alone in standard cages. Thus performance on the learning task showed a strong interaction effect. In this particular case, the ad lib animals were differentially affected by the type of housing, whereas animals fed once a day were uniformly affected by their living conditions.

Let us now turn to an example of an interaction from the research literature. This interaction occurred in an experiment dealing with intimacy, summarized by Rubin (1974). In this experiment, Rubin and Hill wanted to know what effect the amount of perceived freedom or spontaneity has on both high or low levels of intimate behavior. To answer this question, they conducted a laboratory experiment involving written exchanges of self-disclosure statements between dating couples. In other words, the study relates to how you would respond if your boyfriend or girlfriend sent you a message (either very intimate or not very intimate) when you believed that the experimenter told him or her to write the message versus how you would respond when you believed that your boyfriend or girlfriend sent the message spontaneously. As you might predict, the return message (your message back to your boyfriend or girlfriend) was related both to the level of intimacy of the first message and to whether or not the person believed that the boyfriend or girlfriend had produced the message spontaneously or under direction of the experimenter. See if you can draw a graph to illustrate this interaction, generating your own numbers.

When you interpret the results of a factorial experiment, you *always interpret the interaction effects first.* If you think about this for a moment, you will realize that if there is an interaction effect,then the main effects cannot be discussed without a qualifier. This is difficult for some people to understand. However, if you consider the example of the barbiturates and alcohol, you can quickly see that an interaction effect makes it impossible to discuss the effects of either drug alone without qualifying the statement to include the interaction. That is, you can say that moderate drinking does not immediately lead to illness if you include the qualifier that this is true only when barbiturates are not also taken in moderate amounts, and vice versa. To give you another example, if you look at the data in Table 8.1, you can see that it would be inaccurate to conclude that type of housing is an important independent variable without qualifying the statement to say that this is true only if the feeding schedule is ad lib. Thus, the interaction effect must be interpreted before the main effects so that any necessary qualifiers can be added to the main effects.

Let us pause for a moment and examine the form of an analysis of variance summary table that we might see when reading experiments using factorial designs (see Table 8.2). For our present purposes, we are concerned only that you know how to read such a table, and it is not necessary that you understand the calculative procedures. In the first column we see listed the sources of the variance. In a simple experiment such as the cereal experiment described in Chapter 2, there would be two entries in this column. The first would be for the treatment variance due to eating cereal (between-groups variance) and the second would be for the error variance (within-groups variance). In factorial experiments, this column would list the treatment variance due to each independent variable and the interactions. The next column lists the degrees of freedom (*df*) as we discussed in Chapter 4. The third column lists the sum of squares (*SS*). The fourth column lists the mean square (*MS*). *Mean square* is what we call a variance when it comes from the statistic analysis of variance. The fifth column depicts the *F*-ratio, which, as we discussed, is the between-groups variance divided by the within-groups variance (error variance). In a factorial design, you must evaluate the treatment effect for each independent variable and for the interactions involved. Thus, you will have an *F*-ratio for each main effect and interaction. The error term (within-groups variance) remains the same for each *F*-ratio. Often there is an additional column listing the probability ($p$) or if it is nonsignificant (ns). It is based on this probability that we either accept or reject the null hypothesis.

Table 8.2 is the analysis of variance *F*-table for the mouse study presented earlier in this chapter. Based on this table, we would reject the null hypothesis for factor A (housing) and for the A × B interaction (the interaction of housing and feeding schedule). We would not reject the null hypothesis for factor B (feeding). It is rare in actual practice that we obtain an *F*-ratio of less than 1, although it is possible in actual calculations, as was the case for factor B (housing).

After the null hypotheses have been evaluated for the interaction of A × B, the main effect of factor A, and the main effect of factor B, then conceptually one turns to the role of confounds and the independent variable in causing the results. By the way, to make your life interesting, there is a possible confound in the mouse study we just presented. See if you can find it.

**Table 8.2 Analysis of Variance *F*-Table for the Mouse Study**

| *Source of Variance* | *df* | *SS* | *MS* | *F* | *p* |
|---|---|---|---|---|---|
| Housing (factor A) | 1 | 640 | 640 | 245.21 | .001 |
| Feeding (factor B) | 1 | 0 | 0 | 0 | ns |
| A × B (interaction) | 1 | 640 | 640 | 245.21 | .001 |
| Error (within-groups variance) | 36 | 94 | 2.61 | — | — |

Because factorial designs are frequently used in the published reports you will be reading, it will be helpful for you to have some idea of how the main effects and interaction effects are actually manifested in data. With this goal in mind, the next section describes a hypothetical series of eight factorial experimental outcomes. In each case the outcome is depicted in two ways: numerically and graphically. If you are not yet accustomed to dealing with factorial designs, proceed slowly. Allow yourself several careful readings to get a feel for the main effects and interaction effects.

## EIGHT POSSIBLE OUTCOMES OF 2 × 2 FACTORIAL EXPERIMENTS SHOWING DIFFERENT COMBINATIONS OF SIGNIFICANT AND NONSIGNIFICANT MAIN EFFECTS AND INTERACTIONS

The purpose of this section is to clarify the idea of both main effects and interactions in factorial designs. To achieve this goal, we will work directly with specific examples. In each of the examples, a different hypothetical outcome will be described in which either the main effects or the interaction effects may be assumed to be statistically signficant. Box 8.1 presents actual research examples of interaction effects.

The first example is Figure 8.5, in which the same results are shown in two different ways: first numerically and then pictorially. In the left-hand portion of this figure is a matrix. The numbers inside the box represent the outcomes for each of the four groups in a hypothetical experiment. For example, the group that received treatment combination $A_1B_1$ is represented in the upper left-hand cell of the matrix, the group that received condition $A_1B_2$ in the lower left-hand cell, the group that received $A_2B_1$ in the upper right-hand cell, and the group that received $A_2B_2$ in the lower right-hand cell of the matrix. The numbers to the right of the box represent the mean for condition $B_1$ and the mean for condition $B_2$, and the numbers below the box represent the means for conditions $A_1$ and $A_2$, respectively. In the right-hand portion of the figure, the outcome is represented pictorially in graph form. The $x$-axis of this graph—that is, the horizontal axis—indicates groups $A_1$ and $A_2$. The $y$-axis, or vertical axis, of the graph gives the values 10, 20, 30, and so on. In this first example, the outcomes for the four groups are 20, 20, 20, and 20, so obviously there was no main effect and no interaction effect. This same outcome is pictorially represented to the right of Figure 8.5. Those subjects who received treatment combination $A_1B_1$ responded with a dependent variable measure of

---

### *Box 8.1 Research Examples of Interaction Effects*

Bower (1981) summarizes a series of studies on mood and memory. The following graphs were from this 1981 paper.

An experiment by Bower, Monteiro, and Gilligan (1978) produced an interaction similar to that protrayed in Figure 8.8. In this study, college students were hypnotized and put in a happy or sad mood. Once the mood induction had been completed, the students memorized a list of 16 words. After the list was memorized, the opposite mood was induced. The students then learned a second list. At a later time (either 10 minutes or one day), the original mood was again induced and the students recalled the first list. These results are shown below:

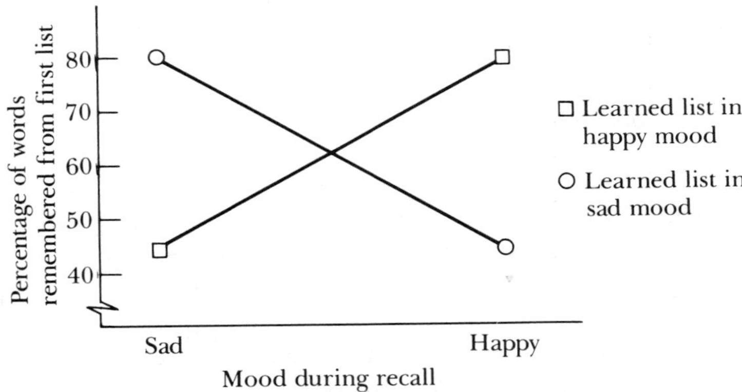


(Figure based on Bower et al., 1978.)

---

20, and this outcome is represented by the triangle above $A_1$ on the $x$-axis. In a similar way, the outcome of group $A_2B_1$ is represented by a triangle above $A_2$ on the $x$-axis. The line connecting these points is intended to highlight the total effect of the first level of condition B. The outcomes from groups $A_1B_2$ and $A_2B_2$ are represented by squares above $A_1$ and $A_2$ on the $x$-axis and are joined by lines to show the total effect of the second level of condition B. In this figure, the results are the same for all groups. Neither the main effects nor the interaction effects are statistically significant. In the right-hand portion, this is indicated by the line representing condition $B_1$ and the line representing $B_2$ falling directly on top of one another. This

---

Does this graph show that subjects could learn more or fewer items when they were in the same mood as when they first learned the list?

A later study by Bower and Gilligan (1979) resulted in an interaction similar to that protrayed in Figure 8.9. In this study subjects were asked to remember personal experiences in either a positive or negative mood. In the description of the remembered event subjects were asked to rate the event as pleasant or unpleasant. These data are presented graphically as follows:

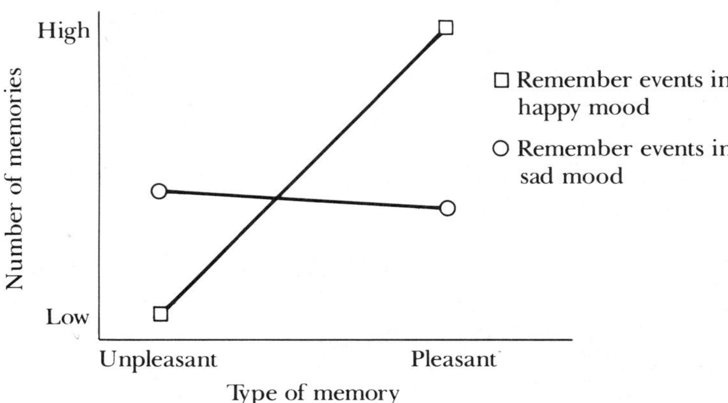


In what type of mood would unpleasant events be most completely remembered?

(Figure based on Bower and Gilligan, 1979.)

---

shows that there is no difference between the main effects of $B_1$ and $B_2$. The fact that $A_1$ and $A_2$ are both equal to 20 is shown by the corresponding points falling at the 20 on the $y$-axis, so in this case nothing is significant.

Figure 8.6 shows a hypothetical condition in which the main effect of A is statistically significant, while the main effect of B and the interaction between A and B are nonsignificant. In the left-hand portion, the mean for condition $B_1$ and the mean for condition $B_2$ are both 30; that is, there is no difference between these two levels of factor B. In contrast, the mean effect of $A_1$ is 20 and the mean effect of $A_2$ is 40. Looking at the figure at the right, we see this graphically. The fact that there is no difference between $B_1$ and $B_2$ is represented by the two lines overlapping. Furthermore, the fact that the midpoint of each line corresponds to a value of 30 on the $y$-axis reflects that 30 is the mean for both levels of condition B. In contrast, the values for $A_1$ and $A_2$ are quite different, which accounts for the slope in the lines

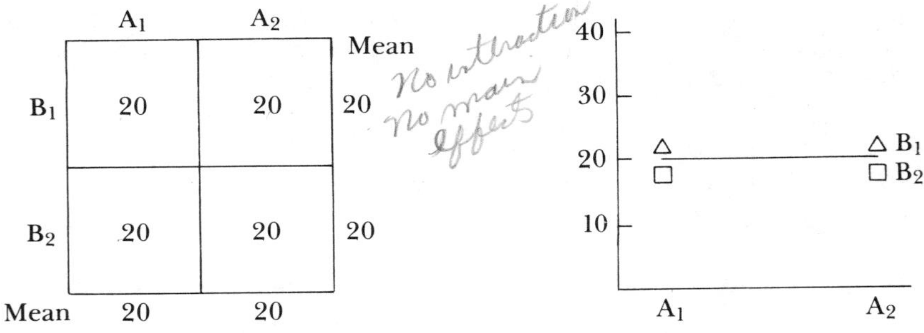


**Figure 8.5** A,B main effects, and interactions are nonsignificant.

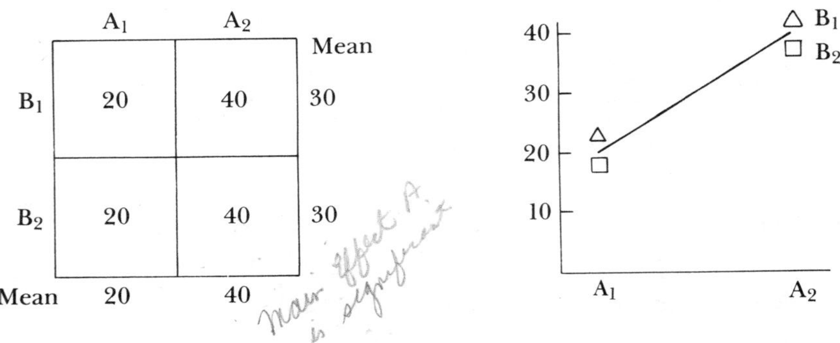


**Figure 8.6** A is significant; B and interactions are nonsignificant.

between 20 and 40 along the *y*-axis. In this case, then, the main effect of A is significant, whereas the main effect of B and the interaction effect are nonsignificant.

Figure 8.7 shows a case in which the main effect of B is significant and the main effect of A and the interaction effect are nonsignificant. There is a large difference between the values of $B_1$ and $B_2$ across conditions $A_1$ and $A_2$. The mean value of $B_1$ is 40. The mean value of $B_2$ is 20. The values of $A_1$ and $A_2$ across both conditions of B are the same—namely 30. In the right-hand portion, these same results are graphically depicted. Two parallel lines occur at 20 and 40 along the *y*-axis. Note also that there is no difference in the mean values of A. The average of both levels is 30.

Figure 8.8 shows a hypothetical example in which the interaction effect is significant and neither A nor B is statistically significant. In this case, the means of levels $A_1$, $A_2$, $B_1$ and $B_2$ are exactly the same—namely 30. This means that $A_1$ and $A_2$ and $B_1$ and $B_2$ are not statistically different from one another. Thus, the main effects of A and B are both nonsignificant. On the other hand, notice that the effect of $B_1$ in the presence of $A_1$ is 40, whereas the effect of $B_1$ in the presence of $A_2$ is 20. For $B_2$, exactly the opposite occurs; that is, for $B_2$ in the presence of $A_1$, the value is 20, whereas in the presence of $A_2$, the value of $B_2$ is 40. Although the mean of each group is the same, the actual value of both levels of B is highly dependent on which level of A is involved. This is what we mean by a strong interaction effect. The same thing is shown in the right-hand portion of the figure. In this case, the line for $B_1$ slopes downward as you move from $A_1$ to $A_2$. In contrast, the line for $B_2$ slopes upward as you move from $A_1$ to $A_2$, and this illustrates that $B_2$ is larger in the presence of $A_2$ so that the effect of $B_1$ and $B_2$ varies depending on whether it occurs in the presence of $A_1$ or $A_2$. Again, this is exactly what we mean by a significant interaction.

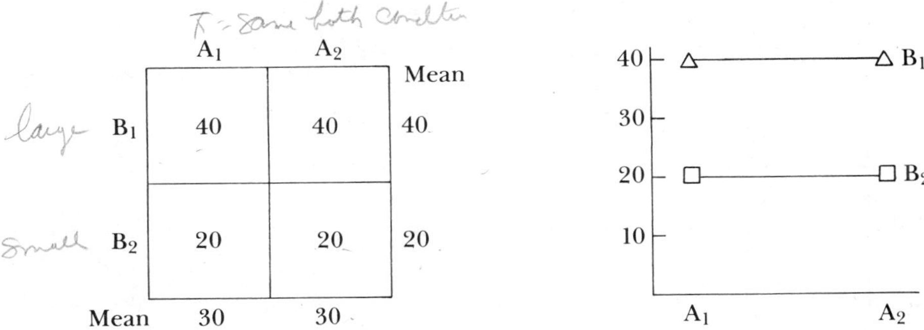


**Figure 8.7** B is significant; A and interactions are nonsignificant.

Before proceeding, note for a moment that in Figures 8.5, 8.6, and 8.7, the lines representing $B_1$ and $B_2$ are parallel. In Figure 8.5 they are parallel and superimposed in the horizontal direction. In Figure 8.6 they are parallel and superimposed in an inclined direction. In Figure 8.7 they are not superimposed but are parallel in the horizontal direction. In each case, the interaction is nonsignificant. In Figure 8.8, however, when the interaction is statistically significant, the lines are not parallel. Indeed, a useful rule of thumb is that whenever the outcome of a factorial experiment involves nonparallel lines, you are probably dealing with a significant interaction effect. This same sort of result can be seen in several of the following examples.

In the next case (Figure 8.9), an example is shown in which the main effect of A and the interaction effect are statistically significant, but the main effect of B is nonsignificant. The means for the two levels of A are 30 and 10, and the means for the two levels of B are 20 and 20. There is also an

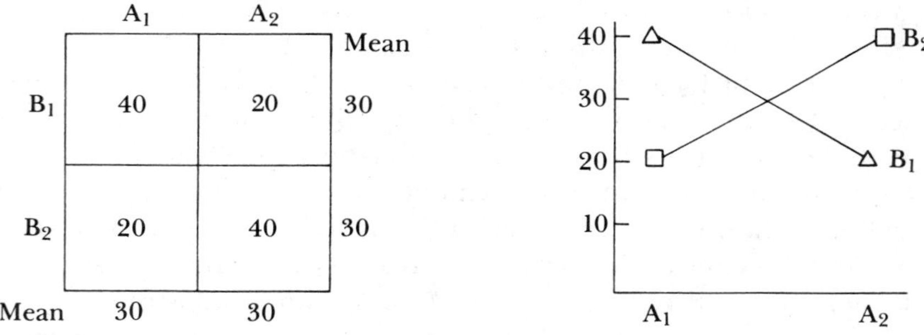

| | $A_1$ | $A_2$ | Mean |
|---|---|---|---|
| $B_1$ | 40 | 20 | 30 |
| $B_2$ | 20 | 40 | 30 |
| Mean | 30 | 30 | |



**Figure 8.8** Interaction is significant; A and B are nonsignificant.

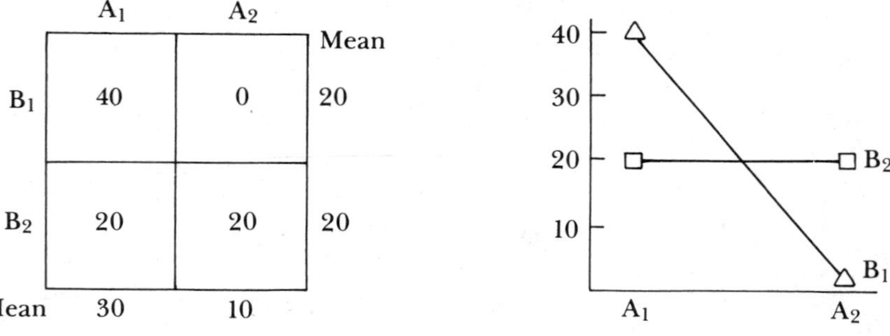

| | $A_1$ | $A_2$ | Mean |
|---|---|---|---|
| $B_1$ | 40 | 0 | 20 |
| $B_2$ | 20 | 20 | 20 |
| Mean | 30 | 10 | |



**Figure 8.9** A and interactions are significant; B is nonsignificant.

interaction effect illustrated by the fact that $B_1$ in the presence of $A_1$ and $A_2$ is markedly different from $B_2$ in the presence of $A_1$ and $A_2$. In one case there is no decrease, and in the other case there is a decrease. The same outcome is depicted in the right-hand portion of the figure. Note that $B_2$ is the same whether in the presence of $A_1$ or $A_2$, whereas the effect of $B_1$ varies considerably depending on whether it is occurring in the presence of $A_1$ or $A_2$. Note also that the lines are not parallel, which, as mentioned above, is a clue that perhaps we are dealing with a significant interaction effect. Remember, interaction simply means that the various levels of the independent variable are not affecting one another in the same way.

Figure 8.10 shows a case in which B and the interaction effect are significant and A is not. The means for $B_1$ and $B_2$ are 10 and 30; the means for $A_1$ and $A_2$ are 20 and 20. In the right-hand portion of the figure, the data are represented by two lines divergent from one another. Note that once again the two lines are not parallel, thus suggesting a possible interaction effect.

In Figure 8.11, the main effects of A and B are statistically significant and the interaction effect is not significant. The mean differences between levels $B_1$ and $B_2$ are 10 and 30, and the means for levels $A_1$ and $A_2$ are also 10 and 30. In the right-hand portion of this figure, this outcome is depicted as two parallel lines rising from left to right. The fact that the lines are parallel demonstrates the lack of an interaction effect.

In Figure 8.12, an outcome is shown in which all main effects and the interaction effects are significant. The means for $B_1$ and $B_2$ are 20 and 30, respectively. The means for $A_1$ and $A_2$ are also 20 and 30, respectively. In the right-hand portion of the figure, we see two nonparallel lines; $B_1$ is the horizontal line representing the scores 20 and 20, and $B_2$ is a rising line from 20 to 40. The fact that at $A_2$ the effect of $B_1$ and $B_2$ is quite different from the effect of $B_1$ and $B_2$ at $A_1$ is consistent with the idea that we are working with a statistically significant interaction.

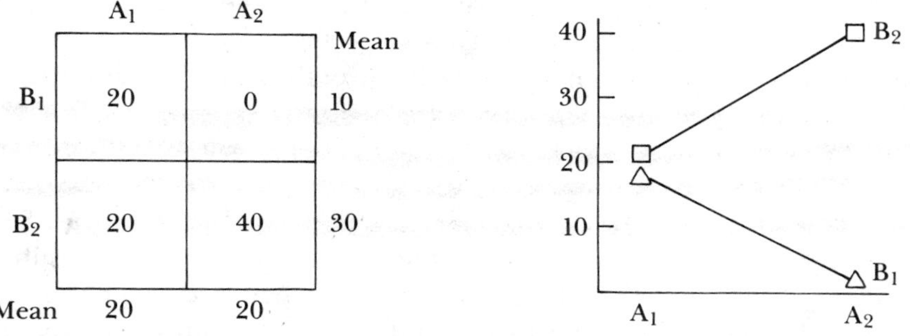


**Figure 8.10** B and interactions are significant; A is nonsignificant.

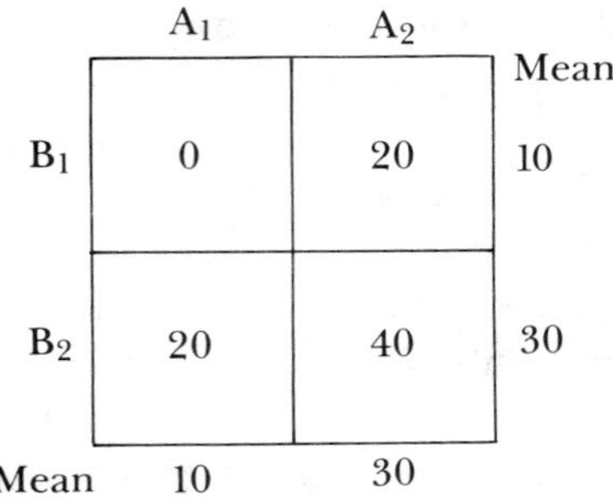

| | $A_1$ | $A_2$ | Mean |
|---|---|---|---|
| $B_1$ | 0 | 20 | 10 |
| $B_2$ | 20 | 40 | 30 |
| Mean | 10 | 30 | |

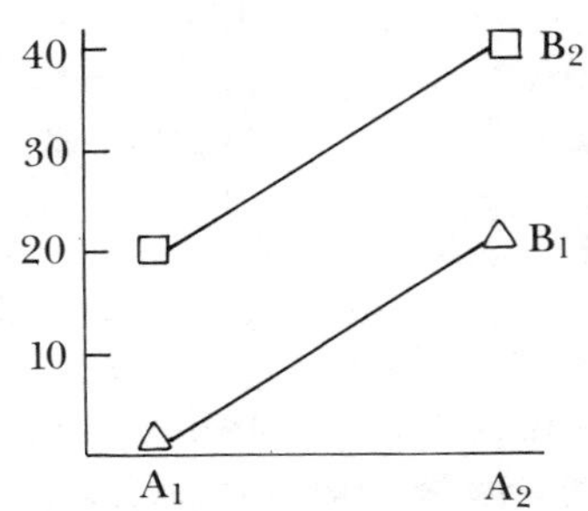


**Figure 8.11** A and B are significant; interaction is nonsignificant.

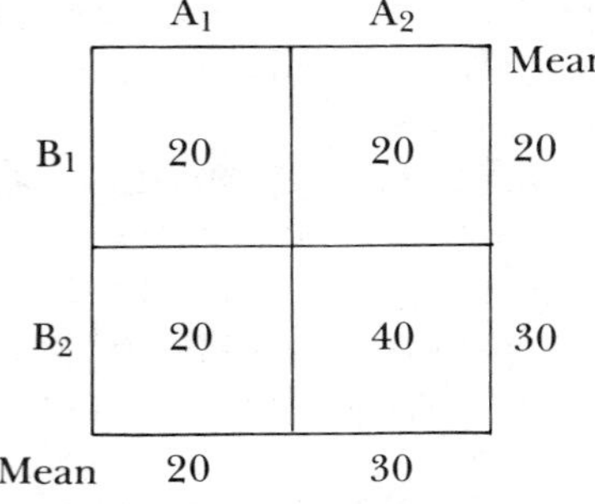

| | $A_1$ | $A_2$ | Mean |
|---|---|---|---|
| $B_1$ | 20 | 20 | 20 |
| $B_2$ | 20 | 40 | 30 |
| Mean | 20 | 30 | |

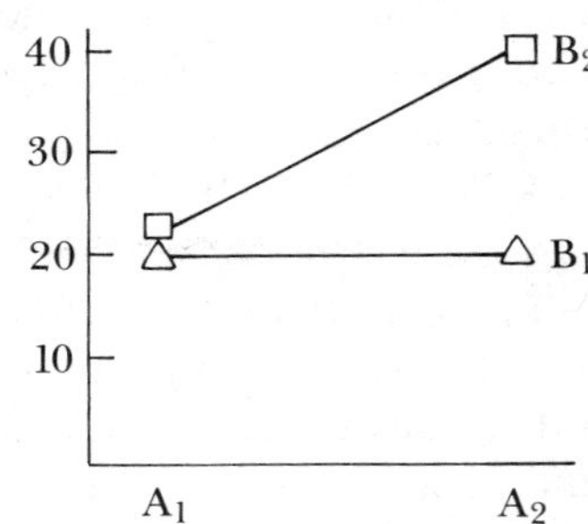


**Figure 8.12** A,B, and interactions are significant.

## THE INTERPRETATION OF SUBJECT VARIABLES WITH FACTORIAL DESIGNS

In this section we want to add a warning based on the type of research in which some students try to use factorial designs. For the logic of experimentation to work best, it is necessary that you be able to randomly assign subjects to groups in such a way that any subject may be placed in any cell of the factorial design. This is not possible if one of the factors in the design is a subject variable. A *subject variable* is a characteristic or condition that a subject is seen to possess in a relatively permanent manner (from the time frame of the experiment). In the broadest sense, any physical or mental characteristic of an individual that can be measured is called a subject variable. Some common examples of subject variables used in research are sex of subject, eye color, being shy or outgoing, having cancer, being schizophrenic, and being intelligent. We could perform a study and choose our subjects according to any of these characteristics. For example, we might ask whether feedback concerning accuracy improves basketball scores differently for men and women. Such a factorial study could be diagramed as follows:

| | No feedback | Feedback |
|---|---|---|
| Males | | |
| Females | | |

Such a design could examine the effect of feedback on making basketball shots. Since the subjects could be randomly assigned to either the feedback or the nonfeedback condition, it would be logical to conclude that feedback did (or did not) affect performance. However, we could not randomly assign subjects to either the male or female condition, since sex is a subject characteristic. Thus if we found differences between men and women, it would not be logical to conclude that the differences were due to sex. For example, men and women may have had different amounts of practice with basketball before the study. As an exercise you might note other possible confounds that could account for differential results between men and women in such a study.

The point we want to make is that when we cannot randomly assign subjects to groups, it is very difficult to control for the previous history of subjects. Thus, the logic of our conclusions becomes weakened and causality is impossible to specify. With this word of caution, we must also point out that the study of subject variables forms a very important part of psychology. For example, many studies in psychology are devoted to the differences between schizophrenics and normals, or males and females, or high-anxiety and low-anxiety subjects, or even children and adults. In such comparisons, the logic of experimentation is considerably weakened and additional control measures are required for a meaningful interpretation of the results. We will return to this point in Chapter 9.

## ADVANTAGES OF FACTORIAL DESIGNS

Before concluding this discussion of factorial designs, it will be useful to point out several strengths of factorial designs. One major strength we have already seen is that we can simultaneously examine more than one hypothesis or factor. This is very important because human behavior is frequently influenced by more than one factor. A second advantage is that because factorial experiments simultaneously evaluate each factor, they are much more economical in number of subjects and total experimenter effort than studying each factor separately. For example, suppose we wanted to investigate two independent variables, each of which has two factors (see Figure 8.13). Furthermore, suppose we wanted 20 subjects to experience each condition. If we used two separate completely randomized designs, a total of 80 subjects would be required, whereas if we used a single 2 × 2 factorial design only 40 subjects would be required. The third and perhaps most important advantage of factorial designs is that by examining the extent of interactions between the different levels of the factors, we can see how the various causal factors influence one another.

## Key Terms and Concepts

1. Between-subjects design
2. Completely randomized design
   a. examples
   b. Bransford and Johnson (1972)
   c. Strupp and Hadley (1979)
3. Factorial designs
   a. 2 × 2
   b. main effects
   c. interaction effect
   d. cells
4. Interpretation of
   a. interaction effects
   b. main effects
5. Advantages of factorial designs

## Summary

1. Between-subjects designs are those that involve comparisons between different groups of subjects.
2. One of the simplest between-subjects design is the completely randomized design, also called the simple randomized design. When such a design contains more than two levels of the independent variable, it is referred to as the multileveled completely randomized design. The Bransford and Johnson memory study presents one illustration of this design.
3. A factoral design allows for the simultaneous assessment of more than one independent variable on the dependent variable. It is one of the most popular designs in psychology.
4. An important aspect of factorial designs is that they allow for the assessment the combined influence of two or more independent variables on the dependent

**A.** Two completely randomized design experiments:

| | Experiment I (money) | | Experiment II (prior knowledge) | |
|---|---|---|---|---|
| | Level 1(1¢) 20 subjects | Level 2 ($1) 20 subjects | Level 1 (no picture) 20 subjects | Level 2 (picture) 20 subjects |
| Total number of subjects for each experiment | 40 | | 40 | |
| Overall total | | | | |

**B.** One 2 × 2 factorial design experiment:

| | | Money: Level 1 (1¢) | Money: Level 2 ($1) | Total subjects across factor A |
|---|---|---|---|---|
| Prior Knowledge | Level 1 (no picture) | 10 | 10 | 20 |
| | Level 2 (picture) | 10 | 10 | 20 |
| | Total subjects across factor B | 20 | 20 | |
| | Overall total | 40 | | |

**Figure 8.13** This figure shows a comparison of subject requirements for (A) two completely randomized experiments and (B) a single 2 × 2 factorial design experiment. Note that the factorial design experiment requires half as many subjects.

variable. This is referred to as an interaction effect. An interaction effect reflects the extent to which one independent variable varies as a function of the level of the other independent variable.

5. Table 8.2 presented an analysis of variance table illustrating the null hypotheses for each independent variable and the interactions between the independent variables.
6. In a factorial design with two independent variables there are three separate null hypotheses—one for each independent variable and one for the interaction effect. A statistically significant interaction may result from a variety of numerical relationships. These were presented graphically toward the end of the chapter.
7. Three advantages of factorial designs are (1) the simultaneous examination of more than one independent variable, (2) economy in the number of subjects and total experimental effort, and (3) the determination of interactions between different levels of effort.

## Review Questions

1. What is a between-subjects design and how is it different from a within-subjects design?
2. What are post hoc tests?
3. What is a factorial design and what is a 2 × 2 design?
4. Describe a 2 × 2 design and explain the terms *main effects* and *interaction effect.*
5. In what order should main effects and interaction effects be interpreted? Why?
6. Describe the different aspects of the analysis of variance table presented in this chapter (Table 8.2).
7. Draw a graph that would reflect a significant interaction effect.
8. What are subject variables and how should they be interpreted in relation to changes in the dependent variable?

## Discussion Questions and Projects

1. Look up the Strupp and Hadley or the Bower research in your library and note how these researchers controlled for possible confounds. (Note: For a review of the Bower research see Bower, 1981.)
2. Develop rules for looking at a graph and determining whether an interaction effect might be present.
3. Develop an experiment in which individuals learn a series of sentences. Before presenting the sentences, give one group something pleasant to drink (e.g., orange juice, cola drink, etc.) and the other group nothing. Graphically present the results and discuss how these data would support the hypothesis that a pleasant experience before a memory task helps recall. When are some alternative ways of interpreting the data that point out potential confounds?

4. Take the design you constructed for the recall experiment in Question 3 and add the variable of the sentences being either simple or complex in meaning. Diagram this study and discuss potential outcomes. Would there be any advantage of performing two separate studies, one looking at the effects of pleasant experiences on recall and one looking at the level of complexity and its effect on recall? Would there be any disadvantages?
5. Construct a study examining factors related to helping behavior. For example you might ask whether the physical appearance of the person in need of help influences how many people help. Now ask whether physical appearance influences men and women differently. How would this study be designed and what conclusion could you draw from the data? What other factors might you need to consider?

CHAPTER NINE

# *Extending the Logic of Experimentation: Within-Subjects and Matched-Subjects Approaches*

## INTRODUCTION

From the onset of our discussion of experimental design in Chapter 6 we have stressed two themes. First, we stressed the logical necessity of beginning our experiments with groups that can be assumed to be equal. Second, we stressed the statistical importance of reducing variation, especially the within-groups variation (error variance) component of the *F*-ratio. In relation to the need for beginning our experiment with equal groups, we suggested that the random assignment of subjects is one of the best techniques for ensuring that no systematic differences are present at the onset of our experiment. In Chapters 7 and 8 we also discussed a number of experimental designs whose logic was based on the random assignment of subjects to groups. However, as we shall see in this chapter, there are times when random assignment alone may not be the most appropriate approach to subject assignment.

In this chapter we will discuss two approaches to experimental design that do not use random assignment alone. The first section of this chapter will be devoted to *within-subjects designs* in which the same subject is used in different experimental conditions. The second section will discuss what are referred to as *matched-subjects designs*. We will discuss how matching can be used both as a control procedure and as an experimental procedure for analyzing differences between groups. As in the previous chapters, we will stress the need for beginning our experiment with equal groups and the importance of reducing the within-groups variance component in the *F*-

ratio. Although the overall logic of experimentation presented in this chapter is similar to that discussed previously, the specific techniques for achieving these goals are slightly different.

## WITHIN-SUBJECTS DESIGNS

In previous chapters we discussed designs that compared the performance of one group of subjects with the performance of a different group of subjects. These designs were referred to as *between-subjects designs.* In *within-subjects designs,* the subject's own performance is the basis of comparison; that is, every subject serves in every group and receives all levels of the independent variable. In these designs, performance on the dependent variable is compared following different treatments on the *same* set of subjects. Let us now quickly illustrate the same experiment performed as both a between-subjects experiment and a within-subjects experiment.

In a simple between-subjects experiment, an experimenter can determine the role of immediate feedback in shooting basketballs by having one group shoot baskets blindfolded (zero level of feedback) and another group shoot without a blindfold (high level of feedback). This is diagramed as follows:

| | | | |
|---|---|---|---|
| R | Group 1 | T(feedback) | M(number of shots made) |
| R | Group 2 | T(zero level of feedback) | M(number of shots made) |

If we further identify individual subjects, this same between-subjects experiment appears as follows:

| | | | | |
|---|---|---|---|---|
| R | Group 1 | Subject 1 | T(feedback) | M(number of shots made) |
| | | Subject 2 | | |
| | | Subject 3 | | |
| | | Subject 4 | | |
| | | Subject 5 | | |
| R | Group 2 | Subject 6 | T(zero level of feedback) | M(number of shots made) |
| | | Subject 7 | | |
| | | Subject 8 | | |
| | | Subject 9 | | |
| | | Subject 10 | | |

We can perform this same study as a within-subjects design in which each subject is exposed to both levels of the independent variable; that is, every subject in the study shoots baskets both with and without a blindfold. We can diagram such a study in a fashion similar to the previous two-group study except that we just list the *same* five subjects in the no-feedback condition, and thus the total experiment is composed of only five subjects.

| | | | |
|---|---|---|---|
| Group 1 | Subject 1 | T(feedback) | M(number of shots made) |
| | Subject 2 | | |
| | Subject 3 | | |
| | Subject 4 | | |
| | Subject 5 | | |
| Group 2 | Subject 1 | T(zero level of feedback) | M(number of shots made) |
| | Subject 2 | | |
| | Subject 3 | | |
| | Subject 4 | | |
| | Subject 5 | | |

For simplicity we usually list the subjects only once in a within-subjects design, as follows:

| | Factor A | |
|---|---|---|
| | Level 1 (zero feedback) | Level 2 (feedback) |
| Subject 1 | | |
| Subject 2 | | |
| Subject 3 | | |
| Subject 4 | | |
| Subject 5 | | |

The within-subjects designs accomplish both of our two goals—equating groups before the presentation of the independent variable and reducing within-groups variance. Since the same subjects are used in each group, we can be certain that before any treatment has been presented, the groups are exactly the same. A within-subjects design also increases the sensitivity of a study by decreasing the within-groups variance (error variance). The logic behind this last statement is that we would expect someone's behavior in a series of different conditions to be more similar than the behavior of various individuals in different conditions. Statistically, the error variance term of the *F*-ratio for a within-subjects design is smaller than that of a comparable between-subjects design. This means that smaller treatment differences are adequate for the rejection of the null hypothesis.

Let us now illustrate a within-subjects design with an actual experiment.

### An Illustration of Within-Subjects Research

The 727 airplane was introduced in the fall of 1965. Although pilots liked the airplane and the early test flights were good, within a year there were four accidents involving the plane (Kraft, 1978). The first accident involved a 727 flying into Chicago from the northeast. This plane began an approach from 22,000 feet and continued to descend until it literally flew into Lake Michigan some 19 miles from the shore. The second accident occurred as a 727 flew into the Cincinnati area from the east. To make the landing, the plane had to fly over the river at night and land on a built-up runway. Unfortunately, the plane attempted to land some 12 feet below the level of the runway. The third accident happened as a 727 approached Salt Lake City from the south. From the airplane, the lights of Salt Lake City could be seen past the runway and to the right. In front of the runway it was dark. This airplane also attempted to land short of the runway. The fourth accident occurred as a 727 attempted to land in Tokyo. It was a clear night so the pilot decided to use the flight rules for visual landings (VFR) rather than for instrument landings (IFR). The pilot began the descent over Tokyo Bay with the lights of the city visible. The descent was abruptly halted when the plane hit the water of Tokyo Bay 6½ miles east of the runway.

What happened? Assume that you are a psychologist called to help determine what caused the accidents. How would you go about this? First, you need to rule out mechanical problems with the airplanes, especially the altimeters (meters that indicate altitude). After other experts eliminate mechanical problems as a cause, you might look to the manner in which the planes were being flown by the pilots. You might also look for any pattern of events present at each of the accidents. The initial clues that you find are (1) all accidents happened at night, (2) the pilots were all operating under visual rather than instrument flight rules, (3) the instruments did not appear to be malfunctioning, and (4) each approach required pilots to fly over dark areas with lights in the distance.

Conrad Kraft, a researcher for the Boeing Company, reports that from this information it was hypothesized that the problem was a miscalculation of space perception on the part of the pilots. This hypothesis suggested that the pilots saw the equivalent of a visual illusion, which resulted in their misjudging the location of the ground. Analysis of the accidents also suggested that for various reasons—for example, looking for another airplane—the pilots had been distracted from their instruments. In the factorial language presented in the preceding chapter, we would guess that the plane crashes were the result of an interaction effect; that is, they were caused by a visual illusion but only when the pilots were distracted from the instruments. To determine whether this was the case, we could perform a simple $2 \times 2$ design with one level of factor A being the necessary conditions for the visual illusion (clear night, no lights before the runway, and lights in the distance) and the second level being a zero level of these conditions. The first level of factor B would be pilot distraction from instruments and the second level would be a zero level of distraction. We could schematically represent this factorial design as follows:

| | | Conditions Necessary for Visual Illusion | |
|---|---|---|---|
| | | Presence $A_1$ | Absence $A_2$ |
| Distraction from Instruments | Presence $B_1$ | | |
| | Absence $B_2$ | | |

The dependent variable in such a factorial design would be the amount of landing error. Because flying can be simulated on flight simulators, this entire study could be performed in the laboratory, which would both save money and control for environmental factors such as wind speed and pressure level. Using a *between-subjects design,* we would randomly assign pilots to one of the four possible conditions ($A_1B_1$, $A_1B_2$, $A_2B_1$, $A_2B_2$). We could then conduct the study and determine any interaction or main effects.

Let us think about the realities of this situation for a moment and see whether a *between-subjects design* is really the best alternative. One factor we must consider is the subject population. In this example we are interested in a rather special population—pilots who fly 727 airplanes. Thus it seems somewhat wasteful, in terms of both time and money, to bring a large number of subjects to the laboratory just to make one landing in the simulator. We would more likely want to collect as much data as possible from the pilots. A second consideration is to make the experimental and control groups as similar as possible. Are there any factors that we do *not* want to vary systematically between our groups? Experience with night flying in general, or with the 727 aircraft in particular, might be one such factor. One solution to both considerations would be to use a *within-subjects* design. This would answer our first consideration by having each pilot serve in every condition. It would address our second consideration by allowing each pilot to serve as his or her own control. Allowing each pilot to serve as a subject in each of the groups would automatically equate the groups for such factors as total flying time and knowledge of the 727 airplane. We can schematically represent such a within-subjects design exactly as we would a between-subjects design *except* that each cell is composed of the same subjects.

### Advantages and Disadvantages of Within-Subjects Designs

There are several advantages to within-subjects designs that have been previously mentioned. To begin, because the same subjects serve in each group, this experimental procedure ensures that all groups are equal on every factor at the beginning of the experiment.

An additional benefit derived from using a within-subjects design is that the total number of subjects can be reduced dramatically. For example, in the simulator study just described, rather than using the 12 subjects per cell (4 cells × 12 subjects = 48 total subjects) that would be necessary in a between-subjects design, we could use a total of 12 in the entire experiment by using a within-subjects design. The advantages in terms of the number of subjects become even greater as the complexity of the design increases (for example, a 2 × 3 × 2 design).

Another advantage to within-subjects designs is that they are statistically more sensitive to changes in the treatment effect. Why is this so? Most of the error variance in psychological studies results from differences between individuals who take part in the study. Within-subjects studies reduce this source of variance by using the same subject in every condition. Because of this, in the *F*-ratio a smaller within-subjects variance term is used. The within-subjects variance term is derived by taking the within-subjects variance as it would be found in a between-subjects design and subtracting an estimate of how consistent subjects are over the different treatment conditions. This means that the *F*-ratio for within-subjects designs is more *sensitive* to changes in the treatments; that is, given the *same* treatment difference, we would be more likely to reject the null hypothesis with a within-subjects design than with a between-subjects design.

Before you throw out the last chapter and center your research career around within-subjects designs, let us consider some of their disadvantages. Remember, experimental designs are plans for helping us to answer research questions, and some questions cannot be appropriately answered by a within-subjects design. For example, if a treatment has any lasting effects on the subjects, then a within-subjects design is inappropriate. To illustrate this point, consider the outcome of the Bransford and Johnson study as a within-subjects design. Each subject would both be shown the picture and not be shown the picture. Clearly, seeing the picture would have a carryover or residual effect when subjects were asked to remember the passage in the no-picture condition. Clinical treatment studies, such as the Strupp and Hadley psychotherapy study or a drug treatment study, would also be difficult to interpret with a within-subjects design. That is, if the same subject in the Strupp and Hadley study received counseling from both an experienced therapist and a college professor, it would be difficult to determine which changes in the subject should be attributed to which counselor. Thus, the within-subjects design is not appropriate either when the treatment has a lasting effect or the purpose of the study is to test for a lasting effect.

Another disadvantage of within-subjects designs is that they are extremely sensitive to time-related effects. To illustrate this, consider a simple learning study in which the independent variable is the complexity of the material learned. The subjects could be given different sets of materials to learn, each set progressively harder. If the material is presented in this order, can you see any confound that would make interpretation difficult? One possible confound might be fatigue; that is, by the time the subjects reach the difficult material, they may be tired. The results would then be due not only to the independent variable (complexity) but also to being tired (a confound). Another confound that could give us an opposite result is practice; that is, each time the subjects perform the experimental tasks, they may become better through practice. The effects brought about through continued repetition of the tasks, whether they are increases or decreases, are referred to as *practice effects*.

In many cases, order and time can be controlled (not eliminated) through such procedures as *counterbalancing*. Counterbalancing assures that every possible sequence appears at each presentation of the treatment. For example, we could counterbalance the complexity learning study mentioned above so that in the first presentation of the independent variable the first subject would receive the easy level, the second subject the medium level, and the third the hard level (assuming there are three levels). In the second presentation the first subject would receive the medium level, the second subject the hard level, and the third subject the easy level. The third presentation would have the first subject receive the hard level, the second the easy, and the third the medium, and so forth. This is illustrated as follows:

| | | | |
|---|---|---|---|
| Subject 1 | easy | medium | hard |
| Subject 2 | medium | hard | easy |
| Subject 3 | hard | easy | medium |
| Subject 4 | easy | hard | medium |
| Subject 5 | hard | medium | easy |
| Subject 6 | medium | easy | hard |

Note that there are only six possible orders in this design. This would control for such time-related effects as improved performance through practice or decreased performance through fatigue or boredom. Counterbalancing will not control for a *differential order* effect, however, such as would be the case if the Bransford and Johnson study was presented as a within-subjects experiment; that is, if one particular order differentially affects the results, then counterbalancing will not control for this confound. For example, to present the picture condition before the no-picture condition in the Bransford and Johnson study would produce a different effect from presenting the no-picture condition first. This type of confound cannot be controlled through counterbalancing and would also be inevitable in drug or clinical treatment studies such as the Strupp and Hadley psychotherapy study.

### Repeated Measures

One common application of within-subjects designs uses repeated measures as one factor in a factorial design. The design is useful in studying psychological processes that occur over time. For example, this design is widely used in studying human and animal learning processes. We might have levels of problem difficulty as one factor (easy versus difficult problems), and the other factor might be the number of trials (the repeated measure factor). The dependent variable in such a study could be the number of problems solved correctly. This design would tell us whether there are differences in the number of problems solved over repeated trials—that is, whether the two levels of difficulty are mastered at different rates. In this case we use repeated measures to study the process of learning or practice effects directly. At other times we use a repeated measures design as a control technique to ensure that learning or practice effects are not present in our study.

## MIXED DESIGNS

Probably the most common design used in psychological research combines a between-subjects design with a within-subjects design. Designs that include both "within" and "between" components are referred to as *mixed designs*. For example, assume we want to perform a biofeedback experiment to determine the effect of feedback on our ability to control heart rate. One factor is the amount of feedback—either total or partial feedback. Should we use a between-subjects or a within-subjects design? If one can learn the ability to control heart rate, there could be a carryover effect or a transfer of training from one condition to the other, especially if a subject learned to control heart rate with total feedback first. This suggests that it would be better to use a between-subjects design and to assign subjects randomly to two groups—one that receives total feedback and one that receives partial feedback. We might also want to look at the effects of this training over a period of days. Thus our second factor would be a repeated measures component consisting of the number of days. Such an experiment is diagramed as follows:

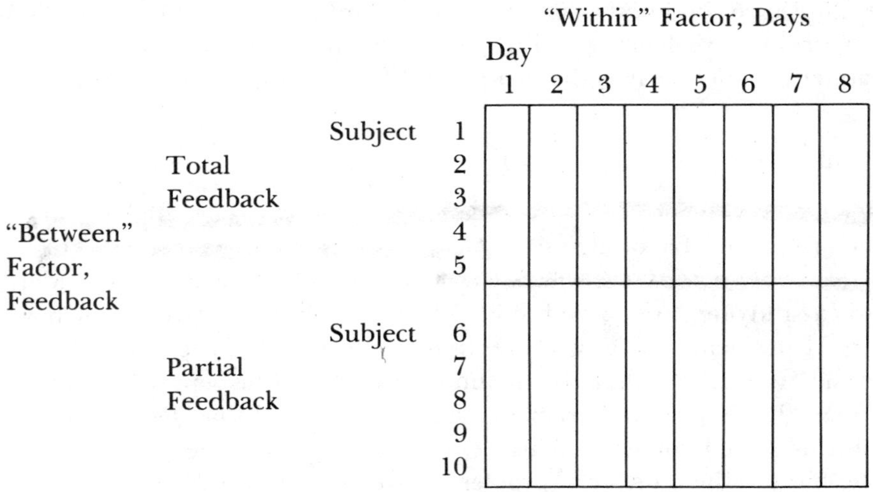

| | | | "Within" Factor, Days | | | | | | | |
|---|---|---|---|---|---|---|---|---|---|---|
| | | | Day 1 | 2 | 3 | 4 | 5 | 6 | 7 | 8 |
| "Between" Factor, Feedback | Total Feedback | Subject 1 | | | | | | | | |
| | | 2 | | | | | | | | |
| | | 3 | | | | | | | | |
| | | 4 | | | | | | | | |
| | | 5 | | | | | | | | |
| | Partial Feedback | Subject 6 | | | | | | | | |
| | | 7 | | | | | | | | |
| | | 8 | | | | | | | | |
| | | 9 | | | | | | | | |
| | | 10 | | | | | | | | |

The "within" factor in a mixed design is not limited to a temporal factor such as days or trials, although this is one of the more common choices.

The statistical analysis of mixed designs is complicated because they use different error terms in the $F$-ratio. The error variance for the "between" comparison (level of feedback in our example) is computed differently from that of the "within" comparison (days in our example). Although a discussion of these statistical procedures is beyond this presentation, the logic of the $F$-ratio remains the same and you must still interpret the role of the independent variable and rule out the role of chance and confounds in the results.

## MATCHED-SUBJECTS PROCEDURES

In this section we will examine matching as a procedure for accomplishing the goals of equating groups in an experiment and of reducing the within-groups variance (error variance). To help us in this discussion, we build upon the logic of the within-subjects design. As you remember, within-subjects experiments equate groups by using the same subject in every treatment condition. Likewise, by using the same subjects in each group, the within-groups variance is reduced since a given individual will perform more consistently in different situations than different individuals will perform in different situations. What if, rather than using the same subjects, we use subjects who are very similar in different groups? By this procedure we could reap some of the advantages of within-subjects designs and simultaneously take advantage of the random assignment of subjects that is possible with a between-subjects design. Our first task would be to find subjects who are very much alike. We might use twins, for example, whom we would expect to perform more similarly on a variety of tasks than strangers since they are more alike physiologically. If we randomly assign one twin to the experimental group and the other twin to the control group, we should be able to equate our groups at the beginning of the experiment as well as reduce within-groups variance (error variance). However, since we cannot use twins in every study we perform, an alternative is to *match* subjects. If we pair subjects along some factor and then randomly assign one subject to each of two groups, we can likewise assume our groups are equal at the beginning of the experiment as well as reduce within-group variance (error variance).

In terms of error variance, by this method we create a type of design that is a hybrid of within-subjects designs and between-subjects designs. We would not have as much error variance as in a between-subjects design or as little error variance as in a within-subjects design. Obviously, the characteristics we use to match our groups of subjects are of central importance to this design.

In the broadest sense, any physical or mental characteristic of an individual that can be measured may be used for matching. Thus, characteristics such as height, weight, intelligence, anxiety level, achievement motivation, hair color, and emotional sensitivity are all subject characteristics that can be measured. Consequently, they are all potential subject variables on which matching can be based. Is there a criterion for choosing the subject variable on which the subjects will be matched? Yes. For a matching procedure to work, there must be a high correlation between the variable used for matching and the dependent variable. If the subjects are matched on a factor that does not correlate with the dependent variable, then the within-groups variance will be no smaller than the variance obtained by random selection alone, and the amount of effort required for matching will have been wasted.

Matching can be used in one of two major ways. First, it can be used as a control procedure. We introduced you to this idea in Chapter 7 in the time estimation experiment. Since there were reported differences between men and women in their ability to estimate time, it was suggested that these differences might be controlled for by assigning an equal number of men and women to each group. In this way the groups were matched by sex. However, we did not analyze the sex factor in that example. If we had analyzed the sex factor, we would have illustrated the second use of matching—that of an experimental procedure. We will discuss this use in more detail as we introduce you to matching as an experimental procedure in this chapter. Although it would be technically correct to refer to this second use of matching only as an experimental design as contrasted with a control procedure, few researchers follow this procedure.

### Matching as a Control Procedure

When we know that a particular subject variable or characteristic has a high correlation with the dependent variable, equal groups may be obtained by matching along this characteristic. The task of actually forming matched groups of subjects consists of two major steps. First, pairs of subjects are matched on some measure that is correlated with performance on the dependent variable. Second, each member of the pair is randomly assigned to either the experimental or the control group. Such a design can be schematically represented as follows:

| | | | |
|---|---|---|---|
| MR | Group 1 | T | M |
| MR | Group 2 | T (zero level) | M |

Notice that we placed an M before the R to denote that the subjects were matched before they were randomly assigned to groups. In essence, we have a completely randomized design.

As you remember from Chapter 7, in the time estimation experiment we matched subjects according to sex and then randomly assigned subjects to groups such that there was an equal number of each sex in each group. In this study, matching took place according to sex—a nominal scale of measurement.

Let us look at another example of matching as a control procedure. In this illustration the matching takes place along an ordinal scale of measurement. Suppose we are interested in neurochemical changes that result from prolonged periods of sensory deprivation. For a number of reasons we decide to use monkeys. Since monkeys are difficult to obtain, we decide to use as few subjects as possible. To control for potential bias in the groups, we might decide to match along a dimension that is highly correlated with our dependent variable—a certain amino acid in the brain, for example. The overall procedure is presented in Figure 9.1. We begin by performing a blood chemistry analysis of our monkeys and then rank order them on the basis of this analysis. After we complete the initial rank ordering, we pair the animals (for a two-group study) according to the rankings. We begin with the two animals that have the highest rankings and then go to the next two and so on. We then randomly assign one member of each pair to one group and the other to the second group and proceed with the experiment.

### Matching as an Experimental Procedure

In the previous examples of matching as a control procedure, subjects are matched according to some factor (subject variable) but the factor itself is not analyzed. It is possible to analyze the matching factor, however. When the matching factor is analyzed, the resulting procedure is traditionally referred to as a *randomized block design*. The term *block* in this case refers back to the development of the design by Sir Ronald Fisher when he studied agricultural procedures on different blocks of land. Let us now discuss how the

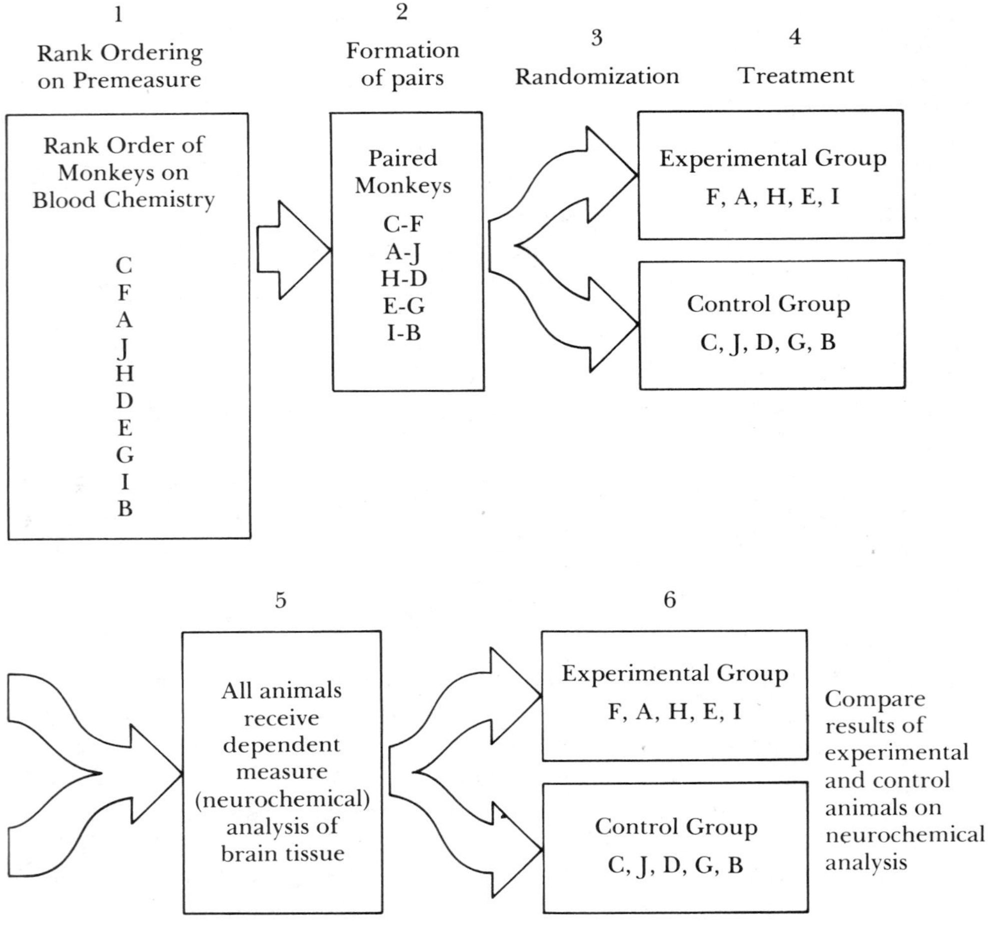


**Figure 9.1** This figure schematically represents the six major steps in a matched-subjects design used to study changes in brain chemistry resulting from prolonged sensory deprivation. (1) Rank order all subjects on the aspects of blood chemistry that are known to be correlated with brain neurochemistry. (2) Form pairs of subjects on the basis of order in the initial ranking. (3) Randomly assign one member of each pair to the experimental group and one member to the control group. (4) Conduct the experimental treatments. (5) Conduct neurochemical analyses. (6) Compare the results for the experimental and control animals. Note that except for our ranking and matching procedures, the design is similar to the completely randomized designs discussed earlier.

matching factor can be described and used experimentally. To begin, let us again schematically represent a randomized design in which matching is used as a control factor. Take the time estimation study, for example, in which an equal number of men and women are placed in each group. We might diagram such a design as follows:

| | | | |
|---|---|---|---|
| MR | Group 1 (males and females) | T | M |
| MR | Group 2 (males and females) | T (zero level) | M |

We could further break down this design as

| | | | |
|---|---|---|---|
| Group 1 | Males | T | M |
| Group 1 | Females | T | M |
| Group 2 | Males | T (zero level) | M |
| Group 2 | Females | T (zero level) | M |

At this point it is possible to convert this experiment into a two-factor factorial design and to analyze the factor of sex. Such a factorial design is diagramed as follows:

| | | Factor A: Level 1 | Factor A: Level 2 (zero level) |
|---|---|---|---|
| Factor B, Sex | Males | | |
| | Females | | |

As we have discussed, we can now analyze for the main effect of Factor A, the main effect of Factor B, and the interaction of A × B. It must be remembered that the factor according to which the subjects are classified is not a factor on which the subjects were randomly selected, and it must be interpreted with caution. If there is a significant main effect for this factor, we may be able to conclude that there is a relationship between this factor and the dependent variable, but we cannot conclude that the relationship is a *causal* one. However, this does not mean that we want to ignore the classification factor. Especially if there is an interaction between the classification variable and the treatment variable, there is much information to be gained. Such an interaction will tell us to what groups and under what conditions the findings of a particular study may be generalized. For example, in a study of the effects of feedback on performance, Ray, Katahn, and Snyder (1971) divided subjects into high- and low-anxiety groups and then randomly assigned them to either a high-feedback condition (feedback on the number correct after each study trial) or a low-feedback condition (feedback only after a series of study trials). It was found in this study that there was no difference between anxiety groups when feedback was given at the end of a series of trials, but there was a difference when feedback was given at the end of each trial. With feedback after each trial, the low-anxiety group increased the number of items learned more than the high-anxiety group. Such an interaction may be valuable in generalizing from this particular study to other studies concerning the role of feedback in learning.

In addition to the knowledge gained from the interaction effect, we have discussed two other advantages acquired through the prior matching of subjects to groups. The first is ensuring that the groups in a study are equal before the introduction of the treatment. This equating of groups is especially valuable for those situations in which we have only a limited number of subjects yet we cannot use a within-subjects design. The second advantage of matching subjects is that it reduces the within-groups variance (error variance) and thus makes our design more sensitive to treatments than a comparable between-subjects design. However, this is possible only when the matching factor has a high correlation with the dependent variable.

Before we leave this section, let us briefly introduce you to more sophisticated terminology concerning what has traditionally been referred to as the randomized block design. Glass and Stanley (1970) suggest that we reserve the term *blocking* for cases in which the matching takes place on a nominal scale factor such as sex. They also suggest that the use of twins be likewise considered a nominal scale factor. When the matching uses ordinal measurements such as ranking, Glass and Stanley suggest that the term *stratifying* be used. An experiment that ranks subjects into high, medium, and low socioeconomic classes is one example of a stratifying variable. When interval or ratio scales are used, then Glass and Stanley suggest that the term *leveling* be used. Some common examples are dividing subjects according to intelligence levels (high, medium, and low), anxiety levels, or depression levels. It must be remembered that although the groups are developed in terms of subject variables—the members of each of the blocks, strata, or levels—it is still necessary to randomly assign subjects to treatment conditions.

## Key Terms and Concepts

1. Within-subjects designs
2. Practice effects
3. Counterbalancing
4. Repeated measures
5. Mixed designs
6. Matched-subjects procedures
   a. as a control procedure
   b. as an experimental procedure
7. Randomized block design
8. Subject factors
9. Terminology of randomized block designs
   a. blocking
   b. stratifying
   c. leveling

## Summary

1. Within-subjects designs are those in which every subject serves in every group and receives all levels of the independent variable. Performance on the dependent variable is compared following different treatments on the same set of subjects.
2. There are a number of advantages to within-subjects designs. Since each subject serves in every group, all groups are equated at the beginning of the experiment. Another advantage is that fewer subjects are needed than would be the case in a similar between-subjects design. Within-subjects designs are statistically more sensitive to changes in the treatment effect and this adds another advantage to within-subjects designs.
3. Problems with within-subjects designs include their sensitivity to time-related factors. Also, they cannot be used when a treatment has a lasting effect on the subject.
4. A mixed design is one that combines both "within" and "between" designs, as illustrated by a study that compared differences between two different groups of subjects over a number of days.
5. A matched subjects procedure may be used either as a control procedure or an experimental procedure, in which case the matching factor is statistically analyzed. Matching used as an experimental procedure has traditionally been referred to as a randomized block design.

## Review Questions

1. Name some advantages of within-subjects designs.
2. In what situations would you not use a within-subjects design?

3. What is a practice effect and why is it important?
4. For which effects will counterbalancing control? For which will it not control?
5. Give an example of the use of repeated measures.
6. What is a mixed design? Give an example.
7. Discuss matching as a control and as an experimental procedure.
8. Discuss random assignment to groups and the results from not assigning subject in this manner.

## Discussion Questions and Projects

1. Discuss those situations in which within-subjects designs are particularly useful.
2. Using an overhead projector and colored pens, it is easy to construct a transparency that will demonstrate the Stroop effect. Construct an experiment to determine whether it is easier for students to read the names of the colors while they are tapping their right index finger or their left index finger. Discuss how you might design this experiment to look for sex differences.
3. What would be advantages of performing the experiment in Question 2 as a within-subjects experiment?
4. Why is error variance reduced in a within-subjects experiment?
5. Discuss research areas in which within-subjects designs would be difficult to use, and explain why.
6. Assume that a company is interested in finding which of three visual illusions airline pilots are most sensitive to, and hires you to help construct such a study. How would you go about it? Would you want to counterbalance? Outline your study and then describe potential confounds and how you controlled for them.
7. A company introduces a new beer. In three identical cups labeled "A", "B", and "C", the new beer and two other brands are placed before the subject. The subject is instructed to taste each beer and chose a preference. What would be the problems with using this procedure, and how could these be corrected?

CHAPTER TEN

# The Ecology of the Experiment: The Scientist and Subject in Relation to Their Environment

## INTRODUCTION

In this chapter we want to move beyond our consideration of specific designs to a discussion of the context in which psychological research takes place. By *context,* we mean not only the particular laboratory or setting where the research is conducted but also the worlds in which scientists and subjects live outside of the experiment. Some of our initial discussions in this book related to performing a science of behavior and experience. We suggested that science can be viewed from three separate perspectives: that of the scientist, the subject, and the witness.

In the previous chapters we emphasized the role of the scientist and the manner in which he or she interacts with the subject matter of psychology through research. As you have learned, it is the scientist who plays an active role in science by the type of questions he or she asks, the methods by which these questions are answered, and the types of answers that are ultimately acceptable. We were particularly interested in helping you learn as a scientist to make accurate statements through experimental procedures. In doing this, we were talking to you from the perspective of the scientist.

We are equally interested in helping you make valid statements from a broader perspective. Not only will we discuss methods for performing more valid experiments as seen from the perspective of the scientist, but we will also give you a clearer picture of how the humanness of both the scientist and the subject influences the actual conduct of the experiment. If these factors are not taken into consideration, both the internal and external validity of an experiment may be severely threatened. To facilitate conveying these issues, we will now shift our perspective to include that of the witness, who observes the interplay between the scientist and the subject.

We realize that for some individuals the perspective of the witness is frustrating, since it reminds us of aspects of science that are beyond our control as methodologists and contradicts the picture of science as completely objective. However, as a careful reading of history will show, science has never been and probably never will be completely objective. Science is, as we have tried to show you throughout this book, a means for helping us as people to explore, passionately at times, the world in which we live and to come to some understanding of this world. In our better moments, science may offer us a means of transcending some of our limitations as human beings. Yet most often science faithfully reflects our humanness and thus our limitations as well. It is the viewpoint of the witness that, through an observation of the interactions of the scientist and the subject, helps us to understand the value and relevance as well as the limitations of any new information that our research produces.

In this chapter we will look at how some of these limitations affect science from the perspective of the witness. As scientists we can control for some limitations; others we can only accept for what they are—limitations. In this vein, we will consider the psychological worlds of the scientist and of the subject and how these might influence either collectively or separately the outcome of psychological research.

The consideration of subject-scientist interactions is so important that some researchers believe all human experimentation is really a social event that should be viewed from a broad perspective (Petrinovich, 1979). This focus is important both for the broad perspective it gives us of psychological research and as a means of understanding and perhaps even eliminating potential biases that enter into the process of research with or without the knowledge of the scientist. To study the relationship among the scientist, the subject, and the experimental environment, we will refer by analogy to the science of ecology.

## ECOLOGY

*Ecology*, a term coined more than 100 years ago, is defined as the scientific study of the relationship of living organisms with each other and their environment (Miller, 1975). Most students are familiar with the word *ecology* as it is applied to the relationship between humans and their environment. For example, we may find by following the food chain that if certain chemicals are used to kill weeds on a farmer's field, the same chemicals might later appear in the breast milk that mothers feed their babies. In the 1970s it was shown that when an atomic explosion took place in China, the fallout could be found in the milk consumed by people in Philadelphia. We have also seen that decreases in the population of one type of animal, the lion for example, have led to increases in another animal such as the deer. The general lesson we have learned from the study of ecology is that all parts of nature are closely interconnected and that it is impossible to make environmental changes without affecting the entire system, at least to some extent.

In the same way that we can discuss the ecology of nature by looking at the interrelationships between humans and their environment, we can discuss the ecology of the psychological experiment and examine the relationships among the scientist, the subject, and the experimental situation. By using the word *ecology*, we emphasize that there are ongoing dynamic interactions among the scientist, subject, and context that must be considered before a complete understanding of experimental psychology is possible. Without this complete understanding of the ecological aspects of the scientific context, our conclusions and theoretical ideas may be invalid. From this perspective, we can introduce the concept of *ecological validity*.

Ecological validity asks whether the impact of the important relationships among the scientist, the subject, and the context has been fully considered in evaluating a given piece of research. As we will see in this chapter, this includes the relationship of the scientist and the subject to each other and to the particular research being conducted, as well as to the greater context of the society in which each lives and works. The motivation of the witness, somewhat like that of a consumer protection agency, is not to suggest that no scientific study can ever be acceptable, but rather to offer considerations and at times outright warnings concerning the ecological validity of science. Just as no consumer product or service has been developed that will give perfect results each time, there will never be the perfect scientific experiment. Remember, our goal in science is not to perform a perfect experiment but *to use science to ask questions and to increase our understanding of a given phenomenon.* When used in an appropriate manner, science is one of the most powerful tools we have. When used out of context or in a haphazard manner, it is important that considerations and even warning labels be prominently attached. Let us now turn to some of the considerations to be made when assessing *ecological validity.*

## EXPERIMENTER FACTORS

One initial warning in the acceptance and generalizability of research is the possibility of scientist or *experimenter effects.* To examine experimenter effects is to ask what portion of the results of an experiment can be said to be affected by the attitudes or behavior of the experimenter. In this section we will discuss two types of experimenter effects: (1) those due to biased data collection by the experimenter and (2) those stemming from the experimenter biasing the subject's performance.

### Biased Data Collection

One very real potential source of experimenter bias in the actual collection of data stems from our individuality; two experimenters may actually see the world differently. In his history of psychology, Boring (1950) tells of an incident in the late 1700s and early 1800s that points up the importance of experimenter variability in scientific research. The story goes that an astronomer, Maskelyne, dismissed his assistant Kinnebrook because the assistant timed the passing of stars almost a second later than Maskelyne did. The method of noting star movement in those days was to observe a clock and then, listening to its ticking, count the ticks to record the time a star crosses wires in the telescope. In reading of this event some 20 years later, another astronomer named Bessel began to compare his own observations with those of others. Bessel found that different observers using the same method differ by a constant amount. In this case, however, Bessel did not fire his assistants. Rather he became one of the first researchers to point to the great effect that inherent differences in experimenters can have on the data we record.

The constant error in the observations of different scientists is what we call the *personal equation* in psychology. The personal equation suggests that because of one's physiological and psychological makeup, there are differences, yet consistent differences, in the way we as experimenters observe the world. And these unique experimenter differences form a very real source of experimenter bias. Because of this, it is a common procedure in an observational or rating experiment for two or more independent observers to be used. To check for inconsistent observations, the observations of these observers are then correlated and this correlation is referred to as *inter-rater reliability*. The higher the correlation between the ratings of two independent observers, the less the ratings represent inconsistent subjective factors of the raters.

In addition to these inherent differences between experimenters in the way they perceive and respond to the world, there is a whole level of personality that may create a source of experimenter bias. Remember, scientists are human and at times their desire to see their hypothesis supported exceeds their honest viewing of the world as it is. In most cases this temporary reversal of priorities exerts itself in an unconscious or unintentional manner. For example, psychologists who have carefully studied other scientists doing research have learned that if an experimenter makes an error recording a single piece of data, that error is most likely to be in support of the research hypothesis (Rosenthal, 1979). In addition there are other, more subtle ways a scientist can influence the outcome of an experiment. For example, any unintended variations from the experimental plan tend to favor the hypothesis; the decision about whether to accept or discard a subject's data tends to be influenced by whether or not the performance supported the hypothesis, and the use of inappropriate statistical techniques such as unplanned ad hoc analyses may be misleading. As it turns out, this confusion of priorities is by no means limited to modern researchers. In fact, Barber (1976) has suggested that some of our more famous scientists including Newton, Dalton, and Mendel may have presented their data as being more precise than was possible during the time in which they lived. There is also the alternative possibility that some of these scientists' assistants, like college students performing an experiment for which the answer is "known," may have "helped" the data to fit the predicted theory in order to please the person for whom they worked.

In the first half of the nineteenth century, a new and exciting field was emerging which represented what intelligence testing is today. The field was called *craniometry*, and one of the leading figures in this field in America was Samuel George Morton, a well-known physician and scientist (Gould, 1978). The basic premise behind craniometry was that there existed a relationship between brain size and intelligence, and that measurements of the skull would correlate with brain size. Although today we know that there is little relationship between brain size and intelligence in humans, at that time it was part of the accepted beliefs. Millions of people are said to have had their heads measured in hopes of learning about their abilities. Morton extended this work by studying the skulls of individuals from various races and countries. He then measured the quantity of BBs that the skull would hold and used this as a measure of intelligence. Before you decide this was a crazy man, you should realize that when he died, the *New York Daily Tribune* proclaimed that "probably no scientific man in America enjoyed a higher reputation among scholars throughout the world than Dr. Morton" (Gould, 1978). Much of his reputation was based on his use of objective scientific measurements much in the tradition of modern-day empiricism. One of his major conclusions was that there is a difference in intelligence among the races of the world and that within races one can also find intelligence differences. For example, Morton described the English and Germans as more intelligent than Jewish people and Jewish people as more intelligent than Hindus. In terms of races, whites were seen at the top of the intelligence ladder, with Indians in the middle and blacks on the bottom. Recently Stephen Jay Gould, a scholar interested in the history of science, reexamined Morton's data and the methods by which he came to his conclusions. Gould found that Morton had "unconsciously" selected his samples in such a way that the head sizes of the Indians would appear smaller and those of the Caucasians larger. Morton also made two errors in his mathematical computations; both favored the view of Caucasian supremacy, which was in vogue at that time.

There are, however, other cases in which scientists did more than unconsciously or consciously "push" the data in the direction of their hypotheses; there are cases of outright fraud. Two representative examples are the studies of Sir Cyril Burt and Walter Levy. Burt was interested in demonstrating that intelligence is the result of genetic factors. One method of testing an idea such as this is to examine the intelligence of monozygotic twins. Monozygotic twins are twins in which both individuals develop from the same egg and thus are genetically identical. As you can imagine, if twins who are genetically identical but have had different environmental influences have similar IQs, then it can be concluded that heredity is more responsible than environment. (These same types of studies are used for determining the genetic component of disorders including schizophrenia.) Recently two findings concerning Burt have come to light. The first is that when his data were reexamined, the results of his studies presented an almost impossible occurrence. The occurrence was that the correlation between the intelligence of monozygotic twins reared apart was .771 in the first sample of sets of twins, .771 in the second sample, and .771 in the third sample. As Burt found more and more twins who could be used in his study, he performed other correlations (how closely the IQs of the twins were similar), and whether the correlation was done using 21, 30, or 51 pairs of twins, the results were always .771. It is extremely unlikely that the correlations in all three studies would be exactly the same; most scientists familiar with his work assume his data were misreported to support his theory (for a discussion of this case, see Hearnshaw, 1979).

The second case is that of Walter Levy, who performed research in parapsychology. Levy was observed to alter data to support his previous research. After this came to light, Levy resigned and admitted that he had "fudged" the data. Barber (1976) not only discusses these cases but points out that in a number of studies, college students who have been asked to run laboratory experiments have been shown to fudge data or to alter the instructions or procedure of the experiment. Whether these students wanted to get a good grade or were in a hurry to finish their midterm exam is not known, but it is important to understand that scientists are people and may inadvertently or purposely alter their data in a biased manner.

More recently, the journal *Science* reported a case that resulted in the resignation of two scientists from two separate major medical centers and the retraction of 11 research reports from the scientific literature (Broad, 1980). The story began with a researcher submitting her paper to a scientific journal for publication. In the journal review process, which we will discuss in Chapter 14, another scientist saw the paper and made a copy of it. During the next month the second scientist wrote a paper that included passages from the first scientist's paper without reference to her. By chance, in the review process for this second paper, the first scientist saw the paper and realized that it included passages from her own work. She then wrote to the journal and to the dean of the medical school where the other scientist worked and accused the other scientist of plagiarism. At first, according to *Science,* the dean felt that the scientist at the medical school had acted improperly in copying from the work of another but that, since the copying was not related to the actual data collection, it did not call into question the research itself. However, further investigation revealed that the original research had never been completely performed and that the results had been fabricated. In the process of the investigation, another scientist was implicated and the results from 11 published papers were called into question.

What we have been calling experimenter bias not only can affect the actual data the experimenter records, but it can also exert a strong infuence on the theoretical interpretation of our findings. As with any human beings, scientists may consciously or unconsciously choose to view their own and other scientists' results from a biased position that supports their earlier viewpoint. Although few people would consider this type of behavior as fraud, it is important to be aware of the possibility when evaluating published theories and review papers or even just reading the discussion sections of published papers.

## Biased Interactions with Subjects

To understand one way an experimenter might unintentionally bias the interactions with subjects, consider yourself a subject in an experiment in which the scientist is testing the hypothesis that more college men than women dream about violating social taboos. Imagine what type of person (male or female, attractive or unattractive, old or young) you would be most willing to tell your uncommon dreams to. Imagine what type of person you would be least likely to tell your dreams to. As you realize that you react differently to different people in your life, you can also see how subjects in a psychological experiment might react differently to different experimenters. To some experimenters subjects would be withholding, and to others they would talk freely. Such experimenter characteristics as sex, attractiveness, dress, race, and age are known to influence many types of psychological experimentation and should be considered when evaluating a set of studies.

Once the experimenter begins to interact with subjects in the actual experiment, additional factors are likely to influence the research. For example, consider your first experiment in which you ask people to serve as subjects. Did you feel anxious? Did you feel ill at ease that you were imposing on these people? Did you want one group to respond differently from another? Most experimenters do want their experimental groups to be different from their control groups. It is only natural, but it is also a source of bias if the experimenter communicates to the subjects that they are to respond in a certain manner or if the experimenter treats one group differently from another.

Let us now consider two examples of this process. As you know, it is possible to breed animals for certain characteristics such as color, temperament, and predisposition for specific diseases. In this first study, students were given rats to train in running a maze. Half the students were told that they had received rats specially bred for being "maze bright" and the other half were told that they were given "maze dull" animals. In reality, all the animals were bred the same and randomly assigned to the two groups of student experimenters. At the end of the study, the authors report that rats that were trained and tested by experimenters expecting brighter behavior showed statistically significant superior learning over that of the rats run by the experimenters expecting dull behavior (Rosenthal & Fode, 1963). A second study showed the same findings with other experimenters and animals, this time using a Skinner box (Rosenthal & Lawson, 1964). Rosenthal and Rubin (1978) have recently reviewed 345 studies of interpersonal expectancy, and it is now apparent that scientists, like people everywhere, have expectations and that these expectations influence the outcomes of their studies. Although we all like to think of ourselves as objective in our research, it is important to realize that our passionate commitment to our own hypotheses leads us to give special attention to our own expectations about the outcome of our research. In this way we create self-fulfilling prophecies; that is, we expect something to happen and we look for confirmation of our expectation. Even researchers who study self-fulfilling prophecies may have self-fulfilling prophecies, as suggested by some who have tried to replicate Rosenthal's research.

In this section we discussed two major sources of experimenter bias: biased data collection by scientists, and effects related to biases conveyed by interactions between the experimenter and the subject. Although research has described various possible sources of experimenter bias, this issue is very complex and our understanding of these sources of bias is far from complete. Consequently, it is difficult to say exactly how various situations bring forth bias. Thus, it becomes the task of the scientist when designing a new study and the witness when evaluating research to ask whether there are situations in which experimenter bias might have influenced either the treatment of subjects or the collection of the data. Perhaps the best way we can minimize this problem is to remind ourselves that the only way we will ever understand human behavior and experience is to examine it in its complexity, which includes the manner in which scientists and subjects interact with one another.

## Some Ways to Avoid Experimenter Bias

There are a number of possible procedures that can help to reduce experimenter bias. As suggested, one of the most common is to use several different experimenters and even to include this as a factor in the study. Maher (1978a) has suggested that it may be necessary, especially in clinical psychology research, to expose the subjects to a number of different experimenters and experimental situations. This is based on Brunswik's notion that we should sample not only from subject populations but from a number of stimulus situations (Brunswik, 1947). By this Brunswik means that not only should the psychological phenomena under study be presented to a representative sample of subjects, but that they should also be presented in a representative sample of situations.

Another procedure to reduce experimenter bias is to keep the person who is interacting with the subject "blind" to the hypothesis and the particular groups with which he or she is working. For example, blind studies are frequently used in drug research where behavioral ratings are made after a certain drug is administered. In this type of study, the raters are not told which subjects received what drugs or even whether they received a drug at all. In this way the experimenter's expectation cannot be conveyed to the subjects nor can it affect the manner in which the data are recorded. For

---

### *Box 10.1 Recommendations for Research*

In an attempt to improve psychological research, Theodore X. Barber (1976) has suggested 13 changes that need to be made in the way research is performed. This is a summary of these changes.

1. Based on Kuhn's analysis of the importance of paradigms, researchers need to be aware of their underlying assumptions and to state these explicitly when possible.
2. There would be less bias if the person who plans the study (the investigator) is not the same person who analyzes the data.
3. There would be less bias if the person who plans the study (the investigator) is not the same person who actually performs the study (the experimenter).
4. Researchers should be pilot subjects in their own experiments to understand the actual experience of experimentation as encountered by the subjects.
5. Investigators (those who plan studies) should specify *exactly* what the experimenters (those who run the studies) should and should not do and when.
6. Pilot studies carried out by experimenters should be run and carefully supervised by investigators to ensure correct and rehearsed procedures before the actual experimental phase begins.
7. Researchers should be trained in the complexity of data analysis and the manner in which different types of analyses may lead to different conclusions.
8. Students should be taught more the value of good research methods in answering questions and less the importance of finding significant results.
9. Teachers in beginning experimental courses should emphasize the importance of following research procedures to the letter and honestly recording the data.
10. When investigators use experimenters to run the experiment, the investigators should monitor carefully to see that the procedures are being followed.
11. Investigators should use multiple experimenters who vary in personal attributes to collect the data.
12. Whenever possible, experiments should be performed "blind," and if possible the experimenter giving the treatment should be different from the experimenter recording the results.
13. One should not rely on any one study for the answer but seek replications performed by different experimenters in different locations. For the beginning student, a replication of a previous experiment should be encouraged and rewarded as a worthwhile activity.

---

more recommendations for improving research, see Box. 10.1. (We discuss double blind studies later in the chapter in more detail.)

The most useful way to begin eliminating experimenter bias from your own experiments is to try, consciously, to see the experiment from varying perspectives. We are always in a stronger position if we accept that we all are human and make mistakes. After all, at one time we all believed the world was flat. The important point for science is not that we were wrong but that we were willing to change.

## SUBJECT FACTORS

Another potential source of misinterpretation is subject factors. Subject factors or bias refer to the fact that the subjects are not behaving *in the way we expect them to behave.* Some of these factors come about because we have not really considered how a particular subject might experience our experiment. In a nutshell, subject factors boil down to the realization that subjects are human. In some cases they are highly motivated to please the experimenter. In other cases they may actually try to figure out the experiment and behave in a way that will support or sabotage the experiment. In many psychology departments, introductory students serve as subjects to get extra points on their final grade. Scientists working in these settings will be quick to tell you that near the end of the term, when students are working under increased pressure, subject bias can become a real problem. At exam time, the available subjects may be harrassed, anxious, tired, and generally negative toward participating in research. From a broader ecological perspective, it is clear that such a subject has little motivation to be part of a psychological experiment. Thus, it is the task of the scientist to consider how the subject experiences the experiment and to look for personal and social factors that might bias the results of an experiment.

One classic example of an initially overlooked subject factor occurred in an experiment conducted in the 1930s. The experiment took place at the Hawthorne plant of Western Electric and was designed to determine how factors such as lighting and working hours affect productivity. The subjects were a group of women who worked at the plant; they were asked to work under varying conditions. The productivity of these women was compared with general productivity. When the data were analyzed, a strange finding emerged. No matter what the experimental condition was, the productivity of these women increased. It even increased under a condition in which the lighting in the experimental condition was not as good as that in the actual plant. What conclusion would you draw from these studies? From an experimental design standpoint it was difficult to understand the data until the experimenters examined how they had treated these women. The answer they came up with was that the women in the experiment had been given special attention just by being in an experiment. These women were able to consider themselves as *special* and this was reflected in the work they performed. Today the Hawthorne effect remains a warning to experimenters that being given attention and considering oneself special may produce either directly or indirectly results much stronger than those of the experimental independent variables. This is not to suggest that you treat the subjects of your experiments in a cold, impersonal manner, but you should take into account the way that the subjects experience your experiment. The easiest way to do this is simply to ask a few people to be a subject in your study and then discuss how they felt and how they reacted to your study.

Another example of subject bias took place during the Depression and involved a group of dental students who were paid to be subjects. The study had been designed to examine a new type of toothpaste and its effects on bacterial concentration and tooth decay. Subjects with high bacterial concentrations were sought to participate. To qualify for the study and earn some needed money, the students ate candy bars to increase bacterial concentration. Once the study was over and the subjects were paid, they quit eating candy and thus the bacterial count decreased. The experimenters did not realize the subjects had been eating candy bars, and in the follow-up reports they believed the decrease in bacterial concentration was due to the new experimental toothpaste (Simon, 1978). This story points out that in psychology we are dealing with human beings, whose behavior may be motivated by any number of factors, many of which we do not even suspect. The overall ecology of the dental study helps to stress that the subjects were reacting not only to the demands of the experimental environment by using the new toothpaste but also to the demands of a larger environment, in this case an economic one.

In the psychological experiment, the witness reminds us that it is not enough to watch the behavior of human beings as one would watch material objects. Although people may *just* react to the experiment as designed, their reaction may involve many factors we are not aware of. It is the delightful complexity of ourselves and others that makes psychological research both difficult and exciting. Psychological scientists have had to learn that subjects are not passive robots; they are active, creative people with definite motives. It is impossible for any experimenter to know exactly which aspects of the study the subjects are responding to and what their motives are. For example, when a subject takes part in a psychological experiment, it is impossible to predict (regardless of the design of the study) whether the subject will react to the experimenter as someone to make contact with, as someone to talk to, as a neutral person just doing his job, or as a person who is keeping the subject away from some important work such as studying for an exam.

Because the subject is an active, creative, complex human being, it is not surprising that the subject may decide not to follow the instructions of the experiment but to second-guess the experimenter and act in a certain manner. Consider an experiment in which the subject is shown erotic films and then a physiological measure such as pulse rate is taken. In reality the subjects might find the films boring, but because they like the experimenter and want to help him or her, they decide to think about someone that does make them feel erotic and thus give the experimenter results. Unfortunately, of course, the results have nothing to do with the research as it was designed. Let us now examine three possible ways a subject might respond. If the experimenter asks subjects to watch an erotic film, they might (1) just watch the film and react "naturally," (2) react out of humanness more to the experimenter than to the film, or (3) consciously construct what they think the experiment is about and respond to the thought rather than to the film. Restated in broad terms, we are saying that subjects may react to themselves, to the experimenter, or to the experimental situation. What makes the interpretation of scientific research even more difficult is that these three possibilities may be brought forth systematically and thus bias the results in any number of complex ways. For example, in the erotic film example, we might find a *sex by experimenter* interaction in which men react differently from women to a female experimenter. As we shall see in the next section, subjects may react differently not only to the experimenter but also to the experimental situation itself. In the next section we will consider two important phenomena: the placebo effect and the demand characteristic. These two processes point out the importance of having a broad ecological understanding of the relationship among the scientist, the subject, and the experimental situation.

## PLACEBO FACTORS

One potential problem is the influence of placebo effects in the experiment. Imagine you have just picked up your newspaper and there is a story that says "Scientists have found a new cure for headache." As you continue to read the story, you are told of a technique called *biofeedback* in which physiological changes from a person's body are fed back to the person, and it is because of this feedback that headaches are being cured. Now, as a consumer of scientific research, how would you go about evaluating this story? First, you might use common sense and note that it seems reasonable that as one learns to relax there should be a decrease in muscle tension and, in turn, the number of headaches that are thought to be related to tension should also decrease. Second, you might check the experimental design to see whether the study included a baseline condition in which the number of headaches per person was recorded before biofeedback was administered. You might at this point, especially if you have headaches yourself, be ready to run out to the local biofeedback practitioner and sign up. Even if the biofeedback treatment worked for you as it did for the people in the study, it still would not have been demonstrated scientifically that biofeedback was the ingredient that caused your headache to decrease. Both the consumer and the scientist would need to consider one important factor, and that is the *placebo factor*.

The term *placebo* comes from the Latin verb "to please." The phenomenon states that some people will show physiological changes just from the suggestion that a change will take place. For example, considering a number of studies that have attempted to treat tension headaches with a variety of procedures, it has been shown that 60% of the people will report signs of improvement when given only placebo treatments such as a pill containing nothing but sugar or other inert ingredients (Hass, Fink, & Hartfelder, 1963). In recent years, however, research has suggested that endorphins (naturally occurring chemical compounds) may be released internally upon the expectation of change. This finding offers an additional level to understanding the placebo-effect.

The placebo phenomenon is so strong with some individuals that a placebo operation (opening up the chest but not performing a heart operation) has been shown to give rise to recovery rates for persons with angina pectoris (pains in the chest) similar to those following an actual coronary bypass operation (see pp. 382–3). To control for the placebo effect in research, various procedures have been used. One is to use a control group that receives either no treatment or a treatment previously shown to be ineffective for the particular disorder under study. A more powerful control is to use a *double blind experiment*. In a double blind experiment the experimental group is divided into two groups. One group is given the actual treatment and the other is given a treatment exactly like the experimental treatment but without the active ingredient. For example, in a study of medication, the placebo group would receive a medicine that looks and tastes like the experimental one but does not contain the medication being tested. Neither the placebo nor the experimental medicine group would know which medications they were receiving, and in this way these subjects are said to be "blind." The double blind part of the procedure is that the physicians or nurses giving the medicaton are also "blind" to which medication is experimental or placebo. A more sophisticated version of this design would allow for the placebo and experimental subjects to be switched systematically during the study, and thus the same subject would receive at times the active treatment and at times the placebo treatment.

## DEMAND CHARACTERISTICS

A phenomenon similar to the placebo effect is that of demand characteristics in psychological research. Demand characteristics occur when a subject's response is influenced more by the research sitting than the independent variable. For example, in a test on the effect of marijuana on behavior or on the effects of hypnosis, most subjects have some idea of how they "should" act and they may respond in this manner. This may include actual faking on the part of the subject. If demand characteristics play an important role in the experiment, then they pose an important threat to internal validity and offer an alternative explanation for understanding the influence of the independent variable.

Orne and Scheibe (1964) sought to understand the role of demand characteristics in a sensory deprivation experiment. Sensory deprivation research has focused on the effects of reducing the amount of stimulation that a person receives from the environment. In such an experiment individuals would be asked to lie in a room with pads on their arms and legs and goggles over their eyes, allowing a constant level of stimulational. Early descriptions of this research that were reported in the popular press suggested that without sensory stimulation subjects would hallucinate, feel disorientated, and have a difficult time working on any type of task. What Orne and Scheibe did was to set up a sensory deprivation experiment without any sensory deprivation. They divided their subjects into two groups. Subjects in the first group received a physical exam and gave a short medical history. Although they were told that the experiment was safe, they were exposed to an "Emergency Tray" that included drugs and medical instruments. This group was also told to report any problems that they might have in concentrating, as well as any unusual visual imagery, fantasies, or feelings (including disorientation) that they might have. The subjects were told that during the experiment they were to work on an arithmetic task. They were then placed in a special room with food, water, and the materials needed for the arithmetic task. Inside the room was a button marked "Emergency Alarm" that they could press if they wanted to get out of the room. The control group was not given a physical exam nor shown the "Emergency Tray." The control group was only told that they were to perform the arithmetic task and that if they needed to get out of the room, they should knock on the window. In actuality neither group received any type of sensory deprivation. However the results reported by the experimental group were similar to those reported in previous sensory deprivation experiments, suggesting that previous results may have been related to expectations of the subjects who were "in the know," either through their own knowledge or through an experimenter's leading questions, rather than sensory deprivation alone. Thus, in any type of research that asks for a subject's subjective reaction such as studies using alcohol, drugs, or hypnosis, it is important to consider the possible influence of demand characteristics. If possible, a demand characteristics condition should be built into the experiment.

One study of hypnosis that attempted to control for demand characteristics was reported by Martin Orne (Orne, 1969; Orne & Evans, 1966). The purpose of the study was to find out what would happen if the hypnotist left the room after deep hypnosis had been induced. This particular experiment had theoretical importance because one theory of hypnosis suggested that the subjects would return to their normal state of awareness rapidly and another predicted that it would take some time; that is, the study was designed to see which of the two theories more accurately reflected reality. In the study a group of hypnotic subjects was compared with a control group that was asked to simulate hypnosis and act as if they were hypnotized. Orne and Evans referred to their control group as a *quasi-control,* since the control group was being used more to check out the experimental conditions than to compare directly with the experimental group.

The experimenters wanted to design a study in which the hypnotist left the room in an apparently accidental manner in order to avoid breaking the implicit agreement that the hypnotist will remain with and take care of the hypnotized subject. To accomplish this end, the experimenters staged a power failure. During the second of two sessions, after the experimental subjects were hypnotized and were tapping their foot to imagined music, a

"IT WAS MORE OF A '<u>TRIPLE</u>-BLIND' TEST. THE PATIENTS DIDN'T KNOW WHICH ONES WERE GETTING THE REAL DRUG, THE DOCTORS DIDN'T KNOW, AND, I'M AFRAID, <u>NOBODY</u> KNEW."

tape recorder in the room stopped and a desk light went off. The experimenter then said that a fuse had blown and left the room. The findings of the study were apparently clear. The quasi-control group continued to act as if hypnotized until the experimenter returned some 30 minutes later. The experimental subjects, on the other hand, brought themselves out from the hypnotic trance. However, this required varying amounts of time and, once out from under the trance, they appeared somewhat confused. During the postexperimental interviews it appeared that the quasi-control subjects believed that the power failure was not real but only contrived. The experimental group, on the other hand, did not seem to suspect the deception. Since the control subjects were aware of the deception, it was difficult to conclude anything directly from the study. The experimenters then considered ways to make the power failure seem more real. They first reexamined the experimental situation and realized that although the tape recorder and the desk lamp had gone off, the room lights as well as a small polygraph continued to be on. Also, the room with the one-way mirror suggested to subjects that they were being observed, which they were.

A new study was then designed. This study also used an experimental and quasi-control group, but the room had changed. There was no one-way mirror, and when the "power failure" occurred, all the equipment as well as the lights in the room went off. The experimenter was blind as to which was the real hypnotic group and which was the simulated one. Under the new conditions the results for the experimental group were the same. However, the quasi-control groups showed just the opposite results. As soon as the experimenter left the room, the great majority of these subjects stopped simulating and acted as if they were not being observed. Orne and Evans concluded from the second study that the power failure was considered real and that their experimental manipulation was meaningful. Without a control for demand characteristics, an experimenter might have concluded that the theories were correct when in fact the results were due to the subjects acting as they believed they should.

When evaluating research, it is important to consider the role of placebo factors and demand characteristics. It is also important for the researcher to check through such techniques as the quasi-control group and the acceptability of the experimental manipulations. *It is not enough to assume that the subjects in an experiment believe what is being said and accept rationales as true; this needs to be checked out, especially in any study that uses deception!*

## CULTURAL AND SOCIAL BIAS

You may think it strange to suggest that the society and environment in which you live could cause significant bias in scientific research. Yet this is certainly the case. The most common manner in which scientific research is influenced is through a shared *paradigm* (Kuhn, 1970). A paradigm is an accepted world view, which may include ideas about the value of what one is doing as well as specific assumptions about how the world is. Before the time of Columbus, map makers drew flat maps because they had never assumed the world to be other than flat. It is important to realize that because a paradigm shapes the way in which you see the world, when it changes, everything seems to change. There have been a number of paradigm changes in science that have altered the manner in which we see the world. One of the first was the change from seeing the earth as the center of the universe to seeing it as just another planet. Once the earth became just another planet, it could be considered as other planets are and a new scientific cosmology became possible, as did a new idea about the place of humans in the universe. In psychology we have seen changes in scientific viewpoints that have allowed for research never considered possible. For example, at one time it was considered impossible for an animal to either learn language or use it to communicate. Today, there are a number of research projects in which chimpanzees are being taught to communicate through either a computer or sign language, thus opening an entire new field of research which a few years ago was considered impossible. Likewise, we are gaining a new view of both very young and old people that suggests they are capable of far greater potential than we had previously assumed. We are now beginning to realize that children immediately after birth can interact with their external environment, which includes a recognition of faces. Not only our children but also we are beginning to be seen in a new light. As recently as the 1960s it was assumed that an individual's autonomic nervous system (cardiac functioning, stomach activity, smooth muscles, and glands) was beyond any type of conscious control. However, once that assumption was challenged, entire new fields such as biofeedback developed. The point to be made is that we introduce a bias into our scientific research by letting the believed limitations of our time restrict the scope of our vision. Consequently, we never consider certain aspects of behavior that lie beyond our limited view. Every scientist and society hold limited views of the world. That is not the point; the point is to realize that this is the case.

## Key Terms and Concepts

1. The role of the witness in science
2. Ecology
3. Experimenter factors
   a. personal equation
   b. inter-rater reliability
   c. experimenter bias
4. Subject factors
   a. Hawthorne effect
5. Placebo factors
6. Demand characteristics
7. Double blind experiment
8. Cultural and social bias

## Summary

1. All research takes place in a specific context, which extends beyond the laboratory. This involves the scientist-subject interactions during an experiment as well as the world of the scientist when he or she is not performing science, and the world of the subject when he or she is not being part of an experiment.
2. Ecology, as a science interested in the relationship of living organisms and their environment, offers a model for studying the overall contextual relationships between the scientist and the subject. This brings forth the term "ecological validity," which considers whether the full impact of the important relationships among the scientist, subject, and context has been considered in evaluating a piece of research.
3. *Experimenter effects* refer to changes in the dependent variable produced by the attitude or behavior of the experimenter and not related to the independent variable. These may be due to biased data collection by the experimenter or by experimenter influence on the subject's performance.
4. The threat of experimenter bias can be reduced by using multiple experimenters and having the experimenter not know (i.e., be blind to) a subject's group.
5. Subjects may also bias an experiment. They live in their own psychological world and this needs to be considered, as illustrated by the Hawthorne experiment. In this experiment the subjects felt themselves to be special and responded accordingly. Some subjects may want to help an experimenter and in so doing give the data that they think the experimenter wants. Other subjects may try to sabotage an experiment.
6. The word *placebo* comes from the Latin word for "to please." *Placebo effect* refers to the phenomenon (especially likely in drug or psychotherapy studies) of a suggestion of change actually producing a change. Recent research suggests there maybe a biochemical basis to the placebo response.

7. The term *demand characteristic* refers to the subject's being more influenced by the experimental setting than by the independent variable. An example of this would be the case in which subjects respond to excessive alcohol consumption by producing behaviors that they believe someone who drinks would produce.

## Review Questions

1. How can the concept of ecology be applied to the experimental situation?
2. Give some examples of experimenter bias. How would you attempt to reduce this bias?
3. What are placebo effects?
4. How might a drug company control for placebo effects?
5. Discuss demand characteristics.
6. What are some potential experimental biases that might result from the interaction between the subject and the experimenter?

## Discussion Questions and Projects

1. Discuss how research results are relative to the context in which they are derived. How do they transcend the context?
2. It is said that experimenter bias does not affect the internal validity of an experiment. What does this mean? In what cases is this statement true and in what cases false?
3. How could the Hawthorne effect play a role in the experiments you perform in class?
4. When does a subject in an experiment know what the independent variable is?
5. Design your own double blind study. What information did you give to the subjects and what information did you give to the experimenters?
6. A researcher is interested on the effects of alpha wave feedback on feelings of well-being. The researcher develops an experiment in which the experimental group receives alpha biofeedback and then fills out a "feeling of well-being" questionnaire before and after the experimental session and again on the next day. The control group is shown a cartoon book and also fills out the questionnaire before and after the session and on the next day. Both the control and experimental groups showed similar positive scores after the session but only the alpha feedback group reported more positive well-being on the next-day questionnaire. The researcher concludes that alpha biofeedback has lasting effects on a person's well-being. Discuss this conclusion.

CHAPTER ELEVEN

# *Quasi-Experimental, Single-Subject, and Naturalistic Observation Designs*

## INTRODUCTION

In this chapter we want to begin a discussion of moving the location of our research from the laboratory to the field. We will consider some examples of field research that have approximated laboratory experiments, as well as research in which little experimental control has been sought or desired. We will examine the transition from the laboratory to the more natural environment as one of both trade-offs and rewards. While increased control is available in a more closed system such as the laboratory, research in a more open system such as the natural environment allows for the study of everyday psychological processes with the potential for greater relevance to our daily lives. We will further consider the balance between internal and external validity as we seek research that is both sound and relevant. In the next chapter we will consider one particular approach that has found an important role in field research, that of the survey.

Throughout the history of science, the importance of having experimental control of the research situation has been a prime objective. You can see this desire for control in classic studies of the physical sciences as well as in psychological research. Scientists create a research environment through which they can control the important factors that influence the topic under study. Said in other terms, they create a *closed system.* For our purposes a closed system is one in which the important factors that influence the environment are controlled by the experimenter. For example, the technique of studying the falling of objects such as feathers and weights in the closed system of a vacuum chamber illustrates the great degree of control achieved in classic physics. Likewise B. F. Skinner's use of the Skinner box and the precise caring and feeding of animals offered the experimenter a high degree of control over the environmental situation that an organism was exposed to and made possible detailed studies of learning. When we have a relatively high degree of control in the environmental situation the types of design that we discussed in Chapters 8 and 9 are extremely important. With these experimental designs we have the greatest confidence that our dependent variable truly reflects the effect of our independent variable. In particular, these designs help us to rule out alternative explanations and rival hypotheses, and in this manner assure us of a greater degree of *internal validity*.

To be sure, sound experimental control and the resulting high degree of internal validity are extremely desirable features in any experiment we might design. Yet, whatever the importance of internal validity, it is equally important that our designs reflect other issues as well. For example, one important issue is the generalizability of our research findings. Can the results of an experiment be generalized beyond our particular research setting to ongoing life situations? As you may remember, *external validity* refers to the generalizability of an experimental outcome. When Campbell and Stanley (1963) first used the term *external validity,* they were asking to what other groups, settings, treatment variables, and measurement variables an experimental outcome could be generalized.

Today many scientists and nonscientists are insisting that research findings also have direct relevance to the everyday psychological issues that affect us all. This growing concern for the applicability of our research findings to the live situations we all face influences our research efforts in two ways. First, the theoretical questions and hypotheses we generate increasingly deal with complex, relevant psychological issues and processes. Second, our research subjects and settings increasingly reflect real-life situations.

One method for increasing the generality and relevance of our research is to move the research from the laboratory to the setting where the phenomenon we are studying naturally occurs. For example you could not study in a laboratory the effect of some unplanned event such as inner-city riot, the nuclear reactor accident at Three Mile Island, an earthquake, or the impact of some federal intervention program such as the Head Start program. If we are studying the effect of anxiety on final examination performance, a possible natural setting would be the actual final examination session of a college course. If, however, our theoretical issue deals with interpersonal relationships between strangers in a large city, then the natural setting is the streets of that city.

As we move outside of the laboratory and its highly controlled environment, we find ourselves able to control fewer of the factors that influence the behavior of our subject. Whereas we often consider the laboratory as a closed system, the world outside the laboratory is more of an *open system,* with the subjects being influenced by a number of factors over which we as experimenters have little control. In some cases we are unable to manipulate the levels of the independent variable, in others we cannot adequately eliminate potentially confounding variables, and in most we have little real control in terms of subject selection and assignment. In summary we have little influence over what human subjects do, feel, or think as they move about in the everyday world. In these situations we cannot achieve the same degree of control that we accomplish in a closed system. Thus we need research designs that are appropriate to situations in which we have greater difficulty ruling out alternative explanations and that give us less certainty that the changes in the dependent variable were really the result of changes in the independent variable. In these situations we may find ourselves relying more on reasoning and logic than on direct control of the experimental situation.

In fact, in some cases the time required for developing control of the experimental situation brings about unforeseen consequences. Let us consider one striking anecdote told to us by the developmental psychologist Dale Harris. When Professor Harris was teaching at the University of Minnesota, one student decided to perform an experiment that used elderly individuals in retirement homes around Minneapolis. To sample subjects randomly, this particular student collected the names of all the residents of the homes and began random selection in such a way that each resident had an equal chance of being selected for the study. However, the time required to complete this sampling process correlated with an event that was unforeseen by the student. During the time in which random sampling was taking place, 12% of the residents in the retirement homes died! This points up the importance and necessarity of reducing tight experimental controls when the phenomenon under study occurs in a changing environment. Additional examples of such a problem are studies performed in a changing work environment or clinical studies performed in hospitals and clinics where both patients and staff change frequently. These changes prevent tight experimental controls if the study is to be completed.

It is possible to perform very useful research in the field even with lowered control. For example, one applied study asked whether rear-end collisions could be reduced by the addition of a warning device to the backs of cars (Voevodsky, 1974). The independent variable was an amber light that reflected the rate of deceleration and was affixed to the rear of taxi cabs in a fleet. A group of cabs that did not have the device served as a control group. At the end of the experimental period the group of cabs with the device had a rear-end collision rate lower than that of the control group. What types of questions might you ask in evaluating this study? One question would relate to the Hawthorne effect which we discussed in Chapter 10. That is, might the experimental group drivers have seen themselves as part of an experiment and been more careful in their driving? The author of the research suggests that if there were such an effect then we would expect to see an overall reduction in accident rates for the cabs; that is, one might expect that both the control and experimental groups would have had lower accident rates during the experimental period than during similar periods in previous years. The rate for front-end accidents was the same for both the experimental taxis and the control taxis. Also, there was no reduction in front-end accidents, in which the taxi runs into another car. The reduction in accidents was for those caused by other cars running into the taxis from behind, and there was a reduction of these rear-end accidents in the experimental group. Thus, it could be assumed that driving a cab with the device did not influence how the driver of the cab responded but that it did influence those drivers who were following the cabs. In summary, the taxi study offers an example of a valid and useful study performed with relatively less control than found in the laboratory. In this study reasoning and logic was used to arrive at the conclusions of the research.

Naturally occurring phenomena also defy true experimental control. For example, suppose we were interested in studying the effects of a disaster such as that at Three Mile Island. To begin with, there is no way we could control the onset or even the site of such an occurrence, nor could we randomly assign people to a "potential meltdown" versus "no meltdown" group. Furthermore, when dealing with the people affected, it would be difficult to eliminate other factors that may have coincided with the disaster itself. Some of these influences may have been positive, such as the concern expressed by friends, relatives, and strangers all over the country. Perhaps others were more negative, such as the fear for the future effects of radiation on one's children or the loss of property values, or concern over the failure of local government to respond. Consequently, whenever we attempt to increase the external validity of our inquiries by studying phenomena in real-life situations, we run a strong risk of decreasing the internal validity of these same experiments.

In most cases the internal validity of our research is jeopardized or even decreased as we move from the laboratory to more natural settings. Yet, at the same time, the overall applicability and relevance of our research may be increased greatly and, in turn, may enhance the value of our work even further. Thus we are always faced with a trade-off between (1) precision and direct control over experimental design and (2) desire for maximum generalizability and relevance to real-life situations. The process of conducting sound and relevant research involves a balance between our concern for *internal* and *external* validity.

One alternative, although it is somewhat ambitious, is to combine naturalistic observation with more experimental-like procedures in a real-life situation. We will briefly present one set of such studies that took place over a number of years. The initial study in the series was performed in the late 1940s and was designed to explain the development and nature of prejudice. Later studies refined the procedure and may be familiar to you from introductory psychology books under the name the "Robber's Cave Experiment" (see Sherif, Harvey, White, Hood, & Sherif, 1961). Portions of our discussion of the research come from an interview we had with one of the participants, Carolyn Wood Sherif. The impetus for performing the research was the experimenters' dissatification with the theoretical notions of that day relating to the development of prejudice. The example of prejudice that many were attempting to understand during that period was that of Germany against Jews. Some of the writers of the day tried to explain Germany's behavior by suggesting that the German people were somehow different from other people. The researchers of this study were not satisfied with this answer. Thus the question remained: what is the nature of prejudice and how does it develop. How might you go about studying prejudice?

We will now tell you about how this particular set of researchers began. The initial hypothesis was that normal, healthy people would develop all of the earmarks of prejudice when (1) they found themselves in situations of strong group identification and (2) their group was placed in such circumstances that it had to destroy the aspirations of another group in order to reach its most cherished goals. In order to test such an hypothesis it was necessary to set up a situation involving groups in which only one group could win. Where might you find such a situation? Many alternatives might come to mind—a college sports event, a business competition between companies, and many others. Since these researchers wanted as much control as possible and were interested in the formation of group prejudice, they chose a summer camp. In order to better understand what naturally happens in a summer camp, one of the researchers (Muzafer Sherif) spent the summer of 1948 visiting camps and watching the daily activities. Unlike many other groups such as businesses or universities, a summer camp offered the potential for few outside influences except for letters from home or visits from parents and thus extended to the researchers the possibility for a high degree of control in a naturalistic setting. The staff of the camp were trained in observational techniques, some of which we will discuss later in this chapter. To allow for access and observation, some of the researchers became part of the staff. One, for example, became a handyman and was thus able to wander around camp without being noticed. For ethical purposes the parents were told of the experiment before they had formally chosen that particular camp. Observations were recorded by the counselors twice a day. To ensure reliability, additional measures were taken by independent raters; that is, when a counselor observed a boy behaving in a certain way over a period of time (he became a leader or a clown for example), then an independent observer was asked to observe that particular person. To further validate the observations, mini-experiments were designed. For example, the researchers at one time created a baseball practice in which campers rated how accurately another camper hit a target with a thrown baseball. Since it was difficult to rate exactly where the ball hit, the researchers wanted to know if there was a systematic error related to status in the group; that is, were the most popular campers in the groups seen as being better at throwing? From these mini-experiment and observations, the researchers could base their conclusions on not only just a single set of data but a combination of measures obtained in different situations.

In the third of the series of camp experiments which has come to be called the "Robber's Cave Experiment," the researchers observed the formation of group leadership structures. As the researchers had postulated, a group culture formed even when individuals had no idea of the existence of another group. After about a week, the existence of another group of campers was learned and the staff then arranged sports competition between the two groups. What the researchers were most interested in was how and whether prejudice would develop between the groups. What do you think happened? Let's let Dr. Sherif tell it in her own words:

> When they found out there was another group in camp they said they would like to compete with them. So the camp staff became the accommodators to arrange this event so that they could compete. They set up a tournament in which there were a series of events and points to be gained cumulatively. Great prizes offered, loving cup, Swiss Army knife for each boy on a winning team and so on, lots of motivational things. The tournament went on for three or four days. The boys . . . they would say 'we will beat you,' but in a very friendly way. They greeted one another and after the first events they would give the cheer "two, four, six, eight, who do we appreciate?" name the other team and all of these good sportsman sort of things. But, this started to evaporate very, very quickly. The extent of the rivalry, the concern that the other group was doing them in, that they weren't playing fair, that things were being stacked against them and so on began to appear very quickly. So when those things would happen they would then start to behave more aggressively toward the other group. These sorts of aggressive actions, in turn, would feed the fuel if you will of the images that they had of the other boys. So that very shortly, rather clear-cut stereotype views of the other group developed. They were cheats, stinkers, you know. And we, of course, are brave, honorable, and true. (After the tournament each group said) they would just as soon never see those guys again.

At this point the researcher sought to intervene and reduce the conflict that had developed. In the first study they arranged for a sporting event with another camp nearby, thus requiring that the two teams work together. This intervention was effective and represents a case in which competition served to reduce group conflict. This result permitted a clearer statement for study in the two later studies. To quote Dr. Sherif, "So the hypothesis stated that in order to reduce inter-group conflict and prejudice once it was generated it would be necessary to have conditions in which there were goals strongly desired by members of both groups, but absolutely not obtainable without the resources and efforts of both groups together. Those were called superordinate goals." Whereas in the first study the researchers used a sporting event with another camp to bring the two groups together, in the third study they used a water shortage for the same purpose.

As you can imagine, this research describes a complex series of interactions outlining the development and reduction of group prejudice. The research supported the notion that given the right situation, prejudice can be part of any person, not just those with psychological problems. Such a conclusion offers us the possibility of generalizing these findings to the present-day world situation and the prejudice that one country faces from another. For our purposes this series of studies presents one approach to using naturalistic settings in answering psychological questions. We have only touched on the surface of the studies and recommend their reading for an interesting account of conducting psychological research in the field.

We hope to encourage you to see the potential of psychological research for asking important theoretical and practical questions outside of the traditional laboratory setting. To this end we introduce you to research designs in this chapter that offer alternatives to the designs presented previously in this book. With the first group of designs we lack sufficient experimental control over the variable under study and over potentially confounding variables to make logically tight statements concerning the relationship between the independent and dependent variables. Consequently, we rely instead on *logically* discounting alternative interpretations of the data. To emphasize that these designs are less rigorous, many researchers refer to them as *quasi-experimental* designs. Furthermore, because these designs are often used to evaluate the impact of some variable on an ongoing process, they are also referred to as evaluation research designs. Although there are many ways in which quasi-experimental designs approximate true experimental designs, when using them we still cannot be as confident about the relationship between the independent and dependent variables as with true experimental designs. Nevertheless, *they are extremely useful in uncovering potential relationships in complex psychological phenomena that occur in natural settings.* Consequently, because of our growing interest in studying psychological processes outside the laboratory, these designs can play an important role in our early study of many complex psychological phenomena that occur in natural settings. In a similar fashion these designs are useful in showing where a relationship does not exist and thus reducing the necessity for performing more highly controlled designs. For example, if a new form of psychotherapy is shown not to work in quasi-experimental situations where a variety of placebo and suggestibility factors would help its effectiveness, it would be difficult to argue that the therapy would work better under highly controlled situations.

The second class of designs that we will consider is *single-subject designs.* These research designs offer an alternative to group designs for examining psychological processing. Single-subject designs are particularly useful when the subject population is limited. For example, when one wants to study a rare disorder, it would be difficult if not impossible to obtain enough subjects for a group design. Even when adequate numbers of subjects are available, some researchers (Sidman, 1960) have argued that single-subject research offers more control and may be preferable to group studies for particular types of research questions.

The final class of designs that we will examine is *naturalistic observation techniques* (also called field research designs). These designs are not focused on discovering relationships between variables (e.g., independent and dependent variables). Instead they provide a powerful tool for describing an ongoing process in its natural setting.

## QUASI-EXPERIMENTAL DESIGNS

### Time Series Design

A time series design is a within-subjects design; that is, the performance of a single group of subjects is measured *both* before and after the experimental treatment. This particular design is useful when we are interested in the effects of an event that has happened to all members of the population we are studying. For example, suppose you decide to become a college guidance counselor, and after obtaining your Ph.D. you take a job at a small college. One day you are talking to your friend who is the women's gymnastics coach and she mentions that her gymnasts perform very well in practice and during warmups but seem to "fall apart" during actual competition. As a psychologist you know that certain relaxation training and simple concentration exercises have been shown to improve test performance in other test situations. You mention this to the coach and she immediately asks you to try these relaxation exercises with the team. You agree, and for the next week you spend time working with each athlete during daily practice. The entire team enjoys the exercises and feels that they are helping. To evaluate the effectiveness of these relaxation procedures more objectively, you decide to simply compare the final score for the team's next meet with the score for their previous meet.

This particular design, which involves comparing a single pretest measure (total score on first meet) with a single posttest measure (total score on second meet), is called a *single-group, pretest-posttest design.* During their next meet, their composure is much improved and their overall score is better than in the previous meet. Because the coach kept a record of each woman's apparent composure during each performance, it is also possible to rate each woman's composure for these two meets. Hypothetical team results of skills performance and composure are shown in Figure 11.1. As you can see, both the total score and the coach's estimate of composure

increased markedly following the relaxation and concentration exercises. Before accepting this conclusion, however, we should keep in mind that because we have utilized only a single pretest and posttest measure, we have no idea how much fluctuation would normally occur between any two meets. In other words, perhaps the sharp increase in the score or the composure ratings shift is independent of the relaxation exercises. This lack of knowledge concerning the normal amount of fluctuation between any two measures is a very serious weakness of this single-group, pretest-posttest design.

### Interrupted Time Series Design

One way to minimize this weakness is to use an *interrupted time series design*. This design involves making several pretest and several posttest measurements. The basic idea behind this type of design is that the additional pretest and posttest scores give us a better estimate of the normal amount of fluctuation from test to test or in this case from gymnastics meet to meet. Once we know the amount of normal fluctuation, we can better interpret the impact of the phenomenon we are studying. Figure 11.2 is a schematic

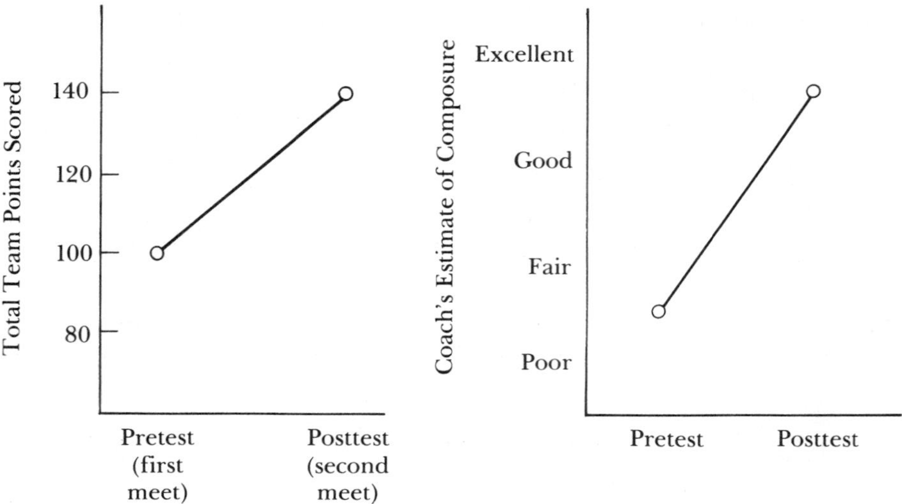


**Figure 11.1** These are the hypothetical results of a single-group, pretest-posttest design studying the effects of relaxation and concentration exercises on the total points scored by a women's gymnastics team and the coach's estimate of the gymnasts' composure.

representation of this design. As a point of notation, the interrupted time series design is also referred to as an ABA design, where A represents baseline measurements and B represents the treatment manipulation. The ABA notation is most often seen in behavioral journals, with B being a specific intervention such as praise for an increase in some target behavior (for example, completing homework or making more positive self-statements).

As an example of a time series design, let us again consider the hypothetical experiment dealing with the effect of relaxation procedures on the performance of gymnasts. In this case a time series design could incorporate the scores for several meets prior to and after the introduction of the relaxation and concentration exercises. Consider for a moment the three possible outcomes depicted in Figure 11.3. In part A the pretest and posttest scores are fairly constant. Consequently, it would be reasonable to assume that the apparent change in performance reflected a real shift. In part B there is considerable fluctuation in the outcome of weekly scores, and consequently our best bet is that the sharp increase in performance after introducing the relaxation procedures is simply chance fluctuation that would have occurred anyway. In each case we gain confidence in our interpretation of the effect of the phenomenon under study by being able to compare its impact with normally occurring fluctuations of weekly meet scores. It is important to note that an *interrupted time series design* can also provide some estimate of how long-lasting the influence of the phenomenon is. For example, Figure 11.3A shows a hypothetical outcome that would lead us to suspect a fairly long-lasting impact of the relaxation procedures. Figure 11.3C shows a hypothetical outcome consistent with the idea that the performance of the gymnasts was only temporarily improved.

Although the interrupted time series design is a great improvement over the simple pretest-posttest design, it still leaves us far short of a clear statement of how one variable influenced the other. For example, if Figure 11.3A represented your data, you could certainly feel confident that a real

| Pretests | Phenomenon under Study | Posttests |
|---|---|---|
| $O_1$ , $O_2$ , $O_3$ , $O_4$ | X | $O_5$ , $O_6$ , $O_7$ , $O_8$ |

**Figure 11.2** In this figure, O represents each observation or test score, and X represents the occurrence of the phenomenon under study. Note that the phenomenon under study, X, interrupts the periodic measurement on our group of subjects (after Campbell & Stanley, 1963).

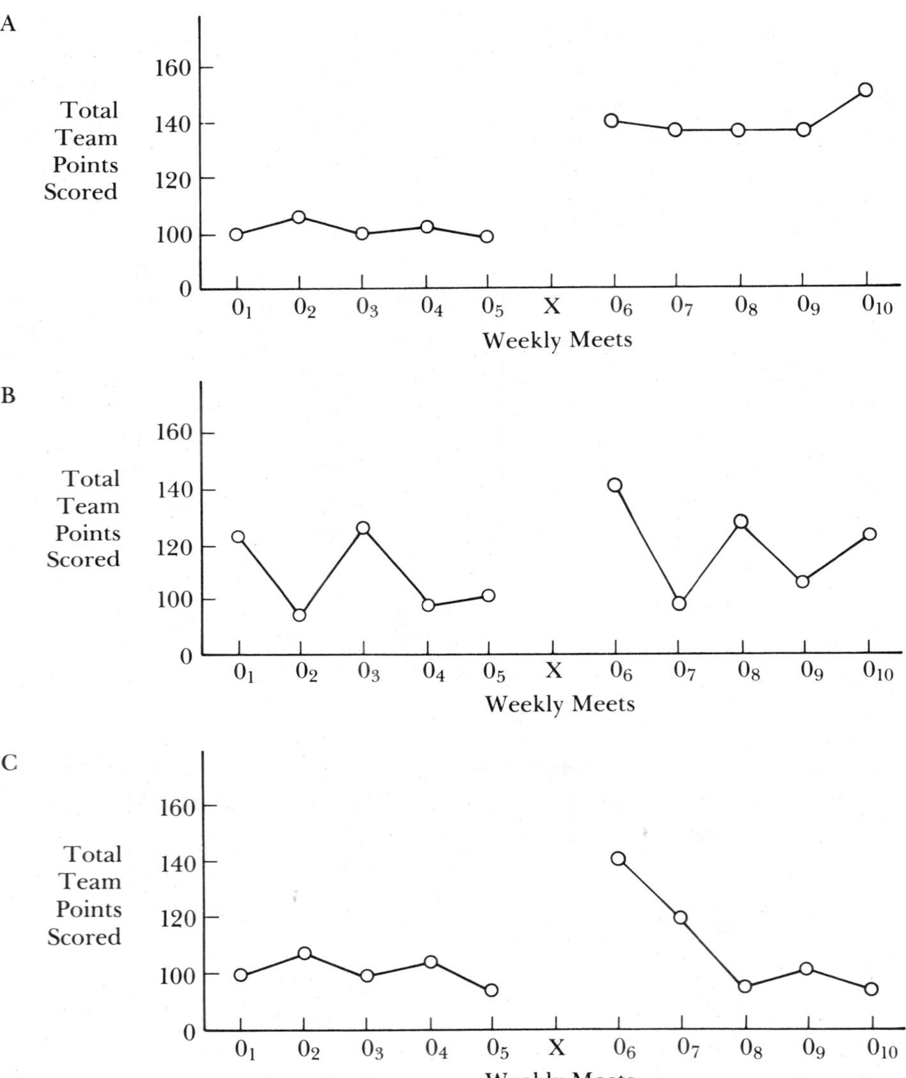


**Figure 11.3** This figure shows the hypothetical outcomes of an interrupted time series design examining the effects of relaxation and concentration exercises on the total points scored by a women's gymnastics team in 10 weekly meets. X marks the point at which the exercises were introduced. Part A shows an outcome in which the pretest and posttest scores are fairly consistent. Part B shows an outcome characterized by much variability in weekly scores. Part C shows what might be a transient effect superimposed on a relatively constant background.

shift in team performance occurred at about the time you introduced your relaxation procedures. However, any number of other events might be contributing to this unusually abrupt shift in team performance. Perhaps the increased care and attention given to each athlete were responsible and not the exercises themselves, or maybe some campus event that occurred about that time caused the shift, or perhaps there was even a television special on women gymnasts bound for the Olympics.

Ideally, we could control for many of these alternative interpretations by including a control group of some sort. However, because *all* members of the population under study have been exposed to the relaxation procedure, it is impossible to select a second group of women gymnasts to serve as a control group. This, of course, is an important limitation of the interrupted time series design, and it must be kept in mind when interpreting the outcome. As it turns out, it is sometimes possible to redefine the population we are studying to utilize control subjects who were not directly exposed to whatever phenomenon is being studied. In this case we might see whether there was a shift in the performance of the men gymnasts or in the performance of women gymnasts from a nearby college. This expanded form of the interrupted time series design is called a multiple times series design.

## Multiple Time Series Design

A *multiple time series design* attempts to rule out some potential alternative interpretations by including a control group that does not receive the experimental treatment. Because of this second group of subjects, the multiple time series design is not a within-subjects design, like the interrupted time series design, but rather is a between-subjects design. A multiple time series design is schematically represented in Figure 11.4

| | Pretests | Phenomenon under Study | Posttests |
|---|---|---|---|
| Experimental group | $O_1, O_2, O_3, O_4, O_5$ | X | $O_6, O_7, O_8, O_9, O_{10}$ |
| Control group | $O_1, O_2, O_3, O_4, O_5$ | | $O_6, O_7, O_8, O_9, O_{10}$ |

**Figure 11.4** Multiple time series design. In the figure, O represents each periodic observation or test score; X represents the occurrence of the phenomenon under study. Note that the phenomenon under study, X, interrupts the periodic measurements of our experimental group but not of our control group (after Campbell & Stanley, 1963).

In our study of the effectiveness of relaxation procedures on the performance of women gymnasts, it might be helpful to utilize a control group of women gymnasts from a neighboring college. We could use their total weekly team scores as control data. To the extent that these subjects are similar to our original subjects in any relevant subject variables and are living under similar social and environmental influences, we can assume that these two groups are equal for factors other than the experience of the relaxation training itself. Figure 11.5 shows two sets of hypothetical data for each team.

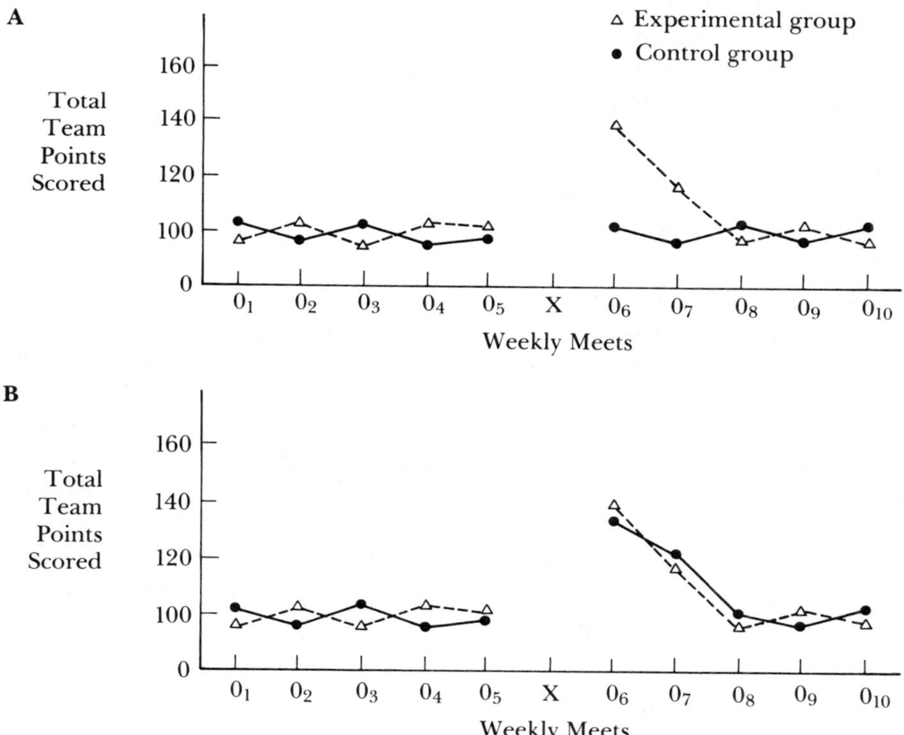


**Figure 11.5** In this figure, two sets of hypothetical data are shown for a multiple time series design used to study the effect of relaxation training on the weekly performance of women gymnasts. The dotted line represents weekly total team scores for the gymnasts who received the relaxation training. The solid line represents weekly scores for the gymnastics team from a neighboring college that did not receive the relaxation training.

In Figure 11.5A the hypothetical scores from Figure 11.3C for the gymnasts who received the relaxation are shown along with the total team score for the women gymnasts from the neighboring college who did not receive the special training. The abrupt difference between the two teams in the two meets following the special training is certainly consistent with the idea that the relaxation procedures had a definite, although transient, influence on the overall performance of the woman gymnasts. Before accepting this conclusion, however, keep in mind that we may have overlooked some social or environmental influence that affected our experimental group and not our control group. For example, it is quite possible that some local campus event or even some independent event among the team members at about the same time influenced their "team spirit" and consequently their performance. This latter interpretation is *always* a real possibility when using the multiple time series design to study complex phenomena in their natural settings.

In Figure 11.5B the hypothetical weekly scores for the two teams show a sharp increase following relaxation training. Because the gymnasts from the neighboring college did not receive the relaxation training, it is likely that some factor other than the relaxation training is responsible for this improvement. One possibility is that both teams were affected by some common event. Can you think of any common events that could account for this parallel performance?

It should be increasingly evident that the interpretation of quasi-experimental designs is a tricky business and that there is *always* a real danger that unknown variables may be contributing to the performance differences between our experimental and control groups. This adds to the difficulty of deciding which of several possible interpretations of our final outcome best reflects the true causal factor. In many cases we will never know which interpretation is correct!

## Nonequivalent Before-After Design

A *nonequivalent before-after design* is used when we want to make comparisons between two groups that we strongly suspect may differ in important ways even before the experiment begins. Because the two groups in this design are initially unequal, there is an unusually high risk of ultimately confusing these initial differences with the effects of the independent variable. Consequently, in this design we avoid simply comparing both groups on a single dependent measure. Instead, each group is first given a pretest and then a posttest, and finally we compare the amount of change in test scores for the experimental and control groups. Thus, by comparing difference scores rather than single dependent measures, we attempt to control more directly for the fact that we are dealing with initially unequal groups. So in a real sense each group's pretest score serves as a sort of baseline from which we estimate the amount of change from pretest to posttest. Then we compare the magnitude of change for each group by comparing difference scores. This design is schematically represented in Figure 11.6.

The nonequivalent before-after design is widely used in educational research where we are frequently interested in comparing different schools, classes, or programs. As an example, let's assume you have just completed your Ph.D. and have taken a job teaching psychology at the college level. One bright spring day your department head asks if you would be willing to develop a new course in human sexuality and, if so, you could teach a morning and afternoon section of it next fall. Having never taught a course on sexuality before, you would like to know whether a lecture or discussion format would be most effective in influencing student attitudes toward human sexuality. Because you will teach two sections, you could begin to answer this question by teaching the morning session with a discussion format and the afternoon session with a lecture format. Then at the end of the term, you could give an attitude questionnaire to each section and directly compare their scores. Because teaching is still a new experience for you, you decide to ask one of the senior professors what she thinks about your idea. To your surprise, she points out that students who voluntarily schedule 8:00 A.M. classes are very different from those who take 4:00 P.M.

| | Pretreatment Measure | Treatment | Posttreatment Measure | Difference |
|---|---|---|---|---|
| Experimental group | $O_1$ | X | $O_2$ | $O_1 - O_2$ |
| Control group | $O_1$ | | $O_2$ | $O_1 - O_2$ |

**Figure 11.6** Example of a nonequivalent before-after design. In this figure, $O_1$ and $O_2$ represent the pre- and posttreatment dependent measures for each group, respectively; X represents the treatment or independent variable. Note that for this design, group comparisons are made between the difference scores for each group rather than directly between posttreatment scores (after Campbell & Stanley, 1963).

classes. Consequently, she warns that a direct comparison of attitudes at the end of the term may reflect these initial subject differences as well as the effects of your discussion and lecture formats. Impressed by her comments, your initial impulse might be simply to assign students randomly to each class as you would do in any experiment you were conducting in our laboratory. In this case, however, you are not in the laboratory, and because your students voluntarily select which section of your course they will enroll in, you have no control over the assignment of subjects. Consequently, you cannot control for these potentially confounding subject differences by randomly assigning subjects to each group.

At this point, while on the verge of abandoning the whole idea and avoiding such applied questions, you recall that quasi-experimental designs can often be used in real-life situations where experimental designs cannot. In this particular case, your major problem is that you strongly suspect that the two groups will be very different at the onset of the experiment. Therefore, you decide to use the nonequivalent before-after design, which was developed for situations in which we cannot randomly assign subjects to groups and are faced with having to compare groups that may differ from the onset of the experiment. The final design you might arrive at is depicted in Figure 11.7.

The nonequivalent before-after design is frequently used in such areas as evaluation research (see Mark, Cook, & Cook, 1984, for more detail). While many of the threats to internal validity such as history are ruled by this design, there are problems such as the threat of selection-maturation. The selection-maturation threat occurs when one group changes at a different rate from the other. For example, if a televised form of learning was shown to disadvantaged children and their progress scores were compared to those of children from higher socioeconomic levels who were not shown the television program, it might be difficult to show a treatment effect for the

| | Pretreatment | Treatment | Posttreatment | Difference |
|---|---|---|---|---|
| Experimental group | Attitude questionnaire | Discussion | Attitude questionnaire | Pretest—posttest score |
| Control group | Attitude questionnaire | Lecture | Attitude questionnaire | Pretest—posttest score |

**Figure 11.7** Example of a nonequivalent before-after design.

television program, it might be difficult to show a treatment effect for the disadvantaged children, since it is common for higher socioeconomic level children to progress faster during a given time period. Thus, we might conclude that the treatment did not have an effect when in fact it did. One of the best ways of ruling out alternative explanations using this design is to have a thorough knowledge of the groups being used and the expected rate of change of each on the variables being measured.

### Ex Post Facto Design

In the designs we have discussed thus far, the experimenter planned a study that would take place in the future. The *ex post facto design* attempts to use empirical procedures for suggesting meaningful relationships from events that have occurred in the past. Some researchers see this procedure as important for suggesting how a significant event in the past (for example, growing up under Hitler or television watching) might have influenced people. Schnelle and Lee (1974) used an ex post facto time series analysis when they studied the manner in which transferring "problem" prisoners to another prison affected the number of offenses committed by the prisoners who were not transferred. From prison records, these authors created an ex post facto A-B-A design, with B being the transfer of problem prisoners and A being the measurement of offenses by the prisoners not transferred. As with other quasi-experimental designs, such studies as this can say *whether* a change took place, but it is impossible to state *why* the change took place.

Other uses of the ex post facto design are found in studies of educational techniques, disease, and psychopathology. For example, Barthell and Holmes (1968) studied the number of listed activites of students in a high school yearbook to determine whether there were differential rates of high school activity between schizophrenics and nonschizophrenics identified later in life. Since the study took place "after the fact," these researchers had to determine a possible control group also after the fact. For their control group they chose students whose pictures appeared next to the schizophrenics in the yearbooks. In one sense you are working backwards in the ex post facto procedure since you know the outcome and wish to determine the antecedents of this outcome. Thus, one of the important questions is: Did you select the correct measure (high school activity in the preceding example) to compare the two groups? This, of course, is an unanswerable question and for this reason the procedure is a very weak form of inference.

Let us consider another example of ex post facto research that points up some additional interpretation problems. You might be interested in people who have a particular disease. If you have a theory that nutrition is important, you might study what healthy and diseased people ate for breakfast. You might then find that the people with the particular disease did not eat breakfast. You could then conclude that eating breakfasts helps one to stay healthy, right? Wrong! Eating may or may not have been the important factor in the disease, but you cannot know from ex post facto designs. The same results may have been brought about because the people with the disease did not feel good when they woke up in the morning and thus chose not to eat breakfast. Thus, subjects may have been self-selected on the treatment variable and in this way invalidate your conclusion that the treatment variable affected the groups. In a true experiment, this objection would have been avoided since you would have selected the subjects and assigned them to groups.

Although ex post facto designs are one of the weakest forms of inference, Kerlinger (1973) suggests that these designs can be used to good advantage in a particular case. This particular case involves testing alternative hypotheses. His ideas are based on those of Chamberlin (1890/1965) and Platt (1964; see Box 5.1). Using ex post facto procedures, one can examine *alternative dependent* variables. For example, retrospectively, cigarette smoking might be shown to be associated with lung cancer more than brain tumors. Although the research still cannot make causal statements, testing alternatives can lead to a greater understanding of the phenomenon under study.

## SINGLE-SUBJECT DESIGNS

In general there are two types of *single-subject designs;* one is primarily descriptive and the other is more experimental in its intent. When our primary goal is to provide a detailed description of an individual, the *case study* design is useful. In contrast, when our primary goal is to begin to focus on a particular aspect of an individual's behavior that may be influenced by some external factor, single-subject designs such as the *reversal* and *multiple baseline designs* may be used.

### Case Study Design

Historically the case study is one of the most widely used methods for studying individual subjects. Indeed for years it has been the primary method for studying phenomena in clinical medicine and clinical psychology. Typically a case study is a brief narrative description of an individual or some aspect of an individual that brings together relevant aspects of the patient's history and present situation. The information that makes up the case study may come from a variety of sources, including the patient's recollection of events, information from friends or relatives, and public records.

In one sense we all use case study techniques when we go to a professional complaining of a pain somewhere in our body. The professional then diagnoses the problem and prescribes some form of therapy. After some time, we then return and give the professional feedback on whether the pain decreased. Since both physical pain such as headaches and psychological distress such as feeling lost or without purpose cannot be seen from behavior alone, the case study technique represents one of the oldest techniques of medical and psychological description. While case studies based solely on the reports of subjects or patients are open to all the problems of self-report such as selective forgetting, the desire to show ourselves in a positive light, and outright deception, there are times in which this can be a useful technique.

For example, Gottmann (1973) suggests that systematic case study observation offers therapists a means of obtaining information concerning specific interventions in therapy during an ongoing series of sessions. As a digression, it should be pointed out that the case study may offer the best type of information when the goal is to note the change of a single individual and the average change of all patients or subjects would give an incorrect picture of change. To illustrate this point, consider a treatment that produced a beneficial change in half the patients and an equally negative change in the other half. If group means or averages were calculated, one might erroneously conclude that the treatment had no effect on patients. Thus in some cases it is more accurate to record a number of systematic single case studies than to record group data. This is true not only for studies of pathology but also for studies of potential. For example, Maslow (1970) used the case study technique to study exceptional people whom he considered to be self-actualizing individuals. Likewise developmental psychologists dating back to the last century have kept records of the development of their own children (Bolgar, 1965). In the case of Piaget, these observations led to his later theories.

In addition to this use of the case study method to provide a general description, there is a second, somewhat more specific use of the case study design. In this instance a case study is a narrative that summarizes an *experimenter's* direct observations of a subject's behavior after some sort of treatment has been performed. This design is represented in Figure 11.8 (sometimes called the one-shot case study). In some instances the case study can be a useful tool in research. The observations may suggest new hypotheses, demonstrate rare phenomena, or even show exceptions to established facts. However, in terms of good design, the case study is very weak; like the single-group, pretest-posttest design, we simply have no assurance that the observations would not be exactly the same without the treatment. Because of the lack of control procedures, we can say absolutely nothing about causal factors and run a high risk of confusing any number of confounding variables with our treatment. In spite of these disadvantages, in some clinical areas, the case study design can provide valuable initial descriptions of new phenomena, which can then be carefully studied with more rigorous experimental methods. One area where the case study method has proved useful is in neuroscience. For example, Scoville and Milner (1957) published a case study describing the effect of removal of the hippocampal region of the brain from an adult male (see Box 11.1). In spite of the weakness of case study designs, this particular case study provided much new information about hippocampal function in humans. Some of these findings have been verified with more rigorous designs in nonhuman primates.

## Reversal Design

As you might imagine, there are times when we want more than a simple description of the relevant behaviors of our single subject. Ideally we want to be able to begin to point toward important relationships. However, with single-subject designs, control groups and randomization are obviously impossible, so the task of controlling for extraneous variables is difficult. We have pointed out that when more rigorous means of experimental control are not possible, we can sometimes logically render alternative hypotheses

| | Treatment | Response |
|---|---|---|
| Single subject | X | O |

**Figure 11.8** In this figure, the X refers to the treatment given to a single subject, and the O refers to whatever observations the experimenter makes.

## *Box 11.1 A Patient with Bilateral Temporal Lobe Damage*

In 1957 Scoville and Milner first described a male patient (H.M.) who underwent bilateral temporal lobe surgery in 1953. The lesions involved the removal of the tissue on the medial surface of both temporal lobes, including large portions of the hippocampi. The purpose of the operation was to relieve very frequent and severe epileptic seizures, which were unrelieved by anticonvulsant medication. (Dr. Scoville was encouraged to attempt this procedure because he had strong reason to believe that some abnormality of this region was responsible for the seizures and because evidence involving nonhuman primates indicated no behavioral abnormalities following removal of this area.) Although the surgical procedure strikingly reduced the number of epileptic seizures, the operation had an unanticipated and awful consequence: The patient was unable to either learn or remember any new material!

Prior to surgery H.M. was a motorwinder who was unable to work because of his epileptic seizures. After surgery he was pleasant and easygoing, as he had been prior to surgery. His measured IQ actually rose from 104 to 119 (presumably it was depressed prior to surgery by the epileptic abnormality). However, H.M. exhibited striking memory deficits for events both before and after surgery. For example, except for Dr. Scoville, whom he had known for many years prior to surgery, he was completely unable to recognize members of the hospital staff; he could not even learn his way to the bathroom. He was unable to remember the death of a close uncle, even though he was repeatedly reminded and became genuinely upset every time he was informed. As the years passed, his ability to remember events has remained severely impaired. H.M. was unable to remember his new house address even after living there for six years. He could not recognize neighbors and when left alone would invite strangers into his house thinking they were friends whom he had forgotten. He was able to perform simple jobs such as mowing the lawn, but could not remember where to find the lawnmower or that he had used it the previous day. He read newspapers over and over, forgetting that he had already read them. He spent many hours resolving the same jigsaw puzzle without any sign of learning it. His memory deficit is paralleled by a total lack of appreciation for the passage of time. His deficit in registering new material has remained severe even many years later (Milner, 1966).

In addition to many informal observations such as these, over the years H.M. and his mother have faithfully cooperated with a number of psychologists in the United States and Canada who have carefully examined the nature of his unfortunate deficit. Taken together, their findings provide a wealth of information about human temporal lobe function. Yet this case obviously raises moral issues which Dr. Scoville (1968) stresses:

> This one case, so carefully studied, has demonstrated to many the grave danger of bilateral resection of the medial parts of the temporal lobes when the hippocampus is included in the removal. Even at this late date, however, scientific publications continue to propose the removal of the hippocampus bilaterally for relief of behavioral disorders, intractable pain, and other reasons; such proposals no longer seem justifiable in view of the profound anterograde amnesia which results.

unlikely. The reversal designs rely primarily on the use of logic to gain at least some control. The rationale behind this design is simple: If a subject behaves one way as a given treatment is presented, then behaves quite differently when it is removed, and finally behaves in the original manner when the treatment is presented a second time, it is reasonable to suspect that this fluctuation in the subject's behavior is due to the treatment. It is extremely hard to even imagine how an extraneous variable might vary in an exactly parallel manner to produce a similar fluctuation in the subject's behavior.

Reversal designs may use any number of reversals. For example a design that measures a subject's behavior before, during, and after a treatment is called an ABA design. During the "before" and "after" conditions, here designated the A conditions, baseline behavior is monitored in the absence of the treatment condition. During the B phase of the design, the subject's behavior is monitored during the treatment conditions. An ABAB reversal design is depicted in Figure 11.9.

In considering the reversal design, it is important to keep in mind that we are using the phenomenon of reversibility of some behavior in the presence or absence of the treatment condition to indicate that these behaviors may be influenced by our treatment condition. One limitation with the reversal design is that it will work only when we are studying the effect of treatment conditions on behaviors that quickly return to baseline levels once the treatment is over. Obviously, the influence of all treatments is not this transient. When we are dealing with treatments that result in more permanent shifts in behavior, this particular design cannot be used. Instead, when we are interested in studying the longer-lasting effects of various independent variables on single subjects, one solution is to use a multiple baseline design.

| | A<br>Baseline | B<br>Treatment<br>X | A<br>Baseline | B<br>Treatment<br>X |
|---|---|---|---|---|
| Single subject | $O_1$ | $O_2$ | $O_3$ | $O_4$ |

**Figure 11.9** This figure represents an ABAB single-subject reversal design. X refers to the administration of the independent variable on observations 2 and 4; O refers to the behavioral observations made on the subject. Note that $O_1$ and $O_3$ reflect the occurrence of the dependent variable in the absence of the treatment condition, and $O_2$ and $O_4$ reflect the measure of the dependent variable in the presence of the treatment condition.

## Multiple Baseline Design

Like the reversal designs just discussed, the multiple baseline, single-subject design relies primarily on logic to gain at least some degree of experimental control. With the multiple baseline design we monitor several behaviors of a single subject simultaneously. Once baseline levels are established for each behavior, we then apply our treatment to one of these behaviors. The likelihood of a causal relation is inferred from the fact that of the several monitored behaviors, *only* the behavior exposed to the experimental treatment changes, while all nontreated behaviors remain unchanged. Once this first behavioral shift is noted, the treatment is then applied to the next behavior and so on. The idea behind this design is that it is very unlikely that the baseline behaviors would successively shift by chance alone as each behavior received the treatment. Consequently in the multiple baseline design it is the successive shifting of baseline levels as the treatment is applied that serves as the basis for suspecting a relationship with the treatment. Unlike the reversal designs, which work only for behaviors that are readily reversible, multiple baseline designs can be used for behaviors that are permanently changed by the experimental treatment. A schematic representation of a multiple baseline, single-subject design is depicted in Figure 11.10.

Hersen and Bellack (1976) used a multiple baseline design to demonstrate the effects of a treatment program for a schizophrenic patient. The patient made little contact with others, rarely engaged in conservation, and was compliant even to unreasonable requests. The treatment consisted of the development of assertive skills and skills for making contact with others.

| | | | | | | |
|---|---|---|---|---|---|---|
| Several | A | Baseline | *Treatment* | Baseline | Baseline | Baseline |
| behaviors | B | Baseline | Baseline | *Treatment* | Baseline | Baseline |
| of a single | C | Baseline | Baseline | Baseline | *Treatment* | Baseline |
| subject | D | Baseline | Baseline | Baseline | Baseline | *Treatment* |

**Figure 11.10** This figure shows a schematic representation of a multiple baseline design. In this design several behaviors (A, B, C, and D) are simultaneously monitored. Whatever treatment condition being used is then successively applied to each of these behaviors. The continuation of baseline measures after treatment is sometimes omitted. Note that evidence suggestive of a causal relationship would consist of a successive shift in baseline activity as each successive behavior receives the treatment condition.

The measures taken over the baseline and treatment sessions were (1) amount of eye contact while talking, (2) speaking without prolonged pauses, (3) making requests of another person, and (4) not complying with unreasonable requests. As illustrated in Figure 11.10, this design requires that baselines be taken for the four measures and then treatments be introduced at different sessions for each of the behaviors to be changed while measurements of all behaviors are continued. This type of design helps us to decide whether the treatment was specific to a particular behavior.

Concerning the limitations of the multiple baseline design, it is important to keep in mind that each behavior being monitored and successively receiving the treatment conditions must be relatively *independent* of the others. That is, the behaviors we are monitoring must not be so highly interrelated that a change in one behavior results in parallel changes in other behaviors even though the subjects did not receive the treatment conditions. If the behaviors under investigation were interdependent, then the successive unfolding of baseline shifts due to the successive application of our treatment condition would be destroyed and this design would lose much of its usefulness. For example, Kazdin (1973) notes that this design may be of limited value in studying inappropriate classroom behaviors because many of these behaviors are interrelated and any treatment that is effective for one behavior is likely to influence other behaviors as well. Although the interrelatedness of these behaviors may eventually facilitate whatever intervention program is implemented, the fact that several of these behaviors may simultaneously be altered by the treatment of any one negates the usefulness of the multiple baseline design in studying these interrelated classroom behaviors.

## NATURALISTIC OBSERVATIONS

In the first two chapters we stressed that our basic scientific methods are direct extensions of ways we normally learn about and interact with the world. In many ways the method of naturalistic observation derives from what may be our most primitive way of learning about the world—simply paying attention and observing what happens. The method of naturalistic observation, sometimes called *field study*, is particularly useful in the early stages of investigating a phenomenon. In this case we usually know very little about the phenomenon and can benefit tremendously from a detailed description of the process we are studying. Natural scientists have made use of this technique for many years. Initially they focused on simply classifying and describing a wide variety of plant and animal life on our planet. More recently they have used this technique to study animal behavior. Perhaps the greatest single application of this technique was Darwin's five-year voyage on the HMS *Beagle,* during which he compiled countless detailed descriptions of plant and animal life over a wide part of the world. As he observed and recorded his observations, ideas about how this great abundance of plant and animal life developed came to him. It was these ideas that he later synthesized to form the foundation of our modern theory of organic evolution. Darwin's early work stressed two functions of naturalistic observation. First, it allows us to compile a mass of descriptive knowledge about a phenomenon. Then, as we become more familiar with it, we may get insight about general patterns or lawful relationships in the phenomenon.

Moving into the present century, we encounter the naturalistic methods of such men as Lorenz and Tinbergen (Lehner, 1979). Initial research may be composed of simply recording in a descriptive manner the behavior that is observed. From these initial observations, new hypotheses and theories may be developed and further explored through observation. In one such study of the herringgull, Tinbergen observed young chicks obtain food from their parent's bill. He was particularly impressed by how fast the young chick could learn to peck the parent's bill and wondered how they could distinguish it from other objects in their environment.

At this point Tinbergen returned to the literature and discovered two conditions that would bring forth the pecking. The first was that a red object must be placed in front of the young bird, and the second was that the red object be kept low to the ground. Using simple quasi-experimental designs, it was shown that the bird would peck at many objects that were both red and low to the ground, including cherries and even the red soles of bathing shoes. This understanding then led Tinbergen into more experimental studies using carved birds as stimuli. This work also led to some beginning hypotheses concerning the sensory apparatus of these birds.

As we have followed this particular work of Tinbergen, we have seen him move from naturalistic observation to more experimental studies. This refinement of ideas is a natural process in which scientists begin with a broad perspective and then focus on a more narrow experimental question. It is equally important to continue to return to the broad perspective of naturalistic observation to add validity to the experimental findings. Both Tinbergen (1972) and Lorenz (1973) have argued that for the study of animal behavior, it is necessary to create a balance between naturalistic and experimental methods as the key to good research.

As we begin to use naturalistic methods to study ourselves, the scientist is faced with greater complexity in both subject matter and the scientist's own role in what is being observed. In some cases the observer may choose to remain undetected or can just blend into the background. Krantz (1979) used this approach when he observed obese and nonobese individuals eating with others in a university cafeteria. In other situations the scientist may find it more useful to become a participant in the situation under study. One classic example of scientists as participants in a naturalistic study is that of D. L. Rosenhan (1973), entitled "On Being Sane in Insane Places."

Rosenhan's research focused on the manner in which mental hospital staffs distinguish sane individuals from insane ones and the types of experiences that patients in these hospitals face. In this study eight sane individuals gained admission to 12 different hospitals across the country. These individuals, or *pseudopatients* as they might be called, called the hospital and reported that they heard voices. Initial interviews were established for admission and, except for the initial complaint of voices and giving a false name and occupation, all other information given was correct. Once admitted to the hospital, the pseudopatients ceased to simulate any symptoms of pathology and followed instructions from the staff as required. Surprising as it may seem, in none of the hospitals were the researchers treated in any way other than as "insane" patients, and their true identities were never realized. This was true even though most of the researchers took notes openly and attempted to have "normal" conversations with the staff. In the published report, Rosenhan discusses his observations and the subjective experiences of powerlessness and depersonalization that the research had on the researchers themselves. This report is extremely interesting reading and points up the role of the scientist as investigative reporter using the methods of naturalistic observation.

## Concerns While Making Naturalistic Observations

Although naturalistic methods do not tell us how one variable influences another, questions of validity are still important. In these designs we also want to know whether our observations are valid and what reasons might account for their not being accurate. In this section we will go through the steps involved in naturalistic observation and consider possible problems in each step.

**Data Collection** One problem any observer faces is that if the subjects realize they are being observed, they may behave differently. When a subject's behavior is influenced by the mere presence of the observer, it is called *reactive behavior*. Reactive behaviors tell us what people are like when they know they are being observed. They tell us nothing about behavior under normal circumstances. To keep our observations free from reactive behaviors, we attempt, by concealing our identity as researchers, to avoid interfering in any way with the process we are studying. These undetected observations, which are called *unobtrusive observations*, greatly facilitate the task of interpreting observations (see Webb, Campbell, Schwartz, & Sechrest, 1966, for an excellent discussion of unobtrusive measures). Researchers attempt to make unobtrusive observations in a variety of ways. In some cases they attempt to conduct their observations without being seen by the subject. Some use one-way mirrors; some use hidden closed-circuit televisions. In some cases ethologists and comparative psychologists have surgically implanted tiny radio transmitters in wandering animals such as wild wolves to study their natural migratory patterns. Obviously this procedure would avoid any reactive behaviors of the wolves such as would occur if they were being tracked across the Arctic by a howling dog sled or a noisy helicopter.

As we mentioned in Chapter 2, simply observing can be difficult. Part of the difficulty is that we do not usually observe for prolonged periods of time without somehow interfering with the process. Our natural tendency is to jump in and influence the process. Try, for example, simply listening to a friend with a minimum of interference other than an occasional supportive statement. Another reason it is difficult to observe accurately is that we are influenced by *selective perception;* that is, the observations of untrained observers are markedly influenced by what they expect to see. Obviously, the extent to which our observations are restricted by our selective perceptions has a great impact on the accuracy of our observations. Fortunately it is possible to teach observers to observe more accurately. One common first step is simply to emphasize the dangers of selective perception. Once we realize that what we expect to see acts as a filtering device, we have come a long way toward seeing things as they are. The use of additional observers can also be a good way to increase the accuracy of observations, particularly if their expectations or selective perceptions are different from our own. One common problem, particularly for new observers, may be boredom. Remember, when you feel bored you are observing boredom and not the phenomenon you are supposed to be observing. So use boredom as a warning sign that you are not focusing on the observation. A useful technique for ensuring a minimum of selective perceptions and boredom is to pretend every few seconds that you have never before witnessed the setting you are observing. In this way you are constantly looking at the scene with a fresh perspective or with a beginner's mind. With this attitude you are constantly reopening yourself to any subtle changes or surprises.

The process of recording observations is equally crucial. Careful, immediately recorded, legible notes are of great value. If you cannot record your observations as they occur, then take sketchy notes and, after the observation session is over, use these highlights to assist recalling as much detail as you can. Obviously, mechanical devices such as video tape and cassette recorders can be useful aids. Remember, though, that these devices are limited; they capture only a portion of what is going on. And although they may involve miles of tape, they will never have a single theoretical insight.

**Data Analysis** The task of processing and analyzing field study data may initially seem monumental. Typically, many data are redundant, so the task of analyzing them is usually not so involved as it initially appears. A good place to begin is to review all your data several times so you get the whole picture of what happened. Next it may be helpful to describe the major patterns of behavior. This initial emphasis on common or invariant behavior is helpful because it provides a baseline of the relevant behavior. Once these primary behavior patterns are outlined, it may be profitable to examine instances of atypical behavior. For example, if you are observing the play behavior of a group of children, ask: Are there a small number who prefer not to play? What do they do instead? Sometimes you will find situations in which no clear patterns of behavior emerge. In these cases it is useful to develop a complete behavioral taxonomy or an organized listing of the behaviors involved along with the relative frequency of each behavior.

Once the major results become apparent, you will have an excellent basis for evaluating any theoretical ideas you may have recorded while directly observing your subjects. You may find that ideas that initially seemed very fruitful simply do not reflect the major patterns of your overall empirical observations. Any incorrect notions can easily be disregarded and replaced by your empirical findings. As you process and analyze your data, you may get insights about possible causal factors that may underlie the natural behaviors you are observing. These can be added to any you thought of while observing your subjects and later evaluated for possible study with formal experimental designs. In some cases you may decide that a simple intervention in a future field setting may provide useful clues to how one variable influences another. If you decide to explore these issues in your field setting, keep in mind that you will no longer be using the method of naturalistic observation. Instead you will most likely be using one of the quasi-experimental designs discussed in the early part of this chapter. As we mentioned, this is precisely what quasi-experimental designs were developed to do!

**To Conceal or Not to Conceal; To Participate or Not to Participate** Before concluding our discussion of naturalistic observation research, there are two issues every observer must face. Both stem from the fact that in actual practice the basic method we just outlined sometimes needs to be modified to fit the realities of the situation we are attempting to study. The first concerns whether to conceal our identity as researchers; the second concerns whether we actually participate in the social process we are observing.

In our previous discussion, we emphasized the importance of unobtrusive observation techniques as a means of minimizing the likelihood of reactive behaviors contaminating our observations. Sometimes, however, the phenomenon we are studying dictates that there is simply no reasonable way to collect data without being seen. In these cases we can best observe the process we are studying by concealing our identity as researchers and becoming actively involved in the process we are studying. For example, Randal Alfred (1976) posed as a member of the Church of Satan for several years while he studied the sociological and psychological aspects of its members. No one knew he was conducting research until he revealed his true purpose to their leader and requested permission to publish a summary of what he had learned.

Other researchers make no attempt to conceal themselves while collecting data. Anthropologists living among and observing people from other cultures typically do not attempt to conceal themselves. In her study of adolescents in Samoa, Margaret Mead (1928) made no attempt to conceal her identity from her subjects. Mead found that Samoan adolescents do not experience the extent of psychological problems seen among adolescents in the United States. And, furthermore, she suggested that their more open attitudes toward sexual behavior may underlie this difference.

The decision about whether to be an active participant in the process we are observing will also depend on the phenomenon we are studying. In the cases of ethologists such as Lorenz and Tinbergen and anthropologists such as Margaret Mead, data are usually collected without the researcher becoming part of the process under study. In contrast, Alfred's valuable contribution was based on his active participation in the process he was observing. Obviously, there is always a danger that the researcher's participation may unintentionally alter the process being observed. On the positive side, participation enables the researcher to experience the process personally. And this introspective data can provide a fruitful source of subjective data and new ideas about underlying psychological processes.

Deciding whether to remain concealed or reveal your identity depends to a large extent on whether you are observing highly reactive behaviors. If you suspect that the behavior of your subjects will be different if they know they are being observed, then use some sort of concealed observation strategy. In a similar way, if you suspect that there is much to be gained by personally experiencing the process you are studying *and* if you feel the overall process would not be significantly influenced by your participation, then you might consider participating directly in the process you are studying.

### Strengths and Weaknesses of Naturalistic Observation

Before proceeding it may be helpful to mention briefly some strengths and weaknesses of the method of naturalistic observation. One advantage is that it attempts to describe behavior as it naturally occurs in real-life settings. This emphasis on observing how things naturally occur enables us to begin our study of a new process with an accurate description of naturally occurring behaviors. As our observations unfold, new ideas about possible relationships or the possible survival value of the behavior we are observing may occur to us. Another advantage to naturalistic observation is that it studies behavioral processes as they unfold over a period of time. This emphasis on observing sequences of behavior provides an important temporal dimension to studying human behavior. This consideration of the flow of ongoing behavior constitutes a valuable complement to experimental and quasi-experimental designs, which focus instead on discovering factors that may be influencing behavior at a given time.

As with any human activity, there are also weaknesses or disadvantages that we must be aware of when using naturalistic observation. Generally this method tends to be qualitative and to rely more on the subjective judgment of the observer than do other research methods. Consequently the problem of *selective perception* can pose a serious threat to the validity of our data.

"OUR REPUTATION FOR LONGEVITY IS BASED ON SEVERAL FACTORS: HARD WORK, SIMPLE FOOD, LACK OF STRESS, AND THE INABILITY TO COUNT CORRECTLY."

If we study a single instance of a process very extensively, we create a potential problem concerning the representativeness of our sample. Unless we also examine other instances of the same phenomenon, we run the risk of making inappropriate generalizations and this would constitute a serious threat to the external validity of our observations. One final point to keep in mind is that naturalistic observations do not provide information about how one variable influences another. Of course, this is not really a weakness, any more than Beethoven is weak compared with Bach. Instead it reminds us that no single technique answers all our questions. We will return to this point later. In the meantime keep in mind that science is a fluid yet pragmatic process, which makes use of a variety of techniques and approaches to answer our questions about reality.

## Key Terms and Concepts

1. Field research
   a. external validity
   b. Voevodsky taxi study
   c. Sherif et al. camp study
2. Time series designs
   a. interrupted time series design
   b. multiple time series design
3. Quasi-experimental designs
   a. nonequivalent before-after design
   b. ex post facto design
4. Single-subject designs
   a. case study
   b. reversal design
      - ABA
      - ABAB
   c. multiple baseline design
5. Naturalistic observation
   a. Tinbergen
   b. Rosenhan
   c. problems of data collection and analysis
   d. role of scientist (to observe, participate, or both)
   e. strengths and weaknesses

## Summary

1. The chapter points out some distinctions that have been made concerning research. One of these distinction reflects whether research is run in a laboratory or out in the field. Another distinction refers to whether the design of the study is

a true experimental design or a quasi-experimental design. Although these are separate dimensions, it is often more difficult to conduct true experiments in the field. Thus, quasi-experimental designs are often presented in the contexts of field research.

2. Quasi-experimental designs are a set of designs that lack necessary controls to rule out important threats to internal validity as true experimental designs can do. Lacking strong experimental control, researchers in quasi-experimental designs attempt to discount logically alternative explanations.
3. Some types of quasi-experimental designs are time series designs, interrupted time series designs, multiple time series designs, and nonequivalent before-after designs.
4. An ex post facto design attempts to use empirical procedures for suggesting meaningful relationships from events that have occurred in the past.
5. Sometimes research is performed on a single subject. Referred to as single subject research, this type of research may be either descriptive (e.g., the case study) or experimental (e.g., reversal and multiple baseline research).
6. Naturalistic observation is the process of observing organisms usually in their natural environment. It is a descriptive procedure, and is illustrated by the work of Lorenz and Tinbergen.

## Review Questions

1. What is gained and what is lost when an experiment is conducted outside of the laboratory?
2. What does it mean to say "there is a trade-off between external and internal validity in any experiment"?
3. What are some of the problems and threats to internal validity with a simple time series design?
4. Describe an ABA design and describe how it might be used.
5. What are some of the problems of interpretation with a multiple time series design?
6. What is ex post facto research and what are the problems with it?
7. What are the major types of single subject designs and when might each be used?
8. How is data collected and analysis performed in a naturalistic observation study?
9. What are the strengths and weaknesses of naturalistic observation methods?

## Discussion Questions and Projects

1. Discuss the advantages and disadvantages of time series designs.
2. Design a naturalistic observation study in which you observe a child at play. What are the different roles you might take in relation to the child and how might this affect your results?

3. Discuss medical research that uses the ex post facto design, and give examples reported in the newspaper.
4. How could an ABAB design be used to study the effects of having no homework on class discussion? What would be some of the problems of interpretation?
5. How are the explorations of Tinbergen and Rosenhan similar and how are they different? How could experimenter bias influence these studies?
6. One student in an experimental class wanted to be more "alive and awake" in the mornings. How might this person use a reversal design to accomplish this end?
7. Another student was interested in determining whether he became less tired when he used a computer with a color screen or a monochrome one. How might he use a single subject design to answer this question?

CHAPTER TWELVE

# Questionnaires, Survey Research, and Sampling

## INTRODUCTION

A psychotherapist might notice that more of the clients coming to see her with problems of depression were women. Puzzled by this observation, she could conduct a research project to help her understand the relationship between gender and depression. That is, she might want to know whether gender was statistically related to being depressed. How might she go about this? One beginning approach would be to gather data from a variety of sources such as counseling centers, private practioners, and so forth concerning the problems that people initially describe when they come to seek therapy. The therapist could then single out depression and simply count the number of males and females who seek help for depression. Can you think of any problem with this approach? Let us assume that the psychotherapist in our example is interested in the question of whether women are more depressed than men using the standard psychiatric definition of depression as the operational definition. One potential problem is that such a study might not tell us whether there are more men than women who are depressed but rather whether more women than men will seek psychological help for any problem in general and depression in particular. That is, the observation that our therapist saw in her office might reflect not more depressed women than depressed men, but more women than men seeking help for the depression. To rule out this alternative and also to learn something about the incidence of depression in the general population, types of research techniques would be required that are different from those we have presented in the first part of this book. One particular alternative would be to use survey research techniques. It is the purpose of this chapter to introduce you to the main considerations in performing survey research. Survey research methods are best seen as helping us to understand the characteristics of some particular group of people, which we refer to as a *population*.

One large-scale survey research project that would have been of benefit to the therapist in the previous example focused on the well-being and life satisfaction of people in the United States at two points in time—1957 and 1976 (Veroff, Douvan, & Kulka, 1981). The 1957 survey and its replicate in 1976 were designed to answer questions about average men and women. These questions included how well or badly adjusted people consider themselves to be; how happy (or unhappy), worried (or not), optimistic (or pessimistic) people are in their outlook; what troubles people in the United States and what they do concerning their problems; whom they turn to for help and how effective that is. Such information would help the researcher in our previous example understand the relationship between help-seeking and gender as well as the specific issue of depression as it relates to differences between women and men. In this chapter we will discuss the survey related to well-being as an exemplar for the types of questions to be considered and the particular steps to be accomplished in performing survey research.

As with any type of research, one of the first questions in designing survey research concerns the general purpose of the research. Veroff et al. (1981, p. 6) report two distinct purposes for conducting their surveys. The first purpose was "to assess the subject mental health, the life experiences of American adults," and the second was "to determine in some detail how American people cope with problems of adjustment which arise in their lives." The second question was of practical concern to the United States Congress, which, through the National Institute of Mental Health, helped to fund this study. Congress was interested in determining whether Americans would use mental health facilities if the government helped to provide them. Thus, in economic terms alone the results of this survey would have far-reaching implications.

In order to fulfill the broad aims of the survey, the researchers addressed more specific questions such as how ready individuals are to seek psychological help, whether going to a mental health professional carries a stigma in someone's mind, and more practical questions, such as how one decides whom to go to, and how individuals decide whether the help they were given was good or bad. In relation to the broad aim of describing the life experiences of American adults, the researchers chose to examine feelings and sources of well-being, self-perceptions, marriage, parenthood, and work as well as patterns of reported problems. The survey researchers also decided to differentiate responses given by men and women offering data concerning the way in which men and women experience and report distress and satisfaction. Once more specific aims have been determined, one is then faced with the task of developing the actual questions that will be used in the survey.

## QUESTION CONSTRUCTION AND FORMATS

Constructing a survey seems at first an incredibly complicated process, with each decision affecting every other decision. Should you ask people general questions or have them compare one viewpoint with another? Have them fill out the questionnaire themselves or call them on the telephone. How would you word a question so that respondents will give you an honest response rather than one that is socially acceptable? These are all important questions. To make things easier for ourselves we will divide the question of survey construction into two parts. The first part will deal with the content of the survey—the actual questions asked and their construction. The second part will focus on the process of giving the survey—the manner in which these particular questions are presented to a person, including both the manner of administration (e.g., face-to-face interview versus mail survey) and the relationship between the interviewer and the respondent. It is important to remember that the manner of administration will often influence the format of the questions being asked. Thus, these two aspects are highly interrelated.

### Types of Questions

There are a number of question forms that may be used in a survey. One of the more common forms is referred to as *open-ended.* An open-ended question, as the name implies, has no fixed answers but allows the respondent to answer in any manner. For example, "What do you like best about college?" is an open-ended question. You could respond to that question by naming a particular course or a good friend, talking about being on your own, or by telling what you do on Saturday night (it's a good thing that surveys are kept confidential). As you can see, an open-ended question is very flexible and this flexibility carries a number of advantages. One advantage of an open-ended question is that it does not impose the researcher's point of view on the respondent. Another advantage is that the person being interviewed may give you information that you had not considered previously, and this information may show you a new way of understanding the issue being investigated. Open-ended questions also offer an important way to begin a survey. For example, the life satisfaction and well-being survey discussed previously used a number of open-ended questions. One of these asked about leisure and was worded as follows:

> One of the things we'd like to know is how people spend their time. For instance—how do you usually spend your time when your work is done—what kind of things do you do, both at home and away from home? (Veroff *et al.,* 1981, p. 552)

The virtue of the open-ended question can also pose a problem when you analyze the data and try to establish meaningful patterns of responding. In other words, it is sometimes difficult to know how to translate a global response to an open-ended question into categories that fit the original research hypothesis. Of course it is possible for researchers to impose their own point of view at this point and thus defeat one of the advantages of open-ended questions. It is important, therefore, to select scoring categories carefully. The life satisfaction and well-being survey made 55 distinctions in order to score responses to the item "What are some of the things you feel pretty happy about these days?"

Another form of question is referred to as *fixed alternative.* A fixed alternative question limits the number of responses that an individual can make. These forms of questions are also referred to as *closed-ended.* The most simple form would be a question that asked:

Do you believe that Puerto Rico should become the fifty-first state?
Yes [ ] No [ ]

With the fixed alternative question respondents are limited in their responses. Respondents cannot give a reason for their response, as they could with the open-ended question. However, in constructing fixed alternative questions you are not limited to just "yes" or "no." For example, a town might ask whether college students should be allowed to vote in local elections. The question could be as follows:

Should students be allowed to vote?

1. Yes, under any circumstances.
2. Yes, but only if they pay local taxes.
3. No.

Qualified answers such as "Yes, but . . ." or "No, but . . ." permit the answering of additional questions that the researchers might be interested in, while retaining an easy-to-score survey question. It is also possible to combine open- and closed-ended questions in a single item. For example, someone might ask who your favorite late-night talk-show host is, and then list Johnny Carson, Ted Koppel, and then "other" followed by a blank for people to write in a choice of their own. Such an item would appear as follows:

Who is your favorite late-night talk-show host?

[ ] Johnny Carson
[ ] Ted Koppel
[ ] Other: Please specify______________________________

It is not uncommon for open-ended and closed-ended questions to be used in the same questionnaire. One technique is to use open-ended questions followed by fixed alternatives to achieve more specific information. For example, in the survey on American life satisfaction, the question concerning leisure time was later followed by this closed-ended question:

Next, how much of your free time do you spend doing things that challenge you? Would you say that you spend *most, a lot, a little, or none* of your free time doing such things.

1. Most 2. A lot 3. Some 4. A little 5. None

When a researcher begins a line of questioning with an open-ended question and then follows this with more specific items as in the previous example, the process is referred to as *funneling*. Like a funnel, the questions initially are very broad and then become more and more specific. However, it is important to begin with open-ended questions, otherwise the closed-ended questions will limit the information that the respondent gives.

It is important to choose responses that fit with the category of question being asked. If the question has to do with frequency, such as "How often do you . . ." then the appropriate alternative answers might be *never, rarely, sometimes, often,* and *very often.* If on the other hand the question asked how true you believe a certain statement is, the alternatives might be *very true, somewhat true, not very true,* and *not at all true.* Although most of the responses that are offered to an item are usually balanced, it is also possible to present an unbalanced response set. That is, in response to the item "Have you ever been dishonest on an exam?" the answers *always* and *almost always* would receive few if any checks. It would be appropriate to offer respondents some alternatives that suggest that they almost never are dishonest or look at anyone else's paper. The responses might be *sometimes, almost never, once or twice,* and *never.* Another important point is that if the response categories ask for specific information, then the categories must not overlap. Consider the following question:

Check how many children you have.
a. 0–1 children
b. 1–2 children
c. 2 or more

Which answer would you check if you had two children? Since the categories overlap, it is difficult to know how to respond. Although the problem may seem obvious in this example, it is commonly seen in other situations, such as those requesting salary information.

The types of items that we previously discussed only begin to touch on the number of possible alternatives that can be used. In the concluding part of this section we want to introduce you briefly to a variety of other response formats. We present them for illustration only and suggest that you consult more in-depth presentations if you design a survey using these formats (cf. Babbie, 1983; Miller, 1977; Oppenheim, 1966). One alternative format is to use a nonverbal mode for describing preference. For example, with special populations such as children, it could be more appropriate to use graphic alternatives rather than verbal ones. For example, children might be asked to point to happy or sad faces to convey how much they like or dislike a certain game. Some other types of formats have been developed for particular purposes in terms of analysis and scaling. We include them in this section since you may hear researchers describe their questionnaires as using "Likert-type items," for example.

Over 50 years ago, Rensis Likert published a technique for measuring attitudes (Likert, 1932). The general format is the same as that of the fixed alternative items that we have presented. One item might be stated as follows:

> If I heard someone calling for help in a large city, I would help them.

| STRONGLY AGREE | AGREE | UNCERTAIN | DISAGREE | STRONGLY DISAGREE |
|---|---|---|---|---|
| (5) | (4) | (3) | (2) | (1) |

As you see, the format of the response is the same as that of items we have discussed. However, what Likert developed was a method of scaling items. Each item could be given a certain weight, represented by the number in parentheses. A number of scale items could then be added together to form an index, such as an index of helping behavior. The original procedure was to perform an *item analysis* to determine which items contributed to the index consistently across subjects. Items that did not contribute consistently could be eliminated from the final version of the questionnaire.

Another type of response format is referred to as the *semantic differential.* The semantic differential uses bipolar adjectives (such as good and bad, soft and hard, modern and old-fashioned, interesting and boring, hot and cold, slow and fast) in relation to a particular concept or idea. These adjectives are usually placed at each end of a seven-point scale. The instructions request the respondent to place a check nearest the adjective that describes the concept or thing to be rated. For example, you could be asked to rate a course you were taking as follows:

> Please rate your course in experimental basketweaving along the following dimensions.

easy ____ : ____ : ____ : ____ : ____ : ____ : ____ hard

fun ____ : ____ : ____ : ____ : ____ : ____ : ____ dull

sexy ____ : ____ : ____ : ____ : ____ : ____ : ____ not sexy

fast ____ : ____ : ____ : ____ : ____ : ____ : ____ slow

For clarity you could list categories (e.g., very much, a lot, somewhat, etc.) at the top of the semantic differential. Since the semantic differential was originally developed for measuring the meaning of objects or what is called the semantic space of experience, it is possible to use adjectives that may be related experientially to a concept. Thus, we can ask if a record is "hot" or a course "sexy" using this technique. When analysis is performed using a number of semantic response lines related to a single concept, then it is possible to arrive at an overall profile (see Osgood, Suci, & Tannenbaum, 1957, for more information about the semantic differential).

## General Considerations

Developing questions for a survey may be more difficult than you may think at first, for a variety of reasons. One reason is the ambiguity of language. For example, we often say such things as "I always eat with my friends" when we are trying to emphasize how close we are to our friends. However, if someone were to ask you the same question on a survey ("Do you always eat with your friends?"), you would probably consider the question to be asking for specific information and might have some difficulty knowing exactly how to answer the question. Thus, it is important in developing questions to be as clear as possible and to avoid unwanted ambiguity. Sometimes the particular question you are asking may be difficult to phrase in a simple sentence, especially if you are asking about how someone feels or thinks about more global concepts such as freedom, love, religion, or their own country or family. Sometimes you may be asking for information that people do not want to give. How you phrase your question may determine whether the person is willing to answer. For example, many people will answer whether their income ranges between $10,000 and $19,999, $20,000 and $29,999, or above $30,000, but they will not tell you the exact figure. If you don't need to know the exact figure, don't ask. One of the first rules for developing questions is to ask only what you need to know. Another important consideration is the order in which the questions are asked. For example, the life satisfaction and well-being survey would probe for positive responses before negative ones. That is, on open-ended questions, such as general questions on marriage, the interviewer would ask about the "nicest things" in marriage before asking about things that were "not quite as nice as you would like them to be." Some researchers who have studied order effects suggest that a person's response to one question has an effect on his or her response to the next question (Schuman & Presser, 1981). These effects seem to be most strong when the questions are of a general or summary type.

Another important guideline is to consider what you are asking not only from your own perspective but also from the perspective of those taking the survey. Questions that seem perfectly clear to use when we are developing a questionnaire may not appear so clear when asked in a survey. The respondent of our survey may even have a different frame of reference. For example, if I asked you about your worth, you would not know whether I wanted to know how much money you had in the bank or how you valued yourself psychologically. Again, it is important to reduce any unwanted ambiguity. One way of doing this is to establish a context in which the question is presented. As you may have noticed in the life satisfaction and well-being survey, the researchers began by saying that they wanted to know how people spend their leisure time. This is a better approach than just asking, "What do you do when you are not working?" Context is also very important when we ask people to give us information that may be at odds with either what is accepted in society or their public image. For example, a question designed to learn about parent's anger toward their small children might begin with the statement, "All parents become angry with their children from time to time. What do you do when you become angry?" The established context—that all parents become angry at times—enables the respondent to feel freer to disclose information in relation to their own angry feelings and actions. By creating a context in which the person can answer the question, we gain more accurate information. However, it is also important not to go to the extreme and create an introduction to your questions that leads the person to answer in a manner that does not reflect his or her real attitude. One should also avoid "leading" in developing questions. In order to avoid potential bias based on their own perceptions, some researchers develop fixed alternative responses based on the initial administration of an open-ended question. That is to say, to ensure that you do not have leading questions in the survey, you may begin by asking the question in an open-ended fashion to a group of individuals. You would tabulate their responses and use these as a basis for fixed alternative items.

At this point it is time to consider one of the most important guidelines for survey research—*PRETEST THE SURVEY!* It is imperative that the questions you have developed be given to people and that you note any unwanted ambiguity in their responses or misunderstanding of the items. Ideally, the survey should be pretested on the population to which it will be given. This is particularly important for helping to determine the adequacy of fixed choice responses. Pretesting helps us to perceive easily that we have worded an item correctly (or incorrectly) and whether the alternatives offered actually do represent the manner in which our target group would respond. It is not uncommon to pretest a survey more than once and to use the feedback from each testing to develop a better survey for answering our original research question.

## METHODS OF ADMINISTERING THE SURVEY

### Face-to-Face Interviews

When someone mentions the word *survey* we often think of census takers coming to our house or of the exit polls that we see on television during political elections. In both of these cases the interviewer presents the person

---

### *Box 12.1 Steps for Designing a Survey Research Project*

Over 30 years ago Campbell and Katona (1953) set up a simple nine-step flow chart describing the steps required for conducting a survey. These steps offer a review and checklist for any surveys you are designing.

(1) General Objectives: The first step is to state why the survey is necessary. What is the broad objective that one is seeking to accomplish? For example, using the case of the psychotherapist presented at the beginning of this chapter, we would say that her overall objective was to describe the relationship between gender and depression.

(2) Specific Objectives: The second step is to be more specific—to state exactly what types of data will be collected and specify the particular hypotheses to be explored. Again using the example of depression, the specific objectives would include a statement of indicators of depression such as feeling state (reporting that one feels blue, etc.), difficulty sleeping, and so forth would be collected in face-to-face interviews. The particular hypotheses could be (1) that women report depression or symptoms of depression more often than men, and (2) that women report seeking help for these symptoms more often than men.

(3) Sample: Two main decisions are needed at this point. The first decision requires that you state which population you are addressing; that is, to which group do you wish to generalize your results? The population that one designates is related to the original question. For example, in a political survey, the population might be all registered voters in a particular state. Once the population is established, the second decision is required. This decision relates to how large a sample one is to use, as well as how the sample is to be chosen. Particular techniques for sample selection are discussed in this chapter.

(4) Questionnaire: This step requires a decision as to how the sample is to be surveyed (e.g., in person, by phone, or by mail), as well as the particular questions that are to be asked. The researcher at this point must decide on the types of questions and responses that will be included. That is, will the questions use an open-ended or fixed alternative format, or some

with a series of questions face-to-face and records their answers. There are a number of advantages to this approach. One of the main advantages of face-to-face interviews, especially if the survey is somewhat complex, is that you are able to achieve a better idea of the psychological set from which the person is answering the questions. That is to say, you can, for example, determine how motivated the person may be to give you answers. You can also judge the respondent's comprehension and clear up any ambiguity or misunderstanding on his or her part. With open-ended questions it is possible to "probe" for additional information if the initial response is very brief, or incomplete. For example, in the survey question concerning what people do with their free time, if the person says only "have fun," it would be

---

combination of both? Once the actual questions are developed, it is important to pretest them to ensure clarity. With fixed alternative questions, the pretest will help to determine whether adequate responses have been provided.

(5) Field Work: This step is related to the people who will actually conduct the survey. The interviewers must be trained and thoroughly practiced. Other considerations such as the inter-relationship between the sex, race, and socioeconomic level of the interviewer and respondent must also be taken into account.

(6) Content Analysis: Some surveys will return data in a qualitative form and this must be transformed into a quantative one. The information must be coded to ensure reliability across subjects, that is to say, there must be a system of coding open-ended questions. Even if the data are presented in a numerical fashion as on a Likert scale, there must exist a systematic manner of grouping data for future analysis.

(7) Analysis Plan: Most surveys contain a large number of questions, each of which could be compared to every other, either singularly or in combination. Before the actual data are collected, it is important to specify a plan of analysis that will answer the research hypotheses. This of course does not preclude later re-analysis of the data for different purposes, but it is important to have an initial plan for data analysis.

(8) Tabulation: This step is required in a large survey. The researcher must decide how the data are to be inputted into the computer, and in what form the data should be stored (e.g., on magnetic tape).

(9) Analysis and Reporting: The final stage is the preparation of a report, which would include not only how the data are related to the specific objectives but also such considerations as the reliability of the data from this study.

As Campbell and Katona point out, these nine steps may be inter-related and thus decisions affecting one step may also have important implications for another step. With this qualification, these steps offer guidelines for design survey research.

---

possible to follow up with a probe such as "tell me more" or "can you name some particular activities" and thus produce a more specific answer. Additionally, the interviewer can make and record observations related to race, sex, socioeconomic level, and so forth without having to ask these questions directly. In comparison to other forms of survey administration such as sending questionnaires through the mail, face-to-face interviews generally give higher completion rates and more complete information.

There are also disadvantages to face-to-face interviews. First, face-to-face interviews are very expensive in time and personnel, thus limiting the number of interviews that can be conducted in comparison to other methods such as mail or phone surveys. Second, although the interviewer may help to clarify information and understanding of the questions, the interviewer can also either consciously or unconsciously bias the results. For example some interviewers may probe more with men than women or may probe less with older than younger individuals, and thus systematically bias the results. It may also happen that the respondent gives different answers to a live person and to a questionnaire. As you can imagine, some individuals find it relatively difficult to discuss with a person in front of them sensitive issues (such as sexuality, drug or alcohol use, or behaviors that might be considered deviant), while they might answer an anonymous questionnaire quite easily. It is also possible that the respondent will not like the interviewer's looks, clothing, race, or sex, and may give biased information. For example, one interviewer reported that after a very productive interview session the respondent said that the interviewer was really a civil rights worker trying to integrate the neighborhood and that the respondent wasn't being fooled (Converse & Schuman, 1974). Thus it is possible his answers were biased by this perception of the interviewer. If you conduct interviews you should consider the possibility that college students will be perceived as having values different from those of the surrounding community. All of these possibilities need to be considered when using face-to-face interviews. As with any piece of research, it is important to walk through each step and determine to the best of your ability whether there could be a potential problem or confound.

### Telephone Interviews

One alternative to face-to-face interviews is the telephone interview. Often surveys that we read about in the newspaper are the result of telephone interviews. For example, in 1983 *The New York Times* interviewed by telephone 1,309 adult men and women, asking them about their attitudes toward work (Dowd, 1983). One of the questions asked was "If you were free to do either, would you prefer to have a job outside the home, or would you prefer to stay home and take care of your house and family?" From this survey, 72% of the men and 45% of the women said they would prefer to have a job outside the home. A telephone interviewer can establish rapport and determine in general both motivational and clarity issues while still being more cost-effective than a face-to-face interviewer. That is, it is possible in a given amount of time to conduct a larger number of telephone interviews than face-to-face interviews, since face-to-face interviewing also requires time for traveling and finding a particular house or apartment. Also, if someone chooses not to participate in a telephone interview all one needs to do is to call the next number, while in a face-to-face situation one must relocate and look for the next address. At one time, telephone interviews were avoided by survey researchers because phones were associated with the higher socioeconomic levels. Today there is the problem, especially in larger cities, that many individuals have unlisted numbers. To avoid the potential bias of leaving out unlisted numbers, some surveys have chosen phone numbers by randomly choosing four numbers and using these with the available prefixes in that area. Although this does avoid the problem of unlisted numbers, it creates others in that it includes businesses and non-working numbers as well. Telephone interviews also have a general time limitation. It is a common rule of thumb that interviews lasting over 15 minutes make some people feel uncomfortable, and these people may actually end the interview by hanging up the phone whether or not you are finished. Thus, telephone interviews will not work when a lengthy session is required.

### Mail Questionnaires

A different type of survey procedure uses self-administered questionnaires delivered through the mail. One of the major advantages of mail questionnaires is that they can be sent almost anywhere in the world for the cost of postage. As you can imagine, however, one of the disadvantages is that they may not always be returned. In fact, the return rate of mail surveys is typically very low in comparison to the completion rate of face-to-face interviews. If you obtain a return rate above 75%, you can consider yourself very fortunate. Although above 50% should be considered acceptable, the typical mail survey probably has a return rate of less than 50%. With a below 50% return rate, you need to reconsider the type of sample that is required, the purpose of the survey, and the manner in which the survey is to be utilized, and evaluate your data accordingly.

Since you want people to respond to a mail survey, it is important that you do everything you can to ensure that they read, complete, and return your questionnaire. Although it is more expensive, it is important that the survey be sent through first class mail; some professionals, for example, open only their first class mail and throw the rest away. Most survey researchers supply postage-paid return envelopes; you would not want your survey to be lost for lack of a stamp. It is also important that the questionnaire look professional. The first impression should be that the questionnaire will be easy to complete and return. It is also important that the respondent understand the importance of the survey; to this end you should include a carefully prepared cover letter explaining the survey and placing it in an appropriate context. One means of increasing response rate is to use follow-up letters reminding the respondent of the survey and enclosing another copy of the survey. Some researchers have also increased compliance by including a shortened version of the original in additional follow-up letters. Although the researchers may lose some information covered in the more detailed version, they are still able to obtain the most important information. They are also able to obtain information on the type of respondent who did not initially fill out the questionnaire. Mail surveys lack some advantages of face-to-face interviews, such as being able to request additional information and personal contact, but sometimes people will be more open and honest with their answers in a mail survey. This is especially true if they believe themselves to be responding anonymously and are reporting areas of personal behavior such as medical problems, sexuality, or attitudes not in keeping with currently held viewpoints.

In conclusion, there are a variety of methods for administering surveys. The three most popular methods are face-to-face, telephone, and mail. There are advantages and disadvantages to each, as we have discussed. Typically one is faced with a trade-off between response rate and cost. In deciding which form of administration you should use, you will need to determine what is important in your survey research. If it is important for you to have a high rate of return on your surveys, then face-to-face or telephone interviews would be good choices. As you will learn in the next section, the ability to have a representive sample will be extremely important in some situations, and will thus rule out mail surveys. Time may also be a factor, as in political surveys taken the day before an election. When cost is an important factor and you need a large number of responses, then a mail survey may be more appropriate. As in any research you need to consider why you are doing the research in the first place as well as what type of information will best answer your research question. (See Dillman, 1978, for more information on telephone and mail surveys.)

## SAMPLING

In discussions of research throughout this book we have raised the question of generalization and considered how the results from a particular experiment could be applied to a larger group. The question of generalization or representiveness is also important for survey research. How can we ensure that the results obtained in giving our questionnaire or interview to a group of individuals will apply to some larger population of people? It should be pointed out that if we were developing a questionnaire for only one group, such as all senior psychology majors in your college, and if we gave it to each senior psychology major, then generalization would not be an issue for our "sample" would represent the entire population. Technically, this type of survey is referred to as a *census*. Like descriptive statistics, a census is aimed at obtaining descriptive information concerning a particular group of individuals and nothing more. However, if we wish to apply the results obtained beyond the specific group from which they were obtained, then we need to be concerned about generalizability. In laboratory experiments one of the ways to accomplish this is through careful experimental controls and the selection of subjects, as discussed in previous chapters. In survey research we place much of the emphasis for generalizability on selection of subjects through sampling procedures. In this section we want to introduce you to sampling techniques. For additional information you can consult text specifically aimed at discussing sampling techniques (e.g., Scheaffer, Mendenhall, & Ott, 1979).

You are probably most familiar with the general idea of sampling in relation to television ratings or attempts to predict who will win a political race. You may have wondered how raters can say that such a television show is highly rated when fewer than 2,000 people are sampled out of millions. You may also wonder what is meant by the statement "78% of the population really wants to take a course in methodology, with a sampling error of 4%"—besides wondering what weird population would have said that. These are two topics that we will cover in this section.

In 1936 asking 2 million people whom they would vote for led one magazine to conclude that Alfred Landon would beat Franklin Roosevelt (Gallup, 1972). George Gallup, on the other hand, conducted a much smaller survey of voters and correctly predicted the winner. What was his secret to success? How did he do more with less? The answer was in the sampling procedures. Although the magazine *Literary Digest* had sampled 2,376,523 individuals, they had drawn the names of the individuals from automobile registration lists and telephone directories. Can you think of any problem with using this method in 1936? Realizing that this was during the Depression, you probably understood the bias in this sampling technique. During the Depression many people did not have money for either cars or telephones and thus would not have been included in the survey. Likewise those who did have telephones and cars tended to be wealthy and also to be Republican. Thus, wealthy Republicans completed the survey, saying they would vote for Landon and against Roosevelt and the New Deal. Gallup used a sampling procedure that did not exclude the poor, who were mainly Democratic and more likely to vote for Roosevelt. He thus had a more accurate representation, and he was right. The situation today seems even more amazing. For example, in 1976 using a sample size of fewer than 2,000 individuals, a New York *Times*-CBS poll correctly predicted that of almost 80 million voters, 51.1% would vote for Jimmy Carter and 48.9% for Gerald Ford. What do you think the actual vote was? Try again; the actual vote was 51.1% for Jimmy Carter and 48.9% for Gerald Ford, the same numbers as the prediction. Of course, not every prediction is that good. However, there is important precision to be gained from understanding and applying the sampling techniques.

The basic idea behind sampling is that we would like to learn about the characteristics of a large group of individuals (referred to as a *population*) by studying a smaller group (referred to as a *sample*). If all people were equal in every way then it would not matter which individuals we chose to study out of a large group. We could use any manner we wished for making a grouping. No matter how individuals were grouped the results would always be the same. However, everyone is not the same in every way, and thus we try to find ways of choosing people from a larger group in such a way that the characteristics found in the smaller group reflect those of the larger group.

One of the first tasks is to define the population that we are interested in, and this is usually related to the research questions being asked. If we are interested in memory and learning across the life span, then we would want to define our population so that people of all ages are included. If we are interested in the drinking habits of college females, then we would have a more narrowly defined population. Once the population is defined, a question arises concerning the appropriate sample that is needed. Since our goal is to perform research or examine a particular sample and from this sample infer to the larger population, it is important that our sample reflects the larger population. The more the sample reflects the larger population the more confidence we have concerning any inference that we make from our smaller sample to the larger population. A variety of sampling techniques are available, and we will present some of the more popular ones, including the major advantages and disadvantages of various sampling procedures.

## Probability Sampling

**Simple Random Sampling** The main characteristic of a randomized procedure is that every member of the population has a known chance of being selected. In a simple random sample, each member has an equal chance of being selected. Conceptually this is like putting the names of everyone in the population in a hat and drawing out a certain number of names. For example, if you were interested in how your campus radio station was rated, you might consider all students in your university as the population and then choose a sample from this population using a random number table (see Box 7.1). You could then conduct a survey on this sample.

**Systematic Sampling** A variation on the random sampling procedure is to choose a person randomly from the list of the total population and then sample some selected number. For example you might sample every fifth person on the list and use them in the survey. This procedure has the advantage of efficiency over total random sampling. However, it is important that the list you use contain the entire population in an unbiased fashion. Although most lists of a population that were alphabetized would not introduce bias into a survey, it is important to consider possible bias from a variety of sources. For example, if you sampled every fifth person in a classroom with 10 seats across, you might produce a biased sample without realizing it. That is, in some classrooms the first seat in each row has a desk designed for someone who writes left-handed and thus if you happened to sample every fifth person beginning with the first seat you would have 50% right-handed people and 50% left-handed people—not a representative sample of the population of students in that class. Of course this is an extreme case of bias but we include it to emphasize that there are types of bias you might not anticipate that can cause problems in the sample.

**Stratified Random Sample** At times we may realize that in order to answer the research question we are interested in, we need to ensure that certain people are systematically represented in our sample, especially if we expect that differences exist in certain groups. For example, we might want to make sure that certain age groups are included or that both males and females are represented. In order to accomplish this end, we could use a stratified sampling procedure. For example, if it was important to us that both males and females were included in our sample in a certain proportion, then we could divide the population according to this category and then randomly sample from each of these divisions separately. Although stratification by sex is an easy example to understand, it is more common to stratify when a group of individuals is likely to be under-represented because the actual numbers of that group are very small. For example, if you conduct a survey requiring that the respondents include all minority groups, then this would be a useful procedure.

**Cluster Sampling** There are situations in which the physical constraints, both in time and money, make it difficult to use a random sampling technique. For example, if you wanted to study language before the introduction of television, you would need countries or areas in which television had yet to be introduced. In those countries that did not have television, it might be impossible to create a random sample from the entire country. It would be more economical to select a few villages and then study these in some depth. Likewise, researchers interested in fear of crime (how individuals feel about the chance of their being victims in a crime) may choose to study the inhabitants of particular blocks in a large city. The general procedure is to randomly select a certain number of blocks in a city and then use local people in the research.

**Multistage Sampling** A multistage sampling procedure, as the name implies, relies on sampling at different stages in the process. At times we may use the same sampling technique but with different populations. For example, if we wanted to study United States college students, we might first randomly sample colleges throughout the country. Then we could randomly sample students in each selected college. Likewise, we might randomly sample cities in the country and then randomly sample individuals within these cities. We might also change the type of sampling procedure from one stage to the next. For example, the study of life satisfaction and well-being discussed previously used a multistage sampling procedure. Before sampling, the researchers decided that the sample would be limited to private households, thus excluding prisons, hospitals, colleges, and other forms of group housing. In the first stage of the sampling procedure, standard metropolitan areas, single counties, and certain county groups within each region of the country were listed. Initial samplings were made proportional to population. That is, the sampling procedure was set up so that areas with larger populations would have a greater chance of being selected. This was changed to an equal probability in the final selection for location. Once specific addresses were selected, a single individual at this address was chosen randomly to be interviewed.

### Nonprobability Sampling

The type of sampling that we have discussed thus far is referred to as probability sampling. The name *probability* refers to the predetermined chance of any individual being selected for the study, given the particular constraints under study. It is also possible to use nonprobability sampling. One common example of this type of sampling is the use of introductory psychology students for research. Since most students do not randomly take a course in introductory psychology—that is, they self-select and in this way form a special group—the question of generalizability arises; that is, what populations can research performed with introductory psychology students be generalized to? This is an important question that should be considered whenever one is using this or any other convenient group for research. Sampling individuals who are convenient is referred to as *convenience sampling*. In convenience sampling we use those individuals who are available to us. Sometimes simple surveys use a convenience sampling procedure when people on the street or in shopping malls are interviewed as they happen to walk by the interviewer. Some students, for example, might choose their sample by picking every tenth person who comes into a snack bar over a two-day period. Although this sample might be useful if the total population was snack bar users, it would not be useful if the survey was to be generalized to all college students. A sample selected in this manner would exclude students who never come to the snack bar and would also overinclude those who come in more than once a day.

Another type of nonprobability sampling is *quota sampling*. A quota sample sets up a quota or number of specific types of individuals. For example, we might decide to give our survey to three biology majors, three psychology majors, and three faculty members. Another type of nonprobability sampling is referred to as *snowball sampling*. This sampling procedure is most often used when no list of the population exists. For example, if a medical researcher was interested in health issues related to prostitution, it would be impossible to obtain a list of prostitutes on which to base the sample. A common procedure is to find one prostitute who would agree to be part of the research and then ask that person to help locate others, and these individuals would help locate others in a snowball fashion.

## SAMPLE SIZE

In this chapter we have said little about one very important matter, the matter of sample size. Sample size in survey research is based on the type of considerations that we discussed in Chapter 4 in our presentation of inferential statistics. We want to be able to choose a sample of individuals who have the same characteristics as the overall population. If we succeed with this goal then we can generalize successfully from our sample to the overall population. Because research is expensive in time and money, we want our sample to be as small as possible. But how do we go about deciding the actual size that we need?

In simple terms we determine the size of the sample that we need by asking two questions. The first question concerns the characteristics of the population to which we want to generalize. Said in other terms, potentially how many people are available to be used in the survey, and how homogeneous or nonhomogeneous are these people? As you can imagine, if the population is very homogeneous on the characteristic we wish to study, then fewer people would be needed for the sample to approximate the population. If there is a wide range of variation, then more individuals would be needed. The second question asks how accurate an answer we need to the question that we are asking. That is, how much difference can we tolerate between the characteristics found in the sample and those of the overall population? These two questions vary together to determine sample size, with the general formulation that the larger the sample to which we want to generalize, or the greater the variability and the more exact we want the results to be, the larger the sample size that is required.

Since we have little control over the size of the population we are interested in, our main concern is with the second question, that of acceptable variations in the estimate of the population parameters. Technically, we establish an upper and lower bound within which we wish the results to fall with some established probability. Said in simple language, we make a statement of how much error we will tolerate. For example, if we were to conduct a survey as to how many students would want an outdoor café built onto the student union, we might decide that we would accept an error of 5%. Thus, if the results of the survey came back saying that 67% of the students were in favor of the outdoor café, we could assume with some established probability that if the entire student body had been questioned the exact percentage in favor of the café would be in the range between 62% (the lower bound) and 72% (the upper bound). This is referred to as a *confidence interval.* In this example we would say there was a *sampling error* of ± 5% (plus or minus 5%). The amount of sampling error that is acceptable is related to the original purpose of the survey. In the beginning of a political campaign, for example, you might be interested only in survey results that give ballpark figures on which candidate is leading. However, as the election draws nearer, it might become important to have more exact estimates of how the vote would go. Thus in an initial survey you might be willing for your survey to report that 40% of the voters liked a particular candidate, when in fact if the election were held that day it would have been 45% who voted for that person. It might have been more acceptable to you to have been off by a greater percentage in the first survey than in the later one which would be nearer the election.

Once we have some idea of the size of our population as well as how variable it is and the amount of error that we are willing to tolerate, then we can determine the sample size that will be needed. The actual formula that we use requires that we establish confidence levels. Traditionally, the 95% level is used. This states that the probability of the results happening by chance is 5 out of 100. The general formula is as follows:

$$\text{Sample Size} = \left( \frac{\text{Confidence Level} \times \text{Variation in Population}}{\text{Desired Precision}} \right)^2$$

Assume we wanted to know how much the average college student pays for books, how many students would we need to survey? Using the formula, we could determine the appropriate number. The variation in the population that we use is the standard deviation (see Chapter 3). The standard deviation for a particular population is often known from previous surveys. (It also can be estimated from the sample standard deviation, although not in advance of performing the survey; for this see advanced survey texts.) Let us assume in this case that we knew it to be $20. The confidence level traditionally used is that for the 95% confidence interval, which is expressed in the formula as a standard score (Z score) of 1.96. For desired precision assume that we wanted the error to be less than $2.00. Solving the formula, we would determine that we needed 384.16 subjects to satisfy our conditions.

$$384.16 \text{ Subjects} = \left( 1.96 \ \frac{20}{2} \right)^2$$

We might also solve this equation using different levels of precision and determine that we would need 1,537 subjects if we wanted the error to be less than $1, but only 96 subjects if we accepted an error of $4. There also exist tables to aid researchers in determining the sample size for

---

### *Box 12.2 Verbal Report as Data: Can We Tell More Than We Know?*

It is often said that if you want to know something, you should ask. In psychological research this simple suggestion has lead to a great deal of debate. The debate centers around a number of themes, one of which asks whether there really is a relationship between attitudes and behaviors. Another asks whether a person can really know about him- or herself. For example, do you really know your attitude concerning the opposite sex? Can you really predict whether you will help someone in distress if you happen into such a situation walking through the streets of New York? Do you actually know how you think as you go about solving a problem, and can you report this to an experimenter? Although our tendency is to say that we know a great deal about ourselves, research has demonstrated that these questions represent very complex considerations which cut across most of psychological research. They are particularly important to survey researchers, since survey research relies heavily on self-report data.

There have been two main approaches that survey researchers have adopted concerning self-report data. The first approach is to seek situations in which it can be assumed that survey responses will give a useful description of a person's attitudes, views, and behaviors. For example, it is assumed that people can report what they do in their leisure time, or whether they would vote for a particular person in an election. The second approach disconnects the attitude from behavior and places an emphasis on attitudes in themselves. For example, it is possible to ask people about their optimism for the future, or their views of capital punishment, or what they think about free trade, all without involving references to a particular behavior.

With regard to the second approach it has been suggested that verbal data are important in their own right and do not have to be related to nonverbal data (cf. Galtung, 1967). This theoretical position suggests that it is not necessary to validate a questionnaire related to behavior by actually observing behavior. To expand on this position, it is important to understand that social and psychological relationships are complex and that all modes of behavior (e.g., cognitive, emotional, and physiological as well as self-report) are not expected to show identical patterns in every situation. This complexity makes psychological research interesting and it is often amazing to discover how widely particular aspects of behavior vary. For example, in one study the task was to listen to a tape recording of different voices and to report after each voice whether the voice was one's own or that of another person. It was shown that individuals would give a psychophysiological response (electrodermal) to hearing their own voice even though they reported that it was not their voice (Gur & Sackeim, 1979). This type of research suggests that the people have multiple response systems and that self-report data cannot be expected to give a single consistent picture across all of these. The research also suggests that when you tap the right channel, it is possible for a person to "tell you more than they know they know."

Whether a person can tell you more than they know they know has been the topic of much debate. Nisbett and Wilson (1977), in a *Psychological Review* article, suggest that people may not be able to use introspection to describe their cognitive processes accurately.

---

survey research (cf. Yamane, 1967). These tables generally assume a large standard deviation and present the desired precision in terms of percent

---

That is to say, people may not actually know why they like someone or why they took a particular course or why they like one color of clothes as opposed to another. According to Nisbett and Wilson, people may also not have access to how they go about making decisions. In particular, these authors suggest that research subjects (1) may be unaware of stimuli that importantly influence a response, (2) may be unaware of the response itself, and (3) may be unaware that a particular stimulus has actually influenced a particular response. If Nisbett and Wilson are correct, then researchers would need to rethink survey research that addresses itself to asking people why they do what what they do, or research that asks people how they go about solving certain problems.

In a later article, Ericsson and Simon (1980) suggest that psychology has always used verbal behavior as data even in nonsense syllable experiments in which the subjects report remembering which syllable was paired with which other syllable. That is, even in those studies that claimed to measure only observable responses, self-report information was still considered valuable. Since Simon and his colleagues often use self-report data to study how people go about solving problems, it would be important to them if subjects could not report how they went about solving problems. In Chapter 1 we discussed one of these studies using novice and expert chess players. Using an information processing model, Ericsson and Simon suggest that situations do exist in which verbal report may not be consistent with behavior, as suggested by Nisbett and Wilson, in particular, those situations that do not require memory processes. If you were asked how you would solve a particular problem had you been given the problem in a different manner, the self-report and the actual behavior (i.e., how you really would have solved the problem) might differ. That is, you would have no actual behavior on which to base your self-report and thus would have to create a hypothetical situation and imagine hypothetical behavior. On the other hand Ericsson and Simon would predict that if you had just solved the problem, then you would have this information in memory and self-report would be valid. Said in simple terms, self-report may be consistent with behavior when the self-report describes an actual set of behaviors that have occurred in the recent past. However, there may be less consistency if the event has not occurred. This is only a statement of the idea that, whether it be solving a problem or responding to cries of help from a person on the streets of New York, we may not be able to predict our own future behavior.

With regard to survey research, the question ultimately becomes: How will the data be used and why do we want the data in the first place? If we are interested in attitudes, then self-report offers a historically important way of tapping into how people feel or think about a certain topic. Likewise, if we are interested in past behavior, self-report also offers a means of obtaining this information as perceived by the person giving it. However, if we want to know about future behavior, self-report may offer a good guess but not certainty. There is one additional point that needs to be made in relation to self-report data and this is that not everyone wants to give you the information that you are seeking. Thus it may be important to include some type of question that assesses how readily that particular person has given out certain information in the past, and to judge your results accordingly.

---

error. From such a table we would learn that if we were to perform such a survey in a national election, we would need 10,000 respondents for a 1% error; 2,500 for a 2% error; 1,111 for a 3% error; 400 for a 5% error; and only 100 respondents for an error of 10% (Yamane, 1967).

## Key Terms and Concepts

1. Survey research
2. Question construction and formats
   a. open-ended questions
   b. closed-ended questions
   c. funneling
   d. Likert scale
   e. semantic differential
3. Methods of administration
   a. face-to-face interviews
   b. telephone interviews
   c. mail questionnaires
4. Probability sampling
   a. simple random sampling
   b. systematic sampling
   c. stratified random sampling
   d. cluster sampling
   e. multistage sampling
5. Nonprobability sampling
   a. convenience sampling
   b. quota sampling
   c. snowball sampling
6. Sample size
   a. confidence interval
   b. sampling error

## Summary

1. A type of research that is gaining popularity in the social sciences is that of survey research. Such research allows for the asking of broad questions, such as "How do Americans view their mental health?"
2. An open-ended question is one in which respondents can respond in any way they wish. An example would be to ask someone "What do you like best about college?"
3. A closed-ended question is one in which respondents are limited in their responses. A multiple choice question is an example of a closed-ended question.
4. In developing questions for a survey it is important to be clear, to avoid unwanted ambiguity, and to ask questions in such a manner that the respondent is able to give the information that you need. It is especially important that you pretest the survey.

5. There are number of methods for administering a survey. Three of the most common ways are (1) face-to-face interviews, (2) telephone interviews, and (3) self-administered questionnaires delivered through the mail.
6. The problem of generalizability is especially critical for survey research. To ensure that the results from a single group can be applied to other groups requires the use of sampling techniques. A broad distinction is made between probability sampling and nonprobability sampling. The more common forms of probability sampling are simple random sampling, systematic sampling, stratified random sampling, cluster sampling, and combining methods in a multistage format. Nonprobability sampling techniques include quota sampling, convenience sampling, and snowball sampling.
7. The sample size that is required is related to three factors: confidence level, variation in the population, and the desired precision (amount of error).

## Review Questions

1. What is the purpose of survey research? Give an example.
2. What is the value of an open-ended question?
3. How might open-ended and closed-ended questions be combined?
4. Give an example of a semantic differential.
5. Why does a survey always need to be pretested?
6. What are the major ways of presenting questionnaires to respondents? What are the advantages of each?
7. Why is sampling important?
8. Describe the major forms of probability sampling.
9. When would nonprobability sampling be appropriate?
10. What are the three major factors in determining sample size?

## Discussion Questions and Projects

1. Many students in experimental psychology classes are interested in how music affects their mood. Discuss how you might determine whether this is an interest mainly of people taking experimental psychology or of all college students.
2. Outline a way to determine how individuals believe music to affect their mood.
3. What could you conclude about how music actually does influence mood from the research conducted in Question 2.
4. Why is sampling so important for surveys and observe how political candidates or others use surveys and what type of sampling procedures they use.
5. How is it possible to know how millions of people will vote in a national election from speaking with only a few thousand? Why would it be no better just to ask as many people as you could?
6. A university wants to know whether the student union should sell beer. How might you help them answer this question? What are some of the issues that would have to be considered from the standpoints of both the university and the students?

CHAPTER THIRTEEN

# Ethics

## INTRODUCTION

In Chapter 10 we discussed the ecology of an experiment. We assumed the viewpoint of the witness and focused on two issues. One issue dealt with the relevance of our research and the other with subject-scientist interactions. Among other things we pointed out that subject-scientist interactions are complex and that these interactions can influence our results in unexpected and sometimes even biased ways. Our concern with subject-scientist interactions focused on the validity of our scientific findings. That is, we examined the subject-scientist interaction hoping that through a fuller understanding of their psychological interaction we could better understand some limitations of the process of experimentation when studying human behavior and experience. Through a clearer understanding of this interaction, we hoped to point out potential confounds and ways to eliminate them so we could eventually increase both the internal and external validity of our conclusions.

In this chapter we will shift our focus. We will again examine the subject-scientist relationship from the viewpoint of the witness, yet we will do so from a new perspective. We will shift our concern from how their interaction influences the scientific validity of our research to the important issue of human ethics. Remember, an experiment is just another form of human interaction. Consequently the witness must also view subject-scientist interactions as if they were interactions between any two people. In making this shift, we move from the world of observation and theory to the world of human values; consequently, we can no longer use the same criteria for making decisions as we did in the world of science. The new criteria will be based on human values. Yet how do we make value judgments? Upon what criteria do we base our ethical behaviors? The study of ethics offers us one answer to these questions.

Ethics is the study of proper action. Ethics examines relationships between human beings and poses suggestions or principles as to how we should treat each other. The ultimate decision in ethical questions resides in judgments of value. Most individuals have either explicitly or implicitly formulated or adopted statements that reflect their values and give direction to their actions. Some of these statements or principles may be based on a religious tradition. One example of this is the golden rule, which states that you should do unto others as you would have them do unto you. Other principles may have a philosophical bias for determining action, such as "Kant's imperative." Immanuel Kant, an eighteenth-century philosopher, suggested that one should "act as to treat humanity, either yourself or others, always as an end also and never as a means only." Although rules of action may be useful in the abstract, problems often arise when one begins to apply these principles to concrete situations. In this chapter we want to look at one particular concrete situation—the scientific experiment—and attempt to determine some guidelines for making ethical decisions within this context.

Before we begin, there are three points we need to make clear. First, although most research scientists are concerned about ethics, actual ethical problems are minimal in most psychological experimentation. As we shall point out, there are exceptions to this and it is the exceptions that require careful consideration. Second, ethical decisions are somewhat regulated in our society by both the federal government and professional societies such as the American Psychological Association. In this chapter we will present their recommended guidelines and procedures. And third, although there are guidelines, there are no hard and fast rules for every situation. *Whether in the role of a scientist or a subject, you, as a human being, must ultimately decide how you will act and then assume responsibility for that action!*

## ETHICAL CONSIDERATION OF PSYCHOLOGICAL EXPERIMENTATION

Ethical consideration of psychological experimentation has at its heart the idea that subjects participating in psychological research should not be harmed or negatively transformed in a way that would result in a lower level of any aspect of human functioning. Additionally, ethical considerations must point up the scientist's right to know and to seek answers to questions; that is, it would also be considered unethical to prevent a scientist from seeking knowledge without consideration of his or her rights. Thus, we begin with the rights of the scientist to know and pursue knowledge and the rights of the subject to protection from undue harm.

In most cases, the scientist has a question that he or she wants to ask and the subject is willing to help. In some cases, the subject learns something about himself or psychology from the experience and is glad to have participated. In psychophysiological experiments, for example, subjects often report that they enjoy seeing their brain wave activity (electroencephalogram—EEG) or heart rate (electrocardiogram—EKG) written out by a polygraph and are willing to participate in research in exchange for these types of experiences. Other subjects, like some travelers to a foreign country, enter the world of experimentation and leave it again without ever realizing the underlying structure of the place they have been. Although ignorant of the underlying structure, they still leave with the *experience* of the event and may become changed by it. If these experiences were always pleasant and any changes in the subject always positive, subjects would gladly participate in experiments and scientist would face few ethical questions.

However, at times the scientist may wish to answer a question that requires that the subject experience either psychological or physiological discomfort. These situations raise a number of questions or issues: What are the responsibilities of the scientist toward the subject? What are the rights of the subject? Are there guidelines for reconciling conflicts between the rights of the subjects for pursuing happiness and the rights of the scientist for pursuing knowledge? What type of relationship or dialogue would be most productive for helping the scientist and the subject to fulfill their needs and desires? These are the questions we will approach in this chapter.

## THE RIGHTS OF THE SCIENTIST AND THE SUBJECT

In our society, individuals have rights to search for that activity or substance that is of importance to them. The Bill of Rights to the Constitution includes the individual's right to "life, liberty, and the pursuit of happiness." We begin with the idea that individuals, whether they later be called scientists or subjects, have the right to pursue those activities that are important to them.

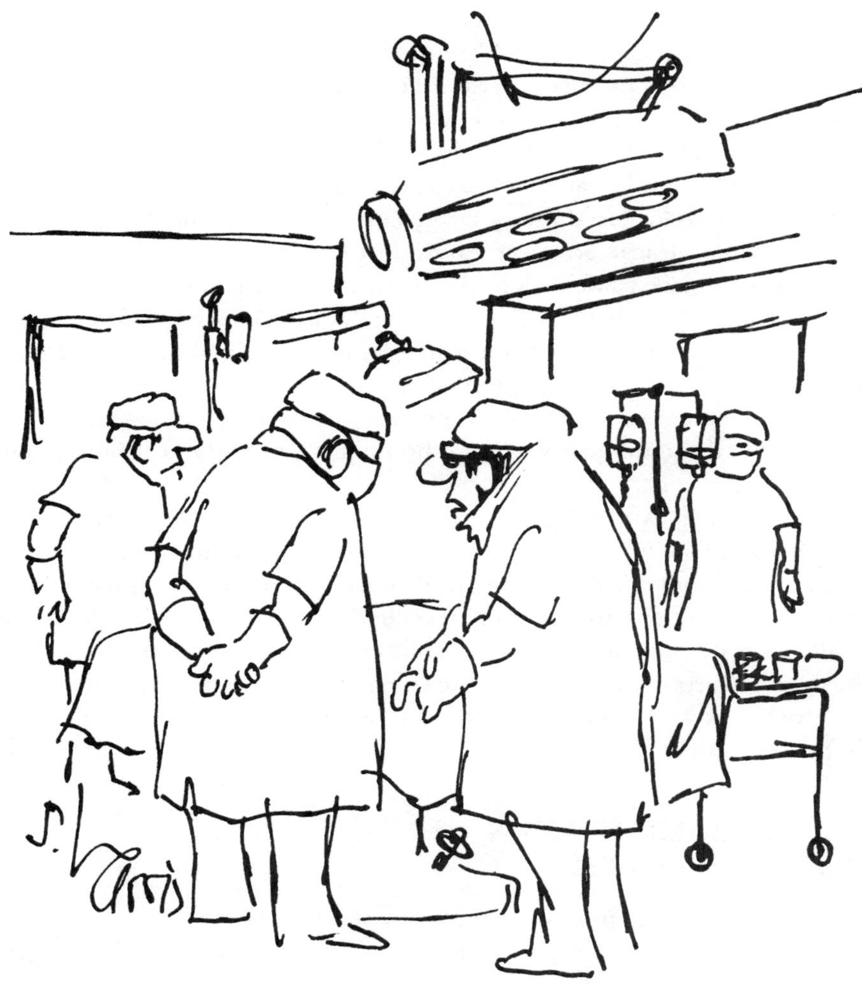


"WE'LL ONLY DO 72% OF IT, SINCE IT'S BEEN REPORTED THAT 28% OF ALL SURGERY IS UNNECESSARY."

There are, however, activities that may infringe on the rights of others. These activities range from the extreme case of murder, which violates your right to life, to less harmful types of activities such as someone's creating noise outside your bedroom window or throwing a cream pie at you across the cafeteria. When a conflict develops between my rights and your rights, we are forced to find a means of arriving at a solution to the problem. The traditional solutions are those of ethics and law; that is, individuals seek to establish some ethical principle to guide their behavior and society may adopt these ethical guidelines in the form of legal sanctions.

What does all this have to do with psychological experimentation? This is exactly the problem. We do not understand completely the relationship between ethics and experimentation, nor do we agree on the manner in which involvement in a scientific experiment infringes on someone's personal rights. Yet this is not to say that we should just ignore the issue and hope it will go away.

Science itself can give us few answers to the question of ethical relationships since science has focused on observation and theory. Thus, we are forced to look outside of science. In this book we used the concept of the witness to help us gain this broad perspective. In this chapter we will imagine ourselves to be the witnesses and examine in more detail the ethical relationship between the scientist and the subject. To accomplish this goal, let us now examine some specific experimental situations and bring forth some of the possible ethical considerations that must be examined.

## THE EXPERIMENT AS AN ETHICAL PROBLEM

Let us begin with the most extreme cases of conflictual experimentation—the Nazi medical experiments during World War II. In several concentration camps during the war, such as Ravensbrueck, Dachau, and Buchenwald, prisoners were injected with a virus or bacteria and then administered drugs to determine their effectiveness. Although "medical facts" were gained from these experiments, the world as a witness judged these experiments to be unethical and criminal. During the trials of these scientist-physicians, held at Nuremberg, it was determined that they themselves were guilty of crimes; seven of them were later hanged and eight received long prison sentences. From these trials a code of medical experimentation was adopted as a guideline for future research with human subjects.

What was unethical about the experiments at the German concentration camps? Was it that human beings were given a virus? The answer to this question would be no, since almost all our current techniques of preventive medicine such as the development of the polio vaccine required that it be tested on human beings at a late phase of its development. Was it unethical to gain scientific knowledge of medical procedures? The answer again would be no, for our society requires that new drugs and treatments be scientifically tested. What were these German physicians convicted of at the trials at Nuremburg? The answer is they were tried for conducting experiments without the *consent* of their subjects. One of the first principles of research is that the subjects must consent to being part of an experiment. Not only is it required that subjects agree to be a part of an experimental procedure, but they must also be informed of what the experiment is about and what the potential risks are. Thus, major ingredients that the witness looks for in the dialogue between the scientist and the subject are *voluntary participation* and *informed consent.*

## INGREDIENTS OF THE INITIAL SCIENTIST-SUBJECT DIALOGUE

In the initial dialogue between the scientist and the subject, the scientist must ask the subject to be a part of the experiment. This is the principle of *voluntary participation.* In essence, this principle suggests that a subject should participate in an experiment of her or his own choice. Additionally, this principle suggests that a subject should be free to leave an experiment at any time whether or not the experiment has been completed.

There are a number of issues involved with the concept of voluntary participation. For example, is it ethical to use prisoners in an experiment? That is, is it really possible for a captive audience to say no without fear of reprisal? One answer to this problem has been to reward subjects by reducing their sentence for participation in research. Yet it has been argued that if a prisoner "agrees" to be in an experiment because he is seeking a lesser sentence, then this agreement would not really be a "free" decision but a form of duress. In the same vein, it has been argued that giving a college student extra credit (points toward the final grade) for participation in psychological experimentation is unethical. What do you think? As you think about this issue, you will become entangled in the question of whether anyone can ever make a "free" decision and, if so, under what circumstances. As you might have already realized, this question becomes even more complicated for someone interested in developmental psychology, which requires research with children, or for someone interested in psychopathology, which requires research with mental patients.

Assuming for a moment that someone can freely agree to participate in research, what information must the scientist give the subject so that he or she can make a sound judgment and consent to be in the experiment? It is suggested that the scientist in the initial dialogue must inform the subject as to what will be required of her or him during the study. The scientist must also inform the subject as to any potential harm that may come from participation. Thus, the subject must be given complete information upon which to make a judgment. This is the principle of *informed consent.* As you can imagine, informed consent also raises a number of issues as to how much information about an experiment is enough. Can you ever tell subjects enough so that they could understand the study? It has been suggested that *informed* consent may not be the same as *educated* consent and that subjects can never really be given enough information. What do you think? Additional problems are raised when the research involves some form of deception, such as when a new drug is being tested against a placebo to determine its effectiveness. Although there are many problems being debated in relation to informed consent, the working procedure at this time is for the scientist to tell subjects as fully as possible without jeopardizing the value of the experiment what will be required of them and any possible risks they might be taking by participating in the experimentation. From the principles of voluntary participation and informed consent, one can see that it is the initial task of the scientist to discuss the experimental procedure fully with subjects and to remind them that they are human beings who do not give their rights away just because they are taking part in a psychological experiment.

## THE RIGHTS OF THE SUBJECT AND THE RESPONSIBILITY OF THE EXPERIMENTER

In our society subjects are considered to have the same rights during an experiment that they have outside of the experimental situation. What are these rights? One major one is the *right to privacy.* What is meant by this right? Most of us at first think of people as having the right to spend time by themselves or with others of their choosing without being disturbed. This is the external manifestation of the right to privacy. But there is also an internal or intrapersonal manifestation to this right (see Raebhausen & Brim, 1967). This is the right to have private thoughts or, as it is sometimes called, a private personality. This means that the thoughts and feelings of a subject should not be made public without the subject's consent. It further suggests that a conversation between a subject and a scientist should be considered as a private and not a public event. But how, you may ask, can the scientist ever report her or his findings? There are two considerations that are part of the scientist's responsibility to the subject. The first is *confidentiality* and the second is *anonymity*. The principle of confidentiality requires that the scientist not release data of a personal nature to other scientists or groups without the subject's consent. The second and related principle of anonymity demands that the personal identity of a given subject and his or her data be kept separately. The easiest way to accomplish this is not to request names in the first place; however, there are times when this may be impossible. Another alternative is to use code numbers that protect the identity of the subject, and to destroy the names of subjects once the data analysis has been completed.

## WHAT IS HARMFUL TO A SUBJECT?

As suggested, it is the right of a subject not to be harmed. But what is harm? In most psychological research, physical pain and harm present no problems since either they are absent completely or the subject is fully informed of the particular stimulus, such as a loud noise or placing one's hand in cold water to measure physiological responsiveness, that will be used. However, the question of psychological harm presents a much larger issue that will continue to be debated for years to come. Is it harmful to show a subject something true but negative about himself? Is it harmful to create situations in which a subject feels negative emotions such as fear or anger? Is it harmful to make a subject feel like a failure in order to determine how this affects his or her performance? These are the types of questions that are currently being asked and debated. As a beginning scientist, where do you go for help? There are two major sources; the first is the APA guidelines on ethics and the second is the human subjects committee in the institution in which you study or work.

## THE AMERICAN PSYCHOLOGICAL ASSOCIATION ETHICAL GUIDELINES

Because it may be unclear and confusing to attempt to determine how to resolve conflicts between the scientist's right to know and the right of the subject not to be harmed psychologically from participating in an experiment, the American Psychological Association has developed a set of guidelines to help individual scientists determine some of their responsibilities toward subjects and the manner in which the scientist-subject dialogue should be conducted. The guidelines were developed by the American Psychological Association after much consideration by the members of the association and subsequent revisions. Detailed ethical guidelines including explication were published in 1982 and may be ordered from the American Psychological Association (122 17th Street, Washington, D.C. 20036) by requesting *Ethical Principles in the Conduct of Research with Human Participants.* Let us now present those guidelines:

> The decision to undertake research rests upon a considered judgment by the individual psychologist about how best to contribute to psychological science and human welfare. Having made the decision to conduct research, the psychologist considers alternative directions in which research energies and resources might be invested. On the basis of this consideration, the psychologist carries out the investigation with respect and concern for the dignity and welfare of the people who participate and with cognizance of federal and state regulations and professional standards governing the conduct of research with human participants.
>
> A. In planning a study, the investigator has the responsibility to make a careful evaluation of its ethical acceptability. To the extent that the weighing of scientific and human values suggests a compromise of any principle, the investigator incurs a correspondingly serious obligation to seek ethical advice and to observe stringent safeguards to protect the rights of human participants.
>
> B. Considering whether a participant in a planned study will be a "subject at risk" or a "subject at minimal risk," according to recognized standards, is of primary ethical concern to the investigator.
>
> C. The investigator always retains the responsibility for ensuring ethical practice in research. The investigator is also responsible for the ethical treatment of research participants by collaborators, assistants, students, and employees, all of whom, however, incur similar obligations.
>
> D. Except in minimal-risk research, the investigator establishes a clear and fair agreement with research participants, prior to their participation, that clarifies the obligations and responsibilities of each. The investigator has the obligation to honor all promises and commitments included in that agreement. The investigator informs the participants of all aspects of the research that might reasonably be expected to influence

willingness to participate and explains all other aspects of the research about which the participants inquire. Failure to make full disclosure prior to obtaining informed consent requires additional safeguards to protect the welfare and dignity of the research participants. Research with children or with participants who have impairments that would limit understanding and/or communication requires special safeguarding procedures.

E. Methodological requirements of a study may make the use of concealment or deception necessary. Before conducting such a study, the investigator has a special responsibility to (1) determine whether the use of such techniques is justified by the study's prospective scientific, educational, or applied value; (2) determine whether alternative procedures are available that do not use concealment or deception; and (3) ensure that the participants are provided with sufficient explanation as soon as possible.

F. The investigator respects the individual's freedom to decline to participate in or to withdraw from the research at any time. The obligation to protect this freedom requires careful thought and consideration when the investigator is in a position of authority or influence over the participant. Such positions of authority include, but are not limited to, situations in which research participation is required as part of employment or in which the participant is a student, client, or employee of the investigator.

G. The investigator protects the participant from physical and mental discomfort, harm, and danger that may arise from research procedures. If risks of such consequences exist, the investigator informs the participant of that fact. Research procedures likely to cause serious or lasting harm to a participant are not used unless the failure to use these procedures might expose the participant to risk of greater harm or unless the research has great potential benefit and fully informed and voluntary consent is obtained from each participant. The participant should be informed of procedures for contacting the investigator within a reasonable time period following participation should stress, potential harm, or related questions or concerns arise.

H. After the data are collected, the investigator provides the participant with information about the nature of the study and attempts to remove any misconceptions that may have arisen. Where scientific or humane values justify delaying or withholding this information, the investigator incurs a special responsibility to monitor the research and to ensure that there are no damaging consequences for the participant.

I. Where research procedures result in undesirable consequences for the individual participant, the investigator has the responsibility to detect and remove or correct these consequences, including long-term effects.

J. Information obtained about a research participant during the course of an investigation is confidential unless otherwise agreed upon in advance. When the possibility exists that others may obtain access to such information, this possibility, together with the plans for protecting confidentiality, is explained to the participant as part of the procedure for obtaining informed consent.

As stated, APA principles should not be considered as laws that a scientist follows, thereby handing over the problems of ethics to another group. Rather, these principles may be considered as *guidelines that direct one's thinking when ethical matters are considered.* In fact, the first and second principles emphasize that the responsibility of research is always with the individual scientist, and it is the scientist who must make decisions as to how to respond to the ethical considerations of an experiment. The APA guidelines do suggest, however, that when an individual scientist does deviate from these principles, she or he should seek advice from other professionals in the field. It should also be noted that the APA has an additional set of guidelines for research with animals.

## INTERNAL REVIEW COMMITTEES

In recent years it has been not only suggested but also required by the Department of Health and Human Services that each scientist whose institution receives federal funds seek a review of the ethical considerations of research with human subjects whether or not there is a deviation from APA guidelines. This type of review is required not only of psychological research but of any type of research with human subjects. The committee that reviews the research is made up of individuals who work at the same university, hospital, school, or other institution with the scientist as well as members of the community where the institution is located.

The main task of the human subjects review committee is to determine whether the subject is adequately protected in terms of both welfare and rights. One major question that the committee asks is: Are there any risks, physical, psychological, or social, that could come about as a result of participating in a given piece of research? As you can imagine, almost everything we do each day involves varying degrees of risk, and thus the committee attempts to determine when a given risk is unreasonable or might have a long-term effect on a person. For example, asking subjects to run a mile, to give a small sample of their blood, to have their heart rate measured, or to discuss their own childhood or sexual preference involves some *risks* in the way the term in used by most internal review committees. However, the committee may decide that these risks are not sufficient to prevent a study from being performed in light of the information that would be gained. Thus, a second major question that a human subjects review committee asks is: Are the risks to the subjects outweighed by the potential benefits to them or by the estimated importance to society of the knowledge to be gained? Once the committee has determined that the answer to this question is yes, a third question is asked: Has the experimenter allowed the subjects to determine freely whether or not they will participate in the experiment through informed consent?

Before we continue, it should be pointed out that not everyone agrees with the principle of informed consent or at least not with the current interpretations of it. For example, in one study using a traditional verbal conditioning paradigm, it was shown that giving the subjects a complete description of the experiment resulted in the subjects not demonstrating conditioning (Resnick & Schwartz, 1973). A complete description actually eliminated the very phenomenon they were studying. These authors also reported that, although the informed subjects took part in the study, they did so in a more uncooperative manner. Another argument against fully informed consent is presented in Box 13.1, in which Loftus and Fries argue that fully informed consent may actually be more harmful than helpful. What do you think? Another consequence of adopting a strict definition of informed consent is that it becomes almost impossible to perform research that involves deception—that is, research in which the subject is not told the complete purpose of an experiment. Let us now examine deception studies and some of the ethical questions involved.

## DECEPTION STUDIES

A deception study is any study in which the subject is deceived about the true purpose of the experiment or experimental procedures. For example, if an experimenter wished to examine the effects of anxiety on performance in college students, the scientist might create an anxiety-provoking situation followed by a performance measure. One method used to create anxiety in college students is to administer a so-called IQ test that cannot be completed in the allotted time, including the statement that most college students who later go to graduate school have no trouble finishing this test. Another type of deception often used in medical research is the placebo treatment. For example, subjects are given a pill made up of sugar or other inactive ingredients and told that it will cause certain physiological changes such as reducing the number of headaches they have been experiencing. Since it is impossible to obtain informed consent in deception research, is it unethical to perform this research?

This is not an easy question to answer and the professionals in the field currently fall into two camps. The first group suggests that any deception is unethical and thus no deception research is possible, while the second group

---

### *Box 13.1 Informed Consent May Be Hazardous to Your Health*

The following was an editorial in *Science,* the journal of the American Association for the Advancement of Science. In this editorial the authors suggest that informed consent may actually harm the subject in some cases. Read the editorial and see what you think (Loftus & Fries, 1979).

> Before human subjects are enrolled in experimental studies, a variety of preliminary rituals are now required. These include an explanation of the nature of the experimental procedure and a specific elaboration of possible adverse reactions. The subjects, in turn, can either withdraw from the experiment or give their "informed consent." These rituals are said to increase the subjects' understanding of the procedures but, perhaps more important, they came into existence because of a strong belief in the fundamental principle that human beings have the right to determine what will be done to their minds and bodies.
>
> Some, on the other hand, consider that the purpose of informed consent is not protection of subjects, but rather protection of investigators and sponsoring institutions from lawsuits based on the charge of subject deception should a misadventure result. But lawsuits arise in any case; subjects simply claim that they did not understand the rituals. It is reasonable, then, to ask whether the putative beneficiary, the subject, might be harmed rather than helped by the current informed consent procedure.
>
> A considerable body of psychological evidence indicates that humans are highly suggestible. Information has been found to change people's attitudes, to change their moods and feelings, and even to make them believe they have experienced events that never in fact occurred. This alone would lead one to suspect that adverse reactions might result from information given during an informed consent discussion.
>
> An examination of the medical evidence demonstrates that there is also a dark side to the placebo effect. Not only can positive therapeutic effects be achieved by suggestion, but negative side effects and complications can similarly result. For example, among subjects who participated in a drug study after the usual informed

argues that certain types of deception research are necessary. The second group further argues that given appropriate safeguards, deception research is the only way to answer certain questions. We will not attempt to determine which group is ethically correct but will present some important questions raised by deception research and ways in which some of these questions have been answered. To do this, we will present three deception studies in further detail.

---

consent procedure, many of those given an injection of a placebo reported physiologically unlikely symptoms such as dizziness, nausea, vomiting, and even mental depression. One subject given the placebo reported that these effects were so strong that they caused an automobile accident. Many other studies provide similar data indicating that to a variable but often scarifying degree, explicit suggestion of possible adverse effects causes subjects to experience these effects. Recent hypotheses that heart attack may follow coronary spasm indicate physiological mechanisms by which explicit suggestions, and the stress that may be produced by them, might prove fatal. Thus, the possible consequences of suggested symptoms range from minor annoyance to, in extreme cases, death.

If protection of the subject is the reason for obtaining informed consent, the possibility of iatrogenic harm [harm brought on by diagnosis or suggestion] to the subject as a direct result of the consent ritual must be considered. This clear cost must be weighed against the potential benefit of giving some people an increased sense of freedom of choice about the use of their bodies. The current legalistic devices, which are designed in part to limit subject recourse, intensify rather than solve a dilemma.

The features of informed consent procedures that do protect subjects should be retained. Experimental procedures should be reviewed by peers and public representatives. A statement to the subject describing the procedure and the general level of risk is reasonable. But detailed information should be reserved for those who request it. Specific slight risks, particularly those resulting from common procedures, should not be routinely disclosed to all subjects. And when a specific risk is disclosed, it should be discussed in the context of placebo effects in general, why they occur and how to guard against them. A growing literature indicates that just as knowledge of possible symptoms can cause those symptoms, so can knowledge of placebo effects be used to defend against those effects. A move in this direction may ensure that a subject will not be at greater risk from self-appointed guardians than from the experimental itself.

---

## Obedience-to-Authority Research

One of the classic deception research studies is Stanley Milgram's obedience-to-authority study (Milgram, 1963, 1977). Using as a background such authority situations as the Old Testament story of God (the authority) commanding Abraham to kill his son, and the situation of war where one person (the authority) tells another to go out and kill (the enemy), Milgram asked the question: Under what conditions would one person (who is not the authority) harm another and how is this related to authority? To examine this question in a concrete situation, Milgram chose the setting of a psychological experiment. He sought to determine whether subjects would harm other subjects on the authority of the experimenter.

The subjects in this experiment were individuals who varied in age and occupation. The general procedure was to have a subject come into the laboratory for a "learning experiment." The subject meets the experimenter and another "subject," who is really an associate of the experimenter. It is explained to the subject that little is known about the effects of punishment on memory and that in the experiment one subject will be the learner and one will be the teacher. A rigged drawing is held in which the associate of the experimenter draws the role of learner and the naive subject draws the role of teacher. Following this, the learner is taken to another room and strapped into a chair with what appear to be shock electrodes (although the subject did not know the electrodes were not connected).

The naive subject is told that it is his or her job to teach the learner a series of words and to administer a shock as punishment whenever the learner makes a mistake. The subject is further instructed to increase the shock with each error made by moving a switch on the control box. The control box along with voltage levels has such verbal labels as "Danger: Severe shock" at the higher levels.

Once the experiment begins, the learner begins to make mistakes and the subject, following the instructions of the experimenter, administers shocks. However, as the voltage levels are increased, the subject begins to hear moans coming from the learner. With more increases in voltage, the learner cries out in pain and later refuses to answer any more questions. The experimenter tells the subject to treat any nonresponse as a wrong answer and to administer additional shocks. When the subject refuses to administer additional shocks, the experiment is concluded. The measure on the shock machine is used as a means of determining the subject's willingness to obey authority even in the face of pressure from the learner not to inflict pain. As presented thus far, would you consider this experiment ethical? Why or why not?

As you might imagine, objections have been raised to this research. One of the first objections to Milgram's work concerned whether or not the subjects were protected in the experiment. In specific, Baumrind (1964) refers to the Milgram study as a case in which the subjects were not treated with respect but rather were manipulated and experienced the discomfort of emotional disturbance.

Milgram responds by suggesting that the emotional distress experienced by the subjects was unexpected. He reports from conversations with colleagues and psychiatrists that they all expected that most subjects would terminate the experiment at an early stage by refusing to give shocks once the learner began to complain. Although Milgram agrees that once a number of subjects had been run he could have terminated the experiment, he decided that "momentary excitement is not the same as harm." Thus Milgram chose to continue the experiment.

Once the experiment had been concluded, it would have been unethical to allow an individual subject to leave the experimental situation without a true understanding of what had taken place. This process is referred to as *debriefing*. In the debriefing procedure, the experimenter, in accord with APA principle H, removes any misconceptions and offers a full discussion of the experiment. Although the ethical principles had not been fully developed when Milgram first ran his experiment, he appears to have followed this principle as follows: First, the subjects were all told the nature of the hoax and that the learner never received any electric shock. Second, each subject had a "friendly reconciliation" with the learner and an opportunity to discuss the experiment. Third, subjects were assured that their behavior was normal and that the tension or emotion they felt was also felt by other subjects.

As required by APA principle I, Milgram also conducted follow-up evaluations. Once the entire study was completed, all the subjects received a report of the experiment. According to Milgram, the subjects' behavior in this follow-up report was treated in a dignified manner. Additionally, all subjects received a questionnaire that allowed them to express their thoughts and feelings concerning their participation in the experiment. As a matter of interest, Milgram reports that 84% of the subjects were glad to have participated in the experiment, 15% were neutral, and 1.3% expressed negative feelings about their participation. In addition, 80% of the subjects believed that this type of research should be carried out and 74% said they had learned something of personal importance from their participation in the experiment. As a further check for possible long-term consequences of the experiment, a psychiatrist interviewed selected subjects seeking any negative long-term effects of the experiment, which he reports not finding.

As you can see, it is not easy to follow APA principles H and I when it comes to deception research since it requires as much, if not more, work to follow up the subjects as it did to run the original experiment. However, when there is a possibility of long-term harm, either psychological or physiological, it is necessary that this type of follow-up be carried out.

## It's Not a Crime the Way I See It

When reading newspaper reports of the break-in at the Watergate as told by the press and by the Nixon Administration, some people felt they were hearing the reports of two different events. West, Gunn, and Chernicky (1975) pointed out the manner in which the differing reports fit into current theory in social psychology. As suggested by the theory of Jones and Nisbett (1971), those involved in Watergate tended to focus on environmental determinants of behavior, such as thinking break-ins were necessary because of the violent nature of the radical left. Members of the press, on the other hand, were observers and tended to explain the break-in in terms of the characteristics of the participants. Other events in history have also shown this trend according to West, et al. For example, those involved in the Nazi armies claimed that they had to follow orders or they would have been shot. Whereas those in the army used situational cues, those who tried these individuals for war crimes saw the problem in terms of the character of the individuals. Likewise, if you remember the story of Kitty Genovese from Chapter 5, you may have thought to yourself, "Why didn't anyone help?" or "what was wrong with those people?" You, as an outside observer, were reacting to the characteristics of the people involved, whereas the people involved seem to have been reacting to the situational characteristics.

Although the three cases of Watergate, Nazi soldiers, and Kitty Genovese lend support to the theory of Jones and Nisbett, a scientist would still like to see the theory tested in a laboratory situation. West, Gunn, and Chernicky set about to do this. They reasoned that if situational factors were important variables in the Watergate crime, then a significant percentage of individuals would agree to break the law if the situational pressure was high. Likewise others, when being told of the "crime," would attribute the event to the person involved and not to the situation. These authors designed the following experiment.

In a field study, subjects were led to believe that they could participate in an illegal burglary. To determine the role of situational variables, rationales for the burglary varied across groups. The first rationale stated that the crime was being sponsored by a government agency. The second rationale offered the subjects in that group a large amount of money for committing the crime. The third rationale offered immunity from prosecution for committing the crime. The fourth rationale served as a control for compliance and offered no money or immunity from prosecution. The last group was designed to give the researchers some indication of how frequently subjects would agree to be part of a crime and thus could be used to assess the demand characteristics of the experiment itself.

A second experiment was performed with another group of subjects who were given booklets describing in detail one of the four conditions from the field experiment. These subjects were asked to estimate how many people out of 100 would agree to participate in the burglary as described by one of the four conditions. They were also asked whether they would participate and were given the opportunity to describe some characteristics of a person who would or would not participate. Based on the theory of Jones and Nisbett (1971), it was predicted that those who participated in the field experiment would attribute their actions to the situational cues, whereas those in the second experiment would focus on the characteristics of the person who agreed or disagreed to be part of the crime.

Imagine yourself in the field study. You do not know you are part of a study. You are approached as you go about your business by someone you know to be a local private investigator. He says to you that he has "a project you might be interested in" and suggests that you meet him at his home or a local restaurant. When you meet the private investigator at the restaurant, he has another person with him and elaborates plans of the burglary of a local advertising firm. The break-in is then explained to you in terms of one of the four rationales presented above. How would you respond? Do you feel your ethics have been violated thus far? Why or why not?

As you might imagine, some professionals believed this study violated the APA ethical principles (Cook, 1975). Cook suggested that the ethical issues should be considered for two major reasons. First, the study has the potential for negative effects on subjects that go beyond the violation of personal moral standards. And second, because the study paralleled the Watergate scandal, it would receive wide publicity.

The authors of the study responded to the concerns of Cook by describing the procedures they included to protect the subjects. First, the field study was carried out in such a manner that the subjects could not leave the experiment feeling that they had become involved in an illegal activity. The subjects in the study were debriefed as to the real nature of the meeting and the concerns of the experimenters over having used deception. Cook points out, and the authors agree, that the subjects should go away from the experiment feeling that their participation aided in gaining new knowledge and that the experimenters were concerned for the welfare of the subjects at all times. Second, the authors point out that the "experimental" meeting was not forced on any subject but took place only after an initial agreement to meet at another location. Third, alternative experimental procedures that did not involve deception were considered and rejected. For example, a study in which people role-played the situation might have been used. However, since the study was to determine the difference between observing and actually participating in the situation, alternative designs were rejected. Fourth, a lawyer-psychologist served as a consultant during the planning and implementation of the field study to protect the rights of the subjects and the experimenters. Also the state's attorney's office found the procedure to be legally acceptable. How would you discuss this study and the ethics involved? If you are interested in the actual results you may look up this article in the library.

## Bypassing the Bypass

Let us examine one other study that required deception. It raised a number of interesting issues, particularly the question of when the information gained is important enough to violate normal ethical standards. This particular study deals with medical research—a heart operation for the treatment of angina (Cobb, Thomas, Dillard, Merendino, & Bruce, 1959). However, the same questions raised by this study are also applicable to studies dealing with the evaluation of new psychotherapy techniques, techniques in biofeedback, and procedures of behavioral medicine, just to name a few. It should be pointed out that this study was reported more than 20 years ago; with the adoption of human subjects review committees, such a study would probably not be permitted today.

In the study, 17 patients with angina pectoris attributed to coronary artery disease were invited to participate in an experimental evaluation of an operation to relieve the angina (pains in the chest). The patients knew that they were part of an experimental evaluation of the operation, but they did not know the nature of the evaluation. Furthermore, most patients knew from the popular press that the operation was considered to be a new and exciting treatment for angina. It should also be pointed out that the angina was severe enough to limit the activities of the patients, with the majority of them reported to be unemployed.

Once the patient was in the operating room and the anesthesia had been given, the surgeon opened an envelope that told him to which experimental group the patient belonged. For half the patients the operation was carried out as usual; that is, there was a ligation of the internal mammary artery. In the other half of the patients, the chest was cut open and the artery of the heart was found, as in the normal procedure, but the artery was not cut and tied in the usual manner. Rather, the cardiac system was left untouched and the patient's chest closed. Both groups of patients were cared for normally without the attending physicians knowing to which group each belonged. Would you consider this experiment a violation of ethics?

Most people would consider it unethical to operate on another human being without his or her consent as to the nature of the operation. However, let us look at the results of the study. During the first six months following the operation, the same number of patients in both the experimental (ligation) and the control (skin incision only) groups showed "significant subjective improvement." Just opening and closing the chest was shown to be associated with the same improvement rate as actually performing the operation. Positive changes were also noted in EKG evaluations. For example, one patient, who before the operation showed irregular heart-wave patterns on an EKG during exercise, showed no irregularities after the operation. Surprising as it may seem, this patient was in the control group.

We are now faced with some very difficult questions. For example, how can we go about testing the value of new therapeutic procedures, whether they be surgical or psychotherapeutic, without violating the ethics of the individual? Are there times when we might consider it ethical to deceive an individual so that knowledge about a procedure might be gained? That is, are there times in which the savings in both patient distress and economic resources justify less than full disclosure? Would you want to "debrief" the patients who received the skin incision only if they were reporting a significant improvement in their disorder? What do you think about this type of research?

## DEBRIEFING—WHEN IS ENOUGH ENOUGH?

Whether or not deception is used in an experiment, an experiment does not end without a completion of the dialogue between the scientist and the subject begun at the start of the experiment. Some researchers call this concluding dialogue *debriefing*. It is the goal of this dialogue to ensure that subjects leave the laboratory with at least as much self-esteem and as little anxiety as when they came to the experiment (Kelman, 1968). Thus, it is suggested that the debriefing process consist of two major aspects. The first is a time for the subjects to tell the experimenter how they felt about being part of the experiment. This not only will be good feedback for the experimenter but will also allow the subjects to express any self-doubt about their performance and to deal with thoughts and feelings that arose during the experiment. The second aspect of debriefing is that it allows the experimenter to explain the study to the subjects in greater detail. It is often difficult for the experimenter to determine how much information should be conveyed to the subjects. For example, the design of the study might be too complex to describe in detail. Or, when children are used as subjects, it might be difficult to convey to the child what was being asked, and the experiment might rely on the parents to help with this task. In the case of deception research, Carlsmith, Ellsworth, and Aronson (1976) suggest that just telling the truth is not enough and may even be more harmful than no explanation at all. These authors suggest that the scientist include a discussion of why deception was necessary and the experimenter's regret for using deception. Furthermore, it is suggested that the researcher lead the subjects to see that the experiment was designed to deceive *anyone* and that it is normal to feel foolish or silly after being taken in by the deception. These authors also suggest that the subjects be given the opportunity to develop and express their own reactions to deception research in general and to the present experiment in particular.

## THE SUBJECT AS COLLEAGUE

Throughout the discussion of ethics it has been suggested that the experimenter value the subjects and respect their rights. A useful metaphor is to consider the subject as a colleague; that is, the subject is best seen as someone who helps with an experiment. As with any colleague, you as a scientist would discuss with the subject what you were interested in doing and the manner in which you would go about doing it. Once the experiment was completed, you would likewise discuss with your colleague and subject the results of the study. This not only would allow for the subject to learn more about the experimentation but would also allow you as scientist to understand the subject's *experience* of the experiment and thus aid in your interpretation of the results. Although more difficult, this same model could be used when performing deception research. For example, if one were using college students in a deception study, Campbell suggests that the student might be told at the beginning of the term that some of the research being performed that term involved some deception. The general nature of the whys and hows of deception studies could be discussed at this time, and the potential subject could be allowed to see the importance of this type of research, whether it be of the placebo type or more straightforward deception. Those students who did not wish ever to participate in a deception study could so indicate in some private manner and then be excluded from future studies of that type. In summary, what is being suggested is that the subject be treated as one treats a colleague; the subject is treated as someone who is valued and respected for the information he or she can offer. Using this approach, many ethical questions of psychological research will remain in the background and arise in only rare and special circumstances.

## Key Terms and Concepts

1. Ethical considerations in research
2. Subject's rights
3. Scientist's rights
4. Voluntary participation
5. Informed consent
6. Right to privacy
   a. confidentiality
   b. anonymity
7. American Psychological Association Guidelines
   a. 10 principles
8. Use of deception in research
   a. Milgram
   b. West, Gunn, and Chernicky
   c. Cobb et al.
9. Debriefing
10. The subject as colleague

## Summary

1. Although the purpose of research is to gain understanding and knowledge, it is necessary to note that this search for knowledge takes place in the context of an interaction between the scientist and the subject. This being the case, it is necessary to ask what the obligation of the scientist and the subject are toward each other, which moves the discussion into the study of proper action and the realm of values, or the study of ethics.

2. Three important points were initially presented. These are (1) although actual ethical problems are minimal in most psychological experiments, there are exceptions that require careful consideration; (2) ethical considerations are partly regulated by both federal agencies and professional societies such as the American Psychological Association; and (3) whether you are a subject or a scientist, you must ultimately decide how you will act and assume responsibility for that action.
3. Ethical consideration of psychological experimentation has at its heart the idea that a subject participating in psychological research should not be harmed or negatively transformed in a way that would result in a lower level of any aspect of human functioning.
4. Two ways in which subject rights are ensured are through the principles of voluntary participation and informed consent. Voluntary participation requires that a subject be part of an experiment without coercion and be able to leave at any time during the experiment. Informed consent requires that the subject be informed about what is to take place in an experiment and about any potential harm, either physical or psychological, that may result from participation in the research.
5. The subject also has the right to privacy and this requires the scientist to maintain the subject's anonymity and not to release any personal information on a particular subject without consent.
6. Questions of an ethical nature arise mainly from research that involves deception. Examples of these studies, such as the Milgram obedience study, point out the problems and promises of such research.
7. In all research except certain deception research, debriefing is a necessary component. In a debriefing session, subjects are told about any deception that occurred as well as the importance of their participation in the research.
8. A simple but important attitude to adopt as a researcher is to treat subjects as colleagues who are there to help give valuable information concerning important psychological processes.

## Review Questions

1. What are the rights of the scientist and the subject in an experiment?
2. Why were the "medical experiments" conducted by the Germans during World War II considered unethical?
3. What do you see as the difference between informed and educated consent?
4. What are the main themes in the APA guidelines on ethics?
5. What is an internal review committee?
6. What are the pros and cons of deception research?
7. What is meant by debriefing and why is it important?
8. In the final analysis, who is responsible for ethical concerns in an experiment?

## Discussion Questions and Projects

1. Discuss the subject's rights and the scientist's rights in performing research.
2. In performing an experiment that uses heart rate as a measure, you notice that the record of one of the subject looks different from every other one you have seen. Although the person told you at the beginning of the experiment that his heart was normal, you think there might be a medical problem. What should you do about your concern?
3. Discuss the ethics of the heart surgery research presented in this chapter. What were the benefits and problems with such research? You could also look in your library for the research published in 1983 and 1984 on the effectiveness of the heart bypass operation. Does knowing the effectiveness of the operation 25 years later make the earlier research more or less ethical?
4. One study not discussed in this chapter that has raised some ethical question is the "prison" experiment conducted by Zimbardo in the 1970s (Zimbardo, Haney, Banks, & Jaffe, 1975). In this study students were assigned the role of guard or prisoner for a week. Before the experiment could be completed, it was stopped since the "guards" were beginning to treat the "prisoners" in a cruel manner and "prisoners" began to obey the guards in what has been called a demeaning manner. Before the experiment began, it is unlikely that any of the students would have claimed they would act as they did. Discuss the ethics of conducting this research and what safeguards should be required. In what ways could it be considered unethical to show someone something true but unpleasant about him or herself? What harm could have been done by this study?
5. Are there times when deception research might be useful or should it be banned altogether?
6. What are the ethical considerations that one would need to consider in using children as research subjects?

# CHAPTER FOURTEEN

# *Sharing the Results*

## INTRODUCTION

In the preceding chapters we traced the unfolding of an experiment from its initial conception through the analysis of the results. Once the final outcome is known, we can integrate this new fact into our understanding of whatever particular phenomenon we are studying and in this way slowly expand our understanding of the world. One important responsibility of the scientist in this process is to communicate new facts to other scientists and, equally important, to nonscientists. In this way not only do we expand our own understanding but we also share our findings with others so that they too may integrate our new findings into their understanding of the world. The idea that science is a shared activity is by no means new. Indeed more than 2,000 years ago Aristotle emphasized that science had two parts: inquiry and argument. *Inquiry* for us includes the actual experiments or observations that generate the new facts. *Argument* includes our responsibility to communicate our findings in either oral or written form.

The particular manner in which we choose to communicate our findings is directed by the audience with whom we wish to communicate. In psychology there are generally two types of audiences to whom we direct our communication. In the majority of instances we are addressing other scientists who are studying related phenomena and might be interested in our findings. The availability of our findings frequently means that other scientists need not repeat our work and can move on to studying a new aspect of the same phenomenon. In addition to making our findings available to other researchers, we have a responsibility to convey the essential direction of our findings and their ethical and moral implications to nonscientists as well. This second responsibility is particularly relevant to psychologists whose findings may have direct bearing on how we relate to one another, interact with our children, and understand ourselves. In this chapter we will describe how scientists communicate with each other by describing how a formal scientific paper is written.

## COMMUNICATION WITH OTHER SCIENTISTS: THE SCIENTIFIC ARTICLE

There are many ways we can share our findings with other scientists. In some cases new facts are shared in informal conversations with colleague-friends over something to drink at the local hangout. In other cases new material is presented orally at scientific meetings or perhaps an entire book is written describing a lengthy series of experiments. In most cases, however, formal communication between scientists takes the form of published journal articles. Consequently we will now describe the process of writing a scientific article and the steps by which an article is accepted for publication and published.

### Preparing Your Article

In simple terms a scientific article is the story of an experiment. This narrative begins with a description of what is already known about the particular phenomenon being studied and a clear statement of the purpose of the experiment. The narrative then describes the manner in which the experiment was performed and the results of the experiment. Finally, the results are interpreted in relation to themselves (are there any confounds or interpretation problems?) and then in relation to what we already know about the phenomenon under study. To facilitate this communication process, a specific format or outline for scientific papers has been developed. Briefly, scientific articles are divided into five parts: (1) abstract, (2) introduction, (3) method, (4) results, and (5) discussion. Detailed descriptions of what should be covered in each section and other guides to writing style are presented in the American Psychological Association *Publication Manual* (1983; available from APA, 1200 17th Street, N.W., Washington, D.C. 20036). An addition to the APA manual was published in 1977 including guidelines for the nonsexist use of language in APA journals. We believe that these are important points to consider and thus we have reproduced this addition in Appendix A. It is important that you become familiar with both format and language style since these are used by scientific journals around the world. Once you are familiar with them, you will find it easier to read articles and to locate information quickly in those you are just skimming. Furthermore, you will undoubtedly use the APA format as a model in preparing your own proposals or papers. Because of the widespread use of the APA format, we will now briefly describe what makes up each of the five parts of a scientific article.

**Abstract** Most scientific papers open with a brief 100–150-word *abstract* or summary of the entire article. The purpose of this abstract is to give an overall description of the experiment so that the readers can quickly decide whether they want to take the time to read the entire paper. In this way we avoid reading halfway through an article before we realize it is not the sort of experiment we thought it was simply from reading the title. With this purpose in mind, the typical abstract provides a very brief, clear statement of purpose, methodology, and results of the experiment. It is written in a concise manner yet describes the essential features of your article. To give you an idea of how an abstract is organized, the following abstract was taken from an article appearing in the *Journal of Consulting and Clinical Psychology* (Gaul, Craighead & Mahoney, 1975):

> A comparison was made of the eating behaviors of obese and nonobese subjects in a naturalistic setting. It was found that obese subjects took more bites, performed fewer chews per bite, and spent less time chewing than did nonobese subjects. The clinical implications of these data are discussed.

**Introduction** The *introduction* of a scientific paper is designed to provide background information about the phenomenon you are studying and to help the reader understand how you arrived at your hypothesis and the experiment you eventually performed. A typical introduction begins with a simple sentence or two explaining the nature of the research problem in broad terms. It then describes what we already know about the phenomenon being studied. As this narrative unfolds, *relevant* facts and theoretical speculations are described. Once this background information has been presented and the reader knows the present status of the research area, the introduction concludes with a clear statement of purpose, which may include the particular hypothesis being evaluated. For example, when Dr. Shotland (Shotland & Straw, 1976) wrote an article describing his research on bystander behavior discussed in Chapter 5, he began his article like this:

> From time to time newspapers report that bystanders have witnessed an attack by a man on a woman without adequately helping the victim.

Shotland continues by describing some current theories that attempt to explain why bystanders do not help. Since the theories were derived from the reports of actual events and after-the-fact reports of witnesses, Shotland sought to test empirically certain aspects of these theories. He concludes his introduction section with a statement of purpose and hypothesis.

> The set of experiments we describe explores the implications and effects of a perceived relationship between a victim and her attacker on helping behavior. Specifically, the hypothesis for Experiment 1 was: If bystanders perceive a relationship between a woman and her attacker, they will be less likely to intervene than if the victim and attacker are perceived as strangers.

Likewise, Dr. Newcombe (Newcombe & Arnkoff, 1979) began her research report on speech styles and the sex of the speaker with the sentence: "Our impressions of other people are derived from many sources: What they say, what they do, what others think of them, and so on." She then continues the introduction by discussing some important research that has been performed in this area and helps the reader to understand why she performed this particular study. The introduction concludes with a statement of why the study was performed. In this particular study the purpose was stated as follows:

> In these initial experiments, the concern was to evaluate the effects, if any, of a variable over which people have some control (speech style) as compared to the effects of a set of variables over many of which they have less or no control (the pitch of their voice, their sex).

Thus, the general formulation of an introduction is to begin with a broad conception of the problem followed by a discussion of previous research related to this topic and then to end with a specific statement of the hypothesis or purpose of the study. Notice that as an introduction unfolds there is a progression from a general topic to a specific purpose. You might think of an introduction as the simple story of relevant published experiments, which leads us from our general topic of interest to our specific purpose or hypothesis.

Introductions may be brief, as we shall see in the following example. Following is the introduction from the study on eating rate and obesity (Gaul et al., 1975). Note again how the last part of the introduction presents the purpose or hypothesis of the study.

**INTRODUCTION**

> In their recent review Stunkard and Mahoney (in press) concluded that behavior modification techniques have demonstrated considerable effectiveness in the treatment of obesity. Many of these techniques were based in part on the behavioral analysis of eating patterns first presented by Ferster, Nurnberger, and Levitt (1962).
>
> An implicit assumption of many behavior modification programs has been that eating patterns differ for obese and nonobese people. Specifically, it has been presumed that overweight individuals eat faster and take fewer bites (cf. Stuart & Davis, 1972). However, virtually no empirical data regarding that assumption have been presented. The purpose of the present study was to determine if obese people consume their food more rapidly than nonobese people, and if consummatory behaviors (chewing and drinking) differ for two groups.

The following example of an introduction is from an exploratory study by Kenneth Ravizza (1977) examining the subjective experience of athletes during sporting events. Again you will see how the author first describes the focus of his study in relation to previous research. He helps the reader to understand how this specific research is both different from and similar to other studies and then concludes with a statement of purpose. Since the research is an exploratory study into an unknown area, the purpose is presented not in the form of a hypothesis but in the form of the goals of the study.

**INTRODUCTION**

> The traditional emphasis of research on sports has been to develop techniques to improve physical performance. One result of this emphasis is that the major focus in sport research has been on motor performance. In contrast, the subjective experience of the athlete has been minimized (Kleinman, 1973; Park, 1973). One explanation for this emphasis on motor performance is that athletes' subjective experiences are difficult to measure and to study scientifically. Some progress has been made in

studying nonpathological, yet extraordinary, psychological experience (Laski, 1961; Maslow, 1968). The limited research dealing with this aspect of sport reveals that participation provides the athlete with a wide domain of subjective experiences (Leonard, 1975; Metheny, 1968; Slusher, 1967; Thomas, 1972). Some of these studies have focused on specific aspects of the subjective experience of the athlete (Beisser, 1967; Csikszentmihalyi, 1975; Gallwey, 1974; Murphy, 1972, 1973; Ravizza, 1973).

The purpose of the present investigation is twofold: first, to use the interview technique to ascertain the personal experiences of athletes; and second, to achieve a general characterization of at least one subjective aspect in sport, those experiences involved in an athlete's "greatest moment" while participating in sport.

**Method** The third section of a scientific paper is called the *method* section and consists of a detailed description of how the experiment was conducted. The goal of this section is to provide enough detail for another researcher to conduct an exact replication of your experiment. Additionally, the procedural details provided in the method section allow the reader to visualize exactly how you conducted your experiment. In this way a careful reader may spot design problems that escaped your attention. The method section is generally divided into three parts (subjects, apparatus, and procedure). Typically, the method section begins with a description of the subjects in the study; that is, were they males or females, college students or patients in a hospital, and so forth. It is important to include the number of subjects who took part in the experiment as well as the manner in which they were recruited. In studies in which a control group was used, how was it selected? Two examples of how subjects might be described are given below. The first is from Harris and Ray (1977).

SUBJECTS. The subjects were 32 students (13 males, 19 females) enrolled in introductory psychology. The subjects were told that they were to keep a dream log for a period of six weeks, and that their dreams would be kept confidential. Participation in the study was voluntary.

The next example of a subjects section comes from the clinical literature and was published in the *Journal of Consulting and Clinical Psychology* (Giannetti, Johnson, Klingler, and Williams, 1978). Notice that this description tells both how subjects were selected and important characteristics of the groups (age and IQ).

> SUBJECTS. The sample was composed of male veterans who were evaluated at the time of application for treatment at the Psychiatric Assessment Unit of the Salt Lake City Veterans Hospital. Subject selection was limited to those veterans who completed the experimental evaluation and testing with 48 hours of referral. In addition, all subjects whose MMPI had more than 30 missing items or had an F-K dissimulation index (Gough, 1950) greater than 14 were eliminated. This resulted in a sample of 572 subjects classified into seven psychotic groups ($n$ = 218), three sociopathic groups ($n$ = 208), three neurotic groups ($n$ = 88) and one "no mental illness" group ($n$ = 58). The mean age for the sample was 37.7 years (SD = 12.4). The mean IQ from the Shipley-Hartford (Paulson & Lin, 1970) was 103.4 (SD = 12.7).

Following the description of the subjects used in the experiment, there is a statement of the experimental situation and any equipment or apparatus that might have been used, including their brand names and model numbers. In physiological studies, psychophysiological studies, and biofeedback studies, this would include a statement of the instrumentation settings that were used in the study.

The final part of the method section is a statement of the procedure utilized in the study. In describing the manner in which the study was conducted, it is important to include everything that the subject was told or was led to believe. Since the experiment is a social situation, it is also important to include some statement of the manner in which the experimenter treated the subject, as well as the important social characteristics of each of the experimenters, such as sex, race, and so forth. When your design calls for dividing subjects into various groups, it is necessary to describe how group assignment was determined (random, matching, and so on). It is also necessary to describe how you operationally defined your independent and dependent variables and how your various groups were tested. For example, if you used a subject variable such as anxiety, you would want to include the mean scores and standard deviations on whatever anxiety scale you used in assigning subjects to either low- or high-anxiety conditions. It should also be stated whether the experimenter who actually tested the subjects knew to which group a given subject belonged. If there is a scoring procedure, was this performed blind? For example, in a study that examined the content of dreams of anxious and nonanxious individuals, did the dream rater know whether a given dream belonged to a high- or low-anxiety subject? To give you an idea of how a method section is written, consider the following section from the obesity study by Gaul et al. (1975). In this example, the subjects and procedure sections describe how the study on the eating rates of obese and nonobese subjects was measured.

## METHOD

SUBJECTS. One hundred subjects were chosen for observation at an eating establishment that specializes in the sale of hamburgers, french fried potatoes, and soft drinks. One criterion for subject selection was that he purchase all three items and only those items. Additionally, for a subject to be included he had to sip his drink through a straw (which nearly all people did). Finally, the subject had to be between the ages of 18 and 35 in the opinion of two trained observers. As each potential subject purchased his food, the two observers independently categorized them on age and obesity. The first 50 males (25 obese, 25 nonobese) to meet joint agreement criteria were included in the study.

PROCEDURE. The consummatory behaviors of each subject were unobtrusively recorded by two trained observers. Any subject who indicated awareness of being observed was excluded from the study. Observations were made, one subject at the time, in order of subjects' appearance until the requisite number ($n = 25$) for each cell was obtained.

Beginning with the subject's first bite or sip of drink, frequency counts were taken by both observers for five minutes. Data were obtained for the following dependent measures: number of bites taken during the five minutes (three french fries were considered equal to one bite of hamburger), number of chews per bite, total number of seconds (of possible 300) spent chewing, and total number of sips of soft drink.

In some psychology experiments, it is necessary to have an extended methods section so that other scientists understand exactly what happened to a subject during the experiment and how particular behaviors were measured. This is particularly true in social psychology experiments in which any type of deception is used. The method section in deception studies includes not only the methodology but also the safeguards such as debriefing and follow-up measures that were involved in the study. The following is one example (Shotland and Straw, 1976).

## METHOD

The first procedure attempted was similar to the one used by Borofsky et al. (1971) in which a male attacked a female during a psychodrama. The fight was actually videotaped and played for each subject, who was told he or she had been arbitrarily selected to act in the next psychodrama pairing of the three participants and was asked to leave the other two participants (the confederates) so as not to inhibit them and to watch their psychodrama on television in the next room. This procedure proved unworkable as approximately 40% of the subjects thought the fight was staged.

A second procedure was needed that was more believable. The local police department was made aware of the impending experiment and their advance was sought. Three of the first author's colleagues in the Department of Psychology were asked to review the procedure for ethical considerations.

SUBJECTS. The subjects were 51 male and female students who participated in order to receive course credit for either an introductory psychology or Man-Environment Relations course during the summer of 1974 at The Pennsylvania State University.

PROCEDURE. Two couples with theatrical training were recruited through the cooperation of a faculty member in the Drama Department. One couple (Team 1) consisted of a man who was 1.70 m, 63.50 kg (5 feet 7 inches, 140 pounds) with brown hair conventionally cut, paired with a woman who was 1.57 m, 49.90 kg (5 feet 2 inches, 110 pounds) with shoulder-length black hair. The second couple (Team 2) consisted of a man who was 1.85 m, 90.72 kg (6 feet 1 inch, 200 pounds) with light brown hair conventionally cut, paired with a 1.70 m, 54.43 kg (5 feet 7 inches, 120 pounds) woman with long blonde hair. All of the college-age actors wore the usual jeans and shirts.

Each couple worked on alternate nights with subjects being randomly assigned to conditions, the only provision being that the conditions contained an equal number of male and female subjects. The subject came to take part in a study of attitudes in which he or she expected to answer a questionnaire and be interviewed. The subject arrived at the appointed room and found a note explaining that the experimenter would arrive later to interview him or her and asking that the subject began filling out the questionnaire. On the table with the questionnaires were what appeared to be a university phone with a standard sticker giving emergency telephone numbers, including the police. The telephone was not functioning and was rigged to provide a dial tone when it was appropriate, and to record any telephone number that the subject might try to call.

Other rooms on the floor had apparent activity in them. From the room across the hall emanated the sound of a computer printer, and in the room next to the experimental room a radio played.

After the subject entered the room 5 minutes passed, during which time the subject proceeded to fill out the questionnaire. The confederates, on a different floor of the building, received a signal by walkie-talkie and took the elevator to the proper floor. Before the doors opened, a loud verbal argument could be heard. The woman was accused by the man of picking up a dollar she claimed to have dropped. After approximately 15 sec of heated discussion, the man physically attacked the woman, violently shaking her while she struggled, resisting and screaming. The screams were loud piercing shrieks, interspersed with pleas to "get away from me." Along with the shrieks one of two conditions was introduced and then repeated several times. In the stranger condition the woman screamed, "I don't know you," and in the married condition, "I don't know why I ever married you." From the first designation of the condition the physical fight lasted a maximum of 45 sec, with the entire incident not lasting more than a minute.

The fight was immediately terminated with the attacker fleeing at any attempt by the subject to intervene. If no one intervened, the fight was terminated by a third confederate (male), who came out of a nearby room and demanded in a loud voice that the attacker stop beating up the woman. The attacker then ran away while the false intervener consoled the woman. Every effort was made to keep a direct intervener away from the actors to insure their safety. Two confederates were placed in concealed locations between the actors and the subject, one to falsely intervene, the other to inform the subject it was an experiment, if necessary.

A subject was considered an intervener if he or she called the police on our phone, asked a person in the computer room to help stop the fight, shouted at the attacker to stop, or acted to intervene directly. The fight was staged 15.85–16.15 m (52–53 feet) away from the room containing the subject. If the subject came down the hall toward the fight some 9.14 m (30 feet) and did not turn into an intersecting hallway, he or she was counted as intervening.

The subjects were interviewed immediately following the experiment and fully debriefed by the first author, who spent up to 45 minutes with each subject. The interviews were unstructured except for several standard questions. First, the subjects were asked to describe what they had seen. If they did not adequately describe the experimental condition to which they were assigned, they were asked: (a) What was the relationship between the two people fighting? (b) How do you know? Subjects were asked (c) What caused the fight? and (d) Did you think it was a rape? They were then asked to describe their thoughts and behavior in the sequence in which they had occurred while witnessing the fight. After the debriefing each subject was specifically asked: (e) Do you think we have done any harm to you by having you go through that experience? and (f) Do you think that the potential results and implications of the research are worth the experience you went through? Each subject was urged to call the first author if he or she wished to discuss any aspect of the experiment in the future.

**Results** The fourth part of a research article is the *results* section. The chief purpose of this section is simply to state the outcome of the experiment and then indicate whether or not the outcome was statistically significant. For example, a results section might begin with the statement that the experimental and control groups did or did not differ significantly in terms of whatever dependent variable was measured. Following this general statement, the actual group scores may be presented and then the manner in which the results were analyzed is briefly described. Quite frequently the results section also contains a figure or table that aids the reader in visualizing the major outcome of the experiment.

Any hypothesis presented in the introduction should have the corresponding results presented in the results section. Although there are no hard-and-fast rules concerning discussion and reference to other studies in the results section, references to other studies are usually saved for the discussion section. The following example is from the eating study presented previously, in which two observers watched obese and nonobese people eat to see whether there were differences in their eating behaviors.

We have changed the statistical results in this example as required by the current APA *Publication Manual.* For example, "$F$ (1, 96) = 68.2, $p < .001$" tells us that an $F$-ratio of 68.2 with 1 and 96 degrees of freedom would be expected to have happened by chance less than one time in 1,000.

## RESULTS

Interobserver agreement was calculated by dividing the number of ratings for which both observers agreed by the number of agreements plus disagreements and multiplying the quotient by 100. Interobserver agreement was 100% for all measures except number of chews per bite, where the average interobserver agreement was 92% (range = 87%–100%).

The means and standard deviations for all the dependent measures are presented in Table 1. The data represent averages between observers for all measures.

All data were submitted to 2 × 2 (Obesity × Sex) analyses of variance. The main effect for obesity was significant for number of bites taken ($F$ (1, 96) = 68.2, $p < .001$), number of chews per bite ($F$ (1, 96) = 126.8, $p < .001$), and for total amount of time spent chewing ($F$ (1, 96) = 70.1, $p < .001$).

Obese subjects took more bites ($M$ = 16.94) than nonobese subjects ($M$ = 12.66), performed fewer chews per bite ($M$ obese = 9.24, $M$ nonobese = 18.60), spent less time chewing ($M$ obese = 104.26, $M$ nonobese = 157.54).

There was a significant main effect for sex ($F$ (1, 96) = 5.8, $p < .018$) and a significant Sex × Obesity interaction effect ($F$ (1, 96) = 3.7, $p < .056$) for total number of sips taken. Males ($M$ = 7.72) took a greater total of sips than did females ($M$ = 6.92); however, this was primarily the result of obese males ($M$ = 8.00) who took a significantly greater number of sips than did the obese female subjects ($M$ = 6.56).

"I THINK YOU SHOULD BE MORE EXPLICIT HERE IN STEP TWO."

**Discussion** The final section is called the *discussion.* In general the discussion is a three-part process. In the first section you simply report the chief finding of the present experiment. Next, you point out any limitations or potential confounds that may affect your interpretation of the results and restate the results in light of these limitations. Quite frequently this second step is omitted lest the article not be accepted for publication. We believe this is an essential step in any discussion, however, and encourage you to make it a part of your scientific papers from the very beginning. In the final part of the discussion, you directly relate the results of your experiment to other published experiments on the same topic and describe how the present experiment expands our understanding of the phenomenon we are studying.

## DISCUSSION

The foregoing results suggest several clinically relevant implications for the behavioral treatment of obesity. To begin with, it does appear that there are differences in the eating styles of obese and nonobese individuals. Obese subjects in the present study spent less time chewing than nonobese subjects and took more bites during the five-minute observation period. This latter finding corroborates the notion that overweight individuals are often rapid eaters (Ferster et al., 1962). Therapeutic strategies aimed at reducing eating pace may therefore be effective. However, the fact that obese subjects took more bites than nonobese subjects is at least partially contradictory to the popular recommendation that overweight individuals increase the number of bites they take (Stuart & Davis, 1972). Unless this increase is accompanied by a slowing of the eating pace, countertherapeutic results might ensue.

The dramatic difference between groups on the mastication variable also deserves comment. Although relatively little therapeutic attention has been paid to this dimension, it seems possible that increased mastication may facilitate weight reduction. This speculation is consistent with recent findings on the role of food texture and mastication in satiety (Balagura, 1973).

The strategy of counting bites (Stuart & David, 1972) may be contraindicated unless obese clients are given specific standards and eating behavior guidelines to pursue. At an intuitive level, the overweight person may interpret this self-monitoring task as suggesting that he should take fewer bites. Were this to result, he might inadvertently develop the maladaptive pattern of rapid, large (but few) bites. A laboratory study subsequent to the one described in this article asked obese and nonobese individuals to eat a standardized meal in a laboratory setting. Within the next three days the subjects were asked to count the bites they took while consuming the same standardized meal. Extensive intersub-

> ject variability was encountered. Self-monitoring did not have any systematic effect on eating pace for either group of individuals. A noteworthy finding, however, was that obese subjects were significantly less accurate in their self-monitoring than nonobese subjects ($U_2 = 4.5$, $n_1 = 6$, $n_2 = 7$, $p < .05$).
>
> One final comment has to do with the assumption that obese individuals will lose weight if they adopt the eating styles of normal persons (Stunkard & Mahoney, in press). While there is strong evidence that modifying *what* people eat (calorically) can result in weight loss, the data on modifying *how* they eat are less conclusive. Further inquiries need to evaluate the relationship between these variables.

In attempting to grasp the fundamental differences among these sections, one rule of thumb is that the method and results sections must be written in an exact manner. The method section must be detailed enough to permit another scientist to perform an exact replication of your experiment; the results section must be an accurate statement of what actually happened in your experiment. In a sense, because these sections are a statement of how you performed your experiment and what your results were, they are a simple record of your experiment and can be expected always to be an accurate description of what happened. In contrast, the discussion is in fact a statement of what you think your finding means for our understanding of the phenomenon you are studying. Although your finding will last forever, your interpretation of your actual data may vary considerably as your understanding of the phenomenon grows with each successive experiment.

Once you have finished writing the five major sections of the article, all that remain are to find a title for your paper and to list your references. The title of your paper is very important because, like the abstract, it describes the nature of your experiment. Consequently many titles are written so that they describe the nature of the independent and dependent variables. For example, in 1958 Silverstine and Klee published an article in the *American Medical Association Archives of Neurology and Psychiatry* entitled: "Effects of lysergic acid diethylamide (LSD-25) on intellectual functions." The title of this paper tells us the independent variable (lysergic acid) and the dependent variables (some measure of intellectual function). Finally, the title, author, and reference information for every study you cite in your paper are listed on a separate page at the end of the paper.

**References** The *reference* section of a paper is important for the valuable information it gives to other scientists. There are no hard-and-fast rules for using references, but general guidelines suggest that you use a reference for one of three purposes. The first is to acknowledge a scientific fact, assumption, or working hypothesis. For example, a research article concerning the functions of the left and right hemispheres of the brain might begin with the statement "Research suggests that the left and right hemispheres of the brain process information differently." Following this sentence the author could give one or more references directing the reader to research articles. A second use of references is to direct the reader to a more detailed discussion of a theoretical concept or a specific experimental or statistical procedure. Since a research report is by its nature short, it is important to direct others to extended discussions of the concept under study, as might be found in *Psychological Bulletin* or *Psychological Review.* The third use of a reference is to give credit to other scientists for developing an idea, technique, or line of research. Finally, we want to point out to you that the particular format for listing references in American Psychological Association journals changed in 1984. In specific, the date of the article or book is now listed directly following the authors. Also a reference to a chapter in a book now includes the page numbers. The following illustrates a reference section including references to journal articles, books, and book chapters.

**REFERENCES**

Bianchi, L. (1895). The function of the frontal lobes. *Brain, 18,* 497–522.

Darwin, C. R. (1965). *The expression of the emotions in man and animals.* Chicago: University of Chicago Press. (Original work published 1872.)

Flynn, J. R. (1984). The mean IQ of Americans: Massive gains 1932 to 1978. *Psychological Bulletin, 95,* 3–28.

Leventhal, H. (1980). Toward a comprehensive theory of emotions. In L. Berkowitz (Ed.), *Advances in experimental psychology* (Vol. 13, pp. 139–207). New York: Academic Press.

Surman, O. S., Gottlieb, S. K., Hackett, T. P., Silverberg, E. (1973). Hypnosis in the treatment of warts. *Archives of General Psychiatry, 28,* 439–441.

A journal article as it was published is presented in Appendix B. For additional help with preparing papers in APA format, we have included a typed copy of selected parts of this article showing the proper spacing, headings, and so forth in Appendix C. This shows both the format a student might use to submit a research paper to a class and the manner in which it *must* be submitted for publication in an APA and other journals. As you may have noticed, the five major parts of this study—the abstract, introduction, method, results, and discussion—along with the title and references are presented in their entirety. Also, if you look at the conclusion of the reference section, you can see the date on which the journal received the article.

Now that you know the sections required for writing an article, we can turn to the next step—submitting the article for publication. Before we do this we want to remind you that proposals for research may also follow the APA format. In a proposal, of course, you would not have actual data. Your results section would describe how your data would be quantified and which specific statistical tests you would use. Likewise the discussion section could discuss possible outcomes and what these might mean scientifically. To aid you in the preparation of proposals, we have included a checklist for preparing a research proposal in Box 14.1 (Holt, 1965).

## Publishing Your Article

Now that we have discussed the basic form of a research article, let us talk about the process of submitting an article for publication. One of the first questions that a scientist asks is: Who or what portion of the scientific community do I want to read my article? For example, suppose someone has performed a study that examines the EEG changes in humans over a period of years and how this correlates with education and psychological development. Depending on the particular hypothesis of the study and its focus, the final article might be sent to a journal that reports physiological research, such as *Psychophysiology, EEG and Clinical Neurology,* or *Neuropsychologia;* or to a journal emphasizing developmental processes, such as *Developmental Psychology;* or even to a journal that discusses educational development. Each of these journals is read by a different group of scientists, and thus publishing an article in one journal will give you a different audience from publishing in another. To help the potential author, most journals include a statement at the beginning as to the type of articles they accept. If your study is a replication and continuation of some of the articles cited in your introduction, probably the same journal that published the other studies would be interested in your work. Once you have decided upon an audience and a journal, it is a good procedure to look through recent issues of the journal to see whether the particular style that is used deviates from the APA recommendation. For example, journals may differ in the reference and results sections. Thus, the particular form of reference citation must be checked carefully, as well as the manner in which statistical significance is reported.

Once you have written the article following the guidelines in the front of the journal, you send the number of copies requested to the editor of the journal and wait. Some journals give information concerning publication decisions very quickly and others take many months. To understand why there is a delay before your article is accepted or rejected, let us examine what happens when an article is received by the editor of a journal. In most cases the editor is a scientist employed by a university or research laboratory, who has agreed to be editor for a few years. To begin with, the editor has another job on which he or she spends considerable time. The day-to-day processes of the journal are generally performed by a paid assistant. Once the manuscript is received by the editor, the editor usually chooses two scientists who are studying phenomena similar to yours and asks them to recommend whether the article should be accepted for publication. The process of review by other scientists is referred to as the *peer review system*. Each reviewer reads your article and evaluates it as to the clarity of presentation, the logic of the experiment, the appropriateness of the data

---

### *Box 14.1 Preparing a Research Proposal*

For some students, there is less emphasis on the writing of formal research papers for publication and more emphasis on the development of sound research proposals. In the development of proposals, there are many conceptual as well as "down to earth" questions that must be considered. In this process a checklist is helpful. The following checklist was developed by Robert Holt. Students who have particular problems with developing a research project will find Dr. Holt's clear-cut advice helpful and should consult his original article (Holt, 1965).

*Checklist of Questions to Be Asked About a Research Proposal*

1. What is the problem?
   a. Is it clearly stated?
   b. Is it focused enough to facilitate efficient work (i.e., are hypotheses directly testable)?
2. What are the underlying objectives?
   a. Is the problem clearly related to the objectives?
3. What is the significance of the proposed research?
   a. How does it tie in with theory?
   b. What are its implications for application?
4. Has the relevant literature been adequately surveyed?
   a. Is the research adequately related to other people's work on the same or similar topics?
5. Are the concepts and variables adequately defined (theoretically and operationally)?
6. Is the design adequate?
   a. Does it meet formal standards for consistency, power, and efficiency?
   b. Is it appropriate to the problem and the objectives?

analysis utilized, and the meaningfulness of the discussion section. This is similar to the type of feedback your professors give you concerning research reports and proposals. In this chapter we will present in more detail some exact evaluative criteria that are used for research evaluation.

After a reviewer has read and evaluated an article, she or he writes a review, which is sent back to the editor. Usually these reviews are a couple of pages long and are designed to give feedback to the author. In some cases the reviewers point out limitations of the experiment itself or of the way the article is written. Frequently, specific suggestions are made to improve your paper. And in each case a general recommendation is made as to whether the article should be published or not. The editor takes these reviews and then makes a final decision about whether to publish the paper and then informs the author of the decision. Sometimes the reviewers differ over the quality of the article and the editor must make a decision. Other times the reviewers suggest publication only if the author agrees to rewrite or

---

   c. Will negative results be meaningful?
   d. Are possibly misleading and confounding variables controlled?
   e. How are the independent and dependent variables measured or specified?
7. What instruments or techniques will be used to gather data?
   a. Are the reliabilities and validities of these techniques well established?
8. Is the sampling of subjects adequately planned for?
   a. Is the population (to which generalizations are to be aimed) specified?
   b. Is there a specific and acceptable method of drawing a sample from this population?
9. Is the sampling of objects (or situations) adequately planned for?
   a. To what population of objects (situations) will generalizations be aimed?
   b. Is there a specific and acceptable method of drawing a sample from this population?
10. What is the setting in which data will be gathered?
    a. Is it feasible and practical to carry out the research plan in this setting?
    b. Is the cooperation of the necessary persons obtainable?
11. How are the data to be analyzed?
    a. What techniques of "data reduction" are contemplated?
    b. Are methods specified for analyzing data qualitatively?
    c. Are methods specified for analyzing data quantitatively?
12. In the light of available resources, how feasible is the design?
    a. What compromises must be made in translating an idealized research design into a practical research design?
    b. What limitations or generalizations will result?
    c. What will be needed in terms of time, money, personnel, and facilities?

---

reanalyze reviewers suggest publication only if the author agrees to rewrite or reanalyze part of the study. Thus, after some wait, you receive the reviews and the editor's disposition as to publication of your article. Even if the editor agrees to publish your article as it stands, there is still another wait for the article to come into print. This delay is referred to as the *publication lag*. This lag is generally brought about because a journal accepts many good articles and is able to publish only a few of them in any given issue. The publication lag may range from a month or two to almost a year and a half.

## WHAT MAKES A GOOD ARTICLE?

One question beginning students ask is: What criteria do editors and reviewers keep in mind as they are reviewing papers for publication? Obviously the answer is important because it should provide you with an idea of what senior scientists consider both good research and a well-written experiment. In August 1978 Brendan Maher, the editor of the *Journal of Consulting and Clinical Psychology*, reported that four out of every five articles submitted to the journal are rejected. Because most of these are rejected for methodological reasons, Maher produced a set of guidelines (reproduced below) that may be used not only by reviewers but also by writers and readers of scientific articles. Some of these guidelines, such as the ones related to factor analysis, you may come to understand after learning more advanced statistical techniques in more advanced courses.

---

### A Reader's, Writer's, and Reviewer's Guide to Assessing Research Reports in Clinical Psychology

**Brendan A. Maher**

*Harvard University*

The Editors of the *Journal of Consulting and Clinical Psychology* who served between 1974 and 1978 have seen some 3,500 manuscripts in the area of consulting and clinical psychology. Working with this number of manuscripts has made it possible to formulate a set of general guidelines that may be helpful in the assessment of research reports. Originally developed by and for journal reviewers, the guidelines are necessarily skeletal and summary and omit many methodological concerns. They do, however, address the methodological concerns that have proved to be significant in a substantial number of cases. In response to a number of requests, the guidelines are being made available here.

### Topic Content

1. Is the article appropriate to this journal? Does it fall within the boundaries mandated in the masthead description?

### Style

1. Does the manuscript conform to APA style in its major aspects?

### Introduction

1. Is the introduction as brief as possible given the topic of the article?
2. Are all of the citations correct and necessary, or is there padding? Are important citations missing? Has the author been careful to cite prior reports contrary to the current hypothesis?
3. Is there an explicit hypothesis?
4. Has the *origin* of the hypothesis been made explicit?
5. Was the hypothesis *correctly* derived from the theory that has been cited? Are other, contrary hypotheses compatible with the same theory?
6. Is there an explicit rationale for the selection of measures, and was it derived logically from the hypothesis?

### Method

1. Is the method so described that replication is possible without further information?
2. Subjects: Were they sampled randomly from the population to which the results will be generalized?
3. Under what circumstances was informed consent obtained?
4. Are there probable biases in sampling (e.g., volunteers, high refusal rates, institution population atypical for the country at large, etc.)?
5. What was the "set" given to subjects? Was there deception? Was there control for experimenter influence and expectancy effects?
6. How were subjects debriefed?
7. Were subjects (patients) led to believe that they were receiving "treatment"?
8. Were there special variables affecting the subjects, such as medication, fatigue, and threat that were not part of the experimental manipulation? In clinical samples, was "organicity" measured and/or eliminated?
9. Controls: Were there appropriate control groups? What was being controlled for?

10. When more than one measure was used, was the order counterbalanced? If so, were order effects actually analyzed statistically?
11. Was there a control task(s) to confirm specificity of results?
12. Measures: For both dependent and independent variable measures—was validity and reliability established and reported? When a measure is tailor-made for a study, this is very important. When validities and reliabilities are already available in the literature, it is less important.
13. Is there adequate description of tasks, materials, apparatus, and so forth?
14. Is there discriminant validity of the measures?
15. Are distributions of scores on measures typical of scores that have been reported for similar samples in previous literature?
16. Are measures free from biases such as
    a. Social desirability?
    b. Yeasaying and naysaying?
    c. Correlations with general responsivity?
    d. Verbal ability, intelligence?
17. If measures are scored by observers using categories or codes, what is the inter-rater reliability?
18. Was administration and scoring of the measures done blind?
19. If short versions, foreign-language translations, and so forth, of common measures are used, has the validity and reliability of these been established?
20. In correlational designs, do the two measures have theoretical and/or methodological independence?

### Representative Design

1. When the stimulus is a human (e.g., in clinical judgments of clients of differing race, sex, etc.), is there a *sample* of stimuli (e.g., more than one client of each race or each sex)?
2. When only one stimulus or a few human stimuli were used, was an adequate explanation of the failure to sample given?

### Statistics

1. Were the statistics used with appropriate assumptions fulfilled by the data (e.g., normalcy of distributions for parametric techniques)? Where necessary, have scores been transformed appropriately?
2. Were tests of significance properly used and reported? For example, did the author use the $p$ value of a correlation to justify conclusions when the actual size of the correlation suggests little common variance between two measures?

3. Have statistical significance levels been accompanied by an analysis of practical significance levels?
4. Has the author considered the effects of a limited range of scores, and so forth, in using correlations?
5. Is the basic statistical strategy that of a "fishing expedition"; that is, if many comparisons are made, were the obtained significance levels predicted in advance? Consider the number of significance levels as a function of the total number of comparisons made.

### Factor Analytic Statistics

1. Have the correlation and factor matrices been made available to the reviewers and to the readers through the National Auxiliary Publications Service or other methods?
2. Is it stated what was used for communalities and is the choice appropriate? Ones in the diagonals are especially undesirable when items are correlated as the variables.
3. Is the method of termination of factor extraction stated, and is it appropriate in this case?
4. Is the method of factor rotation stated, and is it appropriate in this case?
5. If items are used as variables, what are the proportions of yes and no responses for each variable?
6. Is the sample size given, and is it adequate?
7. Are there evidences of distortion in the final solution, such as singlet factors, excessively high communalities, obliqueness when an orthogonal solution is used, linearly dependent variables, or too many complex variables?
8. Are artificial factors evident because of inclusion of variables in the analysis that are alternate forms of each other?

### Figures and Tables

1. Are the figures and tables (a) necessary and (b) self-explanatory? Large tables of nonsignificant differences, for example, should be eliminated if the few obtained significances can be reported in a sentence or two in the text. Could several tables be combined into a smaller number?
2. Are the axes of figures identified clearly?
3. Do graphs correspond logically to the textual argument of the article? (E.g., if the text states that a certain technique leads to an *increment* of mental health and the accompanying graphs shows a *decline* in symptoms, the point is not as clear to the reader as it would be if the text or the graph were amended to achieve visual and verbal congruence.)

### Discussion and Conclusion

1. Is the discussion properly confined to the findings or is it digressive, including new post hoc speculations?
2. Has the author explicitly considered and discussed viable alternative explanations of the findings?
3. Have nonsignificant trends in the data been promoted to "findings"?
4. Are the limits of the generalizations possible from the data made clear? Has the author identified his/her own methodological difficulties in the study?
5. Has the author "accepted" the null hypothesis?
6. Has the author considered the possible methodological bases for discrepancies between the results reported and other findings in the literature?

Requests for reprints should be sent to Brendan A. Maher, Department of Psychology and Social Relations, Harvard University, Cambridge, Massachusetts 02138.



---

## Key Terms and Concepts

1. Parts of an article
   a. abstract
   b. introduction
   c. method
   d. results
   e. discussion
   f. references
2. What makes a good proposal or article

## Summary

1. An important part of research is communicating the results to others, and for this purpose a particular format has evolved. This format includes five parts: (1) abstract, (2) introduction, (3) method, (4) results, and (5) discussion.
2. The abstract is a 100-150-word summary of the article. The typical abstract provides a clear statement of purpose, methodology, and results.
3. The introduction of a paper is designed to review what is already known about the topic being studied, to explain the reasons for the present study, and to outline the hypothesis.

4. The method section consists of a detailed description of what was done, so that another scientist could precisely replicate the experiment. This description covers which subjects were used and how they were selected, what the experimental situation was, any equipment that was used, and the procedures, including what the subjects were told or led to believe.
5. The results section describes the outcome of an experiment and states what statistical procedures were used and the results of these analyses.
6. The discussion section describes the results of the study as they relate to previous research and theoretical interpretation, as well as any potential limitations of the experiment.
7. An excellent set of guidelines for assessing research reports was published by Brendan Maher in the *Journal of Consulting and Clinical Psychology* and is reproduced in this chapter.

## Review Questions

1. What are the major parts of a research article?
2. What is an abstract and where is it located in a paper?
3. How do you determine which references to include in a paper?
4. Where would the research hypothesis be located in a paper?
5. Statistical tests would be reported in which section of a paper?
6. What is the purpose of the discussion section?
7. Why are many articles rejected for publication in the *Journal of Consulting and Clinical Psychology?*
8. How are a proposal and a published article the same and how are they different?

## Discussion Questions and Projects

1. Pick an article published in one of the APA journals (e.g., *Journal of Experimental Psychology, Journal of Personality and Social Psychology, Journal of Abnormal Psychology*). Place a piece of paper over the abstract and read the article. Now write an abstract of your own. How did your abstract differ from the existing one?
2. Pick an article of interest to you (it should not be one published this year). Read the article and write a summary of it. Look up this same article in the appropriate issue of *Psychological Abstracts* and compare your summary with the existing one. What are the differences between yours and the other one?
3. Discuss the function of the discussion section.
4. Why do people use references? What are the reasons for including or excluding a particular article?
5. Take a simple task such as balancing a ruler on the end of your finger (measure amount of time) in two conditions: (1) singing a song to yourself and (2) saying the alphabet backwards. Assume that you have used the appropriate control procedures such as counterbalancing the order of conditions. Write a procedure section of a research article and describe such a task with the various conditions.

CHAPTER FIFTEEN

# *Beyond Method*

## INTRODUCTION

Throughout this book we have sought to teach you more than just methods. This stems from our conviction that the process of science is *more* than the simple application of the scientific method to the study of human behavior and experience. In this chapter we want to move beyond the specific application of particular designs, as important as these approaches are, and to focus on some of the broad themes we have presented throughout this book. To emphasize this point we have entitled this final chapter "Beyond Method." Before beginning this task, let us first review schematically the approaches to research we have presented thus far.

In the preceding chapters we said a great deal about contemporary research methods used to study human behavior and experience. Now we will simply attempt to bring them together in a single schematic representation. To facilitate viewing them together, let's consider three continua (see Figure 15.1). The first continuum refers to the extent to which we directly intervene in the phenomenon we are studying. At one extreme is the experimental method. This is an active method, which involves studying relationships by directly manipulating an independent variable and observing its effect on the dependent variable. Typically experimenters are interested in how one factor affects another at a given point in time. At the other extreme is the method of naturalistic observation. This is typically a passive method, which attempts to describe an ongoing process as it unfolds over time.

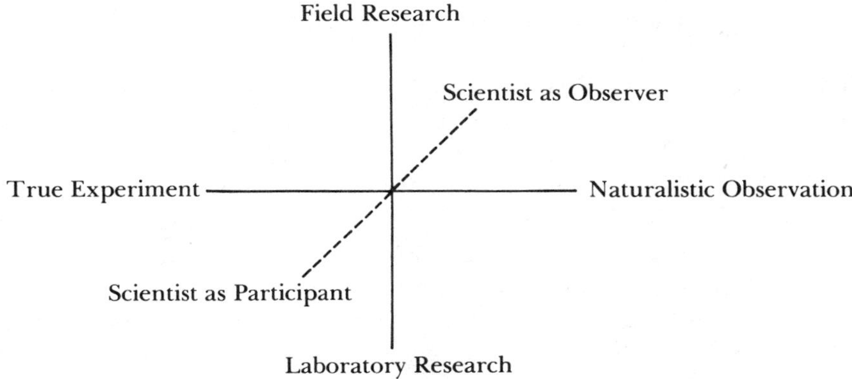


**Figure 15.1** Three-dimensional illustration of research approaches.

It is important to realize that something is gained and something lost whenever we adopt either of these methods. When we use naturalistic observation, we find ourselves unable to point out important relationships. Likewise it is impossible to produce changes in the subjects we study; we must wait until new behaviors and experiences "spontaneously" appear. The experimental methods give us the advantage of increased control and thus the ability to infer important relationships between events. However, *we have to know what we are looking for to use this method successfully.* As soon as we choose a dependent variable, certain information is excluded. In general the information that is excluded is what *we do not know to begin with.* For example, how many of us consider the weather (temperature, pressure, humidity) when we design experiments? We *assume* that weather is not an important factor. But some migraine sufferers, for example, report an increase of episodes before storms.

We would like to suggest using both the experimental method and naturalistic observation simultaneously. When conducting a true experiment, we are interested not only in the dependent variable that is being collected but also in watching the total experiment. Likewise, when observing subjects in naturalistic research, we consider what variables might be related and what variables might affect others. Thus, as one is developing ideas concerning a topic, there is a continuous interplay between naturalistic and experimental methods. This is true for both research and the development of ideas.

The second dimension involves the research setting: laboratory versus field research. Laboratory research refers to our desire to create an experimental situation that includes all the important variables that affect the phenomenon we are studying. By moving our research into the laboratory, we obtain greater control over environmental factors. Field research, on the other hand, gives us less control over environmental factors but allows for more ecologically valid behavior on the part of the subject we are studying. That is, by performing research in the field, many researchers believe the responses of the subjects are more "natural" and thus less controlled by the demand characteristics of the experiment.

There is also a third continuum, which relates to the scientist's actual participation in the experiment. On one extreme is the scientist as observer, in which it is assumed that the scientist is in no way involved in the experiment but only passively records data. On the other extreme is the scientist as participant, in which the scientist is actually part of the study. There is no hard-and-fast rule that suggests whether scientist as observer or scientist as participant gives the greater objectivity. It depends on the questions being asked. If you were studying the social psychology of a motorcycle gang, then more accurate information might be obtained by being part of the group rather than being seen as an outsider. However, if you wanted to see how individuals react to a motorcycle gang driving through their town, then it might be better to be an observer so that you could see the reaction of the town both during and after the gang moved through.

As you look at the continua in Figure 15.1, you can see that you as a scientist have available a variety of methods and approaches to understand the question you are studying. No one approach or method is superior in itself. Methods are useful only in relation to a particular question being asked. To help illustrate this point, let us now divide the three-dimensional illustration of research approaches in Figure 15.1 into the two-dimensional ones in Figure 15.2. As an exercise, try to determine in which quadrant particular research studies discussed throughout this book should be placed.

Depending on the particular topics you study and the particular questions you ask, you are led to one of the methods presented in Figure 15.1 to study it. This brings us to the second aspect of science that we want to address—the questions we study.

## BEGINNING WITH A QUESTION

As we have stressed throughout our discussion, the process of science is more than the mere application of method. In fact, much of the important work of learning to be a scientist lies in the realm of remembering how to ask

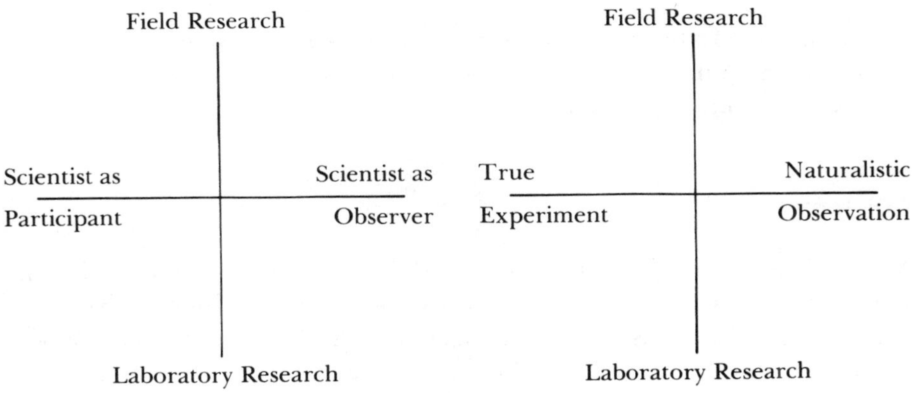


**Figure 15.2** Two-dimensional illustrations of research approaches.

questions. We said *remembering* rather than *learning* because we wanted to remind you that doing science is not some special activity that sets us apart from the rest of humanity but rather an activity that stems from it. To emphasize this in the beginning of this book, we used the metaphor of the scientist being a child out to discover the world. Part of your task on the way to becoming a scientist is to recapture that childlike perspective—to remember how to find the wonder and excitement of asking questions. Once you become fascinated with a process or phenomenon, then you naturally consider it, explore it, and begin to ask questions about it.

Excitement and wonder are not enough, however. Just as the child grows up and matures, the scientist moves beyond the initial excitement of a question and begins to formulate a systematic approach to how the question might be answered. This usually means not just one experiment but a series of directed research studies referred to as a *research program* (see Box 15.1). In formulating such an approach, the scientist draws upon both the previous work of others and his or her own independent ideas. We will discuss the scientist's reliance on others and himself or herself in greater detail later in this chapter. For now we only want to emphasize that being excited about an idea or research question is an important beginning, but it is only the beginning. Then comes hard work.

## LIMITATIONS TO FINDING ANSWERS

The scientist finds many obstacles within the hard work of research that may limit the types of questions that can be asked. Three of the most important limitations are (1) the tools we have available to us, (2) our shared view of the world, and (3) our personal psychological limitations such as fear of making mistakes or being rejected by our colleagues and friends.

## Our Tools

Many of the questions we may wish to ask in science may be limited by the particular techniques that are available to us in the period when we live. This is true of physical tools and technologies as well as methodological sophistication. In the same way that the telescope and the microscope allowed scientists to see worlds that were previously unknown, electronic developments such as the computer and the physiological amplifer allow us to study worlds of human behavior and experience that were previously beyond our limits. With new tools come new methodological advances. However, it is possible to fall in love with a particular tool or research technique, be it methodological, statistical, or mechanical. This often results in someone's trying to make all human behavior and experience conform to measurement by one tool. There is an old saying that if you give a child *only* a hammer, he

---

### *Box 15.1 Philosophy of Science: Imre Lakatos*

Imre Lakatos suggests that the important advances in science are made through the adherence to *research programs.* By saying this, Lakatos means that science is more than following trial-and-error hypotheses. A research program is the examination of a number of major and minor hypotheses concerning a topic. Some examples Lakatos gives of research programs are Newton's theory of gravity, Einstein's relativity theory, and the theories of Freud.

An important point, specifies Lakatos, is whether the research program is progressive or degenerating. How do you tell the difference? The main characteristic of a *progressive* research program is that *it predicts novel facts.* Thus a progressive program leads to the discovery of new facts, whereas a *degenerating* program only reinterprets *known* facts in light of that theory. By this he means that a degenerating research program only explains the results of already existing experiments, whereas a progressive research program leads one into new directions and predicts new facts. In this way, Lakatos proposes that science changes not by sudden revolutions, as Kuhn suggested, but through the replacement of degenerating research programs with progressive ones.

For more information on Lakatos, see Lakatos (1978) and Eysenck (1976).

---

or she will treat everything as if it is a nail. This, of course, is not the fault of the hammer but of the child's view of how a hammer should be used. The same is true for the scientist's view of the purpose of research tools, which leads us to our second point.

## Our Shared View of the World

One of the greatest problems for a scientist interested in discovering new truths is related to our view of the world. Some writers refer to these views as "tacit" or "metaphysical" as well as "unconscious." The real point to be made is that we all have assumptions that guide and direct our behavior, such as "people are evil," "man is an aggressive animal," "all behavior is learned," and "all behavior is innate." Even the law of parsimony (stating that the best explanation in science is the least complicated), which has guided research in science, is itself an untested metaphysical assumption. Having assumptions is not the problem; the real problem, as the biologist David Bohm suggests, occurs when an individual confuses the assumptions themselves with directly observed facts (Bohm, 1969). Take a very common example of this problem: In the morning we "see" the "sunrise" and at night we "see" the "sunset." But of course the sun neither rises nor sets; it is rather we who are turning in space and move into sight of the sun and out of sight of the sun. Once we have pointed it out to you, you will say, yes, of course, and may even actually "see" the next "sunrise" or "sunset" differently.

Looking at scientific examples of the problem, we once all believed that the world was flat and that heavy bodies would reach the ground faster than lighter ones. A more recent example was the belief that organs innervated by the autonomic nervous system (the heart, stomach, and certain glands) were beyond self-regulation. Pioneer work by Neal Miller (1969) and others is beginning to show this assumption to be incorrect. This work has led to the development of new fields such as biofeedback and behavioral medicine. Another example that is currently of great interest is the cognitive processes of nonhumans. Such questions as "Can an ape create a sentence" and "do primates have self-awareness?" have become hotly debated topics among scientists. There has also been a renewed interest in the so-called mind-brain question and the study of consciousness. This has included such traditional issues as how we think, as well as less studied concerns relating to ESP and Eastern approaches to development. How important do you think the concept of the unconscious is for a scientific understanding of cognition? (See Marcel, 1983, for one answer.) Along with this has come an explanation concerning new approaches to studying human functioning. Much traditional scientific research and thought have been directed at so-called normal behavior and the pathological exception as exemplified by neurosis and psychosis. One area yet to be systematically explored is that of human potential. Questions of potential ask what a person can do in the *best of cases.* In relation to this question, researchers are exploring creativity, musical and artistic abilities, genius, and even what makes excellent scientists. In science we have a number of approaches available, yet what we study is largely a personal decision shaped by our shared conceptions and personal perceptions. Even the question of why we study what we do is approachable from a scientific perspective.

## Psychological Limitations

One topic of interest to cognitive psychologists has been emotional blocks toward learning (Bransford, 1979). Included within these blocks are fear of performing poorly, looking stupid in the eyes of others, and feeling foolish. Some authors (Horner, 1972; Maslow, 1971) have even suggested that some of us fear success. In all fairness, if the subjects in our learning experiments and other studies display these fears, then we must entertain the possibility that we as scientists possess these same fears. Thus one major limitation to new discovery is our own fear of what the discovery might mean for us personally.

Some scientists have begun to record their psychological processing as they perform the work of science and thus give us valuable insight into some of our psychological limitations. One famous example is John Watson's book *The Double Helix* (1968). This book records not only the scientific search for the structure of DNA but also the psychological jealousies and ego-motivated strivings that surrounded this search, and something of the manner in which these influenced science. In a formal study, Ian Mitroff has studied scientists and their psychological reaction to science. In particular, he has examined how moon scientists have reacted to new data and rock specimens when these are in conflict with their own theories. Mitroff has also examined how scientists psychologically relate to their families and their work as well as how they express their own emotions (Mitroff, 1974; Mitroff & Fitzgerald, 1977). Mitroff and Fitzgerald end their report by agreeing with Maslow's conclusion that science can serve as a defense and a way of avoiding life, or it can serve as a means of increasing psychological health (Maslow, 1966). Likewise Mahoney (1976) has attempted to examine our myths of the scientist and to replace them with a more accurate picture of science as performed by real people who, like everyone, have real emotions and limitations.

## SCIENCE AS A COMPLEX HUMAN PROCESS

In this section we want to make more explicit some of the themes we have presented throughout this book. Many of these themes have emphasized that science is a complex human process involving (1) a deep commitment to experiencing the world as it is regardless of our preconceived notions or hypotheses about its nature; (2) a strong concern for both the scientist and the subject, involving both ethical and moral issues; and (3) a profound desire to understand better the many issues and problems that confront us and our world. Thus, we are saying that science concerns itself with truth, value, and relevance.

In 1890, T. C. Chamberlin, a scientist and president of the University of Wisconsin, published a paper in the journal *Science* (Chamberlin, 1890/1965) in which he addressed many of the issues we have been indirectly concerned with in this book. In particular he discussed the means for transcending our own preconceptions and pet theories to arrive at a more accurate picture of reality. Chamberlin began his article by suggesting that there are two fundamental approaches to learning about the world. The first consists of "attempting to follow by close imitation the processes of previous thinkers, or to acquire by memorizing the results of their investigations." By this, Chamberlin meant that you learn science by copying the experiments of previously successful scientists and you come to learn the methods that they used. This type of study has constituted the majority of the material in this book. As a beginning student in science, it is your first task to be able to replicate the successful approaches of others, and to do this you must know the accepted methods of study. We outlined many of these approaches in Figures 15.1 and 15.2. The second approach Chamberlin referred to as "primary or creative study." He described this approach as follows:

> In it the effort is to think independently, or at least individually, in the endeavor to discover new truth, or to make new combinations of truth, or at least to develop an individualized aggregation of truth. The endeavor is to think for one's self, whether the thinking lies wholly in the fields of previous thought or not. It is not necessary to this habit of study that the subject-material be new; but the process of thought and its results must

> be individual and independent, not the mere following of previous lines of thought ending in predetermined results. (Chamberlin, 1890/1965, p. 754.)

One clear example in the history of science of someone following this approach is presented by Einstein. In the early 1900s physicists relied on either Newton's theory or Maxwell's equations to help them understand the world. Einstein chose neither approach but began with what he considered a "thought experiment." He imagined a person riding on a streetcar moving away from a town clock. What would happen, Einstein wondered, if the car traveled at the speed of light? Think about this for a moment. Since the light reflected from the clock would be traveling at the speed of light and the person in the car was also traveling at the speed of light, the light reflecting from the clock would be traveling at the speed same speed as the person perceiving the clock. Thus the person would always be "seeing" the same time—time would have stopped. If one could likewise imagine the person in the car going faster than the speed of light, he would actually be going faster than the light reflected from the clock. In this situation he would see the clock going backward. These thought experiments made Einstein see the world in a new and independent way that he himself was unsure of. Since these thought experiments made predictions that Einstein did not initially believe, he turned to other fields, namely philosophy, to consider his predictions. The result was a realization on Einstein's part that our concept of time comes out of the unconscious. That is to say, our concept of time is not something absolute but rather an unconscious conclusion of our mind based on the input of sensory information. We had always *assumed* time to be an absolute. The real absolute, as Einstein was soon to suggest, was not time but the speed of light. Later experimentation supported this conclusion.

Not only does the example of Einstein help us to understand Chamberin's second or creative approach to science, but it is also a good illustraiton of the scientist's willingness to work through a problem logically and to consider surprising outcomes, even when the outcomes go against personal or traditional conceptions of the world.

Chamberlin suggested that a scientist's desire to see the world from a particular perspective can be transcended through a method he referred to as "multiple working hypotheses." For Chamberlin this method could be applied both to one's thinking and to one's research. (In Box 5.1 we presented Platt's interpretation of this method in relation to research.) The method is simply that one considers a family of hypotheses, each leading to different conclusions or interpretations. By considering two or more alternative hypotheses, we are most often able to advance to more sophisticated questions. For example, in the early history of psychology, some scientists argued that all behavior was innate, and they were able to find support for this theory. Other scientists suggested that all behavior was environmentally determined, and they found support for this theory. Today, by considering both theories, it has been possible to move beyond either and to study how environmental and innate factors interact to produce the particular behavior under study. Of course, here again we do not want to consider just one hypothesis but rather a family of hypotheses that compete with each other and offer alternative views of reality. Chamberlin suggested that the method of multiple working hypotheses can be applied not only to hypotheses but also to methods themselves. We will demonstrate this application later in the chapter. In conclusion, by adopting the method of multiple working hypotheses, Chamberlin suggested that one will not accidently place one's motivation in the demonstration that a pet theory is true but rather will search for truth itself. The second theme we have emphasized in this book is the role of value in science. We will now turn to this issue.

## VALUE IN SCIENCE

As we suggested, the domain of value is separate from the domain of science. However, this is not to say there is no overlap between the domains. Consider Figure 15.3. In this illustration the domain of science represents a world in which we test hypotheses and create theory. The domain of value cuts

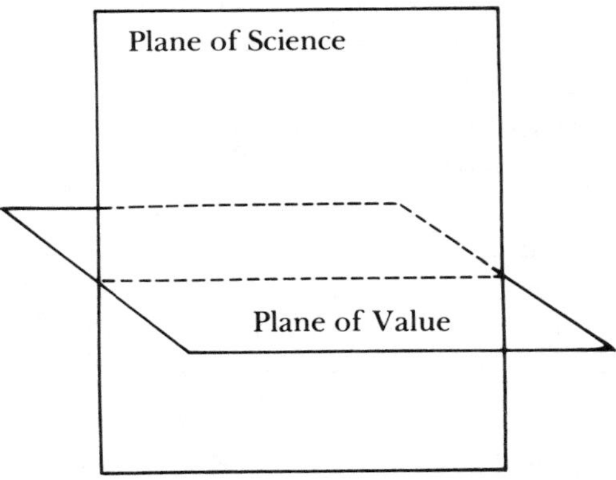


**Figure 15.3** Interception of the planes of science and value.

across the domain of science and thus influences science. The question of ethical research and moral concern for the scientist and the subject is one clear example of the manner in which the world of value influences science. It should be remembered that although we are influenced in science by value, we in no way test the validity of our ethical and moral values; that is, every scientist brings with him or her specific values that remain unexamined in the process of science. However, based on our common human heritage and collective statements such as the American Psychological Association ethical principles, we hope that there is little actual difference between scientists in terms of ethical values.

As important as ethics are, there are other values that individuals bring to the scientific enterprise. Like ethics, these values are untestable from the standpoint of science, but they often enter into the choice of research questions as well as the interpretation of information. For example, many atomic scientists have been committed to the peaceful use of atomic energy, and some of these individuals have refused to work on projects that could lead to weapons of war. Other scientists, on the other hand, have felt that a strong defense system is necessary for maintaining their values, and these individuals have engaged in scientific searches that could lead to better weapons of war. Likewise, in the behavioral sciences, some scientists suggest that behavior modification techniques offer an important means of rehabilitating prisoners, whereas others see these techniques as a denial of freedom and refuse to support such efforts.

Beyond the question of applying scientific knowledge to technological advances, individual scientists also hold personal values not directly connected with their scientific work. For example, Jonas Salk, the developer of the Salk polio vaccine, has concerned himself with humanity and understanding how we shape our own evolution (Salk, 1973). In particular he has stressed how our own ego gives human beings the possibility of destroying our species unless we are willing to become actively involved in trying to understand the value judgments facing us. Other scientists have stressed the importance of universal love or the nonviolent teachings of Gandhi. Einstein, for example, stressed the importance of opposing war. Still others have pursued music or poetry on a personal level. Newton spent much of his time reading the book of Revelations and trying to understand its meaning and relevance for the future. The important point is that the scientist never has been an individual without values—there is no such thing as a completely dispassionate scientist! *Science cannot be performed in a value-free state.* In relation to this point, the historian of science J. Bronowski (1965) has argued "that the practice of science compels the practitioner to form for himself a fundamental set of universal values." An illustration of a scientist's attempt to describe his values in relation to science and the study of consciousness is Roger Sperry's book *Science and Moral Priority* (Sperry, 1983).

## RELEVANCE

The third theme we suggested was that scientists as a group possess a desire to understand better the world in which we all live as well as the organisms (including ourselves) who live in it. For many scientists this desire has manifested itself in a cry for relevance. Some scientists have directed their research toward broad ecological concerns. Others have focused their explorations on understanding both physical and mental pathologies. Still others have attempted to explore new areas that hold promise for the future development of humans as a species. In recent years there have been increasing efforts not only to understand psychological pathologies but also to develop and evaluate new methods of treatments. One example of such work is B. F. Skinner's early attempts, through the application of learning theory techniques, to help neurotic and psychotic individuals. Another is Neal Miller's attempt to apply learning principles to the modification of physiological disorders through biofeedback. Other psychologists have attempted to move beyond normal and pathological processing and ask: What is an individual's potential? Abraham Maslow (1970) has tried to study individuals who are living up to their abilities. He calls these individuals "self-actualized" and has begun initial descriptive explorations into their behavior and experience. Other researchers point out that since we study lessened states of awareness such as sleep and coma, why not also study hyperaware states or altered states of consciousness? Charles Tart is a psychologist interested in this question. In an article in *Science,* Tart (1972) suggested that we need to develop a state-specific science. By this he means that scientific methods and approaches that are appropriate to one state of consciousness (such as sleep) may not be appropriate to the study of other states of consciousness (such as drug experiences or states of ecstasy). Thus each state of consciousness may require different scientific approaches.

Not only does the question of relevance address broad concerns, but it also leads us in evaluating specific research efforts. One case in point is the need to distinguish *scientifically significant* results from results that are *statistically significant.* When researchers compare experimental and control groups in an experiment, it is possible to find statistically significant differences, suggesting that the variations were not the result of chance. *The differences themselves, however, even if statistically significant, may be so small as to have no significant scientific meaning.* Let us look at a simple example to illustrate this point. Assume you developed a new technique for lowering blood pressure through relaxation. After months of testing, you might find that your technique did indeed result in statistically significant differences between experimental and control groups. However, upon close examination, you might discover that members of the experimental group reduced their blood pressure only 2–4 mm Hg and still showed blood pressures in the hypertensive range. Your results, although statistically significant, would not be clinically significant and thus could not be presented as a treatment for high blood pressure. Thus, it is possible to achieve statistical differences in science that are of such small magnitude as to be considered scientifically insignificant.

## SCIENCE AS A MEANS OF TRANSCENDENCE

In the previous sections we suggested that scientists are influenced by considerations of truth, values, and relevance. Thus, science is and always has been something beyond mere methods. We approached these influences from the standpoint of the scientist! However, science can serve another function besides the growth of knowledge. It can aid us in our own growth and development both as individuals and as a society. We are suggesting that one value of science is its ability to aid us in transcending our personal and collective limitations. In the process of science we commit ourselves to the search for truth over and above our personal beliefs. To begin a search for understanding carries with it the commitment to accept the answers that we find and to share these answers with others (See Box 15.2). In this manner scientific knowledge represents a superior knowledge—a knowledge that remains constantly open to question and revision.

We want to be sure you understand the point being made. Scientific knowledge represents superior knowledge not in the sense that it is correct but in the sense that it is open to question, to rebuttal, and to change. Without the willingness to reconsider, to reexamine, and to reevaluate knowledge, that knowledge, however valuable at the moment in which it is presented, becomes dogma and lacks the life to lead us to an increasing understanding of the world in which we live.

As Karl Popper (1959, 1972), G. Spencer Brown (1972), Thomas Kuhn (1970), and others have shown us, we must consider that every theory is

"ALTHOUGH HUMANS MAKE SOUNDS WITH THEIR MOUTHS AND OCCASIONALLY LOOK AT EACH OTHER, THERE IS NO SOLID EVIDENCE THAT THEY ACTUALLY COMMUNICATE WITH EACH OTHER."

inadequate and will one day be refuted. This should cause not despair but hope, however—the hope that through science we can reduce the amount of ignorance we collectively hold. With each new theory we can advance, we give ourselves the opportunity to understand the world in a new way. Each new approach and theory is somewhat like a pair of glasses that shapes our perspective and gives a certain focus to what we view. With a particular pair of glasses we are able to view our world and to draw a map of what we see. As useful as this process is for science, it is equally important that we remember there is a difference between the map and the reality that the map represents. Herein lie both the hope and the limitation of science. The hope is that through science we can reduce the amount of ignorance that we collectively hold and produce maps useful for our times. The limitation is that we may forget that there is a difference and confuse the map we have drawn with the reality in which we live.

To remind you that there is a distinction between the world in which we live and the manner in which we describe it scientifically, we introduced three separate perspectives in this book: the perspectives of the scientist, the subject, and the witness. At this time we can reunite these perspectives and remind ourselves that they are not separate but actually highly interrelated. As single beings incorporating these perspectives, we can begin to understand our world not from a single level but from a multifaceted perspective.

---

### *Box 15.2 Lewis Thomas on the Nature of Science*

It is hard to predict how science is going to turn out, and if it is really good science it is impossible to predict. This is in the nature of the enterprise. If the things to be found are actually new, they are by definition unknown in advance, and there is no way of telling in advance where a really new line of inquiry will lead. You cannot make choices in this matter, selecting things you think you're going to like and shutting off the lines that make for discomfort. You either have science or you don't, and if you have it you are obliged to accept the surprising and disturbing pieces of information, even the overwhelming and upheaving ones, along with the neat and promptly useful bits. It is like that.

The only solid piece of scientific truth about which I feel totally confident is that we are profoundly ignorant about nature. Indeed, I regard this as the major discovery of the past hundred years of biology. It is, in its way, an illuminating piece of news. It would have amazed the brightest minds of the eighteenth-century Enlightenment to be told by any of us how little we know, and how bewildering seems the way ahead. It is this sudden confrontation with the depth and scope of ignorance that represents the most significant contribution of twentieth-century science to the human intellect. We are, at last, facing up to it. In earlier times, we either pretended to under-

---

It is through the interplay of these three aspects that science comes alive. Just as we suggested at the beginning of this book that to understand life we must experience it, we likewise suggest now that to know science we must fully perceive these three aspects: the scientist, the subject, and the witness within ourselves.

It is also important that we reexamine the domains of exploration as presented in Chapter 1. Consider the matrix in Figure 15.4, which represents one way of studying ourselves and others. On one side of the matrix are the categories "I" and "You" and across the top the categories "Experience" and "Behavior." Throughout the brief history of scientific psychology we have focused our energy on the fourth cell—the study of external behavior—although the beginning of psychology included an emphasis on the first cell—personal experience. As the science of psychology developed, the early work directed at the first cell was ignored or discarded, often in the name of being scientific. Psychology almost became a battleground for those who were interested in behavior to fight those who were interested in experience. Today this has begun to change, and we are seeing a new group of scientists coming forth who are interested in the study of both behavior *and* experience, not only in others but also in themselves. Thus, whereas we had been actively attempting to reduce the specific cells in the matrix we were studying, we are now beginning to include topics and approaches from all the cells.

---

stand how things worked or ignored the problem, or simply made up stories to fill the gaps. Now that we have begun exploring in earnest, doing serious science, we are getting glimpses of how huge the questions are, and how far from being answered. Because of this, these are hard times for the human intellect, and it is no wonder that we are depressed. It is not so bad being ignorant if you are totally ignorant; the hard thing is knowing in some detail the reality of ignorance, the worst spots and here and there the not-so-bad spots, but no true light at the end of any tunnel nor even any tunnels that can yet be trusted. Hard times, indeed.

But we are making a beginning, and there ought to be some satisfaction, even exhilaration, in that. The method works. There are probably no questions we can think up that can't be answered, sooner or later, including even the matter of consciousness. To be sure, there may well be questions we can't think up, ever, and therefore limits to the reach of human intellect which we will never know about, but that is another matter. Within our limits, we should be able to work our way through to all our answers, if we keep at it long enough, and pay attention.

From Thomas (1979, pp. 73–74).

---

| | Experience | Behavior (appearance) |
|---|---|---|
| "I" | How do I study my own experiences? 1 | How do I study my own behavior? 3 |
| "You" | How do I study your experiences? 2 | How do I study your behavior? 4 |

**Figure 15.4** Four fields of knowing.

For example, some scientists have recently used the naturalistic approach for the study of the behavior of others and modified this to study their own experience during meditation and psychotherapy (Evans & Robinson, 1978; Walsh, 1976, 1977, 1978). They have used naturalistic observation, an approach associated with Cell 4 (the study of others' behavior), to study their own experience (Cell 1). Premack and Woodruff (1978) have begun to use experimental methods to approach Cell 2 with primates. They are asking whether an ape can infer your mental state from watching your behavior; that is, what is the ape's experience of your experience? In a similar way, Wicklund (1979) has sought to determine the relationship between Cell 1 and Cell 3—how I experience myself and appear to others. He reports that the person who experiences him- or herself as he or she appears to others acts in a more consistent manner and is able to give more accurate self-reports.

As you can imagine, we are just beginning to explore the behavior and experience we have available to us, and there are many gaps in our knowledge that need to be completed. We hope that you have come to see that the topics we study in psychology are complex and defy single-minded approaches. It should be clear that the study of any cell of the matrix, although an important and useful beginning, can never give us a complete and total picture of psychological functioning. As a beginning student, it is your job to understand the traditional methods and approaches and be able to replicate important work. However, it is also your job to look to the future to a fuller understanding of behavior and experience.

## Key Terms and Concepts

1. Type of research and relation of scientist
   a. field
   b. laboratory
   c. true experiment
   d. naturalistic observation
   e. scientist as observer
   f. scientist as participant
2. Limitations to knowing
   a. available tools
   b. shared view of world
   c. personal psychological limitations
3. Lakatos: research programs
4. Science as a complex human process
5. Chamberlin
   a. two types of science
      - imitation
      - primary or creative study
   b. method of multiple working hypotheses
6. Value in science
7. Relevance in science
8. Science as a means of transcendence

## Summary

1. Research is a multifaceted process that can be divided along three continua. The first relates to the research setting—that of the laboratory versus the field. The second continuum relates to the type of methodology used—naturalistic observation versus true experiment. The third continuum relates to the role of the experimenter—either as observer or as participant. A given piece of research may lie anywhere along these three continua.
2. The process of science is more than the mere application of method. It is an important part of our being human and as such requires that we consider both human limitations and human values.

3. Three important limitations are (1) the tools available to us, (2) our shared view of the world, and (3) our personal psychological limitations.
4. In 1890 T. C. Chamberlin suggested two fundamental approaches to learning about the world. The first approach consists of learning about the world through the imitation of other scientists. The second approach involves an effort to think independently in the endeavor to discover new truth. Einstein and the use of thought experiments present an example of this second approach to science.
5. Science cannot be viewed as value-free. All scientists have values and these in turn influence how they go about doing science and what topic they research.
6. The desire for relevance has directed some scientists to attempt a better understanding of our human condition. For example, many scientists have turned their attention toward the question of aging, as more people are living longer. Other researchers are looking not only to questions of psychopathology but also to those of human potential.
7. A distinction can be drawn between those results that are statistically significant and those that are scientifically significant.
8. We are only beginning to understand ourselves as humans. Many questions have yet to be answered, such as those related to consciousness and self-awareness. Many of these questions are complex and defy single-minded approaches.
9. Behavior and experience are two important aspects that need to be included in any attempt to describe and understand human processes.

## Review Questions

1. Why do we have to know what we are looking for to use the experimental method?
2. Give an example of when it would be more useful for a scientist to be a participant in an experiment and when to be an observer.
3. What is a research program?
4. What does this chapter suggest as major limitations to learning about the world? Give examples of each type of limitation.
5. Describe the two approaches to knowing discussed by Chamberlin.
6. What is the difference between statistical significance and scientific significance?
7. According to Lewis Thomas, how has science changed in attitude since the eighteenth century?
8. In what way can it be said that science has the potential of being a superior knowledge?
9. What is your next step in becoming a scientist?

## Discussion Questions and Projects

1. Give some examples of how untested assumption have shaped what we study in psychology.
2. What is meant by the statement "if you give a child *only* a hammer, he or she will treat everything like a nail"? How does this idea apply to research?
3. How are emotional blocks to learning, such as fear of failure or even fear of success, related to performing research?
4. Some people say that science is value-free. Discuss this statement and describe ways in which values enter science.
5. What does Lakatos mean by the term *novel fact?*
6. What is similar to Lakatos's and Lewis Thomas's view of science?
7. What might the study of experience offer psychology?

APPENDIX A

# *Guidelines for Nonsexist Language in APA Journals*

The *Publication Manual* of American Psychological Association (1974, p. 28) suggests that journal authors "be aware of the current move to avoid generic use of male nouns and pronouns when content refers to both sexes . . . [and] avoid overuse of the pronoun *he* when *she* or *they* is equally appropriate." The first change sheet to the *Publication Manual* (1975, p. 2) says: "For some specific suggestions on how to avoid such language, see 'Guidelines for Nonsexist Use of Language,' which was prepared by the APA Task Force on Issues of Sexual Bias in Graduate Education and published in the June 1975 *American Psychologist* (pp. 682–684)." Those guidelines, while helpful, are not specific to journal articles.

This second change sheet states the policy on sexist language in APA journals, offers some general principles for journal authors to consider, and suggests some ways to avoid sexist language.

To obtain single copies of this change sheet, send a stamped, self-addressed envelope to Publication Manual, Change Sheet 2, American Psychological Association, 1200 Seventeenth Street, N.W., Washington, D.C. 20036.

## POLICY STATEMENT

APA as a publisher accepts journal authors' word choices unless those choices are inaccurate, unclear, or ungrammatical. However, because APA as an organization is committed to both science and the fair treatment of individuals and groups, authors of journal articles are expected to avoid writing in a manner that reinforces questionable attitudes and assumptions about people and sex roles.

Language that reinforces sexism can spring from subtle errors in research design, inaccurate interpretation, or imprecise word choices. Faulty logic in design, for example, may lead an investigator to report sex differences when the stimulus materials and measures used give one sex an unwarranted advantage over the other. Or, in interpretation, an investigator may make unwarranted generalizations about all people from data about one sex. Imprecise word choices, which occur frequently in journal writing, may be interpreted as biased, discriminatory, or demeaning even if they are not intended to be.

Advice on research design and interpretation is beyond the scope of the APA *Publication Manual.* However, in the spirit of the guidelines on writing style in Chapter 2, the following guidelines on nonsexist language are intended to help authors recognize and change instances where word choices may be inaccurate, misleading, or discriminatory.

## GUIDELINES

Sexism in journal writing may be classified into two categories that are conceptually different: problems of *designation* and problems of *evaluation.*

### Problems of Designation

An author must use care in choosing words to ensure accuracy, clarity, and freedom from bias. In the case of sexism, long-established cultural practice can exert a powerful insidious influence over even the most conscientious author. Nouns, pronouns, and adjectives that designate persons can be chosen to eliminate, or at least to minimize, the possibility of ambiguity in sex identity or sex role. In the following examples, problems of designation are divided into two subcategories: *ambiguity of referent,* where it is unclear whether the author means one or both sexes, and *stereotyping,* where the writing conveys unsupported or biased connotations about sex roles and identity.

### Problems of Evaluation

By definition, scientific writing should be free of implied or irrelevant evaluation of the sexes. Difficulties may derive from the habitual use of clichés, or familiar expressions, such as "man and wife." The use of *man and wife* together implies differences in the freedom and activities of each, and evaluation of roles can occur. Thus, *husband and wife* are parallel, *man and wife* are not. In the examples that follow, problems of evaluation, like problems of designation, are divided into *ambiguity of referent* and *stereotyping*.

**I. Problems of Designation**

| *Examples of common usage* | *Consider meaning. An alternative may be better.* | *Comment* |
|---|---|---|
| | A. AMBIGUITY OF REFERENT | |
| 1. The *client* is usually the best judge of the value of *his* counseling. | The *client* is usually the best judge of the value of counseling. | *His* deleted. |
| | *Clients* are usually the best judges of the value of the counseling they receive. | Changed to plural. |
| | The best judge of the value of counseling is usually *the client.* | Rephrased. |
| 2. *Man's search* for knowledge has led *him* into ways of learning that bear examination. | *The search* for knowledge has led *us* into ways of learning that bear examination. | Rephrased, using first person. |
| | *People* have continually sought knowledge. The search has led them, etc. . . . | Rewritten in two sentences. |
| 3. man, mankind | people, humanity, human beings, humankind, human species | In this group of examples, a variety of terms may be substituted. |
| man's achievements | human achievements, achievements of the human species | |
| the average man | the average person, people in general | |
| man a project | staff a project, hire personnel, employ staff | |

## I. Problems of Designation

| *Examples of common usage* | *Consider meaning. An alternative may be better.* | *Comment* |
|---|---|---|
| manpower | work force, personnel, workers | |
| Department of Manpower | (No alternative.) | Official titles should not be changed. |
| 4. The use of experiments in psychology presupposes the mechanistic nature of *man.* | The use of experiments in psychology presupposes the mechanistic nature of the *human being.* | Noun substituted. |
| 5. This interference phenomenon, called learned helplessness, has been demonstrated in rats, cats, fish, dogs, monkeys, and *men.* | This interference phenomenon, called learned helplessness, has been demonstrated in rats, cats, fish, dogs, monkeys, and *humans.* | Noun substituted. |
| 6. Issues raised were whether the lack of cardiac responsivity in the premature *infant* is secondary to *his* heightened level of autonomic arousal . . . | . . . responsivity in the premature *infant* is secondary to *the* heightened level . . . | *His* changed to *the.* |
| | . . . responsivity in premature *infants* is secondary to *their* heightened levels . . . | Rewritten in plural. |
| 7. First the *individual* becomes aroused by violations of *his* personal space, and then *he* attributes the cause of this arousal to other people in *his* environment. | First *we* become aroused by violations of *our* personal space, and then *we* attribute the cause of this arousal to other people in *the* environment. | Pronouns substituted, *he* and *his* omitted. |
| 8. Much has been written about the effect that a *child's* position among *his* siblings has on *his* intellectual development. | Much has been written about the relationship between sibling position and intellectual development in *children.* | Rewritten, plural introduced. |

## I. Problems of Designation

| *Examples of common usage* | *Consider meaning. An alternative may be better.* | *Comment* |
|---|---|---|
| 9. Subjects were 16 girls and 16 boys. Each *child* was to place a car on *his* board so that two cars and boards looked alike. | Each child was to place a car on *his* or *her* board so that two cars and boards looked alike. | Changed *his* to *his or her;* however, use sparingly to avoid monotonous repetition. *Her or his* may also be used, but it sounds awkward. In either case, keep pronoun order consistent to avoid ambiguity. |
| 10. Each person's alertness was measured by the difference between *his* obtained relaxation score and *his* obtained arousal score. | Each person's alertness was measured by the difference between *the* obtained relaxation and arousal scores. | *His* deleted, plural introduced. |
| 11. The client's husband *lets* her teach part-time. | The client's husband "*lets*" her teach part-time.<br>The husband says he "*lets*" the client teach part-time.<br>The client *says her husband* "*lets*" her teach part-time. | Punctuation added to clarify location of the bias, that is, with husband and wife, not with author. If necessary, rewrite to clarify as allegation. See Example 24 below. |
| | B. STEREOTYPING | |
| 12. males, females | men, women, boys, girls, adults, children, adolescents | Specific nouns reduce possibility of stereotypic bias and often clarify discussion. Use *male* and *female* as adjectives where appropriate and relevant (female experimenter, male subject). Avoid unparallel usages such as 10 *men* and 16 *females.* |

**I. Problems of Designation**

| *Examples of common usage* | *Consider meaning. An alternative may be better.* | *Comment* |
|---|---|---|
| 13. Research scientists often neglect their *wives* and *children.* | Research scientists often neglect their *families.* | Alternative wording acknowledges that women as well as men are research scientists. |
| 14. When a *test developer or test user* fails to satisfy these requirements, *he* should . . . | When *test developers or test users* fail to satisfy these requirements, *they* should . . . | Same as Example 13. |
| 15. the psychologist . . . *he* | psychologists . . . *they;* the psychologist . . . *she* | Be specific or change to plural if discussing women as well as men. |
| the therapist . . . *he* | therapists . . . *they;* the therapist . . . *she* | |
| the nurse . . . *she* | nurses . . . *they;* nurse . . . *he* | |
| the teacher . . . *she* | teachers . . . *they;* teacher . . . *he* | |
| 16. woman doctor, lady lawyer, male nurse | doctor, physician, lawyer, nurse | Specify sex if it is a variable or if sex designation is necessary to the discussion ("13 female doctors and 22 male doctors"). |
| 17. mothering | parenting, nurturing (or specify exact behavior) | Noun substituted. |
| 18. chairman (of an academic department) | Use *chairperson* or *chair* if it is known that the institution has established either form as an official title. Otherwise use *chairman.* | *Department head* may be appropriate, but the term is not synonymous with *chairman* and *chairperson* at all institutions. |
| chairman (presiding officer of a committee or meeting) | chairperson, moderator, discussion leader | In parliamentary usage *chairman* is the official term. Alternatives are acceptable in most writing. |

## I. Problems of Designation

| *Examples of common usage* | *Consider meaning. An alternative may be better.* | *Comment* |
|---|---|---|
| 19. Only *freshmen* were eligible for the project.<br>All the students had matriculated for three years, but the majority were still *freshmen.* | (No alternative if academic standing is meant.) | *First-year student* is often an acceptable alternative to *freshman,* but in these cases, *freshmen* is used for accuracy. |
| 20. foreman, policeman, stewardess, mailman | supervisor, police officer, flight attendant, postal worker or letter carrier | Noun substituted. |
| | **II. Problems of Evaluation** | |
| | A. AMBIGUITY OF REFERENT | |
| 21. The authors acknowledge the assistance of *Mrs. John Smith.* | The authors acknowledge the assistance of *Jane Smith.* | Use given names in author acknowledgments. When forms of address are used in text, use the appropriate form: Mr., Mrs., Miss, or Ms. |
| 22. men and women, sons and daughters, boys and girls, husbands and wives | women and men, daughters and sons, girls and boys, wives and husbands | Vary the order if content does not require traditional order. |
| | B. STEREOTYPING | |
| 23. men and girls | men and women, woman and men | Use parallel terms. Of course, use *men and girls* if that is literally what is meant. |
| 24. The client's husband lets her teach part-time. | The client teaches part-time. | The author of this example intended to communicate the working status of the woman but inadvertently revealed a stereotype about husband-wife relationships; see Example 11 above. |

## I. Problems of Designation

| *Examples of common usage* | *Consider meaning. An alternative may be better.* | *Comment* |
|---|---|---|
| 25. ambitious men and aggressive women | ambitious women and men or ambitious people<br>aggressive men and women or aggressive people | Some adjectives, depending on whether the person described is a man or a woman, connote bias. The examples illustrate some common usages that may not always convey exact meaning, especially when paired, as in column 1. |
| cautious men and timid women | cautious women and men, cautious people<br>timid men and women or timid people | |
| 26. The boys chose typically male toys. | The boys chose (specify) | Being specific reduces possibility of stereotypic bias. |
| The client's behavior was typically female. | The client's behavior was (specify) | |
| 27. woman driver | driver | If specifying sex is necessary, use *female driver.* |
| 28. The *girls* in the office greeted all clients. | secretaries, office assistants | Noun substituted. |
| 29. coed | female student | Noun substituted. |
| 30. women's lib, women's libber | women's movement, feminist, supporter of women's movement | Noun substituted. |
| 31. Subjects were 16 men and 4 women. *The women were housewives.* | The men were (specify) and the women were (specify). | Describe women and men in parallel terms. *Housewife* indicates sex, marital status, and occupation, and excludes men. *Homemaker* indicates occupation, and includes men. |

## A FINAL WORD

Attempting to introduce nonsexist language at the cost of awkwardness, obscurity, or euphemistic phrasing does not improve scientific communication. An author should make clear that both sexes are under discussion when they are and should indicate sex when only one sex is discussed. Under no circumstances should an author hide sex identity in an attempt to be unbiased, if knowledge of sex may be important to the reader.

Any endeavor to change the language is an awesome task at best. Some aspects of our language that may be considered sexist are firmly embedded in our culture, and we presently have no acceptable substitutes. In English, the use of third-person singular pronouns is one example: the generic use of *he* is misleading, *it* is inaccurate, *one* conveys a different meaning, and *he or she* can become an annoying repetition. Nevertheless, with some rephrasing and careful attention to meaning, even the generic *he* can be avoided most of the time. The result of such efforts is accurate, unbiased communication, the purpose of these guidelines.

## SUGGESTED READING

APA Task Force on Issues of Sexual Bias in Graduate Education. Guidelines for nonsexist use of language. *American Psychologist,* 1975, *30,* 682–684.

Burr, E., Dunn, S., & Farquhar, N. *Guidelines for equal treatment of the sexes in social studies textbooks.* Los Angeles: Westside Women's Committee, 1973. (Available from Westside Women's Committee, P.O. Box 24D20, Los Angeles, California 90024.)

DeBoard, D., Fisher, A. M., Moran, M. C., & Zawodny, L. *Guidelines to promote the awareness of human potential.* Philadelphia, Pa.: Lippincott, undated.

Harper & Row. *Harper & Row guidelines on equal treatment of the sexes in textbooks.* New York: Author, 1976.

Henley, N., & Thorne, B. *She said/he said: An annotated bibliography of sex differences in language, speech, and nonverbal communication.* Pittsburgh, Pa.: Know, 1975. (Available from Know, Inc., P.O. Box 86031, Pittsburgh, Pennsylvania 15221.)

Holt, Rinehart & Winston (College Department). *The treatment of sex roles and minorities.* New York: Author, 1976.

Lakoff, R. *Language and woman's place.* New York: Harper & Row, 1975.

Lerner, H. E. Girls, ladies, or women? The unconscious dynamics of language choice. *Comprehensive Psychiatry,* 1976, *17,* 295–299.

McGraw-Hill. *Guidelines for equal treatment of the sexes in McGraw-Hill Book Company publications.* New York: Author, undated.

Miller, C., & Swift, K. *Words and women.* Garden City, N.Y.: Anchor Press/Doubleday, 1976.

Prentice-Hall. *Prentice-Hall author's guide* (5th ed.). Englewood Cliffs, N.J.: Author, 1975.

Random House. *Guidelines for multiethnic/nonsexist survey.* New York: Author, 1975.

Scott, Foresman. *Guidelines for improving the image of women in textbooks.* Glenview, Ill.: Author, 1974.

John Wiley & Sons. *Wiley guidelines on sexism in language.* New York: Author, 1977.

This change sheet was prepared by the APA Publication Manual Task Force. Members of the task force are Charles N. Cofer (Chairperson), Robert S. Daniel, Frances Y. Dunham, and Walter I. Heimer. Ellen Kimmel served as liaison from the Committee on Women in Psychology, and Anita DeVivo as APA staff liaison. 

# APPENDIX B

# *Printed Article*

Journal of Personality and Social Psychology
1984, Vol. 46, No. 3, 551–560



## Effects of Arousal on Judgments of Others' Emotions

Margaret S. Clark, Sandra Milberg, and Ralph Erber
Carnegie-Mellon University

Based on evidence that arousal cues information from memory associated with a similar level of arousal (Clark, Milberg, & Ross, 1983) and on evidence that people will base judgments on the information that is most available to them (Tversky & Kahneman, 1974), it was hypothesized that (a) increases in arousal would increase the likelihood that subjects would interpret positive statements and positive facial expressions as indicating a positive emotion associated with high arousal (joy) rather than a positive emotion associated with low arousal (serenity), and (b) increases in arousal would increase the likelihood that subjects would interpret negative statements and negative expressions as indicating a negative emotion associated with high arousal (anger) rather than a negative emotion associated with low arousal (sadness or depression). Two studies are reported, each of which support the first hypothesis but not the second. Explanations for why arousal had the predicted effects on positive but not on negative stimuli are offered.

Recently there has been considerable work demonstrating that a perceiver's positive or negative mood state may bias evaluations of stimuli in his or her environment to reflect that mood (e.g., Gouaux, 1971; Isen & Shalker, 1982; Isen, Shalker, Clark, & Karp, 1978). In addition, evidence that perceivers' specific emotions (e.g., fear, disgust) influence judgments about other people's emotional states, such that those judgments become more consistent with the perceiver's own emotional state has been reported (Feshbach & Feshbach, 1963; Feshbach & Singer, 1957; Hornberger, 1960; Murray, 1933; Schiffenbauer, 1974a, 1974b). An explanation for such findings offered by Isen (1975; Isen et al., 1978) and Bower (1981) is that feeling states increase the accessibility of similarly toned material from memory. Thus, if one is evaluating an object while in a positive mood, positive thoughts about the object ought to be more likely to come to mind than usual. On the other hand, if one is in a negative mood, negative thoughts about the object ought to be more likely to come to mind than usual. Then, because these thoughts are more available than other thoughts, they may in turn influence judgments about the objects being evaluated (cf. Tversky & Kahneman, 1974).

Thus far the literature on the influence of mood states on judgments has focused primarily on the positive–negative dimension of moods, whereas the literature on the effects of specific emotions on judgments has tended not to break those emotions down into underlying dimensions. A potentially important dimension of affective states that has been neglected in this work is the level of autonomic arousal associated with a particular emotional state.

Different emotional states do intuitively involve different levels of arousal (e.g., serenity vs. joy, sadness vs. anger). Furthermore research supports the idea that emotional states vary not only in terms of positivity–negativity but also in terms of the level of associated arousal (e.g., Bush, 1973; Russell, 1980; Schwartz, Weinberger, & Singer, 1981). Russell (1980), for instance, had four groups of subjects scale affect stimulus words, each using a different technique: a multidimensional scaling procedure based on the perceived similarity of the terms, a unidimensional scaling of the terms on pleasure–displeasure and arousal dimensions, a principal-components factor

This research was supported by a Ford Motor Company Research Fund grant.

We thank Michael Scheier for helpful suggestions regarding the design of these studies, Charlee Brodsky for aid in collecting stimulus materials, Cyndi Caputo for serving as the first experimenter in Study 2, and Gordon Bower, Susan Fiske, Steve Neuberg, and the reviewers for their helpful comments on earlier versions of this article.

Requests for reprints should be sent to Margaret S. Clark, Department of Psychology, Carnegie-Mellon University, Pittsburgh, Pennsylvania 15213.

analysis of subjects' self-reports of their current affective states, or a category sort technique developed by Ross (1938). Russell's work provided evidence that these adjectives could be represented well as a circle in a two-dimensional bipolar space, the dimensions being pleasure–displeasure and degree of arousal. Schwartz et al. had subjects imagine themselves experiencing happiness, sadness, anger, and fear, and then measured diastolic and systolic blood pressure as well as heart rate. They found that imagining certain emotions (e.g., anger) was associated with higher overall increases on these cardiovascular measures than was imagining other emotions (e.g., sadness).[1]

Given such evidence that emotional states are associated with different levels of arousal, it is reasonable to hypothesize that the level of arousal one is experiencing may influence one's judgments regarding the emotional states being experienced by others. Specifically, people experiencing high levels of arousal may be more likely than usual to perceive others as experiencing high-arousal emotions (e.g., joy or anger). Similarly, people experiencing low levels of arousal may be more likely than usual to perceive others as experiencing low-arousal emotions (e.g., serenity, depression, or sadness). The remainder of the introduction and the two studies reported thereafter are devoted to making a detailed case for this hypothesis.

The case that arousal may bias judgments of others' affective states begins with a recent finding that autonomic arousal cues material from memory associated with a similar level of arousal. Clark, Milberg, and Ross (1983, Studies 1 and 2) conducted two studies in which subjects learned one list of word phrases when experiencing high arousal and a second list when experiencing low arousal. Later, while experiencing either high or low arousal, each subject was unexpectedly asked to recall as many phrases as possible from both lists. In both studies, subjects recalled material best when their level of arousal at recall approximately matched their level of arousal at learning. These effects held even when the manipulations of arousal at learning (exercise for high arousal and relaxation for low arousal) were very different from the manipulations of arousal at recall (viewing a sexually explicit film for high arousal and viewing an educational film for low arousal).

This finding, together with evidence that people base decisions on the information that is most readily available to them (Tversky & Kahneman, 1974), suggests that when people are themselves aroused, they may be more likely to judge others as feeling emotions associated with high arousal than usual. Such biased judgments might result from a two-stage process analogous to the process through which Isen et al. (1978) have suggested that moods may influence judgments. First, when a highly aroused person focuses attention on a stimulus in the environment, the arousal should cue arousal-related information stored in memory and the stimulus should cue stimulus-related information. Consequently, arousal-related thoughts about the stimulus ought to be more likely than usual to come to mind. Second, the increased availability of this information should make it more likely than usual to influence judgments about the stimulus.

Consider the following example of how judgments concerning the emotion being experienced by a smiling person might be influenced by the perceiver's own state of arousal. First, recall that some feelings are associated with higher arousal than are others (Russell, 1980; Schwartz et al., 1981). Joy, for instance, is a high-arousal, positive emotion, whereas serenity is a low-arousal, positive emotion. Next, note that both joy and serenity are associated with some of the same stimuli in the environment (e.g., with smiles). Now think about what should happen when a perceiver sees a smiling person and is asked to judge what emotion that person is experiencing. If the perceiver is highly aroused, arousal combined with the other's smile may bring thoughts of joy to the perceiver's mind, while at the same time the high arousal may block thoughts of serenity. On the other hand, if the

[1] The Schwartz et al. (1981) study also provided clear evidence that different emotional states are associated with different *patterns* of autonomic system arousal, as have many other studies (e.g., Ax, 1953; Sternbach, 1962). Although the variable of primary interest in the present study is the overall level or intensity of arousal rather than the patterning of specific arousal states, the idea that level of arousal can influence psychological judgments does not preclude the possibility that specific patterns of arousal might have effects similar to those we will describe for levels of arousal.

perceiver is experiencing low arousal, the low arousal combined with the smile may bring thoughts of serenity to the perceiver's mind and may simultaneously block thoughts of joy from coming to mind. If the perceiver is then asked to judge what the smiling person is feeling, the highly aroused perceiver may be more likely than usual to say "joy," whereas the perceiver experiencing low arousal may be more likely than usual to say "serenity."

Analogous reasoning yields the prediction that the degree of arousal may bias perception of *negative* stimuli. For example, anger is associated with high levels of arousal; depression and sadness are associated with lower levels of arousal (Russell, 1980; Schwartz et al., 1981). Consequently, a person experiencing high arousal may be more likely than usual to interpret a negative appearance as anger, whereas a person experiencing low arousal may be more likely than usual to interpret the same appearance as indicating depression.

Given this reasoning, we conducted the present studies to test the following specific hypotheses:

1. People experiencing high arousal will be more likely than people experiencing low arousal to interpret positive statements and positive facial expressions as indicating joy rather than serenity.

2. People experiencing high arousal will be more likely than people experiencing low arousal to interpret negative statements and negative facial expressions as indicating anger rather than sadness or depression.

These hypotheses were examined in two studies (a field study and a laboratory study). The first study examined whether arousal would bias interpretations of the emotions indicated by things another might say; the second examined whether arousal would bias interpretations of the emotions indicated by another's physical appearance.

## Study 1

### *Method*

#### *Subjects*

Subjects were 37 adult tennis players, 23 males and 14 females. They were initially identified while waiting to play tennis at a city park. All were recruited by an experimenter who, either before or after their game, asked them to volunteer for a short project. No person refused.

#### *Stimulus Materials*

*Phrases.* For use in the study, we selected a set of five positive phrases that a person who was feeling either serene or joyous might say and a set of five negative phrases that a person who was feeling either depressed or angry might say. The positive phrases were (a) "Just look at that sunset," (b) "I should have more days like today," (c) "For the most part, people are pretty nice," (d) "Life is going well," and (e) "I really like my work." On scales ranging from 1 (indicating serenity) to 7 (indicating joy), 10 pretest judges gave these positive phrases a mean rating of 2.8. The negative phrases were (a) "I'm tired of this," (b) "I'd like to be left alone," (c) "I'm so dumb," (d) "I can't do this," and (e) "Why did that happen?" On scales from 1 (indicating depression) to 7 (indicating anger), 10 pretest judges gave these negative phrases a mean rating of 3.0.[2]

In selecting stimuli, we intentionally selected positive phrases with a slight bias toward serenity and negative phrases with a slight bias toward depression. These biases were sought because if the results did support our hypotheses, they would rule out a Hull-Spence alternative explanation (Hull, 1943, 1952; Spence, 1956). In other words, if arousal biased judgments toward joy or anger, the bias could not be explained by arguing that arousal increased subjects' tendencies to give their dominant response.

*Ratings of terms anchoring the endpoints of scales.* In this research we used scales anchored by the terms *serenity* and *joy* or by the terms *depression* and *anger.* To check our assumptions that people consider serenity and joy to differ in arousal but to be equally positive and that they consider depression and anger to differ in arousal but to be equally negative, we had judges rate these terms for arousal and positivity or negativity. As expected, judges' arousal ratings for serenity on a 7-point scale from low (1) to high (7) arousal ($M = 2.2$) were significantly lower than their arousal ratings for joy ($M = 4.3$), $t(20) = -6.38$, $p < .001$, whereas their positivity ratings of these terms on similar scales (4.6 and 4.9, respectively) did not differ significantly. Also as expected, judges' arousal ratings for depression ($M = 2.2$) were significantly lower than their arousal ratings for anger ($M = 4.7$), $t(16) = 5.63$, $p < .001$, whereas negativity ratings of these terms (4.6 and 3.8, respectively) did not differ significantly.

#### *Procedure*

To conduct the study, the experimenter went to a city park with many tennis courts. Alongside these courts are benches on which people wait until a court becomes free. The experimenter randomly assigned each waiting person

[2] Additional pretesting involving separate ratings of each positive phrase for joy and for serenity and of each negative phrase for depression and for anger indicated that these phrases were not given ratings near the middle of the original scale because judges saw them as indicative of *neither* of the emotions anchoring the ends of the scales.

to either a high- or a low-arousal condition. Those subjects assigned to the low-arousal condition were approached before they played and were asked to participate in a short psychology experiment. Subjects assigned to the high-arousal condition were approached with the same request immediately after having played. Subjects were also randomly assigned to rate either the five positive phrases or the five negative phrases. A total of 17 subjects filled out a questionnaire before playing tennis. Nine (6 males and 3 females) rated the positive statements, and 8 (4 males and 4 females) rated the negative statements. A total of 20 subjects filled out a questionnaire after playing tennis. Ten (6 males and 4 females) rated the positive statements, and 10 (7 males and 3 females) rated the negative statements.

After agreeing to participate, each subject was handed a sheet with five positive or negative phrases. The phrases appeared in the same order on each sheet. Each phrase was followed by a single 7-point scale with 1 indicating serenity or depression and 7 indicating joy or anger. After completing the scales each subject was thanked and debriefed.

### *Results*

The dependent measure was the sum of each subject's ratings of the five phrases. For subjects in the positive conditions, the higher the sum, the greater the tendency to perceive joy rather than serenity. For subjects in the negative conditions, the higher the sum, the greater the tendency to perceive anger rather than depression. Results on each of these measures were examined separately.

#### *Judgments About Positive Statements*

The mean sum of the five ratings for subjects who read the positive statements *before* playing tennis was 15.22, whereas the mean sum for subjects who rated the same statements *after* having played tennis was 27.50. Indeed, among these subjects there was no overlap between scores in the low- and high-arousal conditions. The highest sum in the low-arousal condition was 19 and the lowest sum in the high-arousal condition was 25. Not surprisingly, a two-tailed $t$ test indicated a significant difference between the scores in the pre- and posttennis conditions, $t(17) = 12.9$, $p < .0001$.

#### *Judgments About Negative Statements*

Having played tennis also biased the judgments of people who read the negative statements as predicted. The mean sum of the three ratings for subjects who read the negative statements before playing tennis was 19.50, whereas the mean sum for subjects who rated the same statements after having played tennis was 23.40. A two-tailed $t$ test indicated the expected significant difference between these scores, $t(16) = 3.4$, $p < .004$.

### *Discussion*

The results of the first study are clearly consistent with the hypotheses. High arousal seems to have biased the judgments of positive stimuli toward joy and the judgments of negative stimuli toward anger. However, the results of this study must be interpreted with caution. There is a plausible alternative explanation for these results. Specifically, there is no reason to suspect that before playing tennis, our subjects were feeling either particularly joyous or angry, rather than particularly serene or depressed. After playing, however, subjects who won may have been feeling joyous while subjects who lost may have been feeling angry. Thus the joy of a subset of our posttennis subjects (rather than arousal per se) may have biased our high-arousal, positive group's scores toward joy rather than serenity. Similarly, the anger of a subset of our posttennis subjects (rather than arousal per se) may have biased our high-arousal, negative group's scores toward anger rather than depression.

We did not ask subjects whether they had won or lost, so it was difficult to rule out this alternative explanation. However, recall that in the case of the results obtained for ratings of the positive statements there was no overlap in the scores between the high- and low-arousal subjects. Thus, an alternative explanation involving the assumption that some subset of our subjects were experiencing joy as a result of winning (perhaps as many as half) cannot entirely explain this result. To examine this argument, we eliminated half the data in the high-arousal, positive statements condition, specifically the five *highest* ratings of joy (i.e., the data most favorable to our hypothesis). Then we performed a second two-tailed $t$ test using the data from the five remaining high-arousal subjects and from all the subjects in the low-arousal condition. In this analysis, the mean in the high-arousal condition became 26.2, whereas the mean in the low-arousal condition remained at 15.2. The new test still indicated a significant difference between conditions, $t(12) = 9.61$, $p < .0001$. Thus, despite the potential alternative explanation, the results still support the hypothesis that arousal biases the perception of positive stimuli.

We performed a similar reanalysis to see whether the hypothesis that arousal would bias perception of negative statements would be supported after eliminating the alternative explanation for that result. The five highest scores in the high-arousal condition (i.e., those indicating greatest anger) were eliminated. Then we repeated the analysis using the remaining subjects in that condition and all subjects in the low-arousal condition. The mean in the high-arousal condition became 21.6, whereas the mean in the low-arousal condition remained at 19.5. Although the difference between the means was still in the expected direction, it was no longer significant. Thus the first study did not provide clear evidence that arousal biases perception of negative stimuli.

Despite the results of this first study, however, we were unwilling to conclude that arousal would bias perception of positive but not of negative stimuli. Although we did control for the alternative explanation, only 4 subjects remained in the high-arousal, negative condition. This was not a sufficient number to provide for an adequate test of our hypothesis. Thus it seemed wise to conduct another experiment.

In designing the second experiment we chose an arousal manipulation that was not associated with winning or losing. In addition, several other design improvements were also made. First, the study was designed in such a way that the experimenter collecting the dependent variable was unaware of the subject's arousal condition. Second, the term anchoring the low arousal end of the negative scale, *depressed,* was replaced with the term *sad* because it seemed remotely possible that subjects considered the term *depressed* to mean *clinically depressed,* a state with which the majority probably had had no personal experience. Given that, the absence of any arousal effects on negative judgments might have been due to subjects' feeling forced to make negative judgments on bases other than their personal memories. Finally, instead of using single scales anchored by low- and high-arousal terms for rating stimuli, we rated each positive stimulus on two scales, one for the degree of joy depicted and one for the degree of serenity depicted. Each negative stimulus was also rated on two scales, one for sadness and one for anger. This would allow us to detect whether the effect of arousal observed in the first study was due to an increased tendency to perceive high-arousal emotions, a decreased tendency to perceive low-arousal emotions, or—as we suspected—both tendencies.

## Study 2

### *Method*

#### *Subjects*

Subjects were 38 students (21 males and 17 females) who partly fulfilled a course requirement by participating. The data from three potential subjects were eliminated. One, who was run in the low-arousal, positive condition, clearly indicated to the experimenter that he did not know what "serenity" meant. The remaining two, both in the high-arousal, negative condition were suspicious. They believed that two parts of our study that were presented as being unrelated really were related.

#### *Stimulus Materials*

*Photos.* For use in the study, we selected a set of six positive photographs depicting a person who might be feeling either serenity or joy and a set of six negative photographs depicting a person who might be feeling either sad or angry. The positive photographs included five photographs of women and one of a man. On separate scales ranging from 1 (low) to 5 (high), one for how serene the person was and one for how joyous the person was, 16 pretest judges gave these six positive photographs a mean serenity rating of 3.9 and a mean joy rating of 2.8. The negative photographs included three photographs of women and three of men. On two separate 5-point scales for sadness and anger, 12 to 16 pretest judges (the number varied depending on the particular photograph) gave these photographs mean sadness and anger ratings of 3.1 and 2.7, respectively. As in Study 1, stimuli slightly biased toward the low-arousal ends of the scales were favored. Again, this was done to guard against a Hull-Spence alternative explanation for the results should the results confirm our hypotheses.

*Separate rating of the term sad.* In this study negative scales were anchored by the terms *sadness* and *anger,* which we assumed differed in the degree of associated arousal but not in negativity. Nine judges rated these terms for arousal and positivity/negativity. As expected, judges' arousal ratings for sadness ($M$ = 2.3) were significantly lower than their arousal ratings for anger ($M$ = 4.7), $t(16) = 6.26, p < .0001$. Also as expected, judges' negativity ratings of sadness ($M$ = 3.8) and anger ($M$ = 3.8) did not differ significantly.

#### *Procedure*

Before arrival, each subject was randomly assigned to one of the following four conditions: (a) high-arousal, positive photos (5 males and 3 females), (b) low-arousal, positive photos (7 males, 3 females), (c) high-arousal, negative photos (5 males, 5 females), or (d) low-arousal, negative photos (4 males, 6 females). Upon arrival, each subject was greeted by the first experimenter, who said the research session would include two short studies—pretests for later studies. She would conduct the first session; another person would conduct the second. The two pretests were presented as unrelated projects that were being run together for one credit because each only took 15 minutes.

The first experimenter then explained her pretest. She was interested in how various amounts of exercise and relaxation affected people's pulse rates. Therefore she was going to ask the subject to do some mild exercise as well as to relax in a lounge chair. The subject's pulse rate would be taken before and after each task. All subjects were asked at this point if there was any reason why they should not exercise; they were assured that if there was, they would not have to exercise but they would still receive credit. No subject indicated that he or she should not exercise.

Next, subjects were told they would do one of the first experimenter's two tasks, then participate in the second experimenter's study, and finally return to the first experimenter for the second task. This plan was supposedly being followed to allow the subject's pulse following the first task to return to normal before the start of the second task.[3] Half the subjects (those in the high-arousal condition) began with the exercise task; the other half (those in the low-arousal condition) began with the relaxation task. Subjects in the high-arousal (exercise) condition had their pulse taken, stepped up and down on a cinder block for 7 min and finally had their pulse taken a second time. Subjects in the low-arousal (relaxation) condition had their pulse taken, relaxed in a lounge chair for 7 min, then had their pulse taken a second time.[4]

After completing the first experimenter's first task, all subjects were taken to the second experimenter's room. The first experimenter introduced the subject to the second experimenter, who was unaware of the subjects' arousal condition. The first experimenter then asked the second experimenter to send the subject back when the "second pretest" was over, and finally she left the room.

The second experimenter said he was interested in moods. He wanted to know if it was possible to infer a person's moods from photographs. To study this, he wanted the subject to look at some photographs and to judge the emotion depicted by the people in those photographs. Half the subjects looked at the six positive photos and rated each person's serenity on a scale from 1 (not at all serene) to 7 (very serene). These subjects also rated the joyousness of the people in same photographs on a second scale from 1 (not at all joyous) to 7 (very joyous). The remaining half of the subjects looked at the six negative photos and rated each on two similar 7-point scales, in terms of how angry and in terms of how sad the person seemed to be. The order of presentation of the six photographs was randomized for each subject. Subjects who rated positive photos always rated them in terms of serenity first, then in terms of joy. Subjects who rated negative photos always rated them in terms of sadness first, then in terms of anger. Finally subjects were probed for suspicion and were fully debriefed by the second experimenter.

### *Results*

The dependent measure for the positive stimuli was the difference between the sum of each subject's ratings of the five positive photographs on serenity and the sum of his or her ratings of the same photographs on joy (scores on the serenity scale were subtracted from scores on the joy scale). Higher scores on this measure indicate a greater tendency to judge the photographs as indicating joy than serenity. The dependent measure for the negative stimuli was the difference between the sum of each subject's ratings of the five negative photographs on sadness and the sum of his or her ratings of the same photographs on anger (the sadness score was subtracted from the anger score). Higher scores on this measure indicate a greater tendency to judge the photographs as indicating anger than sadness.

As in Study 1 the effect of arousal on judgments about the positive stimuli was as predicted. The difference scores from the high-arousal subjects indicated a significantly greater tendency to perceive joy relative to serenity ($M = 2.1$) than that shown by the low-arousal subjects ($M = -4.9$), $t(16) = -2.72$, $p < .02$. In contrast, once again analogous evidence was not obtained for negative stimuli. The mean rating of these stimuli by the high-arousal subjects (−1.5) did not differ significantly from the mean rating by the low-arousal subjects (0.2), $t(18) = 0.56$, *ns*.

It is also worth noting the impact of arousal on ratings of joy and on ratings of serenity separately. On the index of joy, the mean for subjects in the high-arousal condition was 27.6,

[3] In fact, as will become evident shortly, at the conclusion of the study, subjects in the high-arousal condition had performed only the exercise task, and subjects in the low-arousal condition had performed only the relaxation task. However, all subjects were led to believe they would do both because we believed that simply being told that one was expected to perform the relaxation or the exercise task might produce an emotional reaction. Given this, we told subjects in both arousal conditions that they would be performing the same two tasks to keep such reactions comparable.

[4] Because it takes some time to locate and count a person's pulse—time during which arousal would be dropping—and because previous research had clearly indicated the effectiveness of these manipulations (Clark et al., 1983), the experimenter actually did not measure pulse rates. She simply pretended to efficiently do so for purposes of the cover story. In the Clark et al. (1983) study a check on the identical manipulations revealed that stepping up and down on the cinder block for 7 min produced significantly greater increases in pulse from pre- to posttask (mean change = 45) than did the relaxation task (mean change = −0.15), $t(4) = 8.1$, $p < .001$.

and the mean for subjects in the low-arousal condition was 25.10. This difference, although it was in the expected direction, was not, by itself, significant. On the index of serenity, the mean for subjects in the high-arousal condition was 25.5 and the mean for subjects in the low-arousal condition was 30.0. This difference, although also in the expected direction, was not by itself significant.

## General Discussion

These two studies taken together provide clear and consistent evidence for increases in arousal biasing judgments of positive stimuli in such a way as to be seen as indicating joy (a positive high-arousal emotion), rather than serenity (a positive low-arousal emotion). These results support our reasoning that this should have occurred because (a) the positive stimuli and arousal would combine to cue positive high-arousal thoughts, increasing the probability that they, rather than positive low-arousal thoughts (which might actually be blocked by the high arousal), would come to mind, and (b) these thoughts, being more available than others, would then bias judgments of others' emotions. The results of the second study not only replicated those of the first study but also extended their generalizability by demonstrating that arousal can bias not only judgments about the emotion indicated by what a person says but also judgments about the emotion indicated by a person's appearance.[5]

### *Explanations for the Lack of an Effect of Arousal on Negative Judgments*

In contrast with the results for positive stimuli, increases in arousal did not bias judgments of negative stimuli as expected.[6] However, concluding that arousal cannot bias judgments of others' negative emotions would be premature. After all, the studies reported here used only one negative emotion term to anchor the high-arousal end of our negative scales and only two to anchor the low-arousal end. Furthermore, only moderate levels of exercise were used to manipulate arousal. Thus our failure to observe an effect of arousal on judgments of negative emotions may be due to the particular pairs of emotional terms used to anchor our scales and/or due to our particular manipulations of arousal. In this regard, consider three possible specific explanations for our failure to observe an effect of arousal on judgments of negative emotions.

The first explanation is suggested by a study by Schwartz et al. (1981), in which subjects who imagined anger experienced greater increases in mean arterial blood pressure and heart rate than did subjects who imagined happiness. This suggests that moderate levels of arousal may be associated with joyful thoughts in memory, whereas high levels of arousal may be associated with angry thoughts in memory. If this is true, then arousal would have to be moderately high to induce joyful thoughts but very high to induce angry thoughts. The arousal in our studies may have been moderate, thus inducing joyful but not angry thoughts.

A second explanation is that the pattern of physiological responses produced by moderate exercise (or more specifically those parts of the pattern that are represented in memory) matches that produced by joy better than that produced by anger. The fact that patterns of sympathetic arousal (as well as of other physiological responses accompanying exercise and various emotional states) differ is well established (e.g., Ax, 1953; Schwartz et al., 1981). Although there is evidence that such patterns do not have to be the same for one to prime another (Clark, Milberg, & Ross, 1983), it is still possible that the more similar two patterns of physiological responses are, the more likely they are to prime one another. Thus moderate exercise may be more likely to prime joy rather than anger. Unfortunately, we do not know enough about the particular patterns of arousal produced by our manipulations of arousal and

[5] Clark, Milberg, and Erber (1983, study 2) replicated a third time the finding that arousal increases people's tendency to judge positive stimuli as indicating joy rather than serenity. In this third study, soccer players rated photographs of smiling others either before or after practicing soccer. Those who rated the photos after practice were significantly more likely than those who rated them before to rate the pictures as indicating joy rather than serenity. This third study is described in a paper (Clark, Milberg, & Erber, 1983, Study 2) that is available from the first author.

[6] This lack of an effect of arousal on judgments of negative photographs in terms of sadness versus anger was also replicated a third time by Clark et al. (1983, Study 2).

that produced by joy and anger to assess the likelihood of this explanation.

A final explanation involves the assumption that serenity and joy differ from one another primarily in terms of the amount of arousal associated with each, whereas depression or sadness and anger differ in more complex ways. For example, a large body of research reveals that angry and sad facial expressions are clearly differentiated, whereas serene and joyous expressions are not (e.g., Izard, 1977; Plutchik, 1962; Schwartz, Fair, Salt, Mandel, & Klerman, 1976; Tomkins & McCarter, 1964; also see Ekman, Friesen, & Ellsworth, 1982, for a review). Given such evidence, it is reasonable to speculate that people's judgments of whether a person is feeling serenity versus joy may be based primarily on their own arousal state, whereas their judgments of whether a person is feeling sadness or depression versus anger may be based primarily on other factors such as facial expressions or the person's particular choice of words.

This last explanation suggests that arousal might bias judgments of negative stimuli if the stimuli were judged in terms of the degree to which they indicated each of two states more qualitatively similar in all respects except the degree of associated arousal than are depression (or sadness) and anger. According to some theorists, terms such as (a) *apprehension, fear,* and *terror;* or (b) *annoyance, anger,* and *rage* describe the same primary emotions experienced at different levels of intensity (Izard, 1977; Plutchik, 1962, p. 138). Thus increased arousal might be capable of biasing people's choice of labels for "fearful" phrases or appearances away from apprehension and toward terror, or of biasing their choice of labels for "angry" phrases or appearances away from annoyance and toward rage.

In any case, all of these possibilities suggest that future work examining the ideas set forth in this article should incorporate not only a variety of materials to be judged, as was the case in the present studies, but also (a) a variety of positive and negative response pairs (e.g., serene vs. joyous; pleased vs. delighted; glad vs. ecstatic; sad vs. distressed; annoyed vs. angry; apprehensive vs. terrified), (b) a variety of levels of arousal (e.g., reduction in arousal, no manipulation, moderate elevation, high elevation) and, finally, (c) a variety of types of arousal manipulations (e.g., for high arousal, exercise vs. caffeine vs. viewing an erotic movie). Work in which such changes are made is needed to detect whether arousal may sometimes bias judgments of negative emotions and specifically when it will, as well as to determine whether the effects of arousal on positive judgments generalize to judgments involving other pairs of positive terms and to arousal produced in ways other than exercise.

### *Importance of Evidence That Arousal Biases Judgments About Positive Emotions*

The finding that arousal can bias at least judgments of positive emotions is important for a number of reasons. First, although early work has already shown that perceivers' specific emotions may bias judgments of the emotions felt by others in such a way as to be consistent with one's own emotion (e.g., Feshbach & Feshbach, 1963; Feshbach & Singer, 1957; Hornberger, 1960; Murray, 1933; Schiffenbauer, 1974a, 1974b), the present work shows that more general states of an observer (states of high or low arousal) may also influence such judgments.

Second, the present work suggests that mood states, at least positive ones, involve more than just a negativity–positivity dimension. They also involve a sympathetic arousal dimension. Thus recent discussions of and research about moods in which moods are referred to primarily in terms of their negativity or positivity may have presented an oversimplified picture of mood states. It may prove profitable in future research to investigate effects of the level of arousal associated with moods as well as effects caused by the evaluative tone of the mood.

Third, our results suggest that the role of arousal in emotion is more complex than previous research has implied. Consider the fact that after reviewing much of the existing literature on arousal and emotion, Eysenck (1982, p. 95) has recently suggested that increases in arousal serve to enhance the degree of negativity or positivity that a person experiences. The present research suggests that the effects of arousal are not always that simple. Although arousal may indeed increase the positivity or probability (or both) of certain *types* of positive feelings (e.g., joy) by cuing joyful thoughts, it may actually decrease the positivity or probability of other types of positive feelings (e.g., serenity) by blocking access to low-arousal thoughts.[7] Of course, since our subjects' *own* emotions were not measured, these ideas remain speculative.

Although we do believe our evidence suggests that the effects of arousal involve more than simply increasing the positivity or negativity of emotions, as Eysenck (1982) suggests, our evidence is not necessarily in conflict with claims that arousal determines the intensity of felt emotion (e.g., Mandler, 1975, p. 67). Joyous thoughts may well be experienced as more intense than serene thoughts. This may occur because of people's awareness of the arousal that accompanies joy, because arousal increases the duration of joy (Clark, 1982), and/or because arousal makes emotions difficult to control. We also believe that these results are not in conflict with Schachter and Singer's (1962) claim that "an individual will react emotionally or describe his feelings as emotions only to the extent that he experiences a state of physiological arousal" (p. 382). One can *experience* low or high arousal, so that does not imply that the higher the arousal the more of any given emotion one will experience. However, the present results do go beyond Schachter and Singer's work to suggest that a person's level of arousal may influence the cognitive label applied to stimuli in the environment, in addition to stimuli in the environment influencing what cognitive label is applied to one's state of arousal.

Finally, the present results, together with past results showing that emotional states influence perception of others' emotions, may shed light on problems of communication in interpersonal relationships. Specifically, such results suggest that people who are "moody" and/or who are especially subject to shifts in their own arousal state for any reason, may experience difficulty in understanding or empathizing with others' emotional states because their own states may bias their perception of those states. Of course, in connection with this last point, when other cues to emotion such as tone of voice (Bugental & Moore, 1979) and context information (Knudsen & Muzekari, in press; Mann, 1940; Muzekari, Knudsen, & Evans, 1983) are present, observers' moods and arousal states may not have as great an impact on their perception of others' emotions as they have been shown to have in laboratory studies.

[7] In connection with this point, it is interesting to note that Reilly & Morris (1983) have very recently reported that exercise-induced arousal *inhibits* the effectiveness of inductions of sadness, a low-arousal emotion.

## References


Ax, A. F. (1953). The physiological differentiation of fear and anger in humans. *Psychosomatic Medicine, 15,* 433–442.

Bower, G. H. (1981). Mood and memory. *American Psychologist, 36,* 129–148.

Bugental, D. B., & Moore, B. S. (1979). Effects of induced moods on voice affect. *Developmental Psychology, 6,* 664–665.

Bush, L. E. (1973). Individual differences multidimensional scaling of attitudes denoting feelings. *Journal of Personality and Social Psychology, 25,* 50–57.

Clark, M. S. (1982). A role for arousal in the link between feeling states, judgments, and behavior. In M. S. Clark & S. T. Fiske (Eds.), *Affect and cognition: The Seventeenth Annual Carnegie Symposium on Cognition* (pp. 263–289). Hillsdale, NJ: Erlbaum.

Clark, M. S., Milberg, S., & Erber, R. (1983, August). *Effects of arousal on judgments about other people's emotions.* Paper presented at the 91st annual meeting of the American Psychological Association, Anaheim, CA.

Clark, M. S., Milberg, S., & Ross, J. (1983). Arousal cues material stored in memory with a similar level of arousal: Implications for understanding the effects of mood on memory. *Journal of Verbal Learning and Verbal Behavior, 22,* 633–649.

Ekman, P., Friesen, W. V., & Ellsworth, P. (1982). What emotion categories or dimensions can observers judge from facial behavior? In P. Ekman (Ed.), *Emotion in the human face* (pp. 39–55). New York: Cambridge University Press.

Eysenck, M. W. (1982). *Attention and arousal: Cognition and performance.* New York: Springer-Verlag.

Feshbach, S., & Feshbach, N. (1963). Influence of the stimulus object upon the complementary and supplementary projection of fear. *Journal of Abnormal and Social Psychology, 66,* 498–502.

Feshbach, S., & Singer, R. D. (1957). The effects of fear arousal and suppression fear upon social perception. *Journal of Abnormal and Social Psychology, 55,* 283–288.

Gouaux, C. (1971). Induced affective states and interpersonal attraction. *Journal of Personality and Social Psychology, 20,* 37–43.

Hornberger, R. H. (1960). The projective effects of fear and sexual arousal on the rating of pictures. *Journal of Clinical Psychology, 16,* 328–331.

Hull, C. L. (1943). *Principles of behavior.* New York: Appleton-Century-Crofts.

Hull, C. L. (1952). *A behavior system: An introduction to behavior theory concerning the individual organism.* New Haven, CT: Yale University Press.

Isen, A. M. (1975). Positive affect, accessibility of cognitions and helping. In J. Piliavin (Chair), *Current directions in theory on helping behavior.* Symposium presented at the meetings of the Eastern Psychological Association, New York.

Isen, A. M., & Shalker, T. (1982). The effect of feeling state on evaluation of positive, neutral and negative stimuli: When you "Accentuate the positive," do you "Eliminate the negative"? *Social Psychology Quarterly, 45,* 58–63.

Isen, A. M., Shalker, T., Clark, M., & Karp, L. (1978). Affect, accessibility of material in memory, and behavior: A cognitive loop? *Journal of Personality and Social Psychology, 36,* 1–12.

Izard, C. E. (1977). *Human emotions.* New York: Plenum Press.

Knudsen, H., & Muzekari, L. H. (in press). The effects of verbal statements of context on facial expressions of emotion. *Journal of Nonverbal Behavior.*

Mandler, G. (1975). *Mind and emotion.* New York: Wiley.

Mann, N. L. (1940). The effect of knowledge of the situation upon judgment of emotion from facial expressions. *Journal of Abnormal and Social Psychology, 35,* 324–338.

Murray, H. A. (1933). The effect of fear upon estimates of the maliciousness of other persons. *Journal of Social Psychology, 4,* 310–339.

Muzekari, L. H., Knudsen, H., & Evans, T. (1983, August). *The effect of context on perception of emotion among psychiatric patients.* Paper presented at the annual meeting of the American Psychological Association, Anaheim, California.

Plutchik, R. (1962). *The emotions: Facts, theories, and a new model.* New York: Random House.

Reilly, N. P., & Morris, W. N. (1983, August). *The role of arousal in the induction of mood.* Paper presented at the annual meeting of the American Psychological Association, Anaheim, California.

Ross, R. T. (1938). A statistic for circular scales. *Journal of Educational Psychology, 29,* 384–389.

Russell, J. A. (1980). A circumplex model of affect. *Journal of Personality and Social Psychology, 39,* 1161–1178.

Schachter, S., & Singer, J. E. (1962). Cognitive, social and physiological determinants of emotional state. *Psychological Review, 69,* 379–399.

Schiffenbauer, A. (1974a). Effect of observer's emotional state on judgments of the emotional state of others. *Journal of Personality and Social Psychology, 30,* 31–35.

Schiffenbauer, A. (1974b). When will people use facial information to attribute emotion?: The effect of judge's emotional state and intensity of facial expression on attribution of emotion. *Representative Research in Social Psychology, 5,* 47–53.

Schwartz, G. E., Fair, P. L., Salt, P., Mandel, M. R., & Klerman, G. L. (1976). Facial muscle patterning to affective imagery in depressed and nondepressed subjects. *Science, 192,* 489–491.

Schwartz, G. E., Weinberger, D. A., & Singer, J. A. (1981). Cardiovascular differentiation of happiness, sadness, anger, and fear following imagery and exercise. *Psychosomatic Medicine, 43,* 343–364.

Spence, K. W. (1956). *Behavior theory and conditioning.* New Haven, CT: Yale University Press.

Sternbach, R. A. (1962). Assessing differential autonomic patterns in emotions. *Journal of Psychosomatic Research, 6,* 87–91.

Tomkins, S. S., & McCarter, R. (1964). What and where are the primary affects? Some evidence for a theory. *Perception and Motor Skills, 18,* 119–158.

Tversky, A., & Kahneman, D. (1974). Judgments under uncertainty: Heuristics and biases. *Science, 185,* 1124–1131.

Received March 3, 1983
Revision received September 28, 1983 ▪

# APPENDIX C

# *Article Manuscript (Selected Pages)*

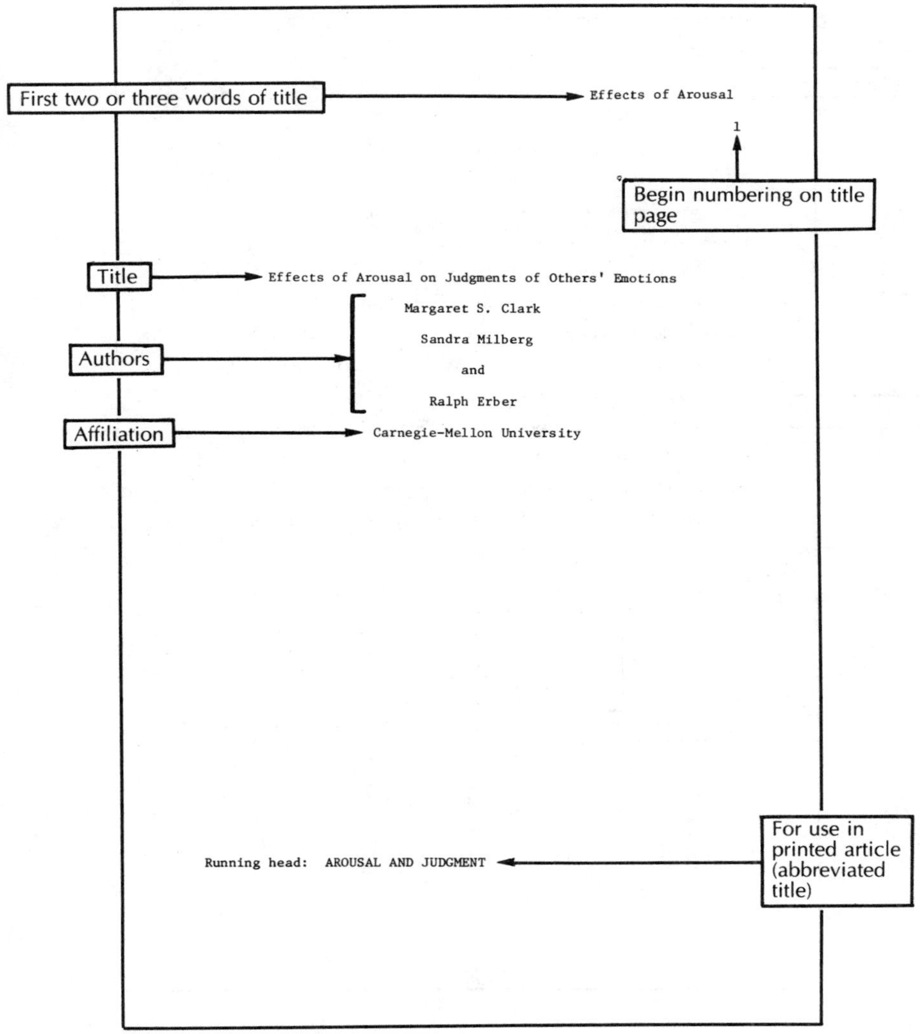

Abstract begins on new page

Not indented

Double space

Single paragraph

Effects of Arousal

2

Abstract

Based on evidence that arousal cues information from memory associated with a similar level of arousal (Clark, Milberg, & Ross, 1983) and on evidence that people will base judgments on the information that is most available to them (Tversky & Kahneman, 1974), it was hypothesized that (a) increases in arousal would increase the likelihood that subjects would interpret positive statements and positive facial expressions as indicating a positive emotion associated with high arousal (joy) rather than a positive emotion associated with low arousal (serenity), and (b) increases in arousal would increase the likelihood that subjects would interpret negative statements and negative expressions as indicating a negative emotion associated with high arousal (anger) rather than a negative emotion associated with low arousal (sadness or depression). Two studies are reported, each of which support the first hypothesis but not the second. Explanations for why arousal had the predicted effects on positive but not on negative stimuli are offered.

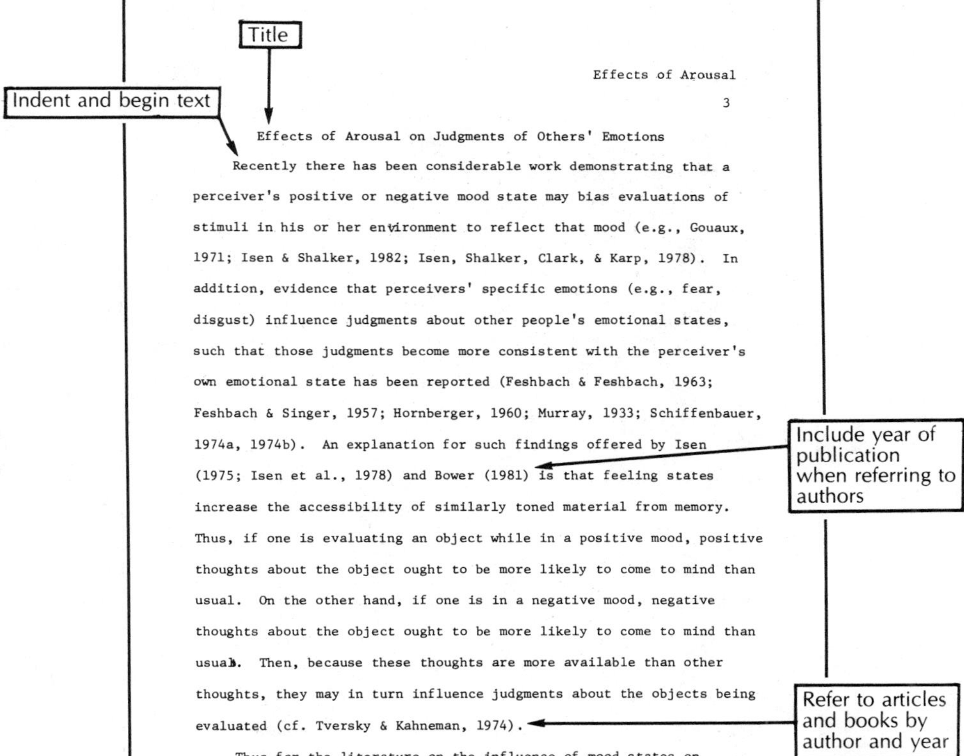
Effects of Arousal

3

Effects of Arousal on Judgments of Others' Emotions

Recently there has been considerable work demonstrating that a perceiver's positive or negative mood state may bias evaluations of stimuli in his or her environment to reflect that mood (e.g., Gouaux, 1971; Isen & Shalker, 1982; Isen, Shalker, Clark, & Karp, 1978). In addition, evidence that perceivers' specific emotions (e.g., fear, disgust) influence judgments about other people's emotional states, such that those judgments become more consistent with the perceiver's own emotional state has been reported (Feshbach & Feshbach, 1963; Feshbach & Singer, 1957; Hornberger, 1960; Murray, 1933; Schiffenbauer, 1974a, 1974b). An explanation for such findings offered by Isen (1975; Isen et al., 1978) and Bower (1981) is that feeling states increase the accessibility of similarly toned material from memory. Thus, if one is evaluating an object while in a positive mood, positive thoughts about the object ought to be more likely to come to mind than usual. On the other hand, if one is in a negative mood, negative thoughts about the object ought to be more likely to come to mind than usual. Then, because these thoughts are more available than other thoughts, they may in turn influence judgments about the objects being evaluated (cf. Tversky & Kahneman, 1974).

Thus far the literature on the influence of mood states on judgments has focused primarily on the positive-negative dimension of moods, whereas the literature on the effects of specific emotions on judgments has tended not to break those emotions down into underlying dimensions. A potentially important dimension of affective states that



* * *

Effects of Arousal

5

Analogous reasoning yields the prediction that the degree of arousal may bias perception of negative stimuli. For example, anger is associated with high levels of arousal; depression and sadness are associated with lower levels of arousal (Russell, 1980; Schwartz et al., 1981). Consequently, a person experiencing high arousal may be more likely than usual to interpret a negative appearance as anger, whereas a person experiencing low arousal may be more likely than usual to interpret the same appearance as indicating depression.

Given this reasoning, we conducted the present studies to test the following specific hypotheses:

1. People experiencing high arousal will be more likely than people experiencing low arousal to interpret positive statements and positive facial expressions as indicating joy rather than serenity.

2. People experiencing high arousal will be more likely than people experiencing low arousal to interpret negative statements and negative facial expressions as indicating anger rather than sadness or depression.

These hypotheses were examined in two studies (a field study and a laboratory study). The first study examined whether arousal would bias interpretations of the emotions indicated by things another might say; the second examined whether arousal would bias interpretations of the emotions indicated by another's physical appearance.

Study 1

Method

Underline and type flush to left margin

Centered and not underlined

Subjects

Subjects were 37 adult tennis players, 23 males and 14 females. They were initially identified while waiting to play tennis at a city

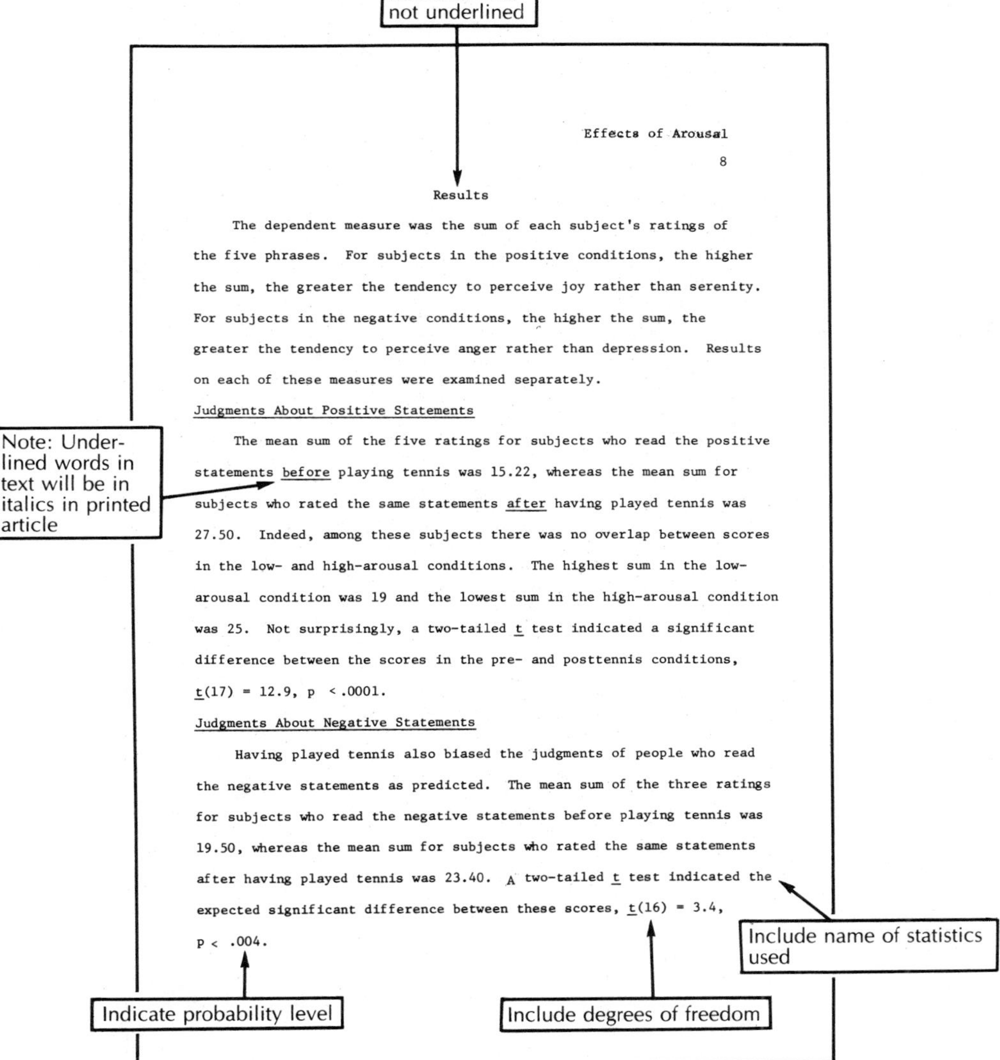


Effects of Arousal

8

Results

The dependent measure was the sum of each subject's ratings of the five phrases. For subjects in the positive conditions, the higher the sum, the greater the tendency to perceive joy rather than serenity. For subjects in the negative conditions, the higher the sum, the greater the tendency to perceive anger rather than depression. Results on each of these measures were examined separately.

Judgments About Positive Statements

The mean sum of the five ratings for subjects who read the positive statements *before* playing tennis was 15.22, whereas the mean sum for subjects who rated the same statements *after* having played tennis was 27.50. Indeed, among these subjects there was no overlap between scores in the low- and high-arousal conditions. The highest sum in the low-arousal condition was 19 and the lowest sum in the high-arousal condition was 25. Not surprisingly, a two-tailed *t* test indicated a significant difference between the scores in the pre- and posttennis conditions, $t(17) = 12.9$, $p < .0001$.

Judgments About Negative Statements

Having played tennis also biased the judgments of people who read the negative statements as predicted. The mean sum of the three ratings for subjects who read the negative statements before playing tennis was 19.50, whereas the mean sum for subjects who rated the same statements after having played tennis was 23.40. A two-tailed *t* test indicated the expected significant difference between these scores, $t(16) = 3.4$, $p < .004$.

Centered and not underlined



Discussion

The results of the first study are clearly consistent with the hypotheses. High arousal seems to have biased the judgments of positive stimuli toward joy and the judgments of negative stimuli toward anger. However, the results of this study must be interpreted with caution. There is a plausible alternative explanation for these results. Specifically, there is no reason to suspect that before playing tennis, our subjects were feeling either particularly joyous or angry, rather than particularly serene or depressed. After playing, however, subjects who won may have been feeling joyous while subjects who lost may have been feeling angry. Thus the joy of a subset of our posttennis subjects (rather than arousal per se) may have biased our high-arousal, positive group's scores toward joy rather than serenity. Similarly, the anger of a subset of our posttennis subjects (rather than arousal per se) may have biased our high-arousal, negative group's scores toward anger rather than depression.

We did not ask subjects whether they had won or lost, so it was difficult to rule out this alternative explanation. However, recall that in the case of the results obtained for ratings of the positive statements there was no overlap in the scores between the high- and low-arousal subjects. Thus an alternative explanation involving the

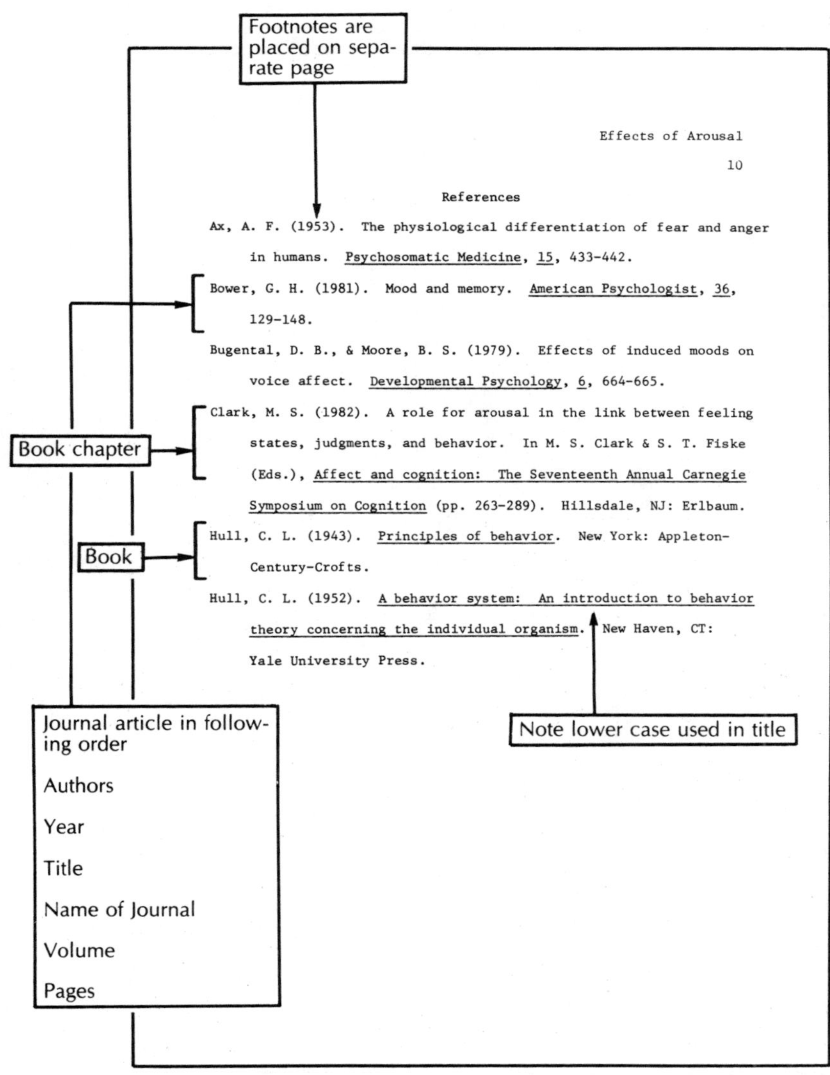


Effects of Arousal

10

References

Ax, A. F. (1953). The physiological differentiation of fear and anger in humans. Psychosomatic Medicine, 15, 433-442.

Bower, G. H. (1981). Mood and memory. American Psychologist, 36, 129-148.

Bugental, D. B., & Moore, B. S. (1979). Effects of induced moods on voice affect. Developmental Psychology, 6, 664-665.

Clark, M. S. (1982). A role for arousal in the link between feeling states, judgments, and behavior. In M. S. Clark & S. T. Fiske (Eds.), Affect and cognition: The Seventeenth Annual Carnegie Symposium on Cognition (pp. 263-289). Hillsdale, NJ: Erlbaum.

Hull, C. L. (1943). Principles of behavior. New York: Appleton-Century-Crofts.

Hull, C. L. (1952). A behavior system: An introduction to behavior theory concerning the individual organism. New Haven, CT: Yale University Press.

Effects of Arousal

11

Footnotes

[1] Additional pretesting involving separate ratings of each positive phrase for joy and for serenity and of each negative phrase for depression and for anger indicated that these phrases were not given ratings near the middle of the original scale because judges saw them as indicative of *neither* of the emotions anchoring the ends of the scales.

Footnotes are placed on separate page

# Bibliography

Alfred, R. The Church of Satan. In C. Glock & R. Bellah (Eds.), *The new religious consciousness.* Berkeley: University of California Press, 1976, pp. 180–202.

American Psychological Association. *Ethical principles in the conduct of research with human participants.* Washington, D.C.: American Psychological Association, 1982.

American Psychological Association. *Publication manual* (3rd ed.). Washington, D.C.: American Psychological Association, 1983.

Babbie, E. R. *Survey research methods.* Belmont, Calif.: Wadsworth, 1973.

Babbie, E. R. *The practice of social research.* Belmont, Calif.: Wadsworth, 1983.

Barber, T. X. *Pitfalls in human research.* New York: Pergamon, 1976.

Barthell, C. N., & Holmes, D. S. High school yearbooks: A nonreactive measure of social isolation in graduates who later became schizophrenic. *Journal of Abnormal Psychology,* 1968, *73,* 313–316.

Baumrind, D. Some thoughts on ethics of research: After reading Milgram's "Behavioral study of obedience." *American Psychologist,* 1964, *19,* 421–423.

Bohm, D. Further remarks on order. In C. H. Waddington (Ed.), *Towards a theoretical biology* (Vol. 2). Edinburgh: Edinburgh University Press, 1969.

Bolgar, H. The case study method. In B. B. Wolman (Ed.), *Handbook of clinical psychology.* New York: McGraw-Hill, 1965, pp. 28–39.

Boring, E. G. *A history of experimental psychology* (2nd ed.). New York: Appleton-Century-Crofts, 1950.

Bower, G. H. Mood and memory. *American Psychologist,* 1981, *36,* 129–148.

Bower, G. H., & Gilligan, S. G. Remembering information related to one's self. *Journal of Research in Personality,* 1979, *13,* 420–432.

Bower, G. H., Monteiro, K. P., & Gilligan, S. G. Emotional mood as a context of learning and recall. *Journal of Verbal Learning and Verbal Behavior,* 1978, *17,* 573–585.

Bransford, J. D. *Human cognition.* Belmont, Calif.: Wadsworth, 1979.

Bransford, J. D., & Johnson, M. K. Contextual prerequisites for understanding: Some investigations of comprehension and recall. *Journal of Verbal Learning and Verbal Behavior,* 1972, *11,* 717–726.

Bridgman, P. W. *The logic of modern physics.* New York: Macmillan, 1927.

Broad, W. J. Imbroglio at Yale (I): Emergence of a fraud. *Science,* 1980, *210,* 38–41.

Bronowski, J. *Science and human values.* New York: Harper & Row, 1965.

Bruning, J. L., & Kintz, B. L. *Computational handbook of statistics.* Glenview, Ill.: Scott, Foresman & Co., 1968.

Brunswik, E. *Systematic and representative design of psychological experiments:* Berkeley: University of California Press, 1947.

Campbell, A. A., & Katona, G. *The sample survey: A technique for social science research.* In L. Festinger & D. Katz (Eds.), *Research methods in the behavioral sciences.* New York: Dryden Press, 1953.

Campbell, D. T., & Stanley, J. C. *Experimental and quasi-experimental designs for research.* Chicago: Rand McNally, 1963.

Carlsmith, J. M., Ellsworth, P. C., & Aronson, E. *Methods of research in social psychology.* Reading, Mass.: Addison-Wesley, 1976.

Chamberlin, T. C. The method of multiple working hypotheses. *Science,* 1965, *148,* 754–759. (Reprint of article originally published in *Science,* 1890.)

Cobb, L. A., Thomas, G. I., Dillard, D. H., Merendino, K. A., & Bruce, R. A. An evaluation of internal-mammary-artery ligation by a double-blind technic. *The New England Journal of Medicine,* 1959, *260,* 1115–1118.

Cohen, L., & Holliday, M. *Statistics for social scientists.* London: Harper & Row, 1982.

Cohen, M., & Nagel, E. *An introduction to logic and scientific method.* New York: Harcourt, 1934.

Converse, J. M., & Schuman, H. *Conversations at random: Survey research as interviewers see it.* New York: Wiley, 1974.

Cook, S. W. A comment on the ethical issues involved in West, Gunn, and Chernicky's "Ubiquitous Watergate: An attributional analysis." *Journal of Personality and Social Psychology,* 1975, *32,* 66–68.

Cook, T. D., & Campbell, D. T. *Quasi-experimentation: Design and analysis issues for field settings.* Chicago: Rand McNally, 1979.

Coombs, C. H., Raiffa, H., & Thrall, R. M. Some views on mathematical models and measurement theory. *Psychological Review,* 1954, *61,* 132–144.

Cronbach, L. J., & Meehl, P. Construct validity in psychological tests. *Psychological Bulletin,* 1955, *52,* 281–302.

Cunningham, M. R. Weather, mood, and helping behavior: Quasi-experiments with the sunshine samaritan. *Journal of Personality and Social Psychology,* 1979, *37,* 1947–1956.

Dillman, D. A. *Mail and telephone surveys: The total design method.* New York: Wiley, 1978.

Dowd, M. Many women in poll equate values of job and family life. *The New York Times,* December 4, 1983.

Edgington, E. S. A new tabulation of statistical procedures used in APA journals. *American Psychologist,* 1974, *29,* 25–26.

Ericsson, K. A., & Simon, H. A. Verbal report as data. *Psychological Review,* 1980, *87,* 215–251.

Evans, I. M., & Robinson, C. H. Behavior therapy observed: The diary of a client. *Cognitive Therapy and Research,* 1978, *2,* 335–355.

Eysenck, H. J. Behavior therapy—dogma or applied science. In M. P. Feldman & A. Broadhurst (Eds.), *Theoretical and experimental bases of the behavior therapies.* London: Wiley, 1976.

Fry, L. W., & Greenfield, S. Examination of attitudinal differences between policemen and policewomen. *Journal of Applied Psychology,* 1980, *65,* 123–126.

Gaito, J. Measurement scales and statistics: Resurgence of an old misconception. *Psychological Bulletin,* 1980, *87,* 564–567.

Galen. De praenotione. In D. C. G. Kuhn (Ed.), *Opera omnia,* cap. vi (Vol. 9) Lipsiae: Officina Libraria Car. Cnoblochii, 1827, pp. 630–635.

Gallup, G. Opinion polling in a democracy. In J. Tanur (Ed.), *Statistics: A guide to the unknown.* San Francisco: Holden-Day, Inc. 1972.

Galtung, J. *Theory and methods of social research.* New York: Columbia University Press, 1967.

Gardner, M. Mathematical games: The combinatorial basis of the "I Ching," the Chinese book of divination and wisdom. *Scientific American,* 1974, *230,* 108–113.

Gaul, D. J., Craighead, W. E., & Mahoney, M. J. Relationship between eating rates and obesity. *Journal of Consulting and Clinical Psychology,* 1975, *43,* 123–125.

Giannetti, R. A., Johnson, J. H., Klingler, D. E., & Williams, T. A. Comparison of linear and configural MMPI diagnostic methods with an uncontaminated criterion. *Journal of Consulting and Clinical Psychology,* 1978, *46,* 1046–1052.

Glass, G. V., & Stanley, J. C. *Statistical methods in education and psychology.* Englewood Cliffs, N.J.: Prentice-Hall, 1970.

Glasser, R. J. *The body is the hero.* New York: Random House, 1976.

Gottmann, J. M. N-of-1 and N-of-2 research in psychotherapy. *Psychological Bulletin,* 1973, *80,* 93–105.

Gould, S. J. The finagle factor. *Human Nature,* 1978, *1,* 80–87.

Guilford, J. P., & Fruchter, B. *Fundamental statistics in psychology and education* (6th ed.). New York: McGraw-Hill, 1978.

Gur, R. C., & Sackeim, H. Self-deception: A concept in search of a phenomenon. *Journal of Personality and Social Psychology,* 1979, *37,* 147–169.

Harris, M. E., & Ray, W. J. Dream content and its relation to self-reported interpersonal behavior. *Psychiatry,* 1977, *40,* 363–368.

Hass, H., Fink, H., & Hartfelder, G. The placebo problem. *Psychopharmacology Service Center Bulletin,* 1963, *2,* 1–65.

Hearnshaw, L. S. *Cyril Burt, psychologist.* Ithaca, N.Y.: Cornell University Press, 1979.

Hersen, M., & Bellack, A. A multiple baseline analysis of social skills training in chronic schizophrenics. *Journal of Applied Behavior Analysis,* 1976, *9,* 239–245.

Herodotus. In F. R. B. Godolphin (Ed.), *The Greek historians.* New York: Random House, 1942.

Holt, R. R. Experimental methods in clinical psychology. In B. B. Wolman (Ed.), *Handbook of clinical psychology.* New York: McGraw-Hill, 1965.

Holton, G. *Introduction to concepts and theories in physical science.* Reading, Mass.: Addison-Wesley, 1952.

Horner, M. S. Toward an understanding of achievement related conflicts in women. *Journal of Social Issues,* 1972, *28,* 157–176.

*I ching* (3rd ed.). (R. Wilhelm, trans., 1924; C. F. Baynes, trans. 1950). Princeton: Princeton University Press, 1967.

Jones, E. E., & Nisbett, R. E. *The actor and the observer: Divergent perceptions of the causes of behavior.* Morristown, N. J.: General Learning Press, 1971.

Kazdin, A. E. Methodological and assessment considerations in evaluating reinforcement programs in applied settings. *Journal of Applied Behavioral Analysis,* 1973, *6,* 517–531.

Kelman, H. C. *A time to speak.* San Francisco: Jossey Bass, 1968.

Keppel, G., & Saufley, W. H. *Introduction to design and analysis: A student's handbook.* San Francisco: W. H. Freeman & Co., 1980.

Kerlinger, F. N. *Foundations of behavioral research* (2nd ed.). New York: Holt, Rinehart & Winston, 1973.

Koestler, A. *The act of creation.* New York: Macmillan, 1964.

Kraft, C. L. A psychophysical contribution to air safety: Simulator studies of visual illusions in night visual approaches. In H. L. Pick, H. W. Leibowitz, J. E. Singer. A. Steinschneider, & H. W. Stevenson (Eds.), *Psychology: From research to practice.* New York: Plenum Press, 1978.

Krantz, D. H., Luce, R. D., Suppes P., & Tversky, A. *Foundations of measurement,* Vol. 1. New York: Academic Press, 1971.

Krantz, D. S. Naturalistic study of social influences on meal size among moderately obese and nonobese subjects. *Psychosomatic Medicine,* 1979, *41,* 19–27.

Kuhn, T. *The structure of scientific revolutions* (2nd ed.). Chicago: University of Chicago Press, 1970.

Lakatos, I. *The methodology of scientific research programs.* Cambridge: Cambridge University Press, 1978.

Landers, D. M., Obermier, G. E., & Patterson, A. H. Iris pigmentation and reactive motor performance. *Journal of Motor Behavior,* 1976, *8,* 171–179.

Lehner, P. N. *Handbook of ethological methods.* New York: Garland STPM Press, 1979.

Likert, R. A technique for the measurement of attitudes. *Archives of Psychology,* 1932, *19,* 44–53.

Linton, M., & Gallo, P. S. *The practical statistician.* Monterey, Calif.: Brooks/Cole, 1975.

Loftus, E. F., & Fries, J. F. Informed consent may be hazardous to your health. *Science,* 1979, *204,* 4388.

Lord, F. M. On the statistical treatment of football numbers. *American Psychologist,* 1953, *8,* 750–751.

Lorenz, K. *King Solomon's ring.* New York: Thomas Y. Crowell, 1952.

Lorenz, K. The fashionable fallacy of dispensing with description. *Naturwissenschaften,* 1973, *60,* 1–9.

Maher, B. A. A reader's, writer's and reviewer's guide to assessing research reports in clinical psychology. *Journal of Consulting and Clinical Psychology,* 1978, *46,* 835–838. (a)

Maher, B. A. Stimulus sampling in clinical research: Representative design reviewed. *Journal of Consulting and Clinical Psychology,* 1978, *46,* 643–647. (b)

Mahoney, M. J. *Scientist as subject.* Cambridge, Mass.: Ballinger, 1976.

Marcel, A. J. Conscious and unconscious perception: An approach to the relations between phenomenal experience and perceptual processes. *Cognitive Psychology,* 1983, *15,* 238–300.

Mark, M., Cook, T. D., & Cook, F. Randomized and quasi-experimental designs in evaluation research. In L. Rutman (Ed.), *Evaluation research methods: A basic guide* (2nd ed.). Beverly Hills, Calif.: Sage, 1984.

Maslow, A. H. *The psychology of science.* New York: Harper & Row, 1966.

Maslow, A. H. *Motivation and personality* (2nd ed.). New York: Harper & Row, 1970.

Maslow, A. H. *The farthest reaches of human nature.* New York: Viking Press, 1971.

McCall, R. B. *Fundamental statistics for psychology* (2nd ed.). New York: Harcourt Brace Jovanovich, 1980.

Mead, M. *Coming of age in Samoa.* New York: Morrow, 1928.

Mesulam, M., & Perry, J. The diagnosis of love-sickness: Experimental psychophysiology without the polygraph. *Psychophysiology,* 1972, *9,* 546–551.

Milgram, S. Behavioral study of obedience. *Journal of Abnormal and Social Psychology,* 1963, *67,* 371–378.

Milgram, S. *The individual in a social world: Essays and experiments.* Reading, Mass.: Addison-Wesley, 1977.

Miller, D. *Handbook of research design and social measurement.* New York: David McKay, 1977.

Miller, G. T. *Living in the environment: Concepts, problems, and alternatives.* Belmont, Calif.: Wadsworth, 1975.

Miller, N. E. Learning of visceral and glandular responses. *Science,* 1969, *163,* 434–445.

Milner, B. Amnesia following operation on the temporal lobes. In C. W. M. Whitty & O. L. Zangwill (Eds.), *Amnesia.* London: Butterworths, 1966, pp. 109–133.

Mitroff, I. I. Norms and counter-norms in a select group of the Apollo moon scientists: A case study of the ambivalence of scientists. *American Sociological Review,* 1974, *39,* 579–595.

Mitroff, I. I., & Fitzgerald, I. On the psychology of the Apollo moon scientists: A chapter in the psychology of science. *Human Relations,* 1977, *30,* 657–674.

Newcombe, N., & Arnkoff, D. Effects of speech style and sex of speaker on person perception. *Journal of Personality and Social Psychology,* 1979, *37,* 1293–1303.

Newton, I. *Mathematical principles.* Andrew Motte translator (1729), revised translation Florian Cajori. New York: Greenwood, 1969.

Nisbett, R. E., & Wilson, T. D. Tell more than we can know: Verbal reports on mental processes. *Psychological Review,* 1977, *84,* 231–259.

Oppenheim, A. N. *Questionnaire design and attitude measurement.* New York: Basic Books, 1966.

Orne, M. Demand characteristics and the concept of quasi-controls. In R. Rosenthal & R. L. Rosnow (Eds.), *Artifact in behavioral research.* New York: Academic Press, 1969.

Orne, M. T., & Evans, F. J. Inadvertent termination of hypnosis on hypnotized and simulating subjects. *International Journal of Clinical and Experimental Hypnosis,* 1966, *14,* 61–78.

Orne, M., & Scheibe, K. The contribution of nondeprivation factors in the production of sensory deprivation effects: The psychology of the "panic button." *Journal of Abnormal and Social Psychology,* 1964, *68,* 3–12.

Ornstein, R. E. *The psychology of consciousness* (2nd ed.). New York: Harcourt Brace Jovanovich, 1977.

Osgood, C., Suci, G., & Tannenbaum, P. *The measurement of meaning.* Urbana: University of Illinois Press, 1957.

Petrinovich, L. Probabilistic functionalism: A conception of research methods. *American Psychologist,* 1979, *34,* 373–390.

Platt, J. R. Strong inference. *Science,* 1964, *146,* 347–353.

Popper, K. R. *The logic of scientific discovery.* New York: Basic Books, 1959.

Popper, K. R. *Objective knowledge.* Oxford: Oxford University Press, 1972.

Premack, D., & Woodruff, G. Does the chimpanzee have a theory of mind? *The Behavioral and Brain Sciences,* 1978, *1,* 515–526.

Raebhausen, O. M., & Brim, O. G. Privacy and behavioral research. *American Psychologist,* 1967, *22,* 423–437.

Ravizza, K. Peak experiences in sports. *Journal of Humanistic Psychology,* 1977, *17,* 35–40.

Ray, W. J., Katahn, M., & Snyder, C. R. Effects of test anxiety on acquisition, retention, and generalization of a complex verbal task in a classroom situation. *Journal of Personality and Social Psychology,* 1971, *20,* 147–154.

Resnick, J. H., & Schwartz, T. Ethical standards as an independent variable in psychological research. *American Psychologist,* 1973, *28,* 134–139.

Roberts, F. S. *Measurement theory with applications to decision making utility and the social sciences.* Reading, Mass.: Addison-Wesley, 1979.

Roechelein, J. E. Sex differences in time estimation. *Perceptual and Motor Skills,* 1972, *35,* 859–862.

Rosenhan, D. L. On being sane in insane places. *Science,* 1973, *179,* 250–258.

Rosenthal, R. How often are our numbers wrong? *American Psychologist,* 1979, *33,* 1005–1008.

Rosenthal, R., & Fode, K. L. The effects of experimenter bias on the performance of the albino rat. *Behavioral Science,* 1963, *8,* 183–189.

Rosenthal, R., & Lawson, R. A longitudinal study of the effects of experimenter bias on the operant learning of operant rats. *Journal of Psychiatric Research,* 1964, *2,* 61–72.

Rosenthal, R., & Rubin, D. B. Interpersonal expectancy effects: The first 345 studies. *The Behavioral and Brain Sciences,* 1978, *1,* 377–386.

Rubin, Z. Lovers and other strangers: The development of intimacy in encounters and relationships. *American Scientist,* 1974, *62,* 182–190.

Salk, J. *The survival of the wisest.* New York: Harper & Row, 1973.

Scheaffer, R. L., Mendenhall, W., & Ott, L. *Elementary survey sampling* (2nd ed.). North Scituate, Mass.; Duxbury Press, 1979.

Schnelle, J. F., & Lee, J. F. Quasi-experimental retrospective evaluation of a prison policy change. *Journal of Applied Behavior Analysis,* 1974, *7,* 483–496.

Schumacher, E. F. *A guide for the perplexed.* New York: Harper & Row, 1977. (In paperback, Perennial Library, 1979.)

Schuman, H., & Presser, S. *Questions and answers in attitude surveys.* New York: Academic Press, 1981.

Scoville, W. B. Amnesia after bilateral mesial temporal-lobe excision: Introduction to case H. M. *Neuropsychologia,* 1968, *6,* 211–213.

Scoville, W. B., & Milner, B. Loss of recent memory after bilateral hippocampal lessions. *Journal of Neurology, Neurosurgery, and Psychiatry,* 1957, *20,* 11–21.

Sherif, M., Harvey, O. J., White, B., Hood, W., & Sherif, C. W. *Intergroup conflict and cooperation: The robber's cave experiment.* Norman, Okla.: The University Book Exchange, 1961.

Sherpard, R. N. Perceptual and analogical bases of cognition. In D. Genter & A. L. Stevens (Eds.), *Mental Models.* Hillsdale, N. J.: Lawrence Earlbaum Associates, 1983.

Shotland, R. L., & Goodstein, L. Just because she doesn't want to doesn't mean it's rape: An experimentally based causal model of the perception of rape in a dating situation. *Social Psychology Quarterly,* 1983, *46,* 220–232.

Shotland, R. L., & Stebbins, C. Bystander response to rape: Can a victim attract help? *Journal of Applied Social Psychology,* 1980, *10,* 510–527.

Shotland, R. L., & Straw, M. K. Bystander response to an assault: When a man attacks a woman. *Journal of Personality and Social Psychology,* 1976, *34,* 990–999.

Sidman, M. *Tactics of scientific research.* New York: Basic Books, 1960.

Simon, J. L. *Basic research methods in social sciences* (2nd ed.). New York: Random House, 1978.

Solomon, R. L. An extension of control group design. *Psychological Bulletin,* 1949, *46,* 137–150.

Spencer-Brown, G. *Laws of form.* New York: Julian, 1972. (In paperback, New York: Bantam Press.)

Sperry, R. *Science and moral priority.* New York: Columbia University Press, 1983.

Stevens, S. S. On the theory of scales of measurement. *Science,* 1946, *103,* 677–680.

Stevens, S. S. Mathematics, measurement, and psychophysics. In S. S. Stevens (Ed.), *Handbook of experimental psycyhology.* New York: Wiley, 1951.

Stevens, S. S. On the psychophysical law. *Psychological Review,* 1957, *64,* 153–181.

Strupp, H. H., & Hadley, S. W. Specific vs. nonspecific factors in psychotherapy. *Archives of General Psychiatry,* 1979, *36,* 1125–1136.

Suppe, F. The structure of scientific theories (2nd ed.). Urbana: University of Illinois Press, 1977.

Tart, C. T. States of consciousness and state specific sciences. *Science,* 1972, *176,* 1203–1210.

Thomas, L. *The medusa and the snail.* New York: Viking, 1979.

Tinbergen, E. A., & Tinbergen, N. *Early childhood autism—an ethological approach.* Berlin: Paul Parey, 1972.

Tinbergen, N. *The animal in its world.* Cambridge, Mass.: Harvard University Press, 1972.

Veroff, J., Douvan, E., & Kulka, R. A. *The inner American.* New York: Basic Books, 1981.

Voevodsky, J. Evaluation of deceleration warning light for reducing rear-end automobile collisions. *Journal of Applied Psychology.* 1974, *59,* 270–273.

Wallas, G. *The art of thought.* New York: Harcourt, Brace & Co., 1926.

Walsh, R. N. Reflections on psychotherapy. *Journal of Transpersonal Psychology,* 1976, *8,* 100–111.

Walsh, R. N. Initial meditative experiences: Part I. *Journal of Transpersonal Psychology,* 1977, *9,* 151–192.

Walsh, R. N. Initial meditative experiences: Part II. *Journal of Transpersonal Psychology,* 1978, *10,* 1–28.

Warren, J. M., Zerweck, C., & Anthony, A. Effects of environmental enrichment on old mice. *Developmental Psychobiology,* 1982, *15,* 13–18.

Wason, P. C. Self-contradictions. In P. N. Johnson-Laird & P. C. Wason (Eds.), *Thinking.* Cambridge: Cambridge University Press, 1977.

Watson, J. D. *The double helix.* New York: Atheneum, 1968.

Webb, E. J., Campbell, D. T., Schwartz, R. D., & Sechrest, L. *Unobtrusive measures.* Chicago: Rand McNally, 1966.

Weimer, W. B. *Notes on the methodology of scientific research.* Hillsdale, N.J.: Lawrence Erlbaum Associates, 1979.

West, S. G., Gunn, S. P., & Chernicky, P. Ubiquitous Watergate: An attributional analysis. *Journal of Personality and Social Psychology,* 1975, *32,* 55–65.

Whitehead, A. N. *Science and the modern world.* New York: Macmillan, 1925.

Wicklund, R. A. Influence of self-awareness on human behavior. *American Scientist,* 1979, *67,* 187–193.

Winer, B. J. *Statistical principles in experimental design.* New York: McGraw-Hill, 1971.

Yamane, T. *Elementary sampling theory.* Englewood Cliffs, N.J.: Prentice-Hall, 1967.

Zimbardo, P. G., Haney, C., Banks, W. C., & Jaffe, D. The psychology of imprisonment: Privation, power and pathology. In D. Rosenhan & P. London (Eds.), *Theory and research in abnormal psychology* (2nd ed.). New York: Holt, Rinehart & Winston, 1975.

# GLOSSARY INDEX